Life of Harriet Beecher Stowe

Compiled from Her Letters and Journals

Charles Edward Stowe

Alpha Editions

Copyright © 2018

ISBN : 9789353292188

Design and Setting By
Alpha Editions
email - alphaedis@gmail.com

Contents

INTRODUCTORY STATEMENT - 1 -

CHAPTER I CHILDHOOD, 1811-1824 - 2 -

CHAPTER II SCHOOL DAYS IN HARTFORD, 1824-1832 - 18 -

CHAPTER III CINCINNATI, 1832-1836. - 41 -

CHAPTER IV EARLY MARRIED LIFE, 1836-1840 - 59 -

CHAPTER V POVERTY AND SICKNESS, 1840-1850 - 75 -

CHAPTER VI REMOVAL TO BRUNSWICK, 1850-1852 - 94 -

CHAPTER VII UNCLE TOM'S CABIN, 1852 - 116 -

CHAPTER VIII FIRST TRIP TO EUROPE, 1853. - 134 -

CHAPTER IX SUNNY MEMORIES, 1853 - 155 -

CHAPTER X FROM OVER THE SEA, 1853 - 173 -

CHAPTER XI HOME AGAIN, 1853-1856 - 189 -

CHAPTER XII DRED, 1856 - 205 -

CHAPTER XIII OLD SCENES REVISITED, 1856

- 223 -

CHAPTER XIV THE MINISTER'S WOOING, 1857-
1859   - 239 -

CHAPTER XV THE THIRD TRIP TO EUROPE, 1859

- 260 -

CHAPTER XVI THE CIVIL WAR, 1860-1865   - 275 -

CHAPTER XVII FLORIDA, 1865-1869   - 300 -

CHAPTER XVIII OLDTOWN FOLKS, 1869   - 318 -

CHAPTER XIX THE BYRON CONTROVERSY,
1869-1870.   - 337 -

CHAPTER XX GEORGE ELIOT   - 348 -

CHAPTER XXI CLOSING SCENES, 1870-1889 - 371 -

FOOTNOTES   - 392 -

INTRODUCTORY STATEMENT

I DESIRE to express my thanks here to Harper & Brothers, of New York, for permission to use letters already published in the "Autobiography and Correspondence of Lyman Beecher." I have availed myself freely of this permission in chapters i. and iii. In chapter xx. I have given letters already published in the "Life of George Eliot," by Mr. Cross; but in every instance I have copied from the original MSS. and not from the published work. In conclusion, I desire to express my indebtedness to Mr. Kirk Munroe, who has been my co-laborer in the work of compilation.

CHARLES E. STOWE.

HARTFORD, *September 30, 1889.*

CHAPTER I

CHILDHOOD, 1811-1824

Death of her Mother.—First Journey from Home.—Life at Nut Plains.—School Days and Hours with Favorite Authors.—The New Mother.—Litchfield Academy and its Influence.—First Literary Efforts.—A Remarkable Composition.—Goes to Hartford.

HARRIET BEECHER (STOWE) was born June 14, 1811, in the characteristic New England town of Litchfield, Conn. Her father was the Rev. Dr. Lyman Beecher, a distinguished Calvinistic divine, her mother Roxanna Foote, his first wife. The little new-comer was ushered into a household of happy, healthy children, and found five brothers and sisters awaiting her. The eldest was Catherine, born September 6, 1800. Following her were two sturdy boys, William and Edward; then came Mary, then George, and at last Harriet. Another little Harriet born three years before had died when only one month old, and the fourth daughter was named, in memory of this sister, Harriet Elizabeth Beecher. Just two years after Harriet was born, in the same month, another brother, Henry Ward, was welcomed to the family circle, and after him came Charles, the last of Roxanna Beecher's children.

The first memorable incident of Harriet's life was the death of her mother, which occurred when she was four years old, and which ever afterwards remained with her as the tenderest, saddest, and most sacred memory of her childhood. Mrs. Stowe's recollections of her mother are found in a letter to her brother Charles, afterwards published in the "Autobiography and Correspondence of Lyman Beecher." She says:—

"I was between three and four years of age when our mother died, and my personal recollections of her are therefore but few. But the deep interest and veneration that she inspired in all who knew her were such that during all my childhood I was constantly hearing her spoken of, and from one friend or another some incident or anecdote of her life was constantly being impressed upon me.

"Mother was one of those strong, restful, yet widely sympathetic natures in whom all around seemed to find comfort and repose. The communion between her and my father was a peculiar one. It was an intimacy throughout the whole range of their being. There was no human mind in whose decisions he had greater confidence. Both intellectually and morally he regarded her as the better and stronger portion of himself, and I remember hearing him say that after her death his first sensation was a sort of terror, like that of a child suddenly shut out alone in the dark.

"In my own childhood only two incidents of my mother twinkle like rays through the darkness. One was of our all running and dancing out before her from the nursery to the sitting-room one Sabbath morning, and her pleasant voice saying after us, 'Remember the Sabbath day to keep it holy, children.'

"Another remembrance is this: mother was an enthusiastic horticulturist in all the small ways that limited means allowed. Her brother John in New York had just sent her a small parcel of fine tulip-bulbs. I remember rummaging these out of an obscure corner of the nursery one day when she was gone out, and being strongly seized with the idea that they were good to eat, using all the little English I then possessed to persuade my brothers that these were onions such as grown people ate and would be very nice for us. So we fell to and devoured the whole, and I recollect being somewhat disappointed in the odd sweetish taste, and thinking that onions were not so nice as I had supposed. Then mother's serene face appeared at the nursery door and we all ran towards her, telling with one voice of our discovery and achievement. We had found a bag of onions and had eaten them all up.

"Also I remember that there was not even a momentary expression of impatience, but that she sat down and said, 'My dear children, what you have done makes mamma very sorry. Those were not onions but roots of beautiful flowers, and if you had let them alone we should have next summer in the garden great beautiful red and yellow flowers such as you never saw.' I remember how drooping and dispirited we all grew at this picture, and how sadly we regarded the empty paper bag.

"Then I have a recollection of her reading aloud to the children Miss Edgeworth's 'Frank,' which had just come out, I believe, and was exciting a good deal of attention among the educational circles of Litchfield. After that came a time when every one said she was sick, and I used to be permitted to go once a day into her room, where she sat bolstered up in bed. I have a vision of a very fair face with a bright red spot on each cheek and her quiet smile. I remember dreaming one night that mamma had got well, and of waking with loud transports of joy that were hushed down by some one who came into the room. My dream was indeed a true one. She was forever well.

"Then came the funeral. Henry was too little to go. I can see his golden curls and little black frock as he frolicked in the sun like a kitten, full of ignorant joy.

"I recollect the mourning dresses, the tears of the older children, the walking to the burial-ground, and somebody's speaking at the grave. Then all was closed, and we little ones, to whom it was so confused, asked where she was gone and would she never come back.

"They told us at one time that she had been laid in the ground, and at another that she had gone to heaven. Thereupon Henry, putting the two things together, resolved to dig through the ground and go to heaven to find her; for being discovered under sister Catherine's window one morning digging with great zeal and earnestness, she called to him to know what he was doing. Lifting his curly head, he answered with great simplicity, 'Why, I'm going to heaven to find mamma.'

"Although our mother's bodily presence thus disappeared from our circle, I think her memory and example had more influence in moulding her family, in deterring from evil and exciting to good, than the living presence of many mothers. It was a memory that met us everywhere, for every person in the town, from the highest to the lowest, seemed to have been so impressed by her character and life that they constantly reflected some portion of it back upon us.

"The passage in 'Uncle Tom' where Augustine St. Clare describes his mother's influence is a simple reproduction of my own mother's influence as it has always been felt in her family."

Of his deceased wife Dr. Beecher said: "Few women have attained to more remarkable piety. Her faith was strong and her prayer prevailing. It was her wish that all her sons should devote themselves to the ministry, and to it she consecrated them with fervent prayer. Her prayers have been heard. All her sons have been converted and are now, according to her wish, ministers of Christ."

Such was Roxanna Beecher, whose influence upon her four-year-old daughter was strong enough to mould the whole after-life of the author of "Uncle Tom's Cabin." After the mother's death the Litchfield home was such a sad, lonely place for the child that her aunt, Harriet Foote, took her away for a long visit at her grandmother's at Nut Plains, near Guilford, Conn., the first journey from home the little one had ever made. Of this visit Mrs. Stowe herself says:—

"Among my earliest recollections are those of a visit to Nut Plains immediately after my mother's death. Aunt Harriet Foote, who was with mother during all her last sickness, took me home to stay with her. At the close of what seemed to me a long day's ride we arrived after dark at a lonely little white farmhouse, and were ushered into a large parlor where a cheerful wood fire was crackling. I was placed in the arms of an old lady, who held me close and wept silently, a thing at which I marveled, for my great loss was already faded from my childish mind.

"I remember being put to bed by my aunt in a large room, on one side of which stood the bed appropriated to her and me, and on the other that of my grandmother. My aunt Harriet was no common character. A more energetic human being never undertook the education of a child. Her ideas of education were those of a vigorous English woman of the old school. She believed in the Church, and had she been born under that *régime* would have believed in the king stoutly, although being of the generation following the Revolution she was a not less stanch supporter of the Declaration of Independence.

"According to her views little girls were to be taught to move very gently, to speak softly and prettily, to say 'yes ma'am,' and 'no ma'am,' never to tear their clothes, to sew, to knit at regular hours, to go to church on Sunday and make all the responses, and to come home and be catechised.

"During these catechisings she used to place my little cousin Mary and myself bolt upright at her knee, while black Dinah and Harry, the bound boy, were ranged at a respectful distance behind us; for Aunt Harriet always impressed it upon her servants 'to order themselves lowly and reverently to all their betters,' a portion of the Church catechism that always pleased me, particularly when applied to them, as it insured their calling me 'Miss Harriet,' and treating me with a degree of consideration such as I never enjoyed in the more democratic circle at home. I became proficient in the Church catechism, and gave my aunt great satisfaction by the old-fashioned gravity and steadiness with which I learned to repeat it.

"As my father was a Congregational minister, I believe Aunt Harriet, though the highest of High Church women, felt some scruples as to whether it was desirable that my religious education should be entirely out of the sphere of my birth. Therefore when this catechetical exercise was finished she would say, 'Now, niece, you have to learn another catechism, because your father is a Presbyterian minister,'—and then she would endeavor to make me commit to memory the Assembly catechism.

"At this lengthening of exercise I secretly murmured. I was rather pleased at the first question in the Church catechism, which is certainly quite on the level of any child's understanding,—'What is your name?' It was such an easy good start, I could say it so loud and clear, and I was accustomed to compare it with the first question in the Primer, 'What is the chief end of man?' as vastly more difficult for me to answer. In fact, between my aunt's secret unbelief and my own childish impatience of too much catechism, the matter was indefinitely postponed after a few ineffectual attempts, and I was overjoyed to hear her announce privately to grandmother that she thought it would be time enough for Harriet to learn the Presbyterian catechism when she went home."

Mingled with this superabundance of catechism and plentiful needlework the child was treated to copious extracts from Lowth's Isaiah, Buchanan's Researches in Asia, Bishop Heber's Life, and Dr. Johnson's Works, which, after her Bible and Prayer Book, were her grandmother's favorite reading. Harriet does not seem to have fully appreciated these; but she did enjoy her grandmother's comments upon their biblical readings. Among the Evangelists especially was the old lady perfectly at home, and her idea of each of the apostles was so distinct and dramatic that she spoke of them as of familiar acquaintances. She would, for instance, always smile indulgently at Peter's remarks and say, "There he is again, now; that's just like Peter. He's always so ready to put in."

It must have been during this winter spent at Nut Plains, amid such surroundings, that Harriet began committing to memory that wonderful assortment of hymns, poems, and scriptural passages from which in after years she quoted so readily and effectively, for her sister Catherine, in writing of her the following November, says:—

"Harriet is a very good girl. She has been to school all this summer, and has learned to read very fluently. She has committed to memory twenty-seven hymns and two long chapters in the Bible. She has a remarkably retentive memory and will make a very good scholar."

At this time the child was five years old, and a regular attendant at "Ma'am Kilbourne's" school on West Street, to which she walked every day hand in hand with her chubby, rosy-faced, bare-footed, four-year-old brother, Henry Ward. With the ability to read germinated the intense literary longing that was to be hers through life. In those days but few books were specially prepared for children, and at six years of age we find the little girl hungrily searching for mental food amid barrels of old sermons and pamphlets stored in a corner of the garret. Here it seemed to her were some thousands of the most unintelligible things. "An appeal on the unlawfulness of a man marrying his wife's sister" turned up in every barrel she investigated, by twos, or threes, or dozens, till her soul despaired of finding an end. At last her patient search was rewarded, for at the very bottom of a barrel of musty sermons she discovered an ancient volume of "The Arabian Nights." With this her fortune was made, for in these most fascinating of fairy tales the imaginative child discovered a well-spring of joy that was all her own. When things went astray with her, when her brothers started off on long excursions, refusing to take her with them, or in any other childish sorrow, she had only to curl herself up in some snug corner and sail forth on her bit of enchanted carpet into fairyland to forget all her griefs.

In recalling her own child-life Mrs. Stowe, among other things, describes her father's library, and gives a vivid bit of her own experiences within its walls. She says: "High above all the noise of the house, this room had to me the air of a refuge and a sanctuary. Its walls were set round from floor to ceiling with the friendly, quiet faces of books, and there stood my father's great writing-chair, on one arm of which lay open always his Cruden's Concordance and his Bible. Here I loved to retreat and niche myself down in a quiet corner with my favorite books around me. I had a kind of sheltered feeling as I thus sat and watched my father writing, turning to his books, and speaking from time to time to himself in a loud, earnest whisper. I vaguely felt that he was about some holy and mysterious work quite beyond my little comprehension, and I was careful never to disturb him by question or remark.

BIRTHPLACE AT LITCHFIELD, CONNECTICUT.

"The books ranged around filled me too with a solemn awe. On the lower shelves were enormous folios, on whose backs I spelled in black letters, 'Lightfoot Opera,' a title whereat I wondered, considering the bulk of the volumes. Above these, grouped along in friendly, social rows, were books of all sorts, sizes, and bindings, the titles of which I had read so often that I knew them by heart. There were Bell's Sermons, Bonnett's Inquiries, Bogue's Essays, Toplady on Predestination, Boston's Fourfold State, Law's Serious Call, and other works of that kind. These I looked over wistfully, day after day, without even a hope of getting something interesting out of them. The thought that father could read and understand things like these filled me with a vague awe, and I wondered if I would ever be old enough to know what it was all about.

"But there was one of my father's books that proved a mine of wealth to me. It was a happy hour when he brought home and set up in his bookcase Cotton Mather's 'Magnalia,' in a new edition of two volumes. What wonderful stories those! Stories too about my own country. Stories that made me feel the very ground I trod on to be consecrated by some special dealing of God's Providence."

In continuing these reminiscences Mrs. Stowe describes as follows her sensations upon first hearing the Declaration of Independence: "I had never heard it before, and even now had but a vague idea of what was meant by some parts of it. Still I gathered enough from the recital of the abuses and injuries that had driven my nation to this course to feel myself swelling with indignation, and ready with all my little mind and strength to applaud the concluding passage, which Colonel Talmadge rendered with resounding majesty. I was as ready as any of them to pledge my life, fortune, and sacred honor for such a cause. The heroic element was strong in me, having come down by ordinary generation from a long line of Puritan ancestry, and just now it made me long to do something, I knew not what: to fight for my country, or to make some declaration on my own account."

When Harriet was nearly six years old her father married as his second wife Miss Harriet Porter of Portland, Maine, and Mrs. Stowe thus describes her new mother: "I slept in the nursery with my two younger brothers. We knew that father was gone away somewhere on a journey and was expected home, therefore the sound of a bustle in the house the more easily awoke us. As father came into our room our new mother followed him. She was very fair, with bright blue eyes, and soft auburn hair bound round with a black velvet bandeau, and to us she seemed very beautiful.

"Never did stepmother make a prettier or sweeter impression. The morning following her arrival we looked at her with awe. She seemed to us so fair, so delicate, so elegant, that we were almost afraid to go near her. We must have appeared to her as rough, red-faced, country children, honest, obedient, and bashful. She was peculiarly dainty and neat in all her ways and arrangements, and I used to feel breezy, rough, and rude in her presence.

"In her religion she was distinguished for a most unfaltering Christ-worship. She was of a type noble but severe, naturally hard, correct, exact and exacting, with intense natural and moral ideality. Had it not been that Doctor Payson had set up and kept before her a tender, human, loving Christ, she would have been only a conscientious bigot. This image, however, gave softness and warmth to her religious life, and I have since noticed how her Christ-enthusiasm has sprung up in the hearts of all her children."

In writing to her old home of her first impressions of her new one, Mrs. Beecher says: "It is a very lovely family, and with heartfelt gratitude I observed how cheerful and healthy they were. The sentiment is greatly increased, since I perceive them to be of agreeable habits and some of them of uncommon intellect."

This new mother proved to be indeed all that the name implies to her husband's children, and never did they have occasion to call her aught other than blessed.

Another year finds a new baby brother, Frederick by name, added to the family. At this time too we catch a characteristic glimpse of Harriet in one of her sister Catherine's letters. She says: "Last week we interred Tom junior with funeral honors by the side of old Tom of happy memory. Our Harriet is chief mourner always at their funerals. She asked for what she called an *epithet* for the gravestone of Tom junior, which I gave as follows:—

"Here lies our Kit,
Who had a fit,
And acted queer,
Shot with a gun,
Her race is run,
And she lies here."

In June, 1820, little Frederick died from scarlet fever, and Harriet was seized with a violent attack of the same dread disease; but, after a severe struggle, recovered.

Following her happy, hearty child-life, we find her tramping through the woods or going on fishing excursions with her brothers, sitting thoughtfully in her father's study, listening eagerly to the animated theological discussions of the day, visiting her grandmother at Nut Plains, and figuring as one of the brightest scholars in the Litchfield Academy, taught by Mr. John Brace and Miss Pierce. When she was eleven years old her brother Edward wrote of her: "Harriet reads everything she can lay hands on, and sews and knits diligently."

At this time she was no longer the youngest girl of the family, for another sister (Isabella) had been born in 1822. This event served greatly to mature her, as she was intrusted with much of the care of the baby out of school hours. It was not, however, allowed to interfere in any way with her studies, and, under the skillful direction of her beloved teachers, she seemed to absorb knowledge with every sense. She herself writes: "Much of the training and inspiration of my early days consisted not in the things that I was supposed to be studying, but in hearing, while seated unnoticed at my desk, the conversation of Mr. Brace with the older classes. There, from hour to hour, I listened with eager ears to historical criticisms and discussions, or to recitations in such works as Paley's Moral Philosophy, Blair's Rhetoric, Allison on Taste, all full of most awakening suggestions to my thoughts.

"Mr. Brace exceeded all teachers I ever knew in the faculty of teaching composition. The constant excitement in which he kept the minds of his pupils, the wide and varied regions of thought into which he led them, formed a preparation for composition, the main requisite for which is to have something which one feels interested to say."

In her tenth year Harriet began what to her was the fascinating work of writing compositions, and so rapidly did she progress that at the school exhibition held when she was twelve years old, hers was one of the two or three essays selected to be read aloud before the august assembly of visitors attracted by the occasion.

Of this event Mrs. Stowe writes: "I remember well the scene at that exhibition, to me so eventful. The hall was crowded with all the literati of Litchfield. Before them all our compositions were read aloud. When mine was read I noticed that father, who was sitting on high by Mr. Brace, brightened and looked interested, and at the close I heard him ask, 'Who wrote that composition?' 'Your daughter, sir,' was the answer. It was the proudest moment of my life. There was no mistaking father's face when he was pleased, and to have interested him was past all juvenile triumphs."

That composition has been carefully preserved, and on the old yellow sheets the cramped childish handwriting is still distinctly legible. As the first literary production of one who afterwards attained such distinction as a writer, it is deemed of sufficient value and interest to be embodied in this biography exactly as it was written and read sixty-five years ago. The subject was certainly a grave one to be handled by a child of twelve.

CAN THE IMMORTALITY OF THE SOUL BE PROVED BY THE LIGHT OF NATURE?

It has justly been concluded by the philosophers of every age that "The proper study of mankind is man," and his nature and composition, both physical and mental, have been subjects of the most critical examination. In the course of these researches many have been at a loss to account for the change which takes place in the body at the time of death. By some it has been attributed to the flight of its tenant, and by others to its final annihilation.

The questions, "What becomes of the soul at the time of death?" and, if it be not annihilated, "What is its destiny after death?" are those which, from the interest that we all feel in them, will probably engross universal attention.

In pursuing these inquiries it will be necessary to divest ourselves of all that knowledge which we have obtained from the light which revelation has shed over them, and place ourselves in the same position as the philosophers of past ages when considering the same subject.

The first argument which has been advanced to prove the immortality of the soul is drawn from the nature of the mind itself. It has (say the supporters of this theory) no composition of parts, and therefore, as there are no particles, is not susceptible of divisibility and cannot be acted upon by decay, and therefore if it will not decay it will exist forever.

Now because the mind is not susceptible of decay effected in the ordinary way by a gradual separation of particles, affords no proof that that same omnipotent power which created it cannot by another simple exertion of power again reduce it to nothing. The only reason for belief which this argument affords is that the soul cannot be acted upon by decay. But it does not prove that it cannot destroy its existence. Therefore, for the validity of this argument, it must either be proved that the "Creator" has not the power to destroy it, or that he has not the will; but as neither of these can be established, our immortality is left dependent on the pleasure of the Creator. But it is said that it is evident that the Creator designed the soul for immortality, or he would never have created it so essentially different from the body, for had they both been designed for the same end they would both have been created alike, as there would have been no object in forming them otherwise. This only proves that the soul and body had not the same destinations. Now of what these destinations are we know nothing, and after much useless reasoning we return where we began, our argument depending upon the good pleasure of the Creator.

And here it is said that a being of such infinite wisdom and benevolence as that of which the Creator is possessed would not have formed man with such vast capacities and boundless desires, and would have given him no opportunity for exercising them.

In order to establish the validity of this argument it is necessary to prove by the light of Nature that the Creator *is* benevolent, which, being impracticable, is of itself sufficient to render the argument invalid.

But the argument proceeds upon the supposition that to destroy the soul would be unwise. Now this is arraigning the "All-wise" before the tribunal of his subjects to answer for the mistakes in his government. Can we look into the council of the "Unsearchable" and see what means are made to answer their ends? We do not know but the destruction of the soul may, in the government of God, be made to answer such a purpose that its existence would be contrary to the dictates of wisdom.

The great desire of the soul for immortality, its secret, innate horror of annihilation, has been brought to prove its immortality. But do we always find this horror or this desire? Is it not much more evident that the great majority of mankind have no such dread at all? True that there is a strong feeling of horror excited by the idea of perishing from the earth and being forgotten, of losing all those honors and all that fame awaited them. Many feel this secret horror when they look down upon the vale of futurity and reflect that though now the idols of the world, soon all which will be left them will be the common portion of mankind—oblivion! But this dread does not arise from any idea of their destiny beyond the tomb, and even were this true, it would afford no proof that the mind would exist forever, merely from its strong desires. For it might with as much correctness be argued that the body will exist forever because we have a great dread of dying, and upon this principle nothing which we strongly desire would ever be withheld from us, and no evil that we greatly dread will ever come upon us, a principle evidently false.

Again, it has been said that the constant progression of the powers of the mind affords another proof of its immortality. Concerning this, Addison remarks, "Were a human soul ever thus at a stand in her acquirements, were her faculties to be full blown and incapable of further enlargement, I could imagine that she might fall away insensibly and drop at once into a state of annihilation. But can we believe a thinking being that is in a perpetual progress of improvement, and traveling on from perfection to perfection after having just looked abroad into the works of her Creator and made a few discoveries of his infinite wisdom and goodness, must perish at her first setting out and in the very beginning of her inquiries?"

In answer to this it may be said that the soul is not always progressing in her powers. Is it not rather a subject of general remark that those brilliant talents which in youth expand, in manhood become stationary, and in old age gradually sink to decay? Till when the ancient man descends to the tomb scarce a wreck of that once powerful mind remains.

Who, but upon reading the history of England, does not look with awe upon the effects produced by the talents of her Elizabeth? Who but admires that undaunted firmness in time of peace and that profound depth of policy which she displayed in the cabinet? Yet behold the tragical end of this learned, this politic princess! Behold the triumphs of age and sickness over her once powerful talents, and say not that the faculties of man are always progressing in their powers.

From the activity of the mind at the hour of death has also been deduced its immortality. But it is not true that the mind is always active at the time of death. We find recorded in history numberless instances of those talents, which were once adequate to the government of a nation, being so weakened and palsied by the touch of sickness as scarcely to tell to beholders what they once were. The talents of the statesman, the wisdom of the sage, the courage and might of the warrior, are instantly destroyed by it, and all that remains of them is the waste of idiocy or the madness of insanity.

Some minds there are who at the time of death retain their faculties though much impaired, and if the argument be valid these are the only cases where immortality is conferred. Again, it is urged that the inequality of rewards and punishments in this world demand another in which virtue may be rewarded and vice punished. This argument, in the first place, takes for its foundation that by the light of nature the distinction between virtue and vice can be discovered. By some this is absolutely disbelieved, and by all considered as extremely doubtful. And, secondly, it puts the Creator under an obligation to reward and punish the actions of his creatures. No such obligation exists, and therefore the argument cannot be valid. And this supposes the Creator to be a being of justice, which cannot by the light of nature be proved, and as the whole argument rests upon this foundation it certainly cannot be correct.

This argument also directly impeaches the wisdom of the Creator, for the sense of it is this,—that, forasmuch as he was not able to manage his government in this world, he must have another in which to rectify the mistakes and oversights of this, and what an idea would this give us of our All-wise Creator?

It is also said that all nations have some conceptions of a future state, that the ancient Greeks and Romans believed in it, that no nation has been found but have possessed some idea of a future state of existence. But their belief arose more from the fact that they wished it to be so than from any real ground of belief; for arguments appear much more plausible when the mind wishes to be convinced. But it is said that every nation, however circumstanced, possess some idea of a future state. For this we may account by the fact that it was handed down by tradition from the time of the flood. From all these arguments, which, however plausible at first sight, are found to be futile, may be argued the necessity of a revelation. Without it, the destiny of the noblest of the works of God would have been left in obscurity. Never till the blessed light of the Gospel dawned on the borders of the pit, and the heralds of the Cross proclaimed "Peace on earth and good will to men," was it that bewildered and misled man was enabled to trace his celestial origin and glorious destiny.

The sun of the Gospel has dispelled the darkness that has rested on objects beyond the tomb. In the Gospel man learned that when the dust returned to dust the spirit fled to the God who gave it. He there found that though man has lost the image of his divine Creator, he is still destined, after this earthly house of his tabernacle is dissolved, to an inheritance incorruptible, undefiled, and that fadeth not away, to a house not made with hands, eternal in the heavens.

Soon after the writing of this remarkable composition, Harriet's child-life in Litchfield came to an end, for that same year she went to Hartford to pursue her studies in a school which had been recently established by her sister Catherine in that city.

CHAPTER II

SCHOOL DAYS IN HARTFORD, 1824-1832

MISS CATHERINE BEECHER.—PROFESSOR FISHER.—
THE WRECK OF THE ALBION AND DEATH OF PROFESSOR
FISHER.—"THE MINISTER'S WOOING."—MISS
CATHERINE BEECHER'S SPIRITUAL HISTORY.—MRS.
STOWE'S RECOLLECTIONS OF HER SCHOOL DAYS IN
HARTFORD.—HER CONVERSION.—UNITES WITH THE
FIRST CHURCH IN HARTFORD.—HER DOUBTS AND
SUBSEQUENT RELIGIOUS DEVELOPMENT.—HER FINAL
PEACE.

THE school days in Hartford began a new era in Harriet's life. It was the formative period, and it is therefore important to say a few words concerning her sister Catherine, under whose immediate supervision she was to continue her education. In fact, no one can comprehend either Mrs. Stowe or her writings without some knowledge of the life and character of this remarkable woman, whose strong, vigorous mind and tremendous personality indelibly stamped themselves on the sensitive, yielding, dreamy, and poetic nature of the younger sister. Mrs. Stowe herself has said that the two persons who most strongly influenced her at this period of her life were her brother Edward and her sister Catherine.

Catherine was the oldest child of Lyman Beecher and Roxanna Foote, his wife. In a little battered journal found among her papers is a short sketch of her life, written when she was seventy-six years of age. In a tremulous hand she begins: "I was born at East Hampton, L. I., September 5, 1800, at 5 P. M., in the large parlor opposite father's study. Don't remember much about it myself." The sparkle of wit in this brief notice of the circumstances of her birth is very characteristic. All through her life little ripples of fun were continually playing on the surface of that current of intense thought and feeling in which her deep, earnest nature flowed.

When she was ten years of age her father removed to Litchfield, Conn., and her happy girlhood was passed in that place. Her bright and versatile mind and ready wit enabled her to pass brilliantly through her school days with but little mental exertion, and those who knew her slightly might have imagined her to be only a bright, thoughtless, light-hearted girl. In Boston, at the age of twenty, she took lessons in music and drawing, and became so proficient in these branches as to secure a position as teacher in a young ladies' school, kept by a Rev. Mr. Judd, an Episcopal clergyman, at New London, Conn. About this time she formed the acquaintance of Professor Alexander Metcalf Fisher, of Yale College, one of the most distinguished young men in New England. In January of the year 1822 they became engaged, and the following spring Professor Fisher sailed for Europe to purchase books and scientific apparatus for the use of his department in the college.

In his last letter to Miss Beecher, dated March 31, 1822, he writes:—

"I set out at 10 precisely to-morrow, in the Albion for Liverpool; the ship has no superior in the whole number of excellent vessels belonging to this port, and Captain Williams is regarded as first on their list of commanders. The accommodations are admirable—fare $140. Unless our ship should speak some one bound to America on the passage, you will probably not hear from me under two months."

Before two months had passed came vague rumors of a terrible shipwreck on the coast of Ireland. Then the tidings that the Albion was lost. Then came a letter from Mr. Pond, at Kinsale, Ireland, dated May 2, 1822:—

"You have doubtless heard of the shipwreck of the Albion packet of New York, bound to Liverpool. It was a melancholy shipwreck. It happened about four o'clock on the morning of the 22d of April. Professor Fisher, of Yale College, was one of the passengers. Out of twenty-three cabin passengers, but one reached the shore. He is a Mr. Everhart, of Chester County, Pennsylvania. He informs me that Professor Fisher was injured by things that fetched away in the cabin at the time the ship was knocked down. This was between 8 and 9 o'clock in the evening of the twenty-first. Mr. Fisher, though badly bruised, was calm and resolute, and assisted Captain Williams by taking the injured compass to his berth and repairing it. About five minutes before the vessel struck Captain Williams informed the passengers of their danger, and all went on deck except Professor Fisher, who remained sitting in his berth. Mr. Everhart was the last person who left the cabin, and the last who ever saw Professor Fisher alive."

I should not have spoken of this incident of family history with such minuteness, except for the fact that it is so much a part of Mrs. Stowe's life as to make it impossible to understand either her character or her most important works without it. Without this incident "The Minister's Wooing" never would have been written, for both Mrs. Marvyn's terrible soul struggles and old Candace's direct and effective solution of all religious difficulties find their origin in this stranded, storm-beaten ship on the coast of Ireland, and the terrible mental conflicts through which her sister afterward passed, for she believed Professor Fisher eternally lost. No mind more directly and powerfully influenced Harriet's than that of her sister Catherine, unless it was her brother Edward's, and that which acted with such overwhelming power on the strong, unyielding mind of the older sister must have, in time, a permanent and abiding influence on the mind of the younger.

After Professor Fisher's death his books came into Miss Beecher's possession, and among them was a complete edition of Scott's works. It was an epoch in the family history when Doctor Beecher came down-stairs one day with a copy of "Ivanhoe" in his hand, and said: "I have always said that my children should not read novels, but they must read these."

The two years following the death of Professor Fisher were passed by Miss Catherine Beecher at Franklin, Mass., at the home of Professor Fisher's parents, where she taught his two sisters, studied mathematics with his brother Willard, and listened to Doctor Emmons' fearless and pitiless preaching. Hers was a mind too strong and buoyant to be crushed and prostrated by that which would have driven a weaker and less resolute nature into insanity. Of her it may well be said:—

"She faced the spectres of the mind
And laid them, thus she came at length
To find a stronger faith her own."

Gifted naturally with a capacity for close metaphysical analysis and a robust fearlessness in following her premises to a logical conclusion, she arrived at results startling and original, if not always of permanent value.

In 1840 she published in the "Biblical Repository" an article on Free Agency, which has been acknowledged by competent critics as the ablest refutation of Edwards on "The Will" which has appeared. An amusing incident connected with this publication may not be out of place here. A certain eminent theological professor of New England, visiting a distinguished German theologian and speaking of this production, said: "The ablest refutation of Edwards on 'The Will' which was ever written is the work of a woman, the daughter of Dr. Lyman Beecher." The worthy Teuton raised both hands in undisguised astonishment. "You have a woman that can write an able refutation of Edwards on 'The Will'? God forgive Christopher Columbus for discovering America!"

Not finding herself able to love a God whom she thought of in her own language as "a perfectly happy being, unmoved by my sorrows or tears, and looking upon me only with dislike and aversion," she determined "to find happiness in living to do good." "It was right to pray and read the Bible, so I prayed and read. It was right to try to save others, so I labored for their salvation. I never had any fear of punishment or hope of reward all these years." She was tormented with doubts. "What has the Son of God done which the meanest and most selfish creature upon earth would not have done? After making such a wretched race and placing them in such disastrous circumstances, somehow, without any sorrow or trouble, Jesus Christ had a human nature that suffered and died. If something else besides ourselves will do all the suffering, who would not save millions of wretched beings and receive all the honor and gratitude without any of the trouble? Sometimes when such thoughts passed through my mind, I felt that it was all pride, rebellion, and sin."

So she struggles on, sometimes floundering deep in the mire of doubt, and then lifted for the moment above it by her naturally buoyant spirits, and general tendency to look on the bright side of things. In this condition of mind, she came to Hartford in the winter of 1824, and began a school with eight scholars, and it was in the practical experience of teaching that she found a final solution of all her difficulties. She continues:—

"After two or three years I commenced giving instruction in mental philosophy, and at the same time began a regular course of lectures and instructions from the Bible, and was much occupied with plans for governing my school, and in devising means to lead my pupils to become obedient, amiable, and pious. By degrees I finally arrived at the following principles in the government of my school:—

"First. It is indispensable that my scholars should feel that I am sincerely and deeply interested in their best happiness, and the more I can convince them of this, the more ready will be their obedience.

"Second. The preservation of authority and order depends upon the certainty that unpleasant consequences to themselves will inevitably be the result of doing wrong.

"Third. It is equally necessary, to preserve my own influence and their affection, that they should feel that punishment is the natural result of wrong-doing in such a way that they shall regard themselves, instead of me, as the cause of their punishment.

"Fourth. It is indispensable that my scholars should see that my requisitions are reasonable. In the majority of cases this can be shown, and in this way such confidence will be the result that they will trust to my judgment and knowledge, in cases where no explanation can be given.

"Fifth. The more I can make my scholars feel that I am actuated by a spirit of self-denying benevolence, the more confidence they will feel in me, and the more they will be inclined to submit to self-denying duties for the good of others.

"After a while I began to compare my experience with the government of God. I finally got through the whole subject, and drew out the results, and found that all my difficulties were solved and all my darkness dispelled."

Her solution in brief is nothing more than that view of the divine nature which was for so many years preached by her brother, Henry Ward Beecher, and set forth in the writings of her sister Harriet,—the conception of a being of infinite love, patience, and kindness who suffers with man. The sufferings of Christ on the cross were not the sufferings of his human nature merely, but the sufferings of the divine nature in Him. In Christ we see the only revelation of God, and that is the revelation of one that suffers. This is the fundamental idea in "The Minister's Wooing," and it is the idea of God in which the storm-tossed soul of the older sister at last found rest. All this was directly opposed to that fundamental principle of theologians that God, being the infinitely perfect Being, cannot suffer, because suffering indicates imperfection. To Miss Beecher's mind the lack of ability to suffer with his suffering creatures was a more serious imperfection. Let the reader turn to the twenty-fourth chapter of "The Minister's Wooing" for a complete presentation of this subject, especially the passage that begins, "Sorrow is divine: sorrow is reigning on the throne of the universe."

In the fall of the year 1824, while her sister Catherine was passing through the soul crisis which we have been describing, Harriet came to the school that she had recently established.

In a letter to her son written in 1886, speaking of this period of her life, Mrs. Stowe says: "Somewhere between my twelfth and thirteenth year I was placed under the care of my elder sister Catherine, in the school that she had just started in Hartford, Connecticut. When I entered the school there were not more than twenty-five scholars in it, but it afterwards numbered its pupils by the hundreds. The school-room was on Main Street, nearly opposite Christ Church, over Sheldon & Colton's harness store, at the sign of the two white horses. I never shall forget the pleasure and surprise which these two white horses produced in my mind when I first saw them. One of the young men who worked in the rear of the harness store had a most beautiful tenor voice, and it was my delight to hear him singing in school hours:—

'When in cold oblivion's shade
Beauty, wealth, and power are laid,
When, around the sculptured shrine,
Moss shall cling and ivy twine,
Where immortal spirits reign,
There shall we all meet again.'

Catherine E. Beecher

"As my father's salary was inadequate to the wants of his large family, the expense of my board in Hartford was provided for by a species of exchange. Mr. Isaac D. Bull sent a daughter to Miss Pierce's seminary in Litchfield, and she boarded in my father's family in exchange for my board in her father's family. If my good, refined, neat, particular stepmother could have chosen, she could not have found a family more exactly suited to her desires. The very soul of neatness and order pervaded the whole establishment. Mr. I. D. Bull was a fine, vigorous, white-haired man on the declining slope of life, but full of energy and of kindness. Mr. Samuel Collins, a neighbor who lived next door, used to frequently come in and make most impressive and solemn calls on Miss Mary Anne Bull, who was a brunette and a celebrated beauty of the day. I well remember her long raven curls falling from the comb that held them up on the top of her head. She had a rich soprano voice, and was the leading singer in the Centre Church choir. The two brothers also had fine, manly voices, and the family circle was often enlivened by quartette singing and flute playing. Mr. Bull kept a very large wholesale drug store on Front Street, in which his two sons, Albert and James, were clerks. The oldest son, Watson Bull, had established a retail drug store at the sign of the 'Good Samaritan.' A large picture of the Good Samaritan relieving the wounded traveler formed a striking part of the sign, and was contemplated by me with reverence.

"The mother of the family gave me at once a child's place in her heart. A neat little hall chamber was allotted to me for my own, and a well made and kept single bed was given me, of which I took daily care with awful satisfaction. If I was sick nothing could exceed the watchful care and tender nursing of Mrs. Bull. In school my two most intimate friends were the leading scholars. They had written to me before I came and I had answered their letters, and on my arrival they gave me the warmest welcome. One was Catherine Ledyard Cogswell, daughter of the leading and best-beloved of Hartford physicians. The other was Georgiana May, daughter of a most lovely Christian woman who was a widow. Georgiana was one of many children, having two younger sisters, Mary and Gertrude, and several brothers. Catherine Cogswell was one of the most amiable, sprightly, sunny-tempered individuals I have ever known. She was, in fact, so much beloved that it was difficult for me to see much of her. Her time was all bespoken by different girls. One might walk with her to school, another had the like promise on the way home. And at recess, of which we had every day a short half hour, there was always a suppliant at Katy's shrine, whom she found it hard to refuse. Yet, among all these claimants, she did keep a little place here and there for me. Georgiana was older and graver, and less fascinating to the other girls, but between her and me there grew up the warmest friendship, which proved lifelong in its constancy.

"Catherine and Georgiana were reading 'Virgil' when I came to the school. I began the study of Latin alone, and at the end of the first year made a translation of 'Ovid' in verse, which was read at the final exhibition of the school, and regarded, I believe, as a very creditable performance. I was very much interested in poetry, and it was my dream to be a poet. I began a drama called 'Cleon.' The scene was laid in the court and time of the emperor Nero, and Cleon was a Greek lord residing at Nero's court, who, after much searching and doubting, at last comes to the knowledge of Christianity. I filled blank book after blank book with this drama. It filled my thoughts sleeping and waking. One day sister Catherine pounced down upon me, and said that I must not waste my time writing poetry, but discipline my mind by the study of Butler's 'Analogy.' So after this I wrote out abstracts from the 'Analogy,' and instructed a class of girls as old as myself, being compelled to master each chapter just ahead of the class I was teaching. About this time I read Baxter's 'Saint's Rest.' I do not think any book affected me more powerfully. As I walked the pavements I used to wish that they might sink beneath me if only I might find myself in heaven. I was at the same time very much interested in Butler's 'Analogy,' for Mr. Brace used to lecture on such themes when I was at Miss Pierce's school at Litchfield. I also began the study of French and Italian with a Miss Degan, who was born in Italy.

"It was about this time that I first believed myself to be a Christian. I was spending my summer vacation at home, in Litchfield. I shall ever remember that dewy, fresh summer morning. I knew that it was a sacramental Sunday, and thought with sadness that when all the good people should take the sacrificial bread and wine I should be left out. I tried hard to feel my sins and count them up; but what with the birds, the daisies, and the brooks that rippled by the way, it was impossible. I came into church quite dissatisfied with myself, and as I looked upon the pure white cloth, the snowy bread and shining cups, of the communion table, thought with a sigh: 'There won't be anything for me to-day; it is all for these grown-up Christians.' Nevertheless, when father began to speak, I was drawn to listen by a certain pathetic earnestness in his voice. Most of father's sermons were as unintelligible to me as if he had spoken in Choctaw. But sometimes he preached what he was accustomed to call a 'frame sermon;' that is, a sermon that sprung out of the deep feeling of the occasion, and which consequently could be neither premeditated nor repeated. His text was taken from the Gospel of John, the declaration of Jesus: 'Behold, I call you no longer servants, but friends.' His theme was Jesus as a soul friend offered to every human being.

"Forgetting all his hair-splitting distinctions and dialectic subtleties, he spoke in direct, simple, and tender language of the great love of Christ and his care for the soul. He pictured Him as patient with our errors, compassionate with our weaknesses, and sympathetic for our sorrows. He went on to say how He was ever near us, enlightening our ignorance, guiding our wanderings, comforting our sorrows with a love unwearied by faults, unchilled by ingratitude, till at last He should present us faultless before the throne of his glory with exceeding joy.

"I sat intent and absorbed. Oh! how much I needed just such a friend, I thought to myself. Then the awful fact came over me that I had never had any conviction of my sins, and consequently could not come to Him. I longed to cry out 'I will,' when father made his passionate appeal, 'Come, then, and trust your soul to this faithful friend.' Like a flash it came over me that if I needed conviction of sin, He was able to give me even this also. I would trust Him for the whole. My whole soul was illumined with joy, and as I left the church to walk home, it seemed to me as if Nature herself were hushing her breath to hear the music of heaven.

"As soon as father came home and was seated in his study, I went up to him and fell in his arms saying, 'Father, I have given myself to Jesus, and He has taken me.' I never shall forget the expression of his face as he looked down into my earnest, childish eyes; it was so sweet, so gentle, and like sunlight breaking out upon a landscape. 'Is it so?' he said, holding me silently to his heart, as I felt the hot tears fall on my head. 'Then has a new flower blossomed in the kingdom this day.'"

If she could have been let alone, and taught "to look up and not down, forward and not back, out and not in," this religious experience might have gone on as sweetly and naturally as the opening of a flower in the gentle rays of the sun. But unfortunately this was not possible at that time, when self-examination was carried to an extreme that was calculated to drive a nervous and sensitive mind well-nigh distracted. First, even her sister Catherine was afraid that there might be something wrong in the case of a lamb that had come into the fold without being first chased all over the lot by the shepherd; great stress being laid, in those days, on what was called "being under conviction." Then also the pastor of the First Church in Hartford, a bosom friend of Dr. Beecher, looked with melancholy and suspicious eyes on this unusual and doubtful path to heaven,—but more of this hereafter. Harriet's conversion took place in the summer of 1825, when she was fourteen, and the following year, April, 1826, Dr. Beecher resigned his pastorate in Litchfield to accept a call to the Hanover Street Church, Boston, Mass. In a letter to her grandmother Foote at Guilford, dated Hartford, March 4, 1826, Harriet writes:—

"You have probably heard that our home in Litchfield is broken up. Papa has received a call to Boston, and concluded to accept, because he could not support his family in Litchfield. He was dismissed last week Tuesday, and will be here (Hartford) next Tuesday with mamma and Isabel. Aunt Esther will take Charles and Thomas to her house for the present. Papa's salary is to be $2,000 and $500 settlement.

"I attend school constantly and am making some progress in my studies. I devote most of my attention to Latin and to arithmetic, and hope soon to prepare myself to assist Catherine in the school."

This breaking up of the Litchfield home led Harriet, under her father's advice, to seek to connect herself with the First Church of Hartford. Accordingly, accompanied by two of her school friends, she went one day to the pastor's study to consult with him concerning the contemplated step. The good man listened attentively to the child's simple and modest statement of Christian experience, and then with an awful, though kindly, solemnity of speech and manner said, "Harriet, do you feel that if the universe should be destroyed (awful pause) you could be happy with God alone?" After struggling in vain, in her mental bewilderment, to fix in her mind some definite conception of the meaning of the sounds which fell on her ear like the measured strokes of a bell, the child of fourteen stammered out, "Yes, sir."

"You realize, I trust," continued the doctor, "in some measure at least, the deceitfulness of your heart, and that in punishment for your sins God might justly leave you to make yourself as miserable as you have made yourself sinful?"

"Yes, sir," again stammered Harriet.

Having thus effectually, and to his own satisfaction, fixed the child's attention on the morbid and over-sensitive workings of her own heart, the good and truly kind-hearted man dismissed her with a fatherly benediction. But where was the joyous ecstasy of that beautiful Sabbath morning of a year ago? Where was that heavenly friend? Yet was not this as it should be, and might not God leave her "to make herself as miserable as she had made herself sinful"?

In a letter addressed to her brother Edward, about this time, she writes: "My whole life is one continued struggle: I do nothing right. I yield to temptation almost as soon as it assails me. My deepest feelings are very evanescent. I am beset behind and before, and my sins take away all my happiness. But that which most constantly besets me is pride—I can trace almost all my sins back to it."

In the mean time, the school is prospering. February 16, 1827, Catherine writes to Dr. Beecher: "My affairs go on well. The stock is all taken up, and next week I hope to have out the prospectus of the 'Hartford Female Seminary.' I hope the building will be done, and all things in order, by June. The English lady is coming with twelve pupils from New York." Speaking of Harriet, who was at this time with her father in Boston, she adds: "I have received some letters from Harriet to-day which make me feel uneasy. She says, 'I don't know as I am fit for anything, and I have thought that I could wish to die young, and let the remembrance of me and my faults perish in the grave, rather than live, as I fear I do, a trouble to every one. You don't know how perfectly wretched I often feel: so useless, so weak, so destitute of all energy. Mamma often tells me that I am a strange, inconsistent being. Sometimes I could not sleep, and have groaned and cried till midnight, while in the daytime I tried to appear cheerful and succeeded so well that papa reproved me for laughing so much. I was so absent sometimes that I made strange mistakes, and then they all laughed at me, and I laughed, too, though I felt as though I should go distracted. I wrote rules; made out a regular system for dividing my time; but my feelings vary so much that it is almost impossible for me to be regular.'"

But let Harriet "take courage in her dark sorrows and melancholies," as Carlyle says: "Samuel Johnson too had hypochondrias; all great souls are apt to have, and to be in thick darkness generally till the eternal ways and the celestial guiding stars disclose themselves, and the vague abyss of life knits itself up into firmaments for them."

At the same time (the winter of 1827), Catherine writes to Edward concerning Harriet: "If she could come here (Hartford) it might be the best thing for her, for she can talk freely to me. I can get her books, and Catherine Cogswell, Georgiana May, and her friends here could do more for her than any one in Boston, for they love her and she loves them very much. Georgiana's difficulties are different from Harriet's: she is speculating about doctrines, etc. Harriet will have young society here all the time, which she cannot have at home, and I think cheerful and amusing friends will do much for her. I can do better in preparing her to teach drawing than any one else, for I best know what is needed."

It was evidently necessary that something should be done to restore Harriet to a more tranquil and healthful frame of mind; consequently in the spring of 1827, accompanied by her friend Georgiana May, she went to visit her grandmother Foote at Nut Plains, Guilford. Miss May refers to this visit in a letter to Mrs. Foote, in January of the following winter.

HARTFORD, *January 4, 1828.*

DEAR MRS. FOOTE:— . . . I very often think of you and the happy hours I passed at your house last spring. It seems as if it were but yesterday: now, while I am writing, I can see your pleasant house and the familiar objects around you as distinctly as the day I left them. Harriet and I are very much the same girls we were then. I do not believe we have altered very much, though she is improved in some respects.

The August following this visit to Guilford Harriet writes to her brother Edward in a vein which is still streaked with sadness, but shows some indication of returning health of mind.

"Many of my objections you did remove that afternoon we spent together. After that I was not as unhappy as I had been. I felt, nevertheless, that my views were very indistinct and contradictory, and feared that if you left me thus I might return to the same dark, desolate state in which I had been all summer. I felt that my immortal interest, my happiness for both worlds, was depending on the turn my feelings might take. In my disappointment and distress I called upon God, and it seemed as if I was heard. I felt that He could supply the loss of all earthly love. All misery and darkness were over. I felt as if restored, nevermore to fall. Such sober certainty of waking bliss had long been a stranger to me. But even then I had doubts as to whether these feelings were right, because I felt love to God alone without that ardent love for my fellow-creatures which Christians have often felt. . . . I cannot say exactly what it is makes me reluctant to speak of my feelings. It costs me an effort to express feeling of any kind, but more particularly to speak of my private religious feelings. If any one questions me, my first impulse is to conceal all I can. As for expression of affection towards my brothers and sisters, my companions or friends, the stronger the affection the less inclination have I to express it. Yet sometimes I think myself the most frank, open, and communicative of beings, and at other times the most reserved. If you can resolve all these caprices into general principles, you will do more than I can. Your speaking so much philosophically has a tendency to repress confidence. We never wish to have our feelings analyzed down; and very little, nothing, that we say brought to the test of mathematical demonstration.

"It appears to me that if I only could adopt the views of God you presented to my mind, they would exert a strong and beneficial influence over my character. But I am afraid to accept them for several reasons. First, it seems to be taking from the majesty and dignity of the divine character to suppose that his happiness can be at all affected by the conduct of his sinful, erring creatures. Secondly, it seems to me that such views of God would have an effect on our own minds in lessening that reverence and fear which is one of the greatest motives to us for action. For, although to a generous mind the thought of the love of God would be a sufficient incentive to action, there are times of coldness when that love is not felt, and then there remains no sort of stimulus. I find as I adopt these sentiments I feel less fear of God, and, in view of sin, I feel only a sensation of grief which is more easily dispelled and forgotten than that I formerly felt."

A letter dated January 3, 1828, shows us that Harriet had returned to Hartford and was preparing herself to teach drawing and painting, under the direction of her sister Catherine.

MY DEAR GRANDMOTHER,—I should have written before to assure you of my remembrance of you, but I have been constantly employed, from nine in the morning till after dark at night, in taking lessons of a painting and drawing master, with only an intermission long enough to swallow a little dinner which was sent to me in the school-room. You may easily believe that after spending the day in this manner, I did not feel in a very epistolary humor in the evening, and if I had been, I could not have written, for when I did not go immediately to bed I was obliged to get a long French lesson.

The seminary is finished, and the school going on nicely. Miss Clarissa Brown is assisting Catherine in the school. Besides her, Catherine, and myself, there are two other teachers who both board in the family with us: one is Miss Degan, an Italian lady who teaches French and Italian; she rooms with me, and is very interesting and agreeable. Miss Hawks is rooming with Catherine. In some respects she reminds me very much of my mother. She is gentle, affectionate, modest, and retiring, and much beloved by all the scholars. . . . I am still going on with my French, and carrying two young ladies through Virgil, and if I have time, shall commence Italian.

I am very comfortable and happy.

I propose, my dear grandmamma, to send you by the first opportunity a dish of fruit of my own painting. Pray do not now devour it in anticipation, for I cannot promise that you will not find it sadly tasteless in reality. If so, please excuse it, for the sake of the poor young artist. I admire to cultivate a taste for painting, and I wish to improve it; it was what my dear mother admired and loved, and I cherish it for her sake. I have thought more of this dearest of all earthly friends these late years, since I have been old enough to know her character and appreciate her worth. I sometimes think that, had she lived, I might have been both better and happier than I now am, but God is good and wise in all his ways.

A letter written to her brother Edward in Boston, dated March 27, 1828, shows how slowly she adopted the view of God that finally became one of the most characteristic elements in her writings.

"I think that those views of God which you have presented to me have had an influence in restoring my mind to its natural tone. But still, after all, God is a being afar off. He is so far above us that anything but the most distant reverential affection seems almost sacrilegious. It is that affection that can lead us to be familiar that the heart needs. But easy and familiar expressions of attachment and that sort of confidential communication which I should address to papa or you would be improper for a subject to address to a king, much less for us to address to the King of kings. The language of prayer is of necessity stately and formal, and we cannot clothe all the little minutiæ of our wants and troubles in it. I wish I could describe to you how I feel when I pray. I feel that I love God,—that is, that I love Christ,—that I find comfort and happiness in it, and yet it is not that kind of comfort which would arise from free communication of my wants and sorrows to a friend. I sometimes wish that the Saviour were visibly present in this world, that I might go to Him for a solution of some of my difficulties. . . . Do you think, my dear brother, that there is such a thing as so realizing the presence and character of God that He can supply the place of earthly friends? I really wish to know what you think of this. . . . Do you suppose that God really loves sinners before they come to Him? Some say that we ought to tell them that God hates them, that He looks on them with utter abhorrence, and that they must love Him before He will look on them otherwise. Is it right to say to those who are in deep distress, 'God is interested in you; He feels for and loves you'?"

Appended to this letter is a short note from Miss Catherine Beecher, who evidently read the letter over and answered Harriet's questions herself. She writes: "When the young man came to Jesus, is it not said that Jesus loved him, though he was unrenewed?"

In April, 1828, Harriet again writes to her brother Edward:—

"I have had more reason to be grateful to that friend than ever before. He has not left me in all my weakness. It seems to me that my love to Him is the love of despair. All my communion with

Him, though sorrowful, is soothing. I am painfully sensible of ignorance and deficiency, but still I feel that I am willing that He should know all. He will look on all that is wrong only to purify and reform. He will never be irritated or impatient. He will never show me my faults in such a manner as to irritate without helping me. A friend to whom I would acknowledge all my faults must be perfect. Let any one once be provoked, once speak harshly to me, once sweep all the chords of my soul out of tune, I never could confide there again. It is only to the most perfect Being in the universe that imperfection can look and hope for patience. How strange! . . . You do not know how harsh and forbidding everything seems, compared with his character. All through the day in my intercourse with others, everything has a tendency to destroy the calmness of mind gained by communion with Him. One flatters me, another is angry with me, another is unjust to me.

"You speak of your predilections for literature having been a snare to you. I have found it so myself. I can scarcely think, without tears and indignation, that all that is beautiful and lovely and poetical has been laid on other altars. Oh! will there never be a poet with a heart enlarged and purified by the Holy Spirit, who shall throw all the graces of harmony, all the enchantments of feeling, pathos, and poetry, around sentiments worthy of them? . . . It matters little what service He has for me. . . . I do not mean to live in vain. He has given me talents, and I will lay them at his feet, well satisfied, if He will accept them. All my powers He can enlarge. He made my mind, and He can teach me to cultivate and exert its faculties."

The following November she writes from Groton, Conn., to Miss May:—

"I am in such an uncertain, unsettled state, traveling back and forth, that I have very little time to write. In the first place, on my arrival in Boston I was obliged to spend two days in talking and telling news. Then after that came calling, visiting, etc., and then I came off to Groton to see my poor brother George, who was quite out of spirits and in very trying circumstances. To-morrow I return to Boston and spend four or five days, and then go to Franklin, where I spend the rest of my vacation.

"I found the folks all well on my coming to Boston, and as to my new brother, James, he has nothing to distinguish him from forty other babies, except a very large pair of blue eyes and an uncommonly fair complexion, a thing which is of no sort of use or advantage to a man or boy.

"I am thinking very seriously of remaining in Groton and taking care of the female school, and at the same time being of assistance and company for George. On some accounts it would not be so pleasant as returning to Hartford, for I should be among strangers. Nothing upon this point can be definitely decided till I have returned to Boston, and talked to papa and Catherine."

Evidently papa and Catherine did not approve of the Groton plan, for in February of the following winter Harriet writes from Hartford to Edward, who is at this time with his father in Boston:—

"My situation this winter (1829) is in many respects pleasant. I room with three other teachers, Miss Fisher, Miss Mary Dutton, and Miss Brigham. Ann Fisher you know. Miss Dutton is about twenty, has a fine mathematical mind, and has gone as far into that science perhaps as most students at college. She is also, as I am told, quite learned in the languages. . . . Miss Brigham is somewhat older: is possessed of a fine mind and most unconquerable energy and perseverance of character. From early childhood she has been determined to obtain an education, and to attain to a certain standard. Where persons are determined to be anything, they will be. I think, for this reason, she will make a first-rate character. Such are my companions. We spend our time in school during the day, and in studying in the evening. My plan of study is to read rhetoric and prepare exercises for my class the first half hour in the evening; after that the rest of the evening is divided between French and Italian. Thus you see the plan of my employment and the character of my immediate companions. Besides these, there are others among the teachers and scholars who must exert an influence over my character. Miss Degan, whose constant occupation it is to make others laugh; Mrs. Gamage, her room-mate, a steady, devoted, sincere Christian. . . . Little things have great power over me, and if I meet with the least thing that crosses my feelings, I am often rendered unhappy for days and weeks. . . . I wish I could bring myself to feel perfectly indifferent to the opinions of others. I believe that there never was a person more dependent on the good and evil opinions of those around than I am. This desire to be loved forms, I fear, the great motive for all my actions. . . . I have been reading carefully the book of Job, and I do not think that it contains the views of God which you presented to me. God seems to have stripped a dependent creature of all that renders life desirable, and then to have answered his complaints from the whirlwind; and instead of showing mercy and pity, to have overwhelmed him by a display of his power and justice. . . . With the view I received from you, I should have expected that a being who sympathizes with his guilty, afflicted creatures would not have spoken thus. Yet, after all, I do believe that God is such a being as you represent Him to be, and in the New Testament I find in the character of Jesus Christ a revelation of God as merciful and compassionate; in fact, just such a God as I need.

"Somehow or another you have such a reasonable sort of way of saying things that when I come to reflect I almost always go over to your side. . . . My mind is often perplexed, and such thoughts arise in it that I cannot pray, and I become bewildered. The wonder to me is, how all ministers and all Christians can feel themselves so inexcusably sinful, when it seems to me we all come into the world in such a way that it would be miraculous if we did not sin. Mr. Hawes always says in prayer, 'We have nothing to offer in extenuation of any of our sins,' and I always think when he says it, that we have everything to offer in extenuation. The case seems to me exactly as if I had been brought into the world with such a thirst for ardent spirits that there was just a possibility, though no hope, that I should resist, and then my eternal happiness made dependent on my being temperate. Sometimes when I try to confess my sins, I feel that after all I am more to be pitied than blamed, for I have never known the time when I have not had a temptation within me so strong that it was certain I should not overcome it. This thought shocks me, but it comes with such force, and so appealingly, to all my consciousness, that it stifles all sense of sin. . . .

"Sometimes when I read the Bible, it seems to be wholly grounded on the idea that the sin of man is astonishing, inexcusable, and without palliation or cause, and the atonement is spoken of as such a wonderful and undeserved mercy that I am filled with amazement. Yet if I give up the Bible I gain nothing, for the providence of God in nature is just as full of mystery, and of the two I think that the Bible, with all its difficulties, is preferable to being without it; for the Bible holds out the hope that in a future world all shall be made plain. . . . So you see I am, as Mr. Hawes says, 'on the waves,' and all I can do is to take the word of God that He does do right and there I rest."

The following summer, in July, she writes to Edward: "I have never been so happy as this summer. I began it in more suffering than I ever before have felt, but there is One whom I daily thank for all that suffering, since I hope that it has brought me at last to rest entirely in Him. I do hope that my long, long course of wandering and darkness and unhappiness is over, and that I have found in Him who died for me all, and more than all, I could desire. Oh, Edward, you can feel as I do; you can speak of Him! There are few, very few, who can. Christians in general do not seem to look to Him as their best friend, or realize anything of his unutterable love. They speak with a cold, vague, reverential awe, but do not speak as if in the habit of close and near communion; as if they confided to Him every joy and sorrow and constantly looked to Him for direction and guidance. I cannot express to you, my brother, I cannot tell you, how that Saviour appears to me. To bear with one so imperfect, so weak, so inconsistent, as myself, implied, long-suffering and patience more than words can express. I love most to look on Christ as my teacher, as one who, knowing the utmost of my sinfulness, my waywardness, my folly, can still have patience; can reform, purify, and daily make me more like himself."

So, after four years of struggling and suffering, she returns to the place where she started from as a child of thirteen. It has been like watching a ship with straining masts and storm-beaten sails, buffeted by the waves, making for the harbor, and coming at last to quiet anchorage. There have been, of course, times of darkness and depression, but never any permanent loss of the religious trustfulness and peace of mind indicated by this letter.

The next three years were passed partly in Boston, and partly in Guilford and Hartford. Writing of this period of her life to the Rev. Charles Beecher, she says:—

MY DEAR BROTHER,—The looking over of father's letters in the period of his Boston life brings forcibly to my mind many recollections. At this time I was more with him, and associated in companionship of thought and feeling for a longer period than any other of my experience.

In the summer of 1832 she writes to Miss May, revealing her spiritual and intellectual life in a degree unusual, even for her.

"After the disquisition on myself above cited, you will be prepared to understand the changes through which this wonderful *ego et me ipse* has passed.

"The amount of the matter has been, as this inner world of mine has become worn out and untenable, I have at last concluded to come out of it and live in the external one, and, as F—— S—— once advised me, to give up the pernicious habit of meditation to the first Methodist minister that would take it, and try to mix in society somewhat as another person would.

"'*Horas non numero nisi serenas.*' Uncle Samuel, who sits by me, has just been reading the above motto, the inscription on a sun-dial in Venice. It strikes me as having a distant relationship to what I was going to say. I have come to a firm resolution to count no hours but unclouded ones, and to let all others slip out of my memory and reckoning as quickly as possible. . . .

"I am trying to cultivate a general spirit of kindliness towards everybody. Instead of shrinking into a corner to notice how other people behave, I am holding out my hand to the right and to the left, and forming casual or incidental acquaintances with all who will be acquainted with me. In this way I find society full of interest and pleasure—a pleasure which pleaseth me more because it is not old and worn out. From these friendships I expect little; therefore generally receive more than I expect. From past friendships I have expected everything, and must of necessity have been disappointed. The kind words and looks and smiles I call forth by looking and smiling are not much by themselves, but they form a very pretty flower border to the way of life. They embellish the day or the hour as it passes, and when they fade they only do just as you expected they would. This kind of pleasure in acquaintanceship is new to me. I never tried it before. When I used to meet persons, the first inquiry was, 'Have they such and such a character, or have they anything that might possibly be of use or harm to me?'"

It is striking, the degree of interest a letter had for her.

"Your long letter came this morning. It revived much in my heart. Just think how glad I must have been this morning to hear from you. I was glad. . . . I thought of it through all the vexations of school this morning. . . . I have a letter at home; and when I came home from school, I went leisurely over it.

"This evening I have spent in a little social party,—a dozen or so,—and I have been zealously talking all the evening. When I came to my cold, lonely room, there was your letter lying on the dressing-table. It touched me with a sort of painful pleasure, for it seems to me uncertain, improbable, that I shall ever return and find you as I have found your letter. Oh, my dear G——, it is scarcely well to love friends thus. The greater part that I see cannot move me deeply. They are present, and I enjoy them; they pass and I forget them. But those that I love differently; those that I LOVE; and oh, how much that word means! I feel sadly about them. They may change; they must die; they are separated from me, and I ask myself why should I wish to love with all the pains and penalties of such conditions? I check myself when expressing feelings like this, so much has been said of it by the sentimental, who talk what they could not have felt. But it is so deeply, sincerely so in me, that sometimes it will overflow. Well, there is a heaven,—a heaven,—a world of love, and love after all is the life-blood, the existence, the all in all of mind."

This is the key to her whole life. She was impelled by love, and did what she did, and wrote what she did, under the impulse of love. Never could "Uncle Tom's Cabin" or "The Minister's Wooing" have been written, unless by one to whom love was the "life-blood of existence, the all in all of mind." Years afterwards Mrs. Browning was to express this same thought in the language of poetry.

"But when a soul by choice and conscience doth
Throw out her full force on another soul,

The conscience and the concentration both
Make mere life love. For life in perfect whole
And aim consummated is love in sooth,
As nature's magnet heat rounds pole with pole."

CHAPTER III

CINCINNATI, 1832-1836.

DR. BEECHER CALLED TO CINCINNATI.—THE
WESTWARD JOURNEY.—FIRST LETTER FROM HOME.—
DESCRIPTION OF WALNUT HILLS.—STARTING A NEW
SCHOOL.—INWARD GLIMPSES.—THE SEMI-COLON
CLUB.—EARLY IMPRESSIONS OF SLAVERY.—A JOURNEY
TO THE EAST.—THOUGHTS AROUSED BY FIRST VISIT TO
NIAGARA.—MARRIAGE TO PROFESSOR STOWE.

IN 1832, after having been settled for six years over the
Hanover Street Church in Boston, Dr. Beecher received and finally
accepted a most urgent call to become President of Lane
Theological Seminary in Cincinnati. This institution had been
chartered in 1829, and in 1831 funds to the amount of nearly
$70,000 had been promised to it provided that Dr. Beecher
accepted the presidency. It was hard for this New England family
to sever the ties of a lifetime and enter on so long a journey to the
far distant West of those days; but being fully persuaded that their
duty lay in this direction, they undertook to perform it cheerfully
and willingly. With Dr. Beecher and his wife were to go Miss
Catherine Beecher, who had conceived the scheme of founding in
Cincinnati, then considered the capital of the West, a female
college, and Harriet, who was to act as her principal assistant. In
the party were also George, who was to enter Lane as a student,
Isabella, James, the youngest son, and Miss Esther Beecher, the
"Aunt Esther" of the children.

Before making his final decision, Dr. Beecher, accompanied by
his daughter Catherine, visited Cincinnati to take a general survey
of their proposed battlefield, and their impressions of the city are
given in the following letter written by the latter to Harriet in
Boston:—

"Here we are at last at our journey's end, alive and well. We are staying with Uncle Samuel (Foote), whose establishment I will try and sketch for you. It is on a height in the upper part of the city, and commands a fine view of the whole of the lower town. The city does not impress me as being so very new. It is true everything looks neat and clean, but it is compact, and many of the houses are of brick and very handsomely built. The streets run at right angles to each other, and are wide and well paved. We reached here in three days from Wheeling, and soon felt ourselves at home. The next day father and I, with three gentlemen, walked out to Walnut Hills. The country around the city consists of a constant succession and variety of hills of all shapes and sizes, forming an extensive amphitheatre. The site of the seminary is very beautiful and picturesque, though I was disappointed to find that both river and city are hidden by intervening hills. I never saw a place so capable of being rendered a paradise by the improvements of taste as the environs of this city. Walnut Hills are so elevated and cool that people have to leave there to be sick, it is said. The seminary is located on a farm of one hundred and twenty-five acres of fine land, with groves of superb trees around it, about two miles from the city. We have finally decided on the spot where our house shall stand in case we decide to come, and you cannot (where running water or the seashore is wanting) find another more delightful spot for a residence. It is on an eminence, with a grove running up from the back to the very doors, another grove across the street in front, and fine openings through which distant hills and the richest landscapes appear.

"I have become somewhat acquainted with those ladies we shall have the most to do with, and find them intelligent, New England sort of folks. Indeed, this is a New England city in all its habits, and its inhabitants are more than half from New England. The Second Church, which is the best in the city, will give father a unanimous call to be their minister, with the understanding that he will give them what time he can spare from the seminary.

"I know of no place in the world where there is so fair a prospect of finding everything that makes social and domestic life pleasant. Uncle John and Uncle Samuel are just the intelligent, sociable, free, and hospitable sort of folk that everybody likes and everybody feels at home with.

"The folks are very anxious to have a school on our plan set on foot here. We can have fine rooms in the city college building, which is now unoccupied, and everybody is ready to lend a helping hand. As to father, I never saw such a field of usefulness and influence as is offered to him here."

This, then, was the field of labor in which the next eighteen years of the life of Mrs. Stowe were to be passed. At this time her sister Mary was married and living in Hartford, her brothers Henry Ward and Charles were in college, while William and Edward, already licensed to preach, were preparing to follow their father to the West.

THE HOME AT WALNUT HILLS, CINCINNATI.

Mr. Beecher's preliminary journey to Cincinnati was undertaken in the early spring of 1832, but he was not ready to remove his family until October of that year. An interesting account of this westward journey is given by Mrs. Stowe in a letter sent back to Hartford from Cincinnati, as follows:—

"Well, my dear, the great sheet is out and the letter is begun. All our family are here (in New York), and in good health.

"Father is to perform to-night in the Chatham Theatre! 'positively for the *last* time this season!' I don't know, I'm sure, as we shall ever get to Pittsburgh. Father is staying here begging money for the Biblical Literature professorship; the incumbent is to be C. Stowe. Last night we had a call from Arthur Tappan and Mr. Eastman. Father begged $2,000 yesterday, and now the good people are praying him to abide certain days, as he succeeds so well. They are talking of sending us off and keeping him here. I really dare not go and see Aunt Esther and mother now; they were in the depths of tribulation before at staying so long, and now,

'In the lowest depths, *another* deep!'

Father is in high spirits. He is all in his own element,—dipping into books; consulting authorities for his oration; going round here, there, everywhere; begging, borrowing, and spoiling the Egyptians; delighted with past success and confident for the future.

"Wednesday. Still in New York. I believe it would kill me dead to live long in the way I have been doing since I have been here. It is a sort of agreeable delirium. There's only one thing about it, it is too *scattering*. I begin to be athirst for the waters of quietness."

Writing from Philadelphia, she adds:—

"Well, we did get away from New York at last, but it was through much tribulation. The truckman carried all the family baggage to the wrong wharf, and, after waiting and waiting on board the boat, we were obliged to start without it, George remaining to look it up. Arrived here late Saturday evening,—dull, drizzling weather; poor Aunt Esther in dismay,—not a clean cap to put on,—mother in like state; all of us destitute. We went, half to Dr. Skinner's and half to Mrs. Elmes's: mother, Aunt Esther, father, and James to the former; Kate, Bella, and myself to Mr. Elmes's. They are rich, hospitable folks, and act the part of Gaius in apostolic times. . . . Our trunks came this morning. Father stood and saw them all brought into Dr. Skinner's entry, and then he swung his hat and gave a 'hurrah,' as any man would whose wife had not had a clean cap or ruffle for a week. Father does not succeed very well in opening purses here. Mr. Eastman says, however, that this is not of much consequence. I saw to-day a notice in the 'Philadelphian' about father, setting forth how 'this distinguished brother, with his large family, having torn themselves from the endearing scenes of their home,' etc., etc., 'were going, like Jacob,' etc.,—a very scriptural and appropriate flourish. It is too much after the manner of men, or, as Paul says, speaking 'as a fool.' A number of the pious people of this city are coming here this evening to hold a prayer-meeting with reference to the journey and its object. For *this* I thank them."

From Downington she writes:—

"Here we all are,—Noah and his wife and his sons and his daughters, with the cattle and creeping things, all dropped down in the front parlor of this tavern, about thirty miles from Philadelphia. If to-day is a fair specimen of our journey, it will be a very pleasant, obliging driver, good roads, good spirits, good dinner, fine scenery, and now and then some 'psalms and hymns and spiritual songs;' for with George on board you may be sure of music of some kind. Moreover, George has provided himself with a quantity of tracts, and he and the children have kept up a regular discharge at all the wayfaring people we encountered. I tell him he is *peppering* the land with moral influence.

"We are all well; all in good spirits. Just let me give you a peep into our traveling household. Behold us, then, in the front parlor of this country inn, all as much at home as if we were in Boston. Father is sitting opposite to me at this table, reading; Kate is writing a billet-doux to Mary on a sheet like this; Thomas is opposite, writing in a little journal that he keeps; Sister Bell, too, has her little record; George is waiting for a seat that he may produce his paper and write. As for me, among the multitude of my present friends, my heart still makes occasional visits to absent ones,—visits full of pleasure, and full of cause of gratitude to Him who gives us friends. I have thought of you often to-day, my G. We stopped this noon at a substantial Pennsylvania tavern, and among the flowers in the garden was a late monthly honeysuckle like the one at North Guilford. I made a spring for it, but George secured the finest bunch, which he wore in his button-hole the rest of the noon.

"This afternoon, as we were traveling, we struck up and sang 'Jubilee.' It put me in mind of the time when we used to ride along the rough North Guilford roads and make the air vocal as we went along. Pleasant times those. Those were blue skies, and that was a beautiful lake and noble pine-trees and rocks they were that hung over it. But those we shall look upon 'na mair.'

"Well, my dear, there is a land where we shall not *love* and *leave*. Those skies shall never cease to shine, the waters of life we shall *never* be called upon *to leave*. We have here no continuing city, but we seek one to come. In such thoughts as these I desire ever to rest, and with such words as these let us 'comfort one another and edify one another.'"

"Harrisburg, Sunday evening. Mother, Aunt Esther, George, and the little folks have just gathered into Kate's room, and we have just been singing. Father has gone to preach for Mr. De Witt. To-morrow we expect to travel sixty-two miles, and in two more days shall reach Wheeling; there we shall take the steamboat to Cincinnati."

On the same journey George Beecher writes:—

"We had poor horses in crossing the mountains. Our average rate for the last four days to Wheeling was forty-four miles. The journey, which takes the mail-stage forty-eight hours, took us eight days. At Wheeling we deliberated long whether to go on board a boat for Cincinnati, but the prevalence of the cholera there at last decided us to remain. While at Wheeling father preached eleven times,—nearly every evening,—and gave them the Taylorite heresy on sin and decrees to the highest notch; and what amused me most was to hear him establish it from the Confession of Faith. It went high and dry, however, above all objections, and they were delighted with it, even the old school men, since it had not been christened 'heresy' in their hearing. After remaining in Wheeling eight days, we chartered a stage for Cincinnati, and started next morning.

"At Granville, Ohio, we were invited to stop and attend a protracted meeting. Being in no great hurry to enter Cincinnati till the cholera had left, we consented. We spent the remainder of the week there, and I preached five times and father four. The interest was increasingly deep and solemn each day, and when we left there were forty-five cases of conversion in the town, besides those from the surrounding towns. The people were astonished at the doctrine; said they never saw the truth so plain in their lives."

Although the new-comers were cordially welcomed in Cincinnati, and everything possible was done for their comfort and to make them feel at home, they felt themselves to be strangers in a strange land. Their homesickness and yearnings for New England are set forth by the following extracts from Mrs. Stowe's answer to the first letter they received from Hartford after leaving there:—

MY DEAR SISTER (Mary),—The Hartford letter from all and sundry has just arrived, and after cutting all manner of capers expressive of thankfulness, I have skipped three stairs at a time up to the study to begin an answer. My notions of answering letters are according to the literal sense of the word; not waiting six months and then scrawling a lazy reply, but sitting down the moment you have read a letter, and telling, as Dr. Woods says, "How the subject strikes you." I wish I could be clear that the path of duty lay in talking to you this afternoon, but as I find a loud call to consider the heels of George's stockings, I must only write a word or two, and then resume my darning-needle. You don't know how anxiously we all have watched for some intelligence from Hartford. Not a day has passed when I have not been the efficient agent in getting somebody to the post-office, and every day my heart has sunk at the sound of "no letters." I felt a tremor quite sufficient for a lover when I saw your handwriting once more, so you see that in your old age you can excite quite as much emotion as did the admirable Miss Byron in her adoring Sir Charles. I hope the consideration and digestion of this fact will have its due weight in encouraging you to proceed.

The fact of our having received said letter is as yet a state secret, not to be made known till all our family circle "in full assembly meet" at the tea-table. Then what an illumination! "How we shall be edified and fructified," as that old Methodist said. It seems too bad to keep it from mother and Aunt Esther a whole afternoon, but then I have the comfort of thinking that we are consulting for their greatest happiness "on the whole," which is metaphysical benevolence.

So kind Mrs. Parsons stopped in the very midst of her pumpkin pies to think of us? Seems to me I can see her bright, cheerful face now! And then those well known handwritings! We *do* love our Hartford friends dearly; there can be, I think, no controverting that fact. Kate says that the word *love* is used in *six senses*, and I am sure in some one of them they will all come in. Well, good-by for the present.

Evening. Having finished the last hole on George's black vest, I stick in my needle and sit down to be sociable. You don't know how coming away from New England has sentimentalized us all! Never was there such an abundance of meditation on our native land, on the joys of friendship, the pains of separation. Catherine had an alarming paroxysm in Philadelphia which expended itself in "The Emigrant's Farewell." After this was sent off she felt considerably relieved. My symptoms have been of a less acute kind, but, I fear, more enduring. There! the tea-bell rings. Too bad! I was just going to say something bright. Now to take your letter and run! How they will stare when I produce it!

After tea. Well, we have had a fine time. When supper was about half over, Catherine began: "We have a dessert that we have been saving all the afternoon," and then I held up my letter. "See here, this is from Hartford!" I wish you could have seen Aunt Esther's eyes brighten, and mother's pale face all in a smile, and father, as I unfolded the letter and began. Mrs. Parsons's notice of her Thanksgiving predicament caused just a laugh, and then one or two sighs (I told you we were growing sentimental!). We did talk some of keeping it (Thanksgiving), but perhaps we should all have felt something of the text, "How shall we sing the Lord's song in a strange land?" Your praises of Aunt Esther I read twice in an audible voice, as the children made some noise the first time. I think I detected a visible blush, though she found at that time a great deal to do in spreading bread and butter for James, and shuffling his plate; and, indeed, it was rather a vehement attack on her humility, since it gave her at least "angelic perfection," if not "Adamic" (to use Methodist technics). Jamie began his Sunday-school career yesterday. The superintendent asked him how old he was. "I'm four years old now, and when it *snows very hard* I shall be five," he answered. I have just been trying to make him interpret his meaning; but he says, "Oh, I said so because I could not think of anything else to say." By the by, Mary, speaking of the temptations of cities, I have much solicitude on Jamie's account lest he should form improper intimacies, for yesterday or day before we saw him parading by the house with his arm over the neck of a great hog, apparently on the most amicable terms possible; and the other day he actually got upon the back of one, and rode some distance. So much for allowing these animals to promenade the streets, a particular in which Mrs. Cincinnati has imitated the domestic arrangements of some of her elder sisters, and a very disgusting one it is.

Our family physician is one Dr. Drake, a man of a good deal of science, theory, and reputed skill, but a sort of general mark for the opposition of all the medical cloth of the city. He is a tall, rectangular, perpendicular sort of a body, as stiff as a poker, and enunciates his prescriptions very much as though he were delivering a discourse on the doctrine of election. The other evening he was detained from visiting Kate, and he sent a very polite, ceremonious note containing a prescription, with Dr. D.'s compliments to Miss Beecher, requesting that she would take the inclosed in a little molasses at nine o'clock precisely.

The house we are at present inhabiting is the most inconvenient, ill-arranged, good-for-nothing, and altogether to be execrated affair that ever was put together. It was evidently built without a thought of a winter season. The kitchen is so disposed that it cannot be reached from any part of the house without going out into the air. Mother is actually obliged to put on a bonnet and cloak every time she goes into it. In the house are two parlors with folding doors between them. The back parlor has but one window, which opens on a veranda and has its lower half painted to keep out what little light there is. I need scarcely add that our landlord is an old bachelor and of course acted up to the light he had, though he left little enough of it for his tenants.

During this early Cincinnati life Harriet suffered much from ill-health accompanied by great mental depression; but in spite of both she labored diligently with her sister Catherine in establishing their school. They called it the Western Female Institute, and proposed to conduct it upon the college plan, with a faculty of instructors. As all these things are treated at length in letters written by Mrs. Stowe to her friend, Miss Georgiana May, we cannot do better than turn to them. In May, 1833, she writes:—

"Bishop Purcell visited our school to-day and expressed himself as greatly pleased that we had opened such an one here. He spoke of my poor little geography, and thanked me for the unprejudiced manner in which I had handled the Catholic question in it. I was of course flattered that he should have known anything of the book.

"How I wish you could see Walnut Hills. It is about two miles from the city, and the road to it is as picturesque as you can imagine a road to be without 'springs that run among the hills.' Every possible variety of hill and vale of beautiful slope, and undulations of land set off by velvet richness of turf and broken up by groves and forests of every outline of foliage, make the scene Arcadian. You might ride over the same road a dozen times a day untired, for the constant variation of view caused by ascending and descending hills relieves you from all tedium. Much of the wooding is beech of a noble growth. The straight, beautiful shafts of these trees as one looks up the cool green recesses of the woods seems as though they might form very proper columns for a Dryad temple. There! Catherine is growling at me for sitting up so late; so 'adieu to music, moonlight, and you.' I meant to tell you an abundance of classical things that I have been thinking to-night, but 'woe's me.'

"Since writing the above my whole time has been taken up in the labor of our new school, or wasted in the fatigue and lassitude following such labor. To-day is Sunday, and I am staying at home because I think it is time to take some efficient means to dissipate the illness and bad feelings of divers kinds that have for some time been growing upon me. At present there is and can be very little system or regularity about me. About half of my time I am scarcely alive, and a great part of the rest the slave and sport of morbid feeling and unreasonable prejudice. I have everything but good health.

"I still rejoice that this letter will find you in good old Connecticut—thrice blessed—'oh, had I the wings of a dove' I would be there too. Give my love to Mary H. I remember well how gently she used to speak to and smile on that forlorn old daddy that boarded at your house one summer. It was associating with her that first put into my head the idea of saying something to people who were not agreeable, and of saying something when I had nothing to say, as is generally the case on such occasions."

Again she writes to the same friend: "Your letter, my dear G., I have just received, and read through three times. Now for my meditations upon it. What a woman of the world you are grown. How good it would be for me to be put into a place which so breaks up and precludes thought. Thought, intense emotional thought, has been my disease. How much good it might do me to be where I could not but be thoughtless. . . .

"Now, Georgiana, let me copy for your delectation a list of matters that I have jotted down for consideration at a teachers' meeting to be held to-morrow night. It runneth as follows. Just hear! 'About quills and paper on the floor; forming classes; drinking in the entry (cold water, mind you); giving leave to speak; recess-bell, etc., etc.' 'You are tired, I see,' says Gilpin, 'so am I,' and I spare you.

"I have just been hearing a class of little girls recite, and telling them a fairy story which I had to spin out as it went along, beginning with 'once upon a time there was,' etc., in the good old-fashioned way of stories.

"Recently I have been reading the life of Madame de Staël and 'Corinne.' I have felt an intense sympathy with many parts of that book, with many parts of her character. But in America feelings vehement and absorbing like hers become still more deep, morbid, and impassioned by the constant habits of self-government which the rigid forms of our society demand. They are repressed, and they burn inward till they burn the very soul, leaving only dust and ashes. It seems to me the intensity with which my mind has thought and felt on every subject presented to it has had this effect. It has withered and exhausted it, and though young I have no sympathy with the feelings of youth. All that is enthusiastic, all that is impassioned in admiration of nature, of writing, of character, in devotional thought and emotion, or in the emotions of affection, I have felt with vehement and absorbing intensity,— felt till my mind is exhausted, and seems to be sinking into deadness. Half of my time I am glad to remain in a listless vacancy, to busy myself with trifles, since thought is pain, and emotion is pain."

During the winter of 1833-34 the young school-teacher became so distressed at her own mental listlessness that she made a vigorous effort to throw it off. She forced herself to mingle in society, and, stimulated by the offer of a prize of fifty dollars by Mr. James Hall, editor of the "Western Monthly," a newly established magazine, for the best short story, she entered into the competition. Her story, which was entitled "Uncle Lot," afterwards republished in the "Mayflower," was by far the best submitted, and was awarded the prize without hesitation. This success gave a new direction to her thoughts, gave her an insight into her own ability, and so encouraged her that from that time on she devoted most of her leisure moments to writing.

Her literary efforts were further stimulated at this time by the congenial society of the Semi-Colon Club, a little social circle that met on alternate weeks at Mr. Samuel Foote's and Dr. Drake's. The name of the club originated with a roundabout and rather weak bit of logic set forth by one of its promoters. He said: "You know that in Spanish Columbus is called 'Colon.' Now he who discovers a new pleasure is certainly half as great as he who discovers a new continent. Therefore if Colon discovered a continent, we who have discovered in this club a new pleasure should at least be entitled to the name of 'Semi-Colons.'" So Semi-Colons they became and remained for some years.

At some meetings compositions were read, and at others nothing was read, but the time was passed in a general discussion of some interesting topic previously announced. Among the members of the club were Professor Stowe, unsurpassed in Biblical learning; Judge James Hall, editor of the "Western Monthly;" General Edward King; Mrs. Peters, afterwards founder of the Philadelphia School of Design; Miss Catherine Beecher; Mrs. Caroline Lee Hentz; E. P. Cranch; Dr. Drake; S. P. Chase, and many others who afterwards became prominent in their several walks of life.

In one of her letters to Miss May, Mrs. Stowe describes one of her methods for entertaining the members of the Semi-Colon as follows:—

"I am wondering as to what I shall do next. I have been writing a piece to be read next Monday evening at Uncle Sam's *soirée* (the Semi-Colon). It is a letter purporting to be from Dr. Johnson. I have been stilting about in his style so long that it is a relief to me to come down to the jog of common English. Now I think of it I will just give you a history of my campaign in this circle.

"My first piece was a letter from Bishop Butler, written in his outrageous style of parentheses and foggification. My second a satirical essay on the modern uses of languages. This I shall send to you, as some of the gentlemen, it seems, took a fancy to it and requested leave to put it in the 'Western Magazine,' and so it is in print. It is ascribed to *Catherine*, or I don't know that I should have let it go. I have no notion of appearing in *propria personæ*.

"The next piece was a satire on certain members who were getting very much into the way of joking on the worn-out subjects of matrimony and old maid and old bachelorism. I therefore wrote a set of legislative enactments purporting to be from the ladies of the society, forbidding all such allusions in future. It made some sport at the time. I try not to be personal, and to be courteous, even in satire.

"But I have written a piece this week that is making me some disquiet. I did not like it that there was so little that was serious and rational about the reading. So I conceived the design of writing a *set of letters*, and throwing them in, as being the letters of a friend. I wrote a letter this week for the first of the set,—easy, not very sprightly,—describing an imaginary situation, a house in the country, a gentleman and lady, Mr. and Mrs. Howard, as being pious, literary, and agreeable. I threw into the letter a number of little particulars and incidental allusions to give it the air of having been really a letter. I meant thus to give myself an opportunity for the introduction of different subjects and the discussion of different characters in future letters.

"I meant to write on a great number of subjects in future. Cousin Elisabeth, only, was in the secret; Uncle Samuel and Sarah Elliot were not to know.

"Yesterday morning I finished my letter, smoked it to make it look yellow, tore it to make it look old, directed it and scratched out the direction, postmarked it with red ink, sealed it and broke the seal, all this to give credibility to the fact of its being a real letter. Then I inclosed it in an envelope, stating that it was a part of a *set* which had incidentally fallen into my hands. This envelope was written in a scrawny, scrawly, gentleman's hand.

"I put it into the office in the morning, directed to 'Mrs. Samuel E. Foote,' and then sent word to Sis that it was coming, so that she might be ready to enact the part.

"Well, the deception took. Uncle Sam examined it and pronounced, *ex cathedra*, that it must have been a real letter. Mr. Greene (the gentleman who reads) declared that it must have come from Mrs. Hall, and elucidated the theory by spelling out the names and dates which I had erased, which, of course, he accommodated to his own tastes. But then, what makes me feel uneasy is that Elisabeth, after reading it, did not seem to be exactly satisfied. She thought it had too much sentiment, too much particularity of incident,—she did not exactly know what. She was afraid that it would be criticised unmercifully. Now Elisabeth has a tact and quickness of perception that I trust to, and her remarks have made me uneasy enough. I am unused to being criticised, and don't know how I shall bear it."

In 1833 Mrs. Stowe first had the subject of slavery brought to her personal notice by taking a trip across the river from Cincinnati into Kentucky in company with Miss Dutton, one of the associate teachers in the Western Institute. They visited an estate that afterwards figured as that of Colonel Shelby in "Uncle Tom's Cabin," and here the young authoress first came into personal contact with the negro slaves of the South. In speaking, many years afterwards, of this visit, Miss Dutton said: "Harriet did not seem to notice anything in particular that happened, but sat much of the time as though abstracted in thought. When the negroes did funny things and cut up capers, she did not seem to pay the slightest attention to them. Afterwards, however, in reading 'Uncle Tom.' I recognized scene after scene of that visit portrayed with the most minute fidelity, and knew at once where the material for that portion of the story had been gathered."

At this time, however, Mrs. Stowe was more deeply interested in the subject of education than in that of slavery, as is shown by the following extract from one of her letters to Miss May, who was herself a teacher. She says:—

"We mean to turn over the West by means of *model schools* in this, its capital. We mean to have a young lady's school of about fifty or sixty, a primary school of little girls to the same amount, and then a primary school for *boys*. We have come to the conclusion that the work of teaching will never be rightly done till it passes into *female* hands. This is especially true with regard to boys. To govern boys by moral influences requires tact and talent and versatility it requires also the same division of labor that female education does. But men of tact, versatility, talent, and piety will not devote their lives to teaching. They must be ministers and missionaries, and all that, and while there is such a thrilling call for action in this way, every man who is merely teaching feels as if he were a Hercules with a distaff, ready to spring to the first trumpet that calls him away. As for division of labor, men must have salaries that can support wife and family, and, of course, a revenue would be required to support a requisite number of teachers if they could be found.

"Then, if men have more knowledge they have less talent at communicating it, nor have they the patience, the long-suffering, and gentleness necessary to superintend the formation of character. We intend to make these principles understood, and ourselves to set the example of what females can do in this way. You see that first-rate talent is necessary for all that we mean to do, especially for the last, because here we must face down the prejudices of society and we must have exemplary success to be believed. We want original, planning minds, and you do not know how few there are among females, and how few we can command of those that exist."

During the summer of 1834 the young teacher and writer made her first visit East since leaving New England two years before. Its object was mainly to be present at the graduation of her favorite brother, Henry Ward, from Amherst College. The earlier part of this journey was performed by means of stage to Toledo, and thence by steamer to Buffalo. A pleasant bit of personal description, and also of impressions of Niagara, seen for the first time on this journey, are given in a letter sent back to Cincinnati during its progress. In it she says of her fellow-travelers:—

"Then there was a portly, rosy, clever Mr. Smith, or Jones, or something the like; and a New Orleans girl looking like distraction, as far as dress is concerned, but with the prettiest language and softest intonations in the world, and one of those faces which, while you say it isn't handsome, keeps you looking all the time to see what it can be that is so pretty about it. Then there was Miss B., an independent, good-natured, do-as-I-please sort of a body, who seemed of perpetual motion from morning till night. Poor Miss D. said, when we stopped at night, 'Oh, dear! I suppose Lydia will be fiddling about our room till morning, and we shall not one of us sleep.' Then, by way of contrast, there was a Mr. Mitchell, the most gentlemanly, obliging man that ever changed his seat forty times a day to please a lady. Oh, yes, he could ride outside,—or, oh, certainly, he could ride inside,—he had no objection to this, or that, or the other. Indeed, it was difficult to say what could come amiss to him. He speaks in a soft, quiet manner, with something of a drawl, using very correct, well-chosen language, and pronouncing all his words with carefulness; has everything in his dress and traveling appointments *comme il faut*; and seems to think there is abundant time for everything that is to be done in this world, without, as he says, 'any unnecessary excitement.' Before the party had fully discovered his name he was usually designated as 'the obliging gentleman,' or 'that gentleman who is so accommodating.' Yet our friend, withal, is of Irish extraction, and I have seen him roused to talk with both hands and a dozen words in a breath. He fell into a little talk about abolition and slavery with our good Mr. Jones, a man whose mode of reasoning consists in repeating the same sentence at regular intervals as long as you choose to answer it. This man, who was finally convinced that negroes were black, used it as an irrefragable argument to all that could be said, and at last began to deduce from it that they might just as well be slaves as anything else, and so he proceeded till all the philanthropy of our friend was roused, and he sprung up all lively and oratorical and gesticulatory and indignant to my heart's content. I like to see a quiet man that can be roused."

In the same letter she gives her impressions of Niagara, as follows:—

"I have seen it (Niagara) and yet live. Oh, where is your soul? Never mind, though. Let me tell, if I can, what is unutterable. Elisabeth, it is not *like* anything; it did not look like anything I expected; it did not look like a waterfall. I did not once think whether it was high or low; whether it roared or didn't roar; whether it equaled my expectations or not. My mind whirled off, it seemed to me, in a new, strange world. It seemed unearthly, like the strange, dim images in the Revelation. I thought of the great white throne; the rainbow around it; the throne in sight like unto an emerald; and oh! that beautiful water rising like moonlight, falling as the soul sinks when it dies, to rise refined, spiritualized, and pure. That rainbow, breaking out, trembling, fading, and again coming like a beautiful spirit walking the waters. Oh, it is lovelier than it is great; it is like the Mind that made it: great, but so veiled in beauty that we gaze without terror. I felt as if I could have *gone over* with the waters; it would be so beautiful a death; there would be no fear in it. I felt the rock tremble under me with a sort of joy. I was so maddened that I could have gone too, if it had gone."

While at the East she was greatly affected by hearing of the death of her dear friend, Eliza Tyler, the wife of Professor Stowe. This lady was the daughter of Dr. Bennett Tyler, president of the Theological Institute of Connecticut, at East Windsor; but twenty-five years of age at the time of her death, a very beautiful woman gifted with a wonderful voice. She was also possessed of a well-stored mind and a personal magnetism that made her one of the most popular members of the Semi-Colon Club, in the proceedings of which she took an active interest.

Her death left Professor Stowe a childless widower, and his forlorn condition greatly excited the sympathy of her who had been his wife's most intimate friend. It was easy for sympathy to ripen into love, and after a short engagement Harriet E. Beecher became the wife of Professor Calvin E. Stowe.

Her last act before the wedding was to write the following note to the friend of her girlhood, Miss Georgiana May:—

January 6, 1836.

Well, my dear G., about half an hour more and your old friend, companion, schoolmate, sister, etc., will cease to be Hatty Beecher and change to nobody knows who. My dear, you are engaged, and pledged in a year or two to encounter a similar fate, and do you wish to know how you shall feel? Well, my dear, I have been dreading and dreading the time, and lying awake all last week wondering how I should live through this overwhelming crisis, and lo! it has come and I feel *nothing at all.*

The wedding is to be altogether domestic; nobody present but my own brothers and sisters, and my old colleague, Mary Dutton; and as there is a sufficiency of the ministry in our family we have not even to call in the foreign aid of a minister. Sister Katy is not here, so she will not witness my departure from her care and guidance to that of another. None of my numerous friends and acquaintances who have taken such a deep interest in making the connection for me even know the day, and it will be all done and over before they know anything about it.

Well, it is really a mercy to have this entire stupidity come over one at such a time. I should be crazy to feel as I did yesterday, or indeed to feel anything at all. But I inwardly vowed that my last feelings and reflections on this subject should be yours, and as I have not got any, it is just as well to tell you *that.* Well, here comes Mr. S., so farewell, and for the last time I subscribe

Your own
H. E. B.

CHAPTER IV

EARLY MARRIED LIFE, 1836-1840

PROFESSOR STOWE'S INTEREST IN POPULAR EDUCATION.—HIS DEPARTURE FOR EUROPE.—SLAVERY RIOTS IN CINCINNATI.—BIRTH OF TWIN DAUGHTERS.— PROFESSOR STOWE'S RETURN AND VISIT TO COLUMBUS.—DOMESTIC TRIALS.—AIDING A FUGITIVE SLAVE.—AUTHORSHIP UNDER DIFFICULTIES.—A BEECHER ROUND ROBIN.

THE letter to her friend Georgiana May, begun half an hour before her wedding, was not completed until nearly two months after that event. Taking it from her portfolio, she adds:—

"Three weeks have passed since writing the above, and my husband and self are now quietly seated by our own fireside, as domestic as any pair of tame fowl you ever saw; he writing to his mother, and I to you. Two days after our marriage we took a wedding excursion, so called, though we would most gladly have been excused this conformity to ordinary custom had not necessity required Mr. Stowe to visit Columbus, and I had too much adhesiveness not to go too. Ohio roads at this season are no joke, I can tell you, though we were, on the whole, wonderfully taken care of, and our expedition included as many pleasures as an expedition at this time of the year *ever* could.

"And now, my dear, perhaps the wonder to you, as to me, is how this momentous crisis in the life of such a wisp of nerve as myself has been transacted so quietly. My dear, it is a wonder to myself. I am tranquil, quiet, and happy. I look *only* on the present, and leave the future with Him who has hitherto been so kind to me. 'Take no thought for the morrow' is my motto, and my comfort is to rest on Him in whose house there are many mansions provided when these fleeting earthly ones pass away.

"Dear Georgy, naughty girl that I am, it is a month that I have let the above lie by, because I got into a strain of emotion in it that I dreaded to return to. Well, so it shall be no longer. In about five weeks Mr. Stowe and myself start for New England. He sails the first of May. I am going with him to Boston, New York, and other places, and shall stop finally at Hartford, whence, as soon as he is gone, it is my intention to return westward."

This reference to her husband as about to leave her relates to his sailing for Europe to purchase books for Lane Seminary, and also as a commissioner appointed by the State of Ohio to investigate the public school systems of the old world. He had long been convinced that higher education was impossible in the West without a higher grade of public schools, and had in 1833 been one of the founders in Cincinnati of "The College of Teachers," an institution that existed for ten years, and exerted a widespread influence. Its objects were to popularize the common schools, raise the standard of teachers, and create a demand for education among the people. Professor Stowe was associated in this movement with many of the leading intellects of Ohio at that time, and among them were Albert Pickett, Dr. Drake, Smith Grimke, Archbishop Purcell, President A. H. McGuffey, Dr. Beecher, Lydia Sigourney, Caroline Lee Hentz, and others. Their influence finally extended to the state legislature, and it was concluded to authorize Professor Stowe, when abroad, to investigate and report upon the common school systems of Europe, especially Prussia.

He sailed from New York for London in the ship Montreal, Captain Champlin, on June 8, 1836, and carried with him, to be opened only after he was at sea, a letter from his wife, from which the following extract is made:—

"Now, my dear, that you are gone where you are out of the reach of my care, advice, and good management, it is fitting that you should have something under my hand and seal for your comfort and furtherance in the new world you are going to. Firstly, I must caution you to set your face as a flint against the 'cultivation of indigo,' as Elisabeth calls it, in any way or shape. Keep yourself from it most scrupulously, and though you are unprovided with that precious and savory treatise entitled 'Kemper's Consolations,' yet you can exercise yourself to recall and set in order such parts thereof as would more particularly suit your case, particularly those portions wherewith you so much consoled Kate, Aunt Esther, and your unworthy handmaid, while you yet tarried at Walnut Hills. But seriously, dear one, you must give more way to hope than to memory. You are going to a new scene now, and one that I hope will be full of enjoyment to you. I want you to take the good of it.

"Only think of all you expect to see: the great libraries and beautiful paintings, fine churches, and, above all, think of seeing Tholuck, your great Apollo. My dear, I wish I were a man in your place; if I wouldn't have a grand time!"

During her husband's absence abroad Mrs. Stowe lived quietly in Cincinnati with her father and brothers. She wrote occasionally short stories, articles, and essays for publication in the "Western Monthly Magazine" or the "New York Evangelist," and maintained a constant correspondence with her husband by means of a daily journal, which was forwarded to him once a month. She also assisted her brother, Henry Ward, who had accepted a temporary position as editor of the "Journal," a small daily paper published in the city.

At this time the question of slavery was an exciting one in Cincinnati, and Lane Seminary had become a hotbed of abolition. The anti-slavery movement among the students was headed by Theodore D. Weld, one of their number, who had procured funds to complete his education by lecturing through the South. While thus engaged he had been so impressed with the evils and horrors of slavery that he had become a radical abolitionist, and had succeeded in converting several Southerners to his views of the subject. Among them was Mr. J. G. Birney of Huntsville, Alabama, who not only liberated his slaves, but in connection with Dr. Gamaliel Bailey of Cincinnati founded in that city an anti-slavery paper called "The Philanthropist." This paper was finally suppressed, and its office wrecked by a mob instigated by Kentucky slaveholders, and it is of this event that Mrs. Stowe writes to her husband as follows:—

"Yesterday evening I spent scribbling for Henry's newspaper (the 'Journal') in this wise: 'Birney's printing-press has been mobbed, and many of the respectable citizens are disposed to wink at the outrage in consideration of its moving in the line of their prejudices.'

"I wrote a conversational sketch, in which I rather satirized this inconsistent spirit, and brought out the effects of patronizing *any* violation of private rights. It was in a light, sketchy style, designed to draw attention to a long editorial of Henry's in which he considers the subject fully and seriously. His piece is, I think, a powerful one; indeed, he does write very strongly. I am quite proud of his editorials; they are well studied, earnest, and dignified. I think he will make a first-rate writer. Both our pieces have gone to press to-day, with Charles's article on music, and we have had not a little diversion about our *family newspaper*.

"I thought, when I was writing last night, that I was, like a good wife, defending one of your principles in your absence, and wanted you to see how manfully I talked about it. Henry has also taken up and examined the question of the Seminole Indians, and done it very nobly."

Again:—

"The excitement about Birney continues to increase. The keeper of the Franklin Hotel was assailed by a document subscribed to by many of his boarders demanding that Birney should be turned out of doors. He chose to negative the demand, and twelve of his boarders immediately left, Dr. F. among the number. A meeting has been convoked by means of a handbill, in which some of the most respectable men of the city are invited by name to come together and consider the question whether they will allow Mr. Birney to continue his paper in the city. Mr. Greene says that, to his utter surprise, many of the most respectable and influential citizens gave out that they should go.

"He was one of the number they invited, but he told those who came to him that he would have nothing to do with disorderly public meetings or mobs in any shape, and that he was entirely opposed to the whole thing.

"I presume they will have a hot meeting, if they have any at all.

"I wish father were at home to preach a sermon to his church, for many of its members do not frown on these things as they ought."

"Later: The meeting was held, and was headed by Morgan, Neville, Judge Burke, and I know not who else. Judge Burnet was present and consented to their acts. The mob madness is certainly upon this city when men of sense and standing will pass resolutions approving in so many words of things done contrary to law, as one of the resolutions of this meeting did. It quoted the demolition of the tea in Boston harbor as being authority and precedent.

"A large body, perhaps the majority of citizens, disapprove, but I fear there will not be public disavowal. Even N. Wright but faintly opposes, and Dr. Fore has been exceedingly violent. Mr. Hammond (editor of the 'Gazette') in a very dignified and judicious manner has condemned the whole thing, and Henry has opposed, but otherwise the papers have either been silent or in favor of mobs. We shall see what the result will be in a few days.

"For my part, I can easily see how such proceedings may make converts to abolitionism, for already my sympathies are strongly enlisted for Mr. Birney, and I hope that he will stand his ground and assert his rights. The office is fire-proof, and inclosed by high walls. I wish he would man it with armed men and see what can be done. If I were a man I would go, for one, and take good care of at least one window. Henry sits opposite me writing a most valiant editorial, and tells me to tell you he is waxing mighty in battle."

In another letter she writes:—

"I told you in my last that the mob broke into Birney's press, where, however, the mischief done was but slight. The object appeared to be principally to terrify. Immediately there followed a general excitement in which even good men in their panic and prejudice about abolitionism forgot that mobs were worse evils than these, talked against Birney, and winked at the outrage; N. Wright and Judge Burnet, for example. Meanwhile the turbulent spirits went beyond this and talked of revolution and of righting things without law that could not be righted by it. At the head of these were Morgan, Neville, Longworth, Joseph Graham, and Judge Burke. A meeting was convoked at Lower Market Street to decide whether they would permit the publishing of an abolition paper, and to this meeting all the most respectable citizens were by name summoned.

"There were four classes in the city then: Those who meant to go as revolutionists and support the mob; those who meant to put down Birney, but rather hoped to do it without a mob; those who felt ashamed to go, foreseeing the probable consequence, and yet did not decidedly frown upon it; and those who sternly and decidedly reprehended it.

"The first class was headed by Neville, Longworth, Graham, etc.; the second class, though of some numbers, was less conspicuous; of the third, Judge Burnet, Dr. Fore, and N. Wright were specimens; and in the last such men as Hammond, Mansfield, S. P. Chase, and Chester were prominent. The meeting in so many words voted a mob, nevertheless a committee was appointed to wait on Mr. Birney and ascertain what he proposed to do; and, strange to tell, men as sensible as Uncle John and Judge Burnet were so short-sighted as to act on that committee.

"All the newspapers in the city, except Hammond's ('Gazette') and Henry's (the 'Journal'), were either silent or openly 'mobocratic.' As might have been expected, Birney refused to leave, and that night the mob tore down his press, scattered the types, dragged the whole to the river, threw it in, and then came back to demolish the office.

"They then went to the houses of Dr. Bailey, Mr. Donaldson, and Mr. Birney; but the persons they sought were not at home, having been aware of what was intended. The mayor was a silent spectator of these proceedings, and was heard to say, 'Well, lads, you have done well, so far; go home now before you disgrace yourselves;' but the 'lads' spent the rest of the night and a greater part of the next day (Sunday) in pulling down the houses of inoffensive and respectable blacks. The 'Gazette' office was threatened, the 'Journal' office was to go next; Lane Seminary and the water-works also were mentioned as probable points to be attacked by the mob.

"By Tuesday morning the city was pretty well alarmed. A regular corps of volunteers was organized, who for three nights patrolled the streets with firearms and with legal warrant from the mayor, who by this time was glad to give it, to put down the mob even by bloodshed.

"For a day or two we did not know but there would actually be war to the knife, as was threatened by the mob, and we really saw Henry depart with his pistols with daily alarm, only we were all too full of patriotism not to have sent every brother we had rather than not have had the principles of freedom and order defended.

"But here the tide turned. The mob, unsupported by a now frightened community, slunk into their dens and were still; and then Hammond, who, during the few days of its prevalence, had made no comments, but published simply the Sermon on the Mount, the Constitution of Ohio, and the Declaration of Independence, without any comment, now came out and gave a simple, concise history of the mob, tracing it to the market-house meeting, telling the whole history of the meeting, with the names of those who got it up, throwing on them and on those who had acted on the committee the whole responsibility of the following mob. It makes a terrible sensation, but it 'cuts its way,' and all who took other stand than that of steady opposition from the first are beginning to feel the reaction of public sentiment, while newspapers from abroad are pouring in their reprehensions of the disgraceful conduct of Cincinnati. Another time, I suspect, such men as Judge Burnet, Mr. Greene, and Uncle John will keep their fingers out of such a trap, and people will all learn better than to wink at a mob that happens to please them at the outset, or in any way to give it their countenance. Mr. Greene and Uncle John were full of wrath against mobs, and would not go to the meeting, and yet were cajoled into acting on that committee in the vain hope of getting Birney to go away and thus preventing the outrage.

"They are justly punished, I think, for what was very irresolute and foolish conduct, to say the least."

The general tone of her letters at this time would seem to show that, while Mrs. Stowe was anti-slavery in her sympathies, she was not a declared abolitionist. This is still further borne out in a letter written in 1837 from Putnam, Ohio, whither she had gone for a short visit to her brother William. In it she says:—

"The good people here, you know, are about half abolitionists. A lady who takes a leading part in the female society in this place yesterday called and brought Catherine the proceedings of the Female Anti-Slavery Convention.

"I should think them about as ultra as to measures as anything that has been attempted, though I am glad to see a better spirit than marks such proceedings generally.

"To-day I read some in Mr. Birney's 'Philanthropist.' Abolitionism being the fashion here, it is natural to look at its papers.

"It does seem to me that there needs to be an *intermediate* society. If not, as light increases, all the excesses of the abolition party will not prevent humane and conscientious men from joining it.

"Pray what is there in Cincinnati to satisfy one whose mind is awakened on this subject? No one can have the system of slavery brought before him without an irrepressible desire to *do* something, and what is there to be done?"

On September 29, 1836, while Professor Stowe was still absent in Europe, his wife gave birth to twin daughters, Eliza and Isabella, as she named them; but Eliza Tyler and Harriet Beecher, as her husband insisted they should be called, when, upon reaching New York, he was greeted by the joyful news. His trip from London in the ship Gladiator had been unusually long, even for those days of sailing vessels, and extended from November 19, 1836, to January 20, 1837.

During the summer of 1837 Mrs. Stowe suffered much from ill health, on which account, and to relieve her from domestic cares, she was sent to make a long visit at Putnam with her brother, Rev. William Beecher. While here she received a letter from her husband, in which he says:—

"We all of course feel proper indignation at the doings of last General Assembly, and shall treat them with merited contempt. This alliance between the old school (Presbyterians) and slaveholders will make more abolitionists than anything that has been done yet."

In December Professor Stowe went to Columbus with the extended educational report that he had devoted the summer to preparing; and in writing from there to his wife he says:—

"To-day I have been visiting the governor and legislators. They received me with the utmost kindness, and are evidently anticipating much from my report. The governor communicated it to the legislature to-day, and it is concluded that I read it in Dr. Hodges' church on two evenings, to-morrow and the day after, before both houses of the legislature and the citizens. The governor (Vance) will preside at both meetings. I like him (the governor) much. He is just such a plain, simple-hearted, sturdy body as old Fritz (Kaiser Frederick), with more of natural talent than his predecessor in the gubernatorial chair. For my year's work in this matter I am to receive $500."

On January 14, 1838, Mrs. Stowe's third child, Henry Ellis, was born.

It was about this time that the famous reunion of the Beecher family described in Lyman Beecher's "Autobiography" occurred. Edward made a visit to the East, and when he returned he brought Mary (Mrs. Thomas Perkins) from Hartford with him. William came down from Putnam, Ohio, and George from Batavia, New York, while Catherine, Harriet, Henry, Charles, Isabella, Thomas, and James were already at home. It was the first time they had ever all met together. Mary had never seen James, and had seen Thomas but once. The old doctor was almost transported with joy as they all gathered about him, and his cup of happiness was filled to overflowing when, the next day, which was Sunday, his pulpit was filled by Edward in the morning, William in the afternoon, and George in the evening.

Side by side with this charming picture we have another of domestic life outlined by Mrs. Stowe's own hand. It is contained in the following letter, written June 21, 1838, to Miss May, at New Haven, Conn.:—

MY DEAR, DEAR GEORGIANA,—Only think how long it is since I have written to you, and how changed I am since then—the mother of three children! Well, if I have not kept the reckoning of old times, let this last circumstance prove my apology, for I have been hand, heart, and head full since I saw you.

Now, to-day, for example, I'll tell you what I had on my mind from dawn to dewy eve. In the first place I waked about half after four and thought, "Bless me, how light it is! I must get out of bed and rap to wake up Mina, for breakfast must be had at six o'clock this morning." So out of bed I jump and seize the tongs and pound, pound, pound over poor Mina's sleepy head, charitably allowing her about half an hour to get waked up in,—that being the quantum of time that it takes me,—or used to. Well, then baby wakes—quâ, quâ, quâ, so I give him his breakfast, dozing meanwhile and soliloquizing as follows: "Now I must not forget to tell Mr. Stowe about the starch and dried apples"—doze—"ah, um, dear me! why doesn't Mina get up? I don't hear her,"—doze—"a, um,—I wonder if Mina has soap enough! I think there were two bars left on Saturday"—doze again—I wake again. "Dear me, broad daylight! I must get up and go down and see if Mina is getting breakfast." Up I jump and up wakes baby. "Now, little boy, be good and let mother dress, because she is in a hurry." I get my frock half on and baby by that time has kicked himself down off his pillow, and is crying and fisting the bed-clothes in great order. I stop with one sleeve off and one on to settle matters with him. Having planted him bolt upright and gone all up and down the chamber barefoot to get pillows and blankets to prop him up, I finish putting my frock on and hurry down to satisfy myself by actual observation that the breakfast is in progress. Then back I come into the nursery, where, remembering that it is washing day and that there is a great deal of work to be done, I apply myself vigorously to sweeping, dusting, and the setting to rights so necessary where there are three little mischiefs always pulling down as fast as one can put up.

Then there are Miss H—— and Miss E——, concerning whom Mary will furnish you with all suitable particulars, who are chattering, hallooing, or singing at the tops of their voices, as may suit their various states of mind, while the nurse is getting their breakfast ready. This meal being cleared away, Mr. Stowe dispatched to market with various memoranda of provisions, etc., and the baby being washed and dressed, I begin to think what next must be done. I start to cut out some little dresses, have just calculated the length and got one breadth torn off when Master Henry makes a doleful lip and falls to crying with might and main. I catch him up and turning round see one of his sisters flourishing the things out of my workbox in fine style. Moving it away and looking the other side I see the second little mischief seated by the hearth chewing coals and scraping up ashes with great apparent relish. Grandmother lays hold upon her and charitably offers to endeavor to quiet baby while I go on with my work. I set at it again, pick up a dozen pieces, measure them once more to see which is the right one, and proceed to cut out some others, when I see the twins on the point of quarreling with each other. Number one pushes number two over. Number two screams: that frightens the baby and he joins in. I call number one a naughty girl, take the persecuted one in my arms, and endeavor to comfort her by trotting to the old lyric:—

> "So ride the gentlefolk,
> And so do we, so do we."

Meanwhile number one makes her way to the slop jar and forthwith proceeds to wash her apron in it. Grandmother catches her by one shoulder, drags her away, and sets the jar up out of her reach. By and by the nurse comes up from her sweeping. I commit the children to her, and finish cutting out the frocks.

But let this suffice, for of such details as these are all my days made up. Indeed, my dear, I am but a mere drudge with few ideas beyond babies and housekeeping. As for thoughts, reflections, and sentiments, good lack! good lack!

I suppose I am a dolefully uninteresting person at present, but I hope I shall grow young again one of these days, for it seems to me that matters cannot always stand exactly as they do now.

Well, Georgy, this marriage is—yes, I will speak well of it, after all; for when I can stop and think long enough to discriminate my head from my heels, I must say that I think myself a fortunate woman both in husband and children. My children I would not change for all the ease, leisure, and pleasure that I could have without them. They are money on interest whose value will be constantly increasing.

In 1839 Mrs. Stowe received into her family as a servant a colored girl from Kentucky. By the laws of Ohio she was free, having been brought into the State and left there by her mistress. In spite of this, Professor Stowe received word, after she had lived with them some months, that the girl's master was in the city looking for her, and that if she were not careful she would be seized and conveyed back into slavery. Finding that this could be accomplished by boldness, perjury, and the connivance of some unscrupulous justice, Professor Stowe determined to remove the girl to some place of security where she might remain until the search for her should be given up. Accordingly he and his brother-in-law, Henry Ward Beecher, both armed, drove the fugitive, in a covered wagon, at night, by unfrequented roads, twelve miles back into the country, and left her in safety with the family of old John Van Zandt, the fugitive's friend.

It is from this incident of real life and personal experience that Mrs. Stowe conceived the thrilling episode of the fugitives' escape from Tom Loker and Marks in "Uncle Tom's Cabin."

An amusing and at the same time most interesting account of her struggles to accomplish literary work amid her distracting domestic duties at this time is furnished by the letter of one of her intimate friends, who writes:—

"It was my good fortune to number Mrs. Stowe among my friends, and during a visit to her I had an opportunity one day of witnessing the combined exercise of her literary and domestic genius in a style that to me was quite amusing.

"'Come Harriet,' said I, as I found her tending one baby and watching two others just able to walk, 'where is that piece for the "Souvenir" which I promised the editor I would get from you and send on next week? You have only this one day left to finish it, and have it I must.'

"'And how will you get it, friend of mine?' said Harriet. 'You will at least have to wait till I get house-cleaning over and baby's teeth through.'

"'As to house-cleaning, you can defer it one day longer; and as to baby's teeth, there is to be no end to them, as I can see. No, no; to-day that story must be ended. There Frederick has been sitting by Ellen and saying all those pretty things for more than a month now, and she has been turning and blushing till I am sure it is time to go to her relief. Come, it would not take you three hours at the rate you can write to finish the courtship, marriage, catastrophe, éclaircissement, and all; and this three hours' labor of your brains will earn enough to pay for all the sewing your fingers could do for a year to come. Two dollars a page, my dear, and you can write a page in fifteen minutes! Come, then, my lady housekeeper, economy is a cardinal virtue; consider the economy of the thing.'

"'But, my dear, here is a baby in my arms and two little pussies by my side, and there is a great baking down in the kitchen, and there is a "new girl" for "help," besides preparations to be made for house-cleaning next week. It is really out of the question, you see.'

"'I see no such thing. I do not know what genius is given for, if it is not to help a woman out of a scrape. Come, set your wits to work, let me have my way, and you shall have all the work done and finish the story too.'

"'Well, but kitchen affairs?'

"'We can manage them too. You know you can write anywhere and anyhow. Just take your seat at the kitchen table with your writing weapons, and while you superintend Mina fill up the odd snatches of time with the labors of your pen.'

"I carried my point. In ten minutes she was seated; a table with flour, rolling-pin, ginger, and lard on one side, a dresser with eggs, pork, and beans and various cooking utensils on the other, near her an oven heating, and beside her a dark-skinned nymph, waiting orders.

"'Here, Harriet,' said I, 'you can write on this atlas in your lap; no matter how the writing looks, I will copy it.'

"'Well, well,' said she, with a resigned sort of amused look. 'Mina, you may do what I told you, while I write a few minutes, till it is time to mould up the bread. Where is the inkstand?'

"'Here it is, close by, on the top of the tea-kettle,' said I.

"At this Mina giggled, and we both laughed to see her merriment at our literary proceedings.

"I began to overhaul the portfolio to find the right sheet.

"'Here it is,' said I. 'Here is Frederick sitting by Ellen, glancing at her brilliant face, and saying something about "guardian angel," and all that—you remember?'

"'Yes, yes,' said she, falling into a muse, as she attempted to recover the thread of her story.

"'Ma'am, shall I put the pork on the top of the beans?' asked Mina.

"'Come, come,' said Harriet, laughing. 'You see how it is. Mina is a new hand and cannot do anything without me to direct her. We must give up the writing for to-day.'

"'No, no; let us have another trial. You can dictate as easily as you can write. Come, I can set the baby in this clothes-basket and give him some mischief or other to keep him quiet; you shall dictate and I will write. Now, this is the place where you left off: you were describing the scene between Ellen and her lover; the last sentence was, "Borne down by the tide of agony, she leaned her head on her hands, the tears streamed through her fingers, and her whole frame shook with convulsive sobs." What shall I write next?'

"'Mina, pour a little milk into this pearlash,' said Harriet.

"'Come,' said I. '"The tears streamed through her fingers and her whole frame shook with convulsive sobs." What next?'

"Harriet paused and looked musingly out of the window, as she turned her mind to her story. 'You may write now,' said she, and she dictated as follows:

"'"Her lover wept with her, nor dared he again to touch the point so sacredly guarded"—Mina, roll that crust a little thinner. "He spoke in soothing tones"—Mina, poke the coals in the oven.'

"'Here,' said I, 'let me direct Mina about these matters, and write a while yourself.'

"Harriet took the pen and patiently set herself to the work. For a while my culinary knowledge and skill were proof to all Mina's investigating inquiries, and they did not fail till I saw two pages completed.

"'You have done bravely,' said I, as I read over the manuscript; 'now you must direct Mina a while. Meanwhile dictate and I will write.'

"Never was there a more docile literary lady than my friend. Without a word of objection she followed my request.

"'I am ready to write,' said I. 'The last sentence was: "What is this life to one who has suffered as I have?" What next?'

"'Shall I put in the brown or the white bread first?' said Mina.

"'The brown first,' said Harriet.

"'"What is this life to one who has suffered as I have?"' said I.

"Harriet brushed the flour off her apron and sat down for a moment in a muse. Then she dictated as follows:—

"'"Under the breaking of my heart I have borne up. I have borne up under all that tries a woman,—but this thought,—oh, Henry!"'

"'Ma'am, shall I put ginger into this pumpkin?' queried Mina.

"'No, you may let that alone just now,' replied Harriet. She then proceeded:—

"'"I know my duty to my children. I see the hour must come. You must take them, Henry; they are my last earthly comfort."'

"'Ma'am, what shall I do with these egg-shells and all this truck here?' interrupted Mina.

"'Put them in the pail by you,' answered Harriet.

"'"They are my last earthly comfort,"' said I. 'What next?'

"She continued to dictate,—

"'"You must take them away. It may be—perhaps it *must* be— that I shall soon follow, but the breaking heart of a wife still pleads, 'a little longer, a little longer.'"'

"'How much longer must the gingerbread stay in?' inquired Mina.

"'Five minutes,' said Harriet.

"''A little longer, a little longer,'" I repeated in a dolorous tone, and we burst into a laugh.

"Thus we went on, cooking, writing, nursing, and laughing, till I finally accomplished my object. The piece was finished, copied, and the next day sent to the editor."

The widely scattered members of the Beecher family had a fashion of communicating with each other by means of circular letters. These, begun on great sheets of paper, at either end of the line, were passed along from one to another, each one adding his or her budget of news to the general stock. When the filled sheet reached the last person for whom it was intended, it was finally remailed to its point of departure. Except in the cases of Mrs. Stowe and Mrs. Perkins, the simple address "Rev. Mr. Beecher" was sufficient to insure its safe delivery in any town to which it was sent.

One of these great, closely-written sheets, bearing in faded ink the names of all the Beechers, lies outspread before us as we write. It is postmarked Hartford, Conn., Batavia, N. Y., Chillicothe, Ohio, Zanesville, Ohio, Walnut Hills, Ohio, Indianapolis, Ind., Jacksonville, Ill., and New Orleans, La. In it Mrs. Stowe occupies her allotted space with—

WALNUT HILLS, *April 27, 1839.*

DEAR FRIENDS,—I am going to Hartford myself, and therefore shall not write, but hurry along the preparations for my forward journey. Belle, father says you may go to the White Mountains with Mr. Stowe and me this summer. George, we may look in on you coming back. Good-by.

Affectionately to all, H. E. STOWE.

CHAPTER V

POVERTY AND SICKNESS, 1840-1850

FAMINE IN CINCINNATI.—SUMMER AT THE EAST.—
PLANS FOR LITERARY WORK.—EXPERIENCE ON A
RAILROAD.—DEATH OF HER BROTHER GEORGE.—
SICKNESS AND DESPAIR.—A JOURNEY IN SEARCH OF
HEALTH.—GOES TO BRATTLEBORO' WATERCURE.—
TROUBLES AT LANE SEMINARY.—CHOLERA IN
CINCINNATI.—DEATH OF YOUNGEST CHILD.—
DETERMINED TO LEAVE THE WEST.

ON January 7, 1839, Professor Stowe wrote to his mother in Natick, Mass.: "You left here, I believe, in the right time, for as there has been no navigation on the Ohio River for a year, we are almost in a state of famine as to many of the necessities of life. For example, salt (coarse) has sold in Cincinnati this winter for three dollars a bushel; rice eighteen cents a pound; coffee fifty cents a pound; white sugar the same; brown sugar twenty cents; molasses a dollar a gallon; potatoes a dollar a bushel. We do without such things mostly; as there is yet plenty of bread and bacon (flour six and seven dollars a barrel, and good pork from six to eight cents a pound) we get along very comfortably.

"Our new house is pretty much as it was, but they say it will be finished in July. I expect to visit you next summer, as I shall deliver the Phi Beta Kappa oration at Dartmouth College; but whether wife and children come with me or not is not yet decided."

Mrs. Stowe came on to the East with her husband and children during the following summer, and before her return made a trip through the White Mountains.

In May, 1840, her second son was born and named Frederick William, after the sturdy Prussian king, for whom her husband cherished an unbounded admiration.

Mrs. Stowe has said somewhere: "So we go, dear reader, so long as we have a body and a soul. For worlds must mingle,—the great and the little, the solemn and the trivial, wreathing in and out like the grotesque carvings on a gothic shrine; only did we know it rightly, nothing is trivial, since the human soul, with its awful shadow, makes all things sacred." So in writing a biography it is impossible for us to tell what did and what did not powerfully influence the character. It is safer simply to tell the unvarnished truth. The lily builds up its texture of delicate beauty from mould and decay. So how do we know from what humble material a soul grows in strength and beauty!

In December, 1840, writing to Miss May, Mrs. Stowe says:—

"For a year I have held the pen only to write an occasional business letter such as could not be neglected. This was primarily owing to a severe neuralgic complaint that settled in my eyes, and for two months not only made it impossible for me to use them in writing, but to fix them with attention on anything. I could not even bear the least light of day in my room. Then my dear little Frederick was born, and for two months more I was confined to my bed. Besides all this, we have had an unusual amount of sickness in our family. . . .

"For all that my history of the past year records so many troubles, I cannot on the whole regard it as a very troublous one. I have had so many counterbalancing mercies that I must regard myself as a person greatly blessed. It is true that about six months out of the twelve I have been laid up with sickness, but then I have had every comfort and the kindest of nurses in my faithful Anna. My children have thriven, and on the whole 'come to more,' as the Yankees say, than the care of them. Thus you see my troubles have been but enough to keep me from loving earth too well."

In the spring of 1842 Mrs. Stowe again visited Hartford, taking her six-year-old daughter Hatty with her. In writing from there to her husband she confides some of her literary plans and aspirations to him, and he answers:—

"My dear, you must be a literary woman. It is so written in the book of fate. Make all your calculations accordingly. Get a good stock of health and brush up your mind. Drop the E. out of your name. It only incumbers it and interferes with the flow and euphony. Write yourself fully and always Harriet Beecher Stowe, which is a name euphonious, flowing, and full of meaning. Then my word for it, your husband will lift up his head in the gate, and your children will rise up and call you blessed.

"Our humble dwelling has to-day received a distinguished honor of which I must give you an account. It was a visit from his excellency the Baron de Roenne, ambassador of his majesty the King of Prussia to the United States. He was pleased to assure me of the great satisfaction my report on Prussian schools had afforded the king and members of his court, with much more to the same effect. Of course having a real live lord to exhibit, I was anxious for some one to exhibit him to; but neither Aunt Esther nor Anna dared venture near the study, though they both contrived to get a peep at his lordship from the little chamber window as he was leaving.

"And now, my dear wife, I want you to come home as quick as you can. The fact is I cannot live without you, and if we were not so prodigious poor I would come for you at once. There is no woman like you in this wide world. Who else has so much talent with so little self-conceit; so much reputation with so little affectation; so much literature with so little nonsense; so much enterprise with so little extravagance; so much tongue with so little scold; so much sweetness with so little softness; so much of so many things and so little of so many other things?"

In answer to this letter Mrs. Stowe writes from Hartford:—

"I have seen Johnson of the 'Evangelist.' He is very liberally disposed, and I may safely reckon on being paid for all I do there. Who is that Hale, Jr., that sent me the 'Boston Miscellany,' and will he keep his word with me? His offers are very liberal,—twenty dollars for three pages, not very close print. Is he to be depended on? If so, it is the best offer I have received yet. I shall get something from the Harpers some time this winter or spring. Robertson, the publisher here, says the book ('The Mayflower') will sell, and though the terms they offer me are very low, that I shall make something on it. For a second volume I shall be able to make better terms. On the whole, my dear, if I choose to be a literary lady, I have, I think, as good a chance of making profit by it as any one I know of. But with all this, I have my doubts whether I shall be able to do so.

"Our children are just coming to the age when everything depends on my efforts. They are delicate in health, and nervous and excitable, and need a mother's whole attention. Can I lawfully divide my attention by literary efforts?

"There is one thing I must suggest. If I am to write, I must have a room to myself, which shall be *my* room. I have in my own mind pitched on Mrs. Whipple's room. I can put the stove in it. I have bought a cheap carpet for it, and I have furniture enough at home to furnish it comfortably, and I only beg in addition that you will let me change the glass door from the nursery into that room and keep my plants there, and then I shall be quite happy.

"All last winter I felt the need of some place where I could go and be quiet and satisfied. I could not there, for there was all the setting of tables, and clearing up of tables, and dressing and washing of children, and everything else going on, and the constant falling of soot and coal dust on everything in the room was a constant annoyance to me, and I never felt comfortable there though I tried hard. Then if I came into the parlor where you were I felt as if I were interrupting you, and you know you sometimes thought so too.

"Now this winter let the cooking-stove be put into that room, and let the pipe run up through the floor into the room above. We can eat by our cooking-stove, and the children can be washed and dressed and keep their playthings in the room above, and play there when we don't want them below. You can study by the parlor fire, and I and my plants, etc., will take the other room. I shall keep my work and all my things there and feel settled and quiet. I intend to have a regular part of each day devoted to the children, and then I shall take them in there."

In his reply to this letter Professor Stowe says:—

"The little magazine ('The Souvenir') goes ahead finely. Fisher sent down to Fulton the other day and got sixty subscribers. He will make the June number as handsome as possible, as a specimen number for the students, several of whom will take agencies for it during the coming vacation. You have it in your power by means of this little magazine to form the mind of the West for the coming generation. It is just as I told you in my last letter. God has written it in his book that you must be a literary woman, and who are we that we should contend against God? You must therefore make all your calculations to spend the rest of your life with your pen.

"If you only could come home to-day how happy should I be. I am daily finding out more and more (what I knew very well before) that you are the most intelligent and agreeable woman in the whole circle of my acquaintance."

That Professor Stowe's devoted admiration for his wife was reciprocated, and that a most perfect sympathy of feeling existed between the husband and wife, is shown by a line in one of Mrs. Stowe's letters from Hartford in which she says: "I was telling Belle yesterday that I did not know till I came away how much I was dependent upon you for information. There are a thousand favorite subjects on which I could talk with you better than with any one else. If you were not already my dearly loved husband I should certainly fall in love with you."

In this same letter she writes of herself:—

"One thing more in regard to myself. The absence and wandering of mind and forgetfulness that so often vexes you is a physical infirmity with me. It is the failing of a mind not calculated to endure a great pressure of care, and so much do I feel the pressure I am under, so much is my mind often darkened and troubled by care, that life seriously considered holds out few allurements,—only my children.

"In returning to my family, from whom I have been so long separated, I am impressed with a new and solemn feeling of responsibility. It appears to me that I am not probably destined for long life; at all events, the feeling is strongly impressed upon my mind that a work is put into my hands which I must be earnest to finish shortly. It is nothing great or brilliant in the world's eye; it lies in one small family circle, of which I am called to be the central point."

On her way home from this Eastern visit Mrs. Stowe traveled for the first time by rail, and of this novel experience she writes to Miss Georgiana May:—

BATAVIA, *August 29, 1842.*

Here I am at Brother William's, and our passage along this railroad reminds me of the verse of the psalm:—

"Tho' lions roar and tempests blow,
And rocks and dangers fill the way."

Such confusion of tongues, such shouting and swearing, such want of all sort of system and decency in arrangements, I never desire to see again. I was literally almost trodden down and torn to pieces in the Rochester depot when I went to help my poor, near-sighted spouse in sorting out the baggage. You see there was an accident which happened to the cars leaving Rochester that morning, which kept us two hours and a half at the passing place this side of Auburn, waiting for them to come up and go by us. The consequence was that we got into this Rochester depot aforesaid after dark, and the steamboat, the canal-boat, and the Western train of cars had all been kept waiting three hours beyond their usual time, and they all broke loose upon us the moment we put our heads out of the cars, and such a jerking, and elbowing, and scuffling, and swearing, and protesting, and scolding you never heard, while the great locomotive sailed up and down in the midst thereof, spitting fire and smoke like some great fiend monster diverting himself with our commotions. I do think these steam concerns border a little too much on the supernatural to be agreeable, especially when you are shut up in a great dark depot after sundown.

Well, after all, we had to ride till twelve o'clock at night to get to Batavia, and I've been sick abed, so to speak, ever since.

The winter of 1842 was one of peculiar trial to the family at Walnut Hills; as Mrs. Stowe writes, "It was a season of sickness and gloom." Typhoid fever raged among the students of the seminary, and the house of the president was converted into a hospital, while the members of his family were obliged to devote themselves to nursing the sick and dying.

July 6, 1843, a few weeks before the birth of her third daughter, Georgiana May, a most terrible and overwhelming sorrow came on Mrs. Stowe, in common with all the family, in the sudden death of her brother, the Rev. George Beecher.

He was a young man of unusual talent and ability, and much loved by his church and congregation. The circumstances of his death are related in a letter written by Mrs. Stowe, and are as follows: "Noticing the birds destroying his fruit and injuring his plants, he went for a double-barreled gun, which he scarcely ever had used, out of regard to the timidity and anxiety of his wife in reference to it. Shortly after he left the house, one of the elders of his church in passing saw him discharge one barrel at the birds. Soon after he heard the fatal report and saw the smoke, but the trees shut out the rest from sight. . . . In about half an hour after, the family assembled at breakfast, and the servant was sent out to call him. . . . In a few minutes she returned, exclaiming, 'Oh, Mr. Beecher is dead! Mr. Beecher is dead!' . . . In a short time a visitor in the family, assisted by a passing laborer, raised him up and bore him to the house. His face was pale and but slightly marred, his eyes were closed, and over his countenance rested the sweet expression of peaceful slumber. . . . Then followed the hurried preparations for the funeral and journey, until three o'clock, when, all arrangements being made, he was borne from his newly finished house, through his blooming garden, to the new church, planned and just completed under his directing eye. . . . The sermon and the prayers were finished, the choir he himself had trained sung their parting hymn, and at about five the funeral train started for a journey of over seventy miles. That night will stand alone in the memories of those who witnessed its scenes!

"At ten in the evening heavy clouds gathered lowering behind, and finally rose so as nearly to cover the hemisphere, sending forth mutterings of thunder and constant flashes of lightning.

"The excessive heat of the weather, the darkness of the night, the solitary road, the flaring of the lamps and lanterns, the flashes of the lightning, the roll of approaching thunder, the fear of being overtaken in an unfrequented place and the lights extinguished by the rain, the sad events of the day, the cries of the infant boy sick with the heat and bewailing the father who ever before had soothed his griefs, all combined to awaken the deepest emotions of the sorrowful, the awful, and the sublime. . . .

"And so it is at last; there must come a time when all that the most heart-broken, idolizing love can give us is a coffin and a grave! All that could be done for our brother, with all his means and all the affection of his people and friends, was just this, no more! After all, the deepest and most powerful argument for the religion of Christ is its power in times like this. Take from us Christ and what He taught, and what have we here? What confusion, what agony, what dismay, what wreck and waste! But give Him to us, even the most stricken heart can rise under the blow; yea, even triumph!

"'Thy brother shall rise again,' said Jesus; and to us who weep He speaks: 'Rejoice, inasmuch as ye are made partakers of Christ's sufferings, that when his glory shall be revealed, ye also may be glad with exceeding joy!'"

The advent of Mrs. Stowe's third daughter was followed by a protracted illness and a struggle with great poverty, of which Mrs. Stowe writes in October, 1843:—

"Our straits for money this year are unparalleled even in our annals. Even our bright and cheery neighbor Allen begins to look blue, and says $600 is the very most we can hope to collect of our salary, once $1,200. We have a flock of entirely destitute young men in the seminary, as poor in money as they are rich in mental and spiritual resources. They promise to be as fine a band as those we have just sent off. We have two from Iowa and Wisconsin who were actually crowded from secular pursuits into the ministry by the wants of the people about them. Revivals began, and the people came to them saying, 'We have no minister, and you must preach to us, for you know more than we do.'"

In the spring of 1844 Professor Stowe visited the East to arouse an interest in the struggling seminary and raise funds for its maintenance. While he was there he received the following letter from Mrs. Stowe:—

"I am already half sick with confinement to the house and overwork. If I should sew every day for a month to come I should not be able to accomplish a half of what is to be done, and should be only more unfit for my other duties."

This struggle against ill-health and poverty was continued through that year and well into the next, when, during her husband's absence to attend a ministerial convention at Detroit, Mrs. Stowe writes to him:—

June 16, 1845.

MY DEAR HUSBAND,—It is a dark, sloppy, rainy, muddy, disagreeable day, and I have been working hard (for me) all day in the kitchen, washing dishes, looking into closets, and seeing a great deal of that dark side of domestic life which a housekeeper may who will investigate too curiously into minutiæ in warm, damp weather, especially after a girl who keeps all clean on the *outside* of cup and platter, and is very apt to make good the rest of the text in the *inside* of things.

I am sick of the smell of sour milk, and sour meat, and sour everything, and then the clothes *will* not dry, and no wet thing does, and everything smells mouldy; and altogether I feel as if I never wanted to eat again.

Your letter, which was neither sour nor mouldy, formed a very agreeable contrast to all these things; the more so for being unexpected. I am much obliged to you for it. As to my health, it gives me very little solicitude, although I am bad enough and daily growing worse. I feel no life, no energy, no appetite, or rather a growing distaste for food; in fact, I am becoming quite ethereal. Upon reflection I perceive that it pleases my Father to keep me in the fire, for my whole situation is excessively harassing and painful. I suffer with sensible distress in the brain, as I have done more or less since my sickness last winter, a distress which some days takes from me all power of planning or executing anything; and you know that, except this poor head, my unfortunate household has no mainspring, for nobody feels any kind of responsibility to do a thing in time, place, or manner, except as I oversee it.

Georgiana is so excessively weak, nervous, cross, and fretful, night and day, that she takes all Anna's strength and time with her; and then the children are, like other little sons and daughters of Adam, full of all kinds of absurdity and folly.

When the brain gives out, as mine often does, and one cannot think or remember anything, then what is to be done? All common fatigue, sickness, and exhaustion is nothing to this distress. Yet do I rejoice in my God and know in whom I believe, and only pray that the fire may consume the dross; as to the gold, that is imperishable. No real evil can happen to me, so I fear nothing for the future, and only suffer in the present tense.

God, the mighty God, is mine, of that I am sure, and I know He knows that though flesh and heart fail, I am all the while desiring and trying for his will alone. As to a journey, I need not ask a physician to see that it is needful to me as far as health is concerned, that is to say, all human appearances are that way, but I feel no particular choice about it. If God wills I go. He can easily find means. Money, I suppose, is as plenty with Him now as it always has been, and if He sees it is really best He will doubtless help me.

That the necessary funds were provided is evident from the fact that the journey was undertaken and the invalid spent the summer of 1845 in Hartford, in Natick, and in Boston. She was not, however, permanently benefited by the change, and in the following spring it was deemed necessary to take more radical measures to arrest the progress of her increasing debility. After many consultations and much correspondence it was finally decided that she should go to Dr. Wesselhoeft's watercure establishment at Brattleboro', Vt.

At this time, under date of March, 1846, she writes:

"For all I have had trouble I can think of nothing but the greatness and richness of God's mercy to me in giving me such friends, and in always caring for us in every strait. There has been no day this winter when I have not had abundant reason to see this. Some friend has always stepped in to cheer and help, so that I have wanted for nothing. My husband has developed wonderfully as house-father and nurse. You would laugh to see him in his spectacles gravely marching the little troop in their nightgowns up to bed, tagging after them, as he says, like an old hen after a flock of ducks. The money for my journey has been sent in from an unknown hand in a wonderful manner. All this shows the care of our Father, and encourages me to rejoice and to hope in Him."

A few days after her departure Professor Stowe wrote to his wife:—

"I was greatly comforted by your brief letter from Pittsburgh. When I returned from the steamer the morning you left I found in the post-office a letter from Mrs. G. W. Bull of New York, inclosing $50 on account of the sickness in my family. There was another inclosing $50 more from a Mrs. Devereaux of Raleigh, N. C., besides some smaller sums from others. My heart went out to God in aspiration and gratitude. None of the donors, so far as I know, have I ever seen or heard of before.

"Henry and I have been living in a Robinson Crusoe and man Friday sort of style, greatly to our satisfaction, ever since you went away."

Mrs. Stowe was accompanied to Brattleboro' by her sisters, Catherine and Mary, who were also suffering from troubles that they felt might be relieved by hydropathic treatment.

From May, 1846, until March, 1847, she remained at Brattleboro' without seeing her husband or children. During these weary months her happiest days were those upon which she received letters from home.

The following extracts, taken from letters written by her during this period, are of value, as revealing what it is possible to know of her habits of thought and mode of life at this time.

BRATTLEBORO', *September, 1846.*

MY DEAR HUSBAND,—I have been thinking of all your trials, and I really pity you in having such a wife. I feel as if I had been only a hindrance to you instead of a help, and most earnestly and daily do I pray to God to restore my health that I may do something for you and my family. I think if I were only at home I could at least sweep and dust, and wash potatoes, and cook a little, and talk some to my children, and should be doing something for my family. But the hope of getting better buoys me up. I go through these tedious and wearisome baths and bear that terrible douche thinking of my children. They never will know how I love them. . . .

There is great truth and good sense in your analysis of the cause of our past failures. We have now come to a sort of crisis. If you and I do as we should for *five years* to come the character of our three oldest children will be established. This is why I am willing to spend so much time and make such efforts to have health. Oh, that God would give me these five years in full possession of mind and body, that I may train my children as they should be trained. I am fully aware of the importance of system and order in a family. I know that nothing can be done without it; it is the keystone, the *sine quâ non*, and in regard to my children I place it next to piety. At the same time it is true that both Anna and I labor under serious natural disadvantages on this subject. It is not all that is necessary to feel the importance of order and system, but it requires a particular kind of talent to carry it through a family. Very much the same kind of talent, as Uncle Samuel said, which is necessary to make a good prime minister. . . .

I think you might make an excellent sermon to Christians on the care of health, in consideration of the various infirmities and impediments to the developing the results of religion, that result from bodily ill health, and I wish you would make one that your own mind may be more vividly impressed with it. The world is too much in a hurry. Ministers think there is no way to serve Christ but to overdraw on their physical capital for four or five years for Christ and then have nothing to give, but become a mere burden on his hands for the next five. . . .

November 18. "The daily course I go through presupposes a degree of vigor beyond anything I ever had before. For this week, I have gone before breakfast to the wave-bath and let all the waves and billows roll over me till every limb ached with cold and my hands would scarcely have feeling enough to dress me. After that I have walked till I was warm, and come home to breakfast with such an appetite! Brown bread and milk are luxuries indeed, and the only fear is that I may eat too much. At eleven comes my douche, to which I have walked in a driving rain for the last two days, and after it walked in the rain again till I was warm. (The umbrella you gave me at Natick answers finely, as well as if it were a silk one.) After dinner I roll ninepins or walk till four, then sitz-bath, and another walk till six.

"I am anxious for your health; do be persuaded to try a long walk before breakfast. You don't know how much good it will do you. Don't sit in your hot study without any ventilation, a stove burning up all the vitality of the air and weakening your nerves, and above all, do *amuse* yourself. Go to Dr. Mussey's and spend an evening, and to father's and Professor Allen's. When you feel worried go off somewhere and forget and throw it off. I should really rejoice to hear that you and father and mother, with Professor and Mrs. Allen, Mrs. K., and a few others of the same calibre would agree to meet together for dancing cotillons. It would do you all good, and if you took Mr. K.'s wife and poor Miss Much-Afraid, her daughter, into the alliance it would do them good. Bless me! what a profane set everybody would think you were, and yet you are the people of all the world most solemnly in need of it. I wish you could be with me in Brattleboro' and coast down hill on a sled, go sliding and snowballing by moonlight! I would snowball every bit of the *hypo* out of you! Now, my dear, if you are going to get sick, I am going to come home. There is no use in my trying to get well if you, in the mean time, are going to run yourself down."

January, 1847.

MY DEAR SOUL,—I received your most melancholy effusion, and I am sorry to find it's just so. I entirely agree and sympathize. Why didn't you engage the two tombstones—one for you and one for me?

Ding, dong! Dead and gone!

I shall have to copy for your edification a "poem on tombstones" which Kate put at Christmas into the stocking of one of our most hypochondriac gentlemen, who had pished and pshawed at his wife and us for trying to get up a little fun. This poem was fronted with the above vignette and embellished with sundry similar ones, and tied with a long black ribbon. There were only two cantos in very concise style, so I shall send you them entire.

CANTO I.
In the kingdom of
Mortin
I had the good fortin'
To find these verses
On tombs and on
hearses,
Which I, being jinglish
Have done into
English.

CANTO II.
The man what's so colickish
When his friends are all
frolickish
As to turn up his noses
And turn on his toses
Shall have only verses
On tombstones and hearses.

But, seriously, my dear husband, you must try and be patient, for this cannot last forever. Be patient and bear it like the toothache, or a driving rain, or anything else that you cannot escape. To see things as through a glass darkly is your infirmity, you know; but the Lord will yet deliver you from this trial. I know how to pity you, for the last three weeks I have suffered from an overwhelming mental depression, a perfect heartsickness. All I wanted was to get home and die. Die I was very sure I should at any rate, but I suppose I was never less prepared to do so.

The long exile was ended in the spring of 1847, and in May Mrs. Stowe returned to her Cincinnati home, where she was welcomed with sincere demonstrations of joy by her husband and children.

Her sixth child, Samuel Charles, was born in January of 1848, and about this time her husband's health became so seriously impaired that it was thought desirable for him in turn to spend a season at the Brattleboro' water-cure. He went in June, 1848, and was compelled by the very precarious state of his health to remain until September, 1849. During this period of more than a year Mrs. Stowe remained in Cincinnati caring for her six children, eking out her slender income by taking boarders and writing when she found time, confronting a terrible epidemic of cholera that carried off one of her little flock, and in every way showing herself to be a brave woman, possessed of a spirit that could rise superior to all adversity. Concerning this time she writes in January, 1849, to her dearest friend:—

MY BELOVED GEORGY,—For six months after my return from Brattleboro' my eyes were so affected that I wrote scarce any, and my health was in so strange a state that I felt no disposition to write. After the birth of little Charley my health improved, but my husband was sick and I have been so loaded and burdened with cares as to drain me dry of all capacity of thought, feeling, memory, or emotion.

Well, Georgy, I am thirty-seven years old! I am glad of it. I like to grow old and have six children and cares endless. I wish you could see me with my flock all around me. They sum up my cares, and were they gone I should ask myself, What now remains to be done? They are my work, over which I fear and tremble.

In the early summer of 1849 cholera broke out in Cincinnati, and soon became epidemic. Professor Stowe, absent in Brattleboro', and filled with anxiety for the safety of his family, was most anxious, in spite of his feeble health, to return and share the danger with them, but this his wife would not consent to, as is shown by her letters to him, written at this time. In one of them, dated June 29, 1849, she says:—

MY DEAR HUSBAND,—This week has been unusually fatal. The disease in the city has been malignant and virulent. Hearse drivers have scarce been allowed to unharness their horses, while furniture carts and common vehicles are often employed for the removal of the dead. The sable trains which pass our windows, the frequent indications of crowding haste, and the absence of reverent decency have, in many cases, been most painful. Of course all these things, whether we will or no, bring very doleful images to the mind.

On Tuesday one hundred and sixteen deaths from cholera were reported, and that night the air was of that peculiarly oppressive, deathly kind that seems to lie like lead on the brain and soul.

As regards your coming home, I am decidedly opposed to it. First, because the chance of your being taken ill is just as great as the chance of your being able to render us any help. To exchange the salubrious air of Brattleboro' for the pestilent atmosphere of this place with your system rendered sensitive by water-cure treatment would be extremely dangerous. It is a source of constant gratitude to me that neither you nor father are exposed to the dangers here.

Second, none of us are sick, and it is very uncertain whether we shall be.

Third, if we were sick there are so many of us that it is not at all likely we shall all be taken at once.

July 1. Yesterday Mr. Stagg went to the city and found all gloomy and discouraged, while a universal panic seemed to be drawing nearer than ever before. Large piles of coal were burning on the cross walks and in the public squares, while those who had talked confidently of the cholera being confined to the lower classes and those who were imprudent began to feel as did the magicians of old, "This is the finger of God."

Yesterday, upon the recommendation of all the clergymen of the city, the mayor issued a proclamation for a day of general fasting, humiliation, and prayer, to be observed on Tuesday next.

July 3. We are all in good health and try to maintain a calm and cheerful frame of mind. The doctors are nearly used up. Dr. Bowen and Dr. Peck are sick in bed. Dr. Potter and Dr. Pulte ought, I suppose, to be there also. The younger physicians have no rest night or day. Mr. Fisher is laid up from his incessant visitations with the sick and dying. Our own Dr. Brown is likewise prostrated, but we are all resolute to stand by each other, and there are so many of us that it is not likely we can all be taken sick together.

July 4. All well. The meeting yesterday was very solemn and interesting. There is more or less sickness about us, but no very dangerous cases. One hundred and twenty burials from cholera alone yesterday, yet to-day we see parties bent on pleasure or senseless carousing, while to-morrow and next day will witness a fresh harvest of death from them. How we can become accustomed to anything! Awhile ago ten a day dying of cholera struck terror to all hearts; but now the tide has surged up gradually until the deaths average over a hundred daily, and everybody is getting accustomed to it. Gentlemen make themselves agreeable to ladies by reciting the number of deaths in this house or that. This together with talk of funerals, cholera medicines, cholera dietetics, and chloride of lime form the ordinary staple of conversation. Serious persons of course throw in moral reflections to their taste.

July 10. Yesterday little Charley was taken ill, not seriously, and at any other season I should not be alarmed. Now, however, a slight illness seems like a death sentence, and I will not dissemble that I feel from the outset very little hope. I still think it best that you should not return. By so doing you might lose all you have gained. You might expose yourself to a fatal incursion of disease. It is decidedly not your duty to do so.

July 12. Yesterday I carried Charley to Dr. Pulte, who spoke in such a manner as discouraged and frightened me. He mentioned dropsy on the brain as a possible result. I came home with a heavy heart, sorrowing, desolate, and wishing my husband and father were here.

About one o'clock this morning Miss Stewart suddenly opened my door crying, "Mrs. Stowe, Henry is vomiting." I was on my feet in an instant, and lifted up my heart for help. He was, however, in a few minutes relieved. Then I turned my attention to Charley, who was also suffering, put him into a wet sheet, and kept him there until he was in a profuse perspiration. He is evidently getting better, and is auspiciously cross. Never was crossness in a baby more admired. Anna and I have said to each other exultingly a score of times, "How cross the little fellow is! How he does scold!"

July 15. Since I last wrote our house has been a perfect hospital. Charley apparently recovering, but still weak and feeble, unable to walk or play, and so miserably fretful and unhappy. Sunday Anna and I were fairly stricken down, as many others are, with no particular illness, but with such miserable prostration. I lay on the bed all day reading my hymn-book and thinking over passages of Scripture.

July 17. To-day we have been attending poor old Aunt Frankie's funeral. She died yesterday morning, taken sick the day before while washing. Good, honest, trustful old soul! She was truly one who hungered and thirsted for righteousness.

Yesterday morning our poor little dog, Daisy, who had been ailing the day before, was suddenly seized with frightful spasms and died in half an hour. Poor little affectionate thing! If I were half as good for my nature as she for hers I should be much better than I am. While we were all mourning over her the news came that Aunt Frankie was breathing her last. Hatty, Eliza, Anna, and I made her shroud yesterday, and this morning I made her cap. We have just come from her grave.

July 23. At last, my dear, the hand of the Lord hath touched us. We have been watching all day by the dying bed of little Charley, who is gradually sinking. After a partial recovery from the attack I described in my last letter he continued for some days very feeble, but still we hoped for recovery. About four days ago he was taken with decided cholera, and now there is no hope of his surviving this night.

Every kindness is shown us by the neighbors. Do not return. All will be over before you could possibly get here, and the epidemic is now said by the physicians to prove fatal to every new case. Bear up. Let us not faint when we are rebuked of Him. I dare not trust myself to say more but shall write again soon.

July 26.

MY DEAR HUSBAND,—At last it is over and our dear little one is gone from us. He is now among the blessed. My Charley—my beautiful, loving, gladsome baby, so loving, so sweet, so full of life and hope and strength—now lies shrouded, pale and cold, in the room below. Never was he anything to me but a comfort. He has been my pride and joy. Many a heartache has he cured for me. Many an anxious night have I held him to my bosom and felt the sorrow and loneliness pass out of me with the touch of his little warm hands. Yet I have just seen him in his death agony, looked on his imploring face when I could not help nor soothe nor do one thing, not one, to mitigate his cruel suffering, do nothing but pray in my anguish that he might die soon. I write as though there were no sorrow like my sorrow, yet there has been in this city, as in the land of Egypt, scarce a house without its dead. This heart-break, this anguish, has been everywhere, and when it will end God alone knows.

With this severest blow of all, the long years of trial and suffering in the West practically end; for in September, 1849, Professor Stowe returned from Brattleboro', and at the same time received a call to the Collins Professorship at Bowdoin College, in Brunswick, Maine, that he decided to accept.

CHAPTER VI

REMOVAL TO BRUNSWICK, 1850-1852

MRS. STOWE'S REMARKS ON WRITING AND UNDERSTANDING BIOGRAPHY.—THEIR APPROPRIATENESS TO HER OWN BIOGRAPHY.—REASONS FOR PROFESSOR STOWE'S LEAVING CINCINNATI.—MRS. STOWE'S JOURNEY TO BROOKLYN.—HER BROTHER'S SUCCESS AS A MINISTER.—LETTERS FROM HARTFORD AND BOSTON.—ARRIVES IN BRUNSWICK.—HISTORY OF THE SLAVERY AGITATION.—PRACTICAL WORKING OF THE FUGITIVE SLAVE LAW.—MRS. EDWARD BEECHER'S LETTER TO MRS. STOWE AND ITS EFFECT.—DOMESTIC TRIALS.—BEGINS TO WRITE "UNCLE TOM'S CABIN" AS A SERIAL FOR THE "NATIONAL ERA."—LETTER TO FREDERICK DOUGLASS.—"UNCLE TOM'S CABIN" A WORK OF RELIGIOUS EMOTION.

EARLY in the winter of 1849 Mrs. Stowe wrote in a private journal in which she recorded thought and feeling concerning religious themes: "It has been said that it takes a man to write the life of a man; that is, there must be similarity of mind in the person who undertakes to present the character of another. This is true, also, of reading and understanding biography. A statesman and general would read the life of Napoleon with the spirit and the understanding, while the commonplace man plods through it as a task. The difference is that the one, being of like mind and spirit with the subject of the biography, is able to sympathize with him in all his thoughts and experiences, and the other is not. The life of Henry Martyn would be tedious and unintelligible to a mind like that of a Richelieu or a Mazarin. They never experienced or saw or heard anything like it, and would be quite at a loss where to place such a man in their mental categories. It is not strange, therefore, that of all biography in the world that of Jesus Christ should be least understood. It is an exception to all the world has ever seen.

'The world knew Him not.' There is, to be sure, a simple grandeur about the life of Jesus which awes almost every mind. The most hardened scoffer, after he has jested and jeered at everything in the temple of Christianity, stands for a moment uncovered and breathless when he comes to the object of its adoration and feels how awful goodness is, and Virtue in her shape how lovely. Yet, after all, the character of the Christ has been looked at and not sympathized with. Men have turned aside to see this great sight. Christians have fallen in adoration, but very few have tried to enter into his sympathies and to feel as He felt."

How little she dreamed that these words were to become profoundly appropriate as a description of her own life in its relation to mankind! How little the countless thousands who read, have read, and will read, "Uncle Tom's Cabin" enter into or sympathize with the feelings out of which it was written! A delicate, sensitive woman struggling with poverty, with weary step and aching head attending to the innumerable demands of a large family of growing children; a devoted Christian seeking with strong crying and tears a kingdom not of this world,—is this the popular conception of the author of "Uncle Tom's Cabin"? Nevertheless it is the reality. When, amid the burning ruins of a besieged city, a mother's voice is heard uttering a cry of anguish over a child killed in her arms by a bursting shell, the attention is arrested, the heart is touched. So "Uncle Tom's Cabin" was a cry of anguish from a mother's heart, and uttered in sad sincerity. It was the bursting forth of deep feeling, with all the intense anguish of wounded love. It will be the purpose of this chapter to show this, and to cause to pass before the reader's mind the time, the household, and the heart from which this cry was heard.

After struggling for seventeen years with ill health and every possible vexation and hindrance in his work, Professor Stowe became convinced that it was his duty to himself and his family to seek some other field of labor.

February 6, 1850, he writes to his mother, in Natick, Mass.: "My health has not been good this winter, and I do not suppose that I should live long were I to stay here. I have done a great deal of hard work here, and practiced no little self-denial. I have seen the seminary carried through a most vexatious series of lawsuits, ecclesiastical and civil, and raised from the depths of poverty to comparative affluence, and I feel at liberty now to leave. During the three months of June, July, and August last, more than nine thousand persons died of cholera within three miles of my house, and this winter, in the same territory, there have been more than ten thousand cases of small-pox, many of them of the very worst kind. Several have died on the hill, and the Jesuits' college near us has been quite broken up by it. There have been, however, no cases in our families or in the seminary.

"I have received many letters from friends in the East expressing great gratification at the offer from Bowdoin College, and the hope that I would accept it. I am quite inclined to do so, but the matter is not yet finally settled, and there are difficulties in the way. They can offer me only $1,000 a year, and I must, out of it, hire my own house, at an expense of $75 to $100 a year. Here the trustees offer me $1,500 a year if I will stay, and a good house besides, which would make the whole salary equivalent to $1,800; and to-day I have had another offer from New York city of $2,300. . . . On the whole, I have written to Bowdoin College, proposing to them if they will give me $500 free and clear in addition to the salary, I will accept their proposition, and I suppose that there is no doubt that they will do it. In that case I should come on next spring, in May or June."

This offer from Bowdoin College was additionally attractive to Professor Stowe from the fact that it was the college from which he graduated, and where some of the happiest years of his life had been passed.

The professorship was one just established through the gift of Mrs. Collins, a member of Bowdoin Street Church in Boston, and named in her honor, the "Collins Professorship of Natural and Revealed Religion."

It was impossible for Professor Stowe to leave Lane Seminary till some one could be found to take his place; so it was determined that Mrs. Stowe, with three of the children, should start for the East in April, and having established the family in Brunswick, Professor Stowe was to come on with the remaining children when his engagements would permit.

The following extracts from a letter written by Mrs. Stowe at her brother Henry's, at Brooklyn, April 29, 1850, show us that the journey was accomplished without special incident.

"The boat got into Pittsburgh between four and five on Wednesday. The agent for the Pennsylvania Canal came on board and soon filled out our tickets, calling my three chicks one and a half. We had a quiet and agreeable passage, and crossed the slides at five o'clock in the morning, amid exclamations of unbounded delight from all the children, to whom the mountain scenery was a new and amazing thing. We reached Hollidaysburg about eleven o'clock, and at two o'clock in the night were called up to get into the cars at Jacktown. Arriving at Philadelphia about three o'clock in the afternoon, we took the boat and railroad line for New York.

"At Lancaster we telegraphed to Brooklyn, and when we arrived in New York, between ten and eleven at night, Cousin Augustus met us and took us over to Brooklyn. We had ridden three hundred miles since two o'clock that morning, and were very tired. . . . I am glad we came that way, for the children have seen some of the finest scenery in our country. . . . Henry's people are more than ever in love with him, and have raised his salary to $3,300, and given him a beautiful horse and carriage worth $600. ... My health is already improved by the journey, and I was able to walk a good deal between the locks on the canal. As to furniture, I think that we may safely afford an outlay of $150, and that will purchase all that may be necessary to set us up, and then we can get more as we have means and opportunity. ... If I got anything for those pieces I wrote before coming away, I would like to be advised thereof by you. ... My plan is to spend this week in Brooklyn, the next in Hartford, the next in Boston, and go on to Brunswick some time in May or June."

May 18, 1850, we find her writing from Boston, where she is staying with her brother, Rev. Edward Beecher:—

> MY DEAR HUSBAND,—I came here from Hartford on Monday, and have since then been busily engaged in the business of buying and packing furniture.
>
> I expect to go to Brunswick next Tuesday night by the Bath steamer, which way I take as the cheaper. My traveling expenses, when I get to Brunswick, including everything, will have been seventy-six dollars. ... And now, lastly, my dear husband, you have never been wanting ... in kindness, consideration, and justice, and I want you to reflect calmly how great a work has been imposed upon me at a time when my situation particularly calls for rest, repose, and quiet.
>
> To come alone such a distance with the whole charge of children, accounts, and baggage; to push my way through hurrying crowds, looking out for trunks, and bargaining with hackmen, has been a very severe trial of my strength, to say nothing of the usual fatigues of traveling.

It was at this time, and as a result of the experiences of this trying period, that Mrs. Stowe wrote that little tract dear to so many Christian hearts, "Earthly Care a Heavenly Discipline."

On the eve of sailing for Brunswick, Mrs. Stowe writes to Mrs. Sykes (Miss May): "I am wearied and worn out with seeing to bedsteads, tables, chairs, mattresses, with thinking about shipping my goods and making out accounts, and I have my trunk yet to pack, as I go on board the Bath steamer this evening. I beg you to look up Brunswick on the map; it is about half a day's ride in the cars from Boston. I expect to reach there by the way of Bath by tomorrow forenoon. There I have a house engaged and kind friends who offer every hospitable assistance. Come, therefore, to see me, and we will have a long talk in the pine woods, and knit up the whole history from the place where we left it."

Before leaving Boston she had written to her husband in Cincinnati: "You are not able just now to bear anything, my dear husband, therefore trust all to me; I never doubt or despair. I am already making arrangements with editors to raise money.

"I have sent some overtures to Wright. If he accepts my pieces and pays you for them, take the money and use it as you see necessary; if not, be sure and bring the pieces back to me. I am strong in spirit, and God who has been with me in so many straits will not forsake me now. I know Him well; He is my Father, and though I may be a blind and erring child, He will help me for all that. My trust through all errors and sins is in Him. He who helped poor timid Jacob through all his fears and apprehensions, who helped Abraham even when he sinned, who was with David in his wanderings, and who held up the too confident Peter when he began to sink,—He will help us, and his arms are about us, so that we shall not sink, my dear husband."

May 29, 1850, she writes from Brunswick: "After a week of most incessant northeast storm, most discouraging and forlorn to the children, the sun has at length come out. . . . There is a fair wind blowing, and every prospect, therefore, that our goods will arrive promptly from Boston, and that we shall be in our own house by next week. Mrs. Upham has done everything for me, giving up time and strength and taking charge of my affairs in a way without which we could not have got along at all in a strange place and in my present helpless condition. This family is delightful, there is such a perfect sweetness and quietude in all its movements. Not a harsh word or hasty expression is ever heard. It is a beautiful pattern of a Christian family, a beautiful exemplification of religion. . . ,"

The events of the first summer in Brunswick are graphically described by Mrs. Stowe in a letter written to her sister-in-law, Mrs. George Beecher, December 17, 1850.

MY DEAR SISTER,—Is it really true that snow is on the ground and Christmas coming, and I have not written unto thee, most dear sister? No, I don't believe it! I haven't been so naughty—it's all a mistake—yes, written I must have—and written I have, too—in the night-watches as I lay on my bed— such beautiful letters—I wish you had only gotten them; but by day it has been hurry, hurry, hurry, and drive, drive, drive! or else the calm of a sick-room, ever since last spring.

I put off writing when your letter first came because I meant to write you a long letter—a full and complete one, and so days slid by,—and became weeks,—and my little Charlie came . . . etc. and etc.!!! Sarah, when I look back, I wonder at myself, not that I forget any one thing that I should remember, but that I have remembered anything. From the time that I left Cincinnati with my children to come forth to a country that I knew not of almost to the present time, it has seemed as if I could scarcely breathe, I was so pressed with care. My head dizzy with the whirl of railroads and steamboats; then ten days' sojourn in Boston, and a constant toil and hurry in buying my furniture and equipments; and then landing in Brunswick in the midst of a drizzly, inexorable northeast storm, and beginning the work of getting in order a deserted, dreary, damp old house. All day long running from one thing to another, as for example, thus:—

Mrs. Stowe, how shall I make this lounge, and what shall I cover the back with first?

Mrs. Stowe. With the coarse cotton in the closet.

Woman. Mrs. Stowe, there isn't any more soap to clean the windows.

Mrs. Stowe. Where shall I get soap?

Here H., run up to the store and get two bars.

There is a man below wants to see Mrs. Stowe about the cistern. Before you go down, Mrs. Stowe, just show me how to cover this round end of the lounge.

There's a man up from the depot, and he says that a box has come for Mrs. Stowe, and it's coming up to the house; will you come down and see about it?

Mrs. Stowe, don't go till you have shown the man how to nail that carpet in the corner. He's nailed it all crooked; what shall he do? The black thread is all used up, and what shall I do about putting gimp on the back of that sofa? Mrs. Stowe, there is a man come with a lot of pails and tinware from Furbish; will you settle the bill now?

Mrs. Stowe, here is a letter just come from Boston inclosing that bill of lading; the man wants to know what he shall do with the goods. If you will tell me what to say I will answer the letter for you.

Mrs. Stowe, the meat-man is at the door. Hadn't we better get a little beefsteak, or something, for dinner?

Shall Hatty go to Boardman's for some more black thread?

Mrs. Stowe, this cushion is an inch too wide for the frame. What shall we do now?

Mrs. Stowe, where are the screws of the black walnut bedstead?

Here's a man has brought in these bills for freight. Will you settle them now?

Mrs. Stowe, I don't understand using this great needle. I can't make it go through the cushion; it sticks in the cotton.

Then comes a letter from my husband saying he is sick abed, and all but dead; don't ever expect to see his family again; wants to know how I shall manage, in case I am left a widow; knows we shall get in debt and never get out; wonders at my courage; thinks I am very sanguine; warns me to be prudent, as there won't be much to live on in case of his death, etc., etc., etc. I read the letter and poke it into the stove, and proceed. . . .

Some of my adventures were quite funny; as for example: I had in my kitchen elect no sink, cistern, or any other water privileges, so I bought at the cotton factory two of the great hogsheads they bring oil in, which here in Brunswick are often used for cisterns, and had them brought up in triumph to my yard, and was congratulating myself on my energy, when lo and behold! it was discovered that there was no cellar door except one in the kitchen, which was truly a strait and narrow way, down a long pair of stairs. Hereupon, as saith John Bunyan, I fell into a muse,—how to get my cisterns into my cellar. In days of chivalry I might have got a knight to make me a breach through the foundation walls, but that was not to be thought of now, and my oil hogsheads standing disconsolately in the yard seemed to reflect no great credit on my foresight. In this strait I fell upon a real honest Yankee cooper, whom I besought, for the reputation of his craft and mine, to take my hogsheads to pieces, carry them down in staves, and set them up again, which the worthy man actually accomplished one fair summer forenoon, to the great astonishment of "us Yankees." When my man came to put up the pump, he stared very hard to see my hogsheads thus translated and standing as innocent and quiet as could be in the cellar, and then I told him, in a very mild, quiet way, that I got 'em taken to pieces and put together—just as if I had been always in the habit of doing such things. Professor Smith came down and looked very hard at them and then said, "Well, nothing can beat a willful woman." Then followed divers negotiations with a very clever, but (with reverence) somewhat lazy gentleman of jobs, who occupieth a carpenter's shop opposite to mine. This same John Titcomb, my very good friend, is a character peculiar to Yankeedom. He is part owner and landlord of the house I rent, and connected by birth with all the best families in town; a man of real intelligence, and good education, a great reader, and quite a thinker. Being of an ingenious turn he does painting, gilding, staining, upholstery jobs, varnishing, all in addition to his primary trade of carpentry. But he is a man studious of ease, and fully possessed with the idea that man wants but little here below; so he boards himself in his workshop on crackers and herring, washed down with cold water, and spends his time working, musing, reading new publications, and taking his comfort. In his shop you shall see a joiner's bench, hammers, planes, saws, gimlets, varnish, paint, picture frames, fence posts, rare old china, one or two fine portraits of his ancestry, a bookcase full of books, the tooth of a whale, an old spinning-wheel and spindle, a lady's parasol frame, a church lamp to be mended, in short, Henry says Mr. Titcomb's shop is like the ocean; there is no end to the curiosities in it.

In all my moving and fussing Mr. Titcomb has been my right-hand man. Whenever a screw was loose, a nail to be driven, a lock mended, a pane of glass set, and these cases were manifold, he was always on hand. But my sink was no fancy job, and I believe nothing but a very particular friendship would have moved him to undertake it. So this same sink lingered in a precarious state for some weeks, and when I had *nothing else to do*, I used to call and do what I could in the way of enlisting the good man's sympathies in its behalf.

How many times I have been in and seated myself in one of the old rocking-chairs, and talked first of the news of the day, the railroad, the last proceedings in Congress, the probabilities about the millennium, and thus brought the conversation by little and little round to my sink! . . . because, till the sink was done, the pump could not be put up, and we couldn't have any rain-water. Sometimes my courage would quite fail me to introduce the subject, and I would talk of everything else, turn and get out of the shop, and then turn back as if a thought had just struck my mind, and say:—

"Oh, Mr. Titcomb! about that sink?"

"Yes, ma'am, I was thinking about going down street this afternoon to look out stuff for it."

"Yes, sir, if you would be good enough to get it done as soon as possible; we are in great need of it."

"I think there's no hurry. I believe we are going to have a dry time now, so that you could not catch any water, and you won't need a pump at present."

These negotiations extended from the first of June to the first of July, and at last my sink was completed, and so also was a new house spout, concerning which I had had divers communings with Deacon Dunning of the Baptist church. Also during this time good Mrs. Mitchell and myself made two sofas, or lounges, a barrel chair, divers bedspreads, pillow cases, pillows, bolsters, mattresses; we painted rooms; we revarnished furniture; we—what *didn't* we do?

Then came on Mr. Stowe; and then came the eighth of July and my little Charley. I was really glad for an excuse to lie in bed, for I was full tired, I can assure you. Well, I was what folks call very comfortable for two weeks, when my nurse had to leave me. . . .

During this time I have employed my leisure hours in making up my engagements with newspaper editors. I have written more than anybody, or I myself, would have thought. I have taught an hour a day in our school, and I have read two hours every evening to the children. The children study English history in school, and I am reading Scott's historic novels in their order. To-night I finish the "Abbot;" shall begin "Kenilworth" next week; yet I am constantly pursued and haunted by the idea that I don't do anything. Since I began this note I have been called off at least a dozen times; once for the fish-man, to buy a codfish; once to see a man who had brought me some barrels of apples; once to see a book-man; then to Mrs. Upham, to see about a drawing I promised to make for her; then to nurse the baby; then into the kitchen to make a chowder for dinner; and now I am at it again, for nothing but deadly determination enables me ever to write; it is rowing against wind and tide.

I suppose you think now I have begun, I am never going to stop, and in truth it looks like it; but the spirit moves now and I must obey.

Christmas is coming, and our little household is all alive with preparations; every one collecting their little gifts with wonderful mystery and secrecy. . . .

To tell the truth, dear, I am getting tired; my neck and back ache, and I must come to a close.

Your ready kindness to me in the spring I felt very much; and *why* I did not have the sense to have sent you one line just by way of acknowledgment, I'm sure I don't know; I felt just as if I had, till I awoke, and behold! I had not. But, my dear, if my wits are somewhat wool-gathering and unsettled, my heart is as true as a star. I love you, and have thought of you often.

This fall I have felt often *sad*, lonesome, both very unusual feelings with me in these busy days; but the breaking away from my old home, and leaving father and mother, and coming to a strange place affected me naturally. In those sad hours my thoughts have often turned to George; I have thought with encouragement of his blessed state, and hoped that I should soon be there too. I have many warm and kind friends here, and have been treated with great attention and kindness. Brunswick is a delightful residence, and if you come East next summer you must come to my new home. George would delight to go a-fishing with the children, and see the ships, and sail in the sailboats, and all that.

Give Aunt Harriet's love to him, and tell him when he gets to be a painter to send me a picture.

Affectionately yours,   H. STOWE.

The year 1850 is one memorable in the history of our nation as well as in the quiet household that we have followed in its pilgrimage from Cincinnati to Brunswick.

The signers of the Declaration of Independence and the statesmen and soldiers of the Revolution were no friends of negro slavery. In fact, the very principles of the Declaration of Independence sounded the death-knell of slavery forever. No stronger utterances against this national sin are to be found anywhere than in the letters and published writings of Jefferson, Washington, Hamilton, and Patrick Henry. "Jefferson encountered difficulties greater than he could overcome, and after vain wrestlings the words that broke from him, 'I tremble for my country when I reflect that God is just and that his justice cannot sleep forever,' were the words of despair.

"It was the desire of Washington's heart that Virginia should remove slavery by a public act; and as the prospects of a general emancipation grew more and more dim . . . he did all that he could by bequeathing freedom to his own slaves."

Hamilton was one of the founders of the Manumission Society, the object of which was the abolition of slaves in the State of New York. Patrick Henry, speaking of slavery, said: "A serious view of this subject gives a gloomy prospect to future times." Slavery was thought by the founders of our Republic to be a dying institution, and all the provisions of the Constitution touching slavery looked towards gradual emancipation as an inevitable result of the growth of the democracy.

From an economic standpoint slave labor had ceased to be profitable. "The whole interior of the Southern States was languishing, and its inhabitants emigrating, for want of some object to engage their attention and employ their industry." The cultivation of cotton was not profitable for the reason that there was no machine for separating the seed from the fibre.

This was the state of affairs in 1793, when Eli Whitney, a New England mechanic, at this time residing in Savannah, Georgia, invented his cotton-gin, or a machine to separate seed and fibre. "The invention of this machine at once set the whole country in active motion." The effect of this invention may to some extent be appreciated when we consider that whereas in 1793 the Southern States produced only about five or ten thousand bales, in 1859 they produced over five millions. But with this increase of the cotton culture the value of slave property was augmented. Slavery grew and spread. In 1818 to 1821 it first became a factor in politics during the Missouri compromise. By this compromise slavery was not to extend north of latitude 36° 30′. From the time of this compromise till the year 1833 the slavery agitation slumbered. This was the year that the British set the slaves free in their West Indian dependencies. This act caused great uneasiness among the slaveholders of the South. The National Anti-Slavery Society met in Philadelphia and pronounced slavery a national sin, which could be atoned for only by immediate emancipation. Such men as Garrison and Lundy began a work of agitation that was soon to set the whole nation in a ferment. From this time on slavery became the central problem of American history, and the line of cleavage in American politics. The invasion of Florida when it was yet the territory of a nation at peace with the United States, and its subsequent purchase from Spain, the annexation of Texas and the war with Mexico, were the direct results of the policy of the pro-slavery party to increase its influence and its territory. In 1849 the State of California knocked at the door of the Union for admission as a free State. This was bitterly opposed by the slaveholders of the South, who saw in it a menace to the slave-power from the fact that no slave State was seeking admission at the same time. Both North and South the feeling ran so high as to threaten the dismemberment of the Union, and the scenes of violence and bloodshed which were to come eleven years afterwards. It was to preserve the Union and avert the danger of the hour that Henry Clay brought forward his celebrated compromise measures in the winter of 1850. To conciliate the North, California was to be admitted as a free State. To pacify the slaveholders of the South, more stringent laws were to be enacted "concerning persons bound to service in one State and escaping into another."

The 7th of March, 1850, Daniel Webster made his celebrated speech, in which he defended this compromise, and the abolitionists of the North were filled with indignation, which found its most fitting expression in Whittier's "Ichabod:" "So fallen, so lost, the glory from his gray hairs gone." . . . "When honor dies the man is dead."

It was in the midst of this excitement that Mrs. Stowe, with her children and her modest hopes for the future, arrived at the house of her brother, Dr. Edward Beecher.

Dr. Beecher had been the intimate friend and supporter of Lovejoy, who had been murdered by the slaveholders at Alton for publishing an anti-slavery paper. His soul was stirred to its very depths by the iniquitous law which was at this time being debated in Congress,—a law which not only gave the slaveholder of the South the right to seek out and bring back into slavery any colored person whom he claimed as a slave, but commanded the people of the free States to assist in this revolting business. The most frequent theme of conversation while Mrs. Stowe was in Boston was this proposed law, and when she arrived in Brunswick her soul was all on fire with indignation at this new indignity and wrong about to be inflicted by the slave-power on the innocent and defenseless.

After the passage of the Fugitive Slave Act, letter after letter was received by Mrs. Stowe in Brunswick from Mrs. Edward Beecher and other friends, describing the heart-rending scenes which were the inevitable results of the enforcement of this terrible law. Cities were more available for the capturing of escaped slaves than the country, and Boston, which claimed to have the cradle of liberty, opened her doors to the slave-hunters. The sorrow and anguish caused thereby no pen could describe. Families were broken up. Some hid in garrets and cellars. Some fled to the wharves and embarked in ships and sailed for Europe. Others went to Canada. One poor fellow who was doing good business as a crockery merchant, and supporting his family well, when he got notice that his master, whom he had left many years before, was after him, set out for Canada in midwinter on foot, as he did not dare to take a public conveyance. He froze both of his feet on the journey, and they had to be amputated. Mrs. Edward Beecher, in a letter to Mrs. Stowe's son, writing of this period, says:—

"I had been nourishing an anti-slavery spirit since Lovejoy was murdered for publishing in his paper articles against slavery and intemperance, when our home was in Illinois. These terrible things which were going on in Boston were well calculated to rouse up this spirit. What can I do? I thought. Not much myself, but I know one who can. So I wrote several letters to your mother, telling her of various heart-rending events caused by the enforcement of the Fugitive Slave Law. I remember distinctly saying in one of them, 'Now, Hattie, if I could use a pen as you can, I would write something that would make this whole nation feel what an accursed thing slavery is.' . . . When we lived in Boston your mother often visited us. . . . Several numbers of 'Uncle Tom's Cabin' were written in your Uncle Edward's study at these times, and read to us from the manuscripts."

A member of Mrs. Stowe's family well remembers the scene in the little parlor in Brunswick when the letter alluded to was received. Mrs. Stowe herself read it aloud to the assembled family, and when she came to the passage, "I would write something that would make this whole nation feel what an accursed thing slavery is," Mrs. Stowe rose up from her chair, crushing the letter in her hand, and with an expression on her face that stamped itself on the mind of her child, said: "I will write something. I will if I live."

This was the origin of "Uncle Tom's Cabin," and Professor Cairnes has well said in his admirable work, "The Slave Power," "The Fugitive Slave Law has been to the slave power a questionable gain. Among its first-fruits was 'Uncle Tom's Cabin.'"

The purpose of writing a story that should make the whole nation feel that slavery was an accursed thing was not immediately carried out. In December, 1850, Mrs. Stowe writes: "Tell sister Katy I thank her for her letter and will answer it. As long as the baby sleeps with me nights I can't do much at anything, but I will do it at last. I will write that thing if I live.

"What are folks in general saying about the slave law, and the stand taken by Boston ministers universally, except Edward?

"To me it is incredible, amazing, mournful!! I feel as if I should be willing to sink with it, were all this sin and misery to sink in the sea. . . . I wish father would come on to Boston, and preach on the Fugitive Slave Law, as he once preached on the slave-trade, when I was a little girl in Litchfield. I sobbed aloud in one pew and Mrs. Judge Reeves in another. I wish some Martin Luther would arise to set this community right."

December 22, 1850, she writes to her husband in Cincinnati: "Christmas has passed, not without many thoughts of our absent one. If you want a description of the scenes in our family preceding it, *vide* a 'New Year's Story,' which I have sent to the 'New York Evangelist.' I am sorry that in the hurry of getting off this piece and one for the 'Era' you were neglected." The piece for the "Era" was a humorous article called "A Scholar's Adventures in the Country," being, in fact, a picture drawn from life and embodying Professor Stowe's efforts in the department of agriculture while in Cincinnati.

December 29, 1850. "We have had terrible weather here. I remember such a storm when I was a child in Litchfield. Father and mother went to Warren, and were almost lost in the snowdrifts.

"Sunday night I rather watched than slept. The wind howled, and the house rocked just as our old Litchfield house used to. The cold has been so intense that the children have kept begging to get up from table at meal-times to warm feet and fingers. Our air-tight stoves warm all but the floor,—heat your head and keep your feet freezing. If I sit by the open fire in the parlor my back freezes, if I sit in my bedroom and try to write my head aches and my feet are cold. I am projecting a sketch for the 'Era' on the capabilities of liberated blacks to take care of themselves. Can't you find out for me how much Willie Watson has paid for the redemption of his friends, and get any items in figures of that kind that you can pick up in Cincinnati? . . . When I have a headache and feel sick, as I do to-day, there is actually not a place in the house where I can lie down and take a nap without being disturbed. Overhead is the school-room, next door is the dining-room, and the girls practice there two hours a day. If I lock my door and lie down some one is sure to be rattling the latch before fifteen minutes have passed. . . . There is no doubt in my mind that our expenses this year will come two hundred dollars, if not three, beyond our salary. We shall be able to come through, notwithstanding; but I don't want to feel obliged to work as hard every year as I have this. I can earn four hundred dollars a year by writing, but I don't want to feel that I must, and when weary with teaching the children, and tending the baby, and buying provisions, and mending dresses, and darning stockings, sit down and write a piece for some paper."

January 12, 1851, Mrs. Stowe again writes to Professor Stowe at Cincinnati: "Ever since we left Cincinnati to come here the good hand of God has been visibly guiding our way. Through what difficulties have we been brought! Though we knew not where means were to come from, yet means have been furnished every step of the way, and in every time of need. I was just in some discouragement with regard to my writing; thinking that the editor of the 'Era' was overstocked with contributors, and would not want my services another year, and lo! he sends me one hundred dollars, and ever so many good words with it. Our income this year will be seventeen hundred dollars in all, and I hope to bring our expenses within thirteen hundred."

It was in the month of February after these words were written that Mrs. Stowe was seated at communion service in the college church at Brunswick. Suddenly, like the unrolling of a picture, the scene of the death of Uncle Tom passed before her mind. So strongly was she affected that it was with difficulty she could keep from weeping aloud. Immediately on returning home she took pen and paper and wrote out the vision which had been as it were blown into her mind as by the rushing of a mighty wind. Gathering her family about her she read what she had written. Her two little ones of ten and twelve years of age broke into convulsions of weeping, one of them saying through his sobs, "Oh, mamma! slavery is the most cruel thing in the world." Thus Uncle Tom was ushered into the world, and it was, as we said at the beginning, a cry, an immediate, an involuntary expression of deep, impassioned feeling.

Twenty-five years afterwards Mrs. Stowe wrote in a letter to one of her children, of this period of her life: "I well remember the winter you were a baby and I was writing 'Uncle Tom's Cabin.' My heart was bursting with the anguish excited by the cruelty and injustice our nation was showing to the slave, and praying God to let me do a little and to cause my cry for them to be heard. I remember many a night weeping over you as you lay sleeping beside me, and I thought of the slave mothers whose babes were torn from them."

It was not till the following April that the first chapter of the story was finished and sent on to the "National Era" at Washington.

In July Mrs. Stowe wrote to Frederick Douglass the following letter, which is given entire as the best possible introduction to the history of the career of that memorable work, "Uncle Tom's Cabin."

BRUNSWICK, *July 9, 1851.*

FREDERICK DOUGLASS, ESQ.:

Sir,—You may perhaps have noticed in your editorial readings a series of articles that I am furnishing for the "Era" under the title of "Uncle Tom's Cabin, or Life among the Lowly."

In the course of my story the scene will fall upon a cotton plantation. I am very desirous, therefore, to gain information from one who has been an actual laborer on one, and it occurred to me that in the circle of your acquaintance there might be one who would be able to communicate to me some such information as I desire. I have before me an able paper written by a Southern planter, in which the details and *modus operandi* are given from his point of sight. I am anxious to have something more from another standpoint. I wish to be able to make a picture that shall be graphic and true to nature in its details. Such a person as Henry Bibb, if in the country, might give me just the kind of information I desire. You may possibly know of some other person. I will subjoin to this letter a list of questions, which in that case you will do me a favor by inclosing to the individual, with the request that he will at earliest convenience answer them.

For some few weeks past I have received your paper through the mail, and have read it with great interest, and desire to return my acknowledgments for it. It will be a pleasure to me at some time when less occupied to contribute something to its columns. I have noticed with regret your sentiments on two subjects—the church and African colonization, . . . with the more regret because I think you have a considerable share of reason for your feelings on both these subjects; but I would willingly, if I could, modify your views on both points.

In the first place you say the church is "pro-slavery." There is a sense in which this may be true. The American church of all denominations, taken as a body, comprises the best and most conscientious people in the country. I do not say it comprises none but these, or that none such are found out of it, but only if a census were taken of the purest and most high principled men and women of the country, the majority of them would be found to be professors of religion in some of the various Christian denominations. This fact has given to the church great weight in this country—the general and predominant spirit of intelligence and probity and piety of its majority has given it that degree of weight that it has the power to decide the great moral questions of the day. Whatever it unitedly and decidedly sets itself against as moral evil it can put down. In this sense the church is responsible for the sin of slavery. Dr. Barnes has beautifully and briefly expressed this on the last page of his work on slavery, when he says: "Not all the force out of the church could sustain slavery an hour if it were not sustained in it." It then appears that the church has the power to put an end to this evil and does not do it. In this sense she may be said to be pro-slavery. But the church has the same power over intemperance, and Sabbath-breaking, and sin of all kinds. There is not a doubt that if the moral power of the church were brought up to the New Testament standpoint it is sufficient to put an end to all these as well as to slavery. But I would ask you, Would you consider it a fair representation of the Christian church in this country to say that it is pro-intemperance, pro-Sabbath-breaking, and pro everything that it might put down if it were in a higher state of moral feeling? If you should make a list of all the abolitionists of the country, I think that you would find a majority of them in the church—certainly some of the most influential and efficient ones are ministers.

I am a minister's daughter, and a minister's wife, and I have had six brothers in the ministry (one is in heaven); I certainly ought to know something of the feelings of ministers on this subject. I was a child in 1820 when the Missouri question was agitated, and one of the strongest and deepest impressions on my mind was that made by my father's sermons and prayers, and the anguish of his soul for the poor slave at that time. I remember his preaching drawing tears down the hardest faces of the old farmers in his congregation.

I well remember his prayers morning and evening in the family for "poor, oppressed, bleeding Africa," that the time of her deliverance might come; prayers offered with strong crying and tears, and which indelibly impressed my heart and made me what I am from my very soul, the enemy of all slavery. Every brother I have has been in his sphere a leading anti-slavery man. One of them was to the last the bosom friend and counselor of Lovejoy. As for myself and husband, we have for the last seventeen years lived on the border of a slave State, and we have never shrunk from the fugitives, and we have helped them with all we had to give. I have received the children of liberated slaves into a family school, and taught them with my own children, and it has been the influence that we found in the church and by the altar that has made us do all this. Gather up all the sermons that have been published on this offensive and unchristian Fugitive Slave Law, and you will find that those against it are numerically more than those in its favor, and yet some of the strongest opponents have not published their sermons. Out of thirteen ministers who meet with my husband weekly for discussion of moral subjects, only three are found who will acknowledge or obey this law in any shape.

After all, my brother, the strength and hope of your oppressed race does lie in the church—in hearts united to Him of whom it is said, "He shall spare the souls of the needy, and precious shall their blood be in his sight." Everything is against you, but Jesus Christ is for you, and He has not forgotten his church, misguided and erring though it be. I have looked all the field over with despairing eyes; I see no hope but in Him. This movement must and will become a purely religious one. The light will spread in churches, the tone of feeling will rise, Christians North and South will give up all connection with, and take up their testimony against, slavery, and thus the work will be done.

This letter gives us a conception of the state of moral and religious exaltation of the heart and mind out of which flowed chapter after chapter of that wonderful story. It all goes to prove the correctness of the position from which we started, that "Uncle Tom's Cabin" came from the heart rather than the head. It was an outburst of deep feeling, a cry in the darkness. The writer no more thought of style or literary excellence than the mother who rushes into the street and cries for help to save her children from a burning house thinks of the teachings of the rhetorician or the elocutionist.

A few years afterwards Mrs. Stowe, writing of this story, said, "This story is to show how Jesus Christ, who liveth and was dead, and now is alive and forevermore, has still a mother's love for the poor and lowly, and that no man can sink so low but that Jesus Christ will stoop to take his hand. Who so low, who so poor, who so despised as the American slave? The law almost denies his existence as a person, and regards him for the most part as less than a man—a mere thing, the property of another. The law forbids him to read or write, to hold property, to make a contract, or even to form a legal marriage. It takes from him all legal right to the wife of his bosom, the children of his body. He can do nothing, possess nothing, acquire nothing, but what must belong to his master. Yet even to this slave Jesus Christ stoops, from where he sits at the right hand of the Father, and says, 'Fear not, thou whom man despiseth, for I am thy brother. Fear not, for I have redeemed thee, I have called thee by thy name, thou art mine.'"

"Uncle Tom's Cabin" is a work of religion; the fundamental principles of the gospel applied to the burning question of negro slavery. It sets forth those principles of the Declaration of Independence that made Jefferson, Hamilton, Washington, and Patrick Henry anti-slavery men; not in the language of the philosopher, but in a series of pictures. Mrs. Stowe spoke to the understanding and moral sense through the imagination.

"Uncle Tom's Cabin" made the enforcement of the Fugitive Slave Law an impossibility. It aroused the public sentiment of the world by presenting in the concrete that which had been a mere series of abstract propositions. It was, as we have already said, an appeal to the imagination through a series of pictures. People are like children, and understand pictures better than words. Some one rushes into your dining-room while you are at breakfast and cries out, "Terrible railroad accident, forty killed and wounded, six were burned alive."

"Oh, shocking! dreadful!" you exclaim, and yet go quietly on with your rolls and coffee. But suppose you stood at that instant by the wreck, and saw the mangled dead, and heard the piercing shrieks of the wounded, you would be faint and dizzy with the intolerable spectacle.

So "Uncle Tom's Cabin" made the crack of the slavedriver's whip, and the cries of the tortured blacks ring in every household in the land, till human hearts could endure it no longer.

CHAPTER VII

UNCLE TOM'S CABIN, 1852

"UNCLE TOM'S CABIN" AS A SERIAL IN THE "NATIONAL ERA."—AN OFFER FOR ITS PUBLICATION IN BOOK FORM.—WILL IT BE A SUCCESS?—AN UNPRECEDENTED CIRCULATION.—CONGRATULATORY MESSAGES.—KIND WORDS FROM ABROAD.—MRS. STOWE TO THE EARL OF CARLISLE.—LETTERS FROM AND TO LORD SHAFTESBURY.—CORRESPONDENCE WITH ARTHUR HELPS.

THE wonderful story that was begun in the "National Era," June 5, 1851, and was announced to run for about three months, was not completed in that paper until April 1, 1852. It had been contemplated as a mere magazine tale of perhaps a dozen chapters, but once begun it could no more be controlled than the waters of the swollen Mississippi, bursting through a crevasse in its levees. The intense interest excited by the story, the demands made upon the author for more facts, the unmeasured words of encouragement to keep on in her good work that poured in from all sides, and above all the ever-growing conviction that she had been intrusted with a great and holy mission, compelled her to keep on until the humble tale had assumed the proportions of a volume prepared to stand among the most notable books in the world. As Mrs. Stowe has since repeatedly said, "I could not control the story; it wrote itself;" or "I the author of 'Uncle Tom's Cabin'? No, indeed. The Lord himself wrote it, and I was but the humblest of instruments in his hand. To Him alone should be given all the praise."

Although the publication of the "National Era" has been long since suspended, the journal was in those days one of decided literary merit and importance. On its title-page, with the name of Dr. Gamaliel Bailey as editor, appeared that of John Greenleaf Whittier as corresponding editor. In its columns Mrs. Southworth made her first literary venture, while Alice and Phœbe Cary, Grace Greenwood, and a host of other well-known names were published with that of Mrs. Stowe, which appeared last of all in its prospectus for 1851.

Before the conclusion of "Uncle Tom's Cabin" Mrs. Stowe had so far outstripped her contemporaries that her work was pronounced by competent judges to be the most powerful production ever contributed to the magazine literature of this country, and she stood in the foremost rank of American writers.

After finishing her story Mrs. Stowe penned the following appeal to its more youthful readers, and its serial publication was concluded:—

"The author of 'Uncle Tom's Cabin' must now take leave of a wide circle of friends whose faces she has never seen, but whose sympathies coming to her from afar have stimulated and cheered her in her work.

"The thought of the pleasant family circles that she has been meeting in spirit week after week has been a constant refreshment to her, and she cannot leave them without a farewell.

"In particular the dear children who have followed her story have her warmest love. Dear children, you will soon be men and women, and I hope that you will learn from this story always to remember and pity the poor and oppressed. When you grow up, show your pity by doing all you can for them. Never, if you can help it, let a colored child be shut out from school or treated with neglect and contempt on account of his color. Remember the sweet example of little Eva, and try to feel the same regard for all that she did. Then, when you grow up, I hope the foolish and unchristian prejudice against people merely on account of their complexion will be done away with.

"Farewell, dear children, until we meet again."

With the completion of the story the editor of the "Era" wrote: "Mrs. Stowe has at last brought her great work to a close. We do not recollect any production of an American writer that has excited more general and profound interest."

For the story as a serial the author received $300. In the mean time, however, it had attracted the attention of Mr. John P. Jewett, a Boston publisher, who promptly made overtures for its publication in book form. He offered Mr. and Mrs. Stowe a half share in the profits, provided they would share with him the expense of publication. This was refused by Professor Stowe, who said he was altogether too poor to assume any such risk; and the agreement finally made was that the author should receive a ten per cent. royalty upon all sales.

Mrs. Stowe had no reason to hope for any large pecuniary gain from this publication, for it was practically her first book. To be sure, she had, in 1832, prepared a small school geography for a Western publisher, and ten years later the Harpers had brought out her "Mayflower." Still, neither of these had been sufficiently remunerative to cause her to regard literary work as a money-making business, and in regard to this new contract she writes: "I did not know until a week afterward precisely what terms Mr. Stowe had made, and I did not care. I had the most perfect indifference to the bargain."

The agreement was signed March 13, 1852, and, as by arrangement with the "National Era" the book publication of the story was authorized before its completion as a serial, the first edition of five thousand copies was issued on the twentieth of the same month.

In looking over the first semi-annual statement presented by her publishers we find Mrs. Stowe charged, a few days before the date of publication of her book, with "one copy U. T. C. cloth $.56," and this was the first copy of "Uncle Tom's Cabin" ever sold in book form. Five days earlier we find her charged with one copy of Horace Mann's speeches. In writing of this critical period of her life Mrs. Stowe says:—

"After sending the last proof-sheet to the office I sat alone reading Horace Mann's eloquent plea for these young men and women, then about to be consigned to the slave warehouse of Bruin & Hill in Alexandria, Va.,—a plea impassioned, eloquent, but vain, as all other pleas on that side had ever proved in all courts hitherto. It seemed that there was no hope, that nobody would hear, nobody would read, nobody pity; that this frightful system, that had already pursued its victims into the free States, might at last even threaten them in Canada."

Filled with this fear, she determined to do all that one woman might to enlist the sympathies of England for the cause, and to avert, even as a remote contingency, the closing of Canada as a haven of refuge for the oppressed. To this end she at once wrote letters to Prince Albert, to the Duke of Argyll, to the Earls of Carlisle and Shaftesbury, to Macaulay, Dickens, and others whom she knew to be interested in the cause of anti-slavery. These she ordered to be sent to their several addresses, accompanied by the very earliest copies of her book that should be printed.

Uncle Tom

The cabin of Uncle Tom was a small log building close adjoining to "the house" — as the negro always par excellence designates the master's dwelling — In front it had a neat garden patch where strawberries raspberries & a variety of fruits flourished under careful tending — down. The whole front of the dwelling was covered with a large big- nonia & a native multiflora rose which entwining & interlacing left scarce a vestige of the building to be seen & in the spring was redundant with its clusters of roses & in summer as tropical with the scarlet tints of the ——— Various gay brilliant annuals such as marigolds four oclocks & petunias found here and there a thrifty corner to ——— unfold their glories & were the delight & pride of aunt Chloe's heart

Let us enter the dwelling — The evening meal at "the house" is over & Aunt Chloe who presides over its preparation as head cook has left to inferior officers in the kitchen the business of clearing away & washing dishes & come out into her own snug territory to "get her old man's supper" & therefore doubt not that it is her you see by the fire place presiding with anxious interest

Then, having done what she could, and committed the result to God, she calmly turned her attention to other affairs.

In the mean time the fears of the author as to whether or not her book would be read were quickly dispelled. Three thousand copies were sold the very first day, a second edition was issued the following week, a third on the 1st of April, and within a year one hundred and twenty editions, or over three hundred thousand copies of the book, had been issued and sold in this country. Almost in a day the poor professor's wife had become the most talked-of woman in the world, her influence for good was spreading to its remotest corners, and henceforth she was to be a public character, whose every movement would be watched with interest, and whose every word would be quoted. The long, weary struggle with poverty was to be hers no longer; for, in seeking to aid the oppressed, she had also so aided herself that within four months from the time her book was published it had yielded her $10,000 in royalties.

Now letters regarding the wonderful book, and expressing all shades of opinion concerning it, began to pour in upon the author. Her lifelong friend, whose words we have already so often quoted, wrote:—

"I sat up last night until long after one o'clock reading and finishing 'Uncle Tom's Cabin.' I could not leave it any more than I could have left a dying child, nor could I restrain an almost hysterical sobbing for an hour after I laid my head upon my pillow. I thought I was a thorough-going abolitionist before, but your book has awakened so strong a feeling of indignation and of compassion that I never seem to have had any feeling on this subject until now."

The poet Longfellow wrote:—

I congratulate you most cordially upon the immense success and influence of "Uncle Tom's Cabin." It is one of the greatest triumphs recorded in literary history, to say nothing of the higher triumph of its moral effect.

With great regard, and friendly remembrance to Mr. Stowe, I remain,

Yours most truly,
HENRY W. LONGFELLOW.

Whittier wrote to Garrison:—

"What a glorious work Harriet Beecher Stowe has wrought. Thanks for the Fugitive Slave Law! Better would it be for slavery if that law had never been enacted; for it gave occasion for 'Uncle Tom's Cabin.'"

Garrison wrote to Mrs. Stowe:—

"I estimate the value of anti-slavery writing by the abuse it brings. Now all the defenders of slavery have let me alone and are abusing you."

To Mrs. Stowe, Whittier wrote:—

Ten thousand thanks for thy immortal book. My young friend Mary Irving (of the "Era") writes me that she has been reading it to some twenty young ladies, daughters of Louisiana slaveholders, near New Orleans, and amid the scenes described in it, and that they, with one accord, pronounce it true.

Truly thy friend,
JOHN G. WHITTIER.

From Thomas Wentworth Higginson came the following:—

To have written at once the most powerful of contemporary fictions and the most efficient of anti-slavery tracts is a double triumph in literature and philanthropy, to which this country has heretofore seen no parallel.

Yours respectfully and gratefully,
T. W. HIGGINSON.

A few days after the publication of the book, Mrs. Stowe, writing from Boston to her husband in Brunswick, says: "I have been in such a whirl ever since I have been here. I found business prosperous. Jewett animated. He has been to Washington and conversed with all the leading senators, Northern and Southern. Seward told him it was the greatest book of the times, or something of that sort, and he and Sumner went around with him to recommend it to Southern men and get them to read it."

It is true that with these congratulatory and commendatory letters came hosts of others, threatening and insulting, from the Haleys and Legrees of the country.

Of them Mrs. Stowe said: "They were so curiously compounded of blasphemy, cruelty, and obscenity, that their like could only be expressed by John Bunyan's account of the speech of Apollyon: 'He spake as a dragon.'"

A correspondent of the "National Era" wrote: "'Uncle Tom's Cabin' is denounced by time-serving preachers as a meretricious work. Will you not come out in defense of it and roll back the tide of vituperation?"

To this the editor answered: "We should as soon think of coming out in defense of Shakespeare."

Several attempts were made in the South to write books controverting "Uncle Tom's Cabin," and showing a much brighter side of the slavery question, but they all fell flat and were left unread. Of one of them, a clergyman of Charleston, S. C., wrote in a private letter:—

"I have read two columns in the 'Southern Press' of Mrs. Eastman's 'Aunt Phillis' Cabin, or Southern Life as it is,' with the remarks of the editor. I have no comment to make on it, as that is done by itself. The editor might have saved himself being writ down an ass by the public if he had withheld his nonsense. If the two columns are a fair specimen of Mrs. Eastman's book, I pity her attempt and her name as an author."

In due time Mrs. Stowe began to receive answers to the letters she had forwarded with copies of her book to prominent men in England, and these were without exception flattering and encouraging. Through his private secretary Prince Albert acknowledged with thanks the receipt of his copy, and promised to read it. Succeeding mails brought scores of letters from English men of letters and statesmen. Lord Carlisle wrote:—

"I return my deep and solemn thanks to Almighty God who has led and enabled you to write such a book. I do feel indeed the most thorough assurance that in his good Providence such a book cannot have been written in vain. I have long felt that slavery is by far the *topping* question of the world and age we live in, including all that is most thrilling in heroism and most touching in distress; in short, the real epic of the universe. The self-interest of the parties most nearly concerned on the one hand, the apathy and ignorance of unconcerned observers on the other, have left these august pretensions to drop very much out of sight. Hence my rejoicing that a writer has appeared who will be read and must be felt, and that happen what may to the transactions of slavery they will no longer be suppressed."

To this letter, of which but an extract has been given, Mrs. Stowe sent the following reply:—

MY LORD,—It is not with the common pleasure of gratified authorship that I say how much I am gratified by the receipt of your very kind communication with regard to my humble efforts in the cause of humanity. The subject is one so grave, so awful—the success of what I have written has been so singular and so unexpected—that I can scarce retain a self-consciousness and am constrained to look upon it all as the work of a Higher Power, who, when He pleases, can accomplish his results by the feeblest instruments. I am glad of anything which gives notoriety to the book, because it is a plea for the dumb and the helpless! I am glad particularly of notoriety in England because I see with what daily increasing power England's opinion is to act on this country. No one can tell but a *native* born here by what an infinite complexity of ties, nerves, and ligaments this terrible evil is bound in one body politic; how the slightest touch upon it causes even the free States to thrill and shiver, what a terribly corrupting and tempting power it has upon the conscience and moral sentiment even of a free community. Nobody can tell the thousand ways in which by trade, by family affinity, or by political expediency, the free part of our country is constantly tempted to complicity with the slaveholding part. It is a terrible thing to become used to hearing the enormities of slavery, to hear of things day after day that one would think the sun should hide his face from, and yet, to *get used to them*, to discuss them coolly, to dismiss them coolly. For example, the sale of intelligent, handsome colored females for vile purposes, facts of the most public nature, have made this a perfectly understood matter in our Northern States. I have now, myself, under charge and educating, two girls of whose character any mother might be proud, who have actually been rescued from this sale in the New Orleans market.

I desire to inclose a tract in which I sketched down a few incidents in the history of the family to which these girls belong; it will show more than words can the kind of incident to which I allude. The tract is not a published document, only *printed* to assist me in raising money, and it would not, at present, be for the good of the parties to have it published even in England.

But though these things are known in the free States, and other things, if possible, worse, yet there is a terrible deadness of moral sense. They are known by clergymen who yet would not on any account so far commit themselves as to preach on the evils of slavery, or pray for the slaves in their pulpits. They are known by politicians who yet give their votes for slavery extension and perpetuation.

This year both our great leading parties voted to suppress all agitation of the subject, and in both those parties were men who knew personally facts of slavery and the internal slave-trade that one would think no man could ever forget. Men *united* in pledging themselves to the Fugitive Slave Law, who yet would tell you in private conversation that it was an abomination, and who do not hesitate to say, that as a matter of practice they always help the fugitive because they *can't* do otherwise.

The moral effect of this constant insincerity, the moral effect of witnessing and becoming accustomed to the most appalling forms of crime and oppression, is to me the most awful and distressing part of the subject. Nothing makes me feel it so painfully as to see with how much more keenness the English feel the disclosures of my book than the Americans. I myself am blunted by use—by seeing, touching, handling the details. In dealing even for the ransom of slaves, in learning market prices of men, women, and children, I feel that I acquire a horrible familiarity with evil.

Here, then, the great, wise, and powerful mind of England, if she will but fully master the subject, may greatly help us. Hers is the same kind of mind as our own, but disembarrassed from our temptations and unnerved by the thousands of influences that blind and deaden us. There is a healthful vivacity of moral feeling on this subject that must electrify our paralyzed vitality. For this reason, therefore, I rejoice when I see minds like your lordship's turning to this subject; and I feel an intensity of emotion, as if I could say, Do not for Christ's sake let go; you know not what you may do.

Your lordship will permit me to send you two of the most characteristic documents of the present struggle, written by two men who are, in their way, as eloquent for the slave as Chatham was for us in our hour of need.

I am now preparing some additional notes to my book, in which I shall further confirm what I have said by facts and statistics, and in particular by extracts from the *codes of slaveholding States*, and the *records of their courts*. These are documents that cannot be disputed, and I pray your lordship to give them your attention. No disconnected facts can be so terrible as these legal decisions. They will soon appear in England.

It is so far from being irrelevant for England to notice slavery that I already see indications that this subject, on *both sides*, is yet to be presented there, and the battle fought on *English ground*. I see that my friend the South Carolinian gentleman has sent to "Fraser's Magazine" an article; before published in this country, on "Uncle Tom's Cabin." The article in the London "Times" was eagerly reprinted in this country, was issued as a tract and sold by the hundred, headed, "What they think of 'Uncle Tom' in England." If I mistake not, a strong effort will be made to pervert the public mind of England, and to do away the impression which the book has left.

For a time after it was issued it seemed to go by acclamation. From quarters the most unexpected, from all political parties, came an almost unbroken chorus of approbation. I was very much surprised, knowing the explosive nature of the subject. It was not till the sale had run to over a hundred thousand copies that reaction began, and the reaction was led off by the London "Times." Instantly, as by a preconcerted signal, all papers of a certain class began to abuse; and some who had at first issued articles entirely commendatory, now issued others equally depreciatory. Religious papers, notably the "New York Observer," came out and denounced the book as *anti-Christian*, anti-evangelical, resorting even to personal slander on the author as a means of diverting attention from the work.

All this has a meaning, but I think it comes too late. I can think of no reason why it was not tried sooner, excepting that God had intended that the cause should have a hearing. It is strange that they should have waited so long for the political effect of a book which they might have foreseen at first; but not strange that they should, now they *do* see what it is doing, attempt to root it up.

The effects of the book so far have been, I think, these: 1st. To soften and moderate the bitterness of feeling in *extreme abolitionists*. 2d. To convert to abolitionist views many whom this same bitterness had repelled. 3d. To inspire the free colored people with self-respect, hope, and confidence. 4th. To inspire universally through the country a kindlier feeling toward the negro race.

It was unfortunate for the cause of freedom that the first agitators of this subject were of that class which your lordship describes in your note as "well-meaning men." I speak sadly of their faults, for they were men of *noble* hearts. "But oppression maketh a wise man *mad*," and they spoke and did many things in the frenzy of outraged humanity that repelled sympathy and threw multitudes off to a hopeless distance. It is mournful to think of all the absurdities that have been said and done in the name and for the sake of this holy cause, that have so long and so fatally retarded it.

I confess that I expected for myself nothing but abuse from extreme abolitionists, especially as I dared to name a forbidden shibboleth, "Liberia," and the fact that the wildest and extremest abolitionists united with the coldest conservatives, at first, to welcome and advance the book is a thing that I have never ceased to wonder at.

I have written this long letter because I am extremely desirous that some leading minds in England should know how *we* stand. The subject is now on trial at the bar of a civilized world—a Christian world! and I feel sure that God has not ordered this without a design. Yours for the cause,

HARRIET BEECHER STOWE.

In December the Earl of Shaftesbury wrote to Mrs. Stowe:—

MADAM,—It is very possible that the writer of this letter may be wholly unknown to you. But whether my name be familiar to your ears, or whether you now read it for the first time, I cannot refrain from expressing to you the deep gratitude that I feel to Almighty God who has inspired both your heart and your head in the composition of "Uncle Tom's Cabin." None but a Christian believer could have produced such a book as yours, which has absolutely startled the whole world, and impressed many thousands by revelations of cruelty and sin that give us an idea of what would be the uncontrolled dominion of Satan on this fallen earth.

To this letter Mrs. Stowe replied as follows:—

ANDOVER, *January 6, 1853.*

TO THE EARL OF SHAFTESBURY:

My Lord,—The few lines I have received from you are a comfort and an encouragement to me, feeble as I now am in health, and pressed oftentimes with sorrowful thoughts.

It is a comfort to know that in other lands there are those who feel as we feel, and who are looking with simplicity to the gospel of Jesus, and prayerfully hoping his final coming.

My lord, before you wrote me I read with deep emotion your letter to the ladies of England, and subsequently the noble address of the Duchess of Sutherland, and I could not but feel that such movements, originating in such a quarter, prompted by a spirit so devout and benevolent, were truly of God, and must result in a blessing to the world.

I grieve to see that both in England and this country there are those who are entirely incapable of appreciating the Christian and truly friendly feeling that prompted this movement, and that there are even those who meet it with coarse personalities such as I had not thought possible in an English or American paper.

When I wrote my work it was in simplicity and in the love of Christ, and if I felt anything that seemed to me like a call to undertake it, it was this, that I had a true heart of love for the Southern people, a feeling appreciation of their trials, and a sincere admiration of their many excellent traits, and that I thus felt, I think, must appear to every impartial reader of the work.

It was my hope that a book so kindly intended, so favorable in many respects, might be permitted free circulation among them, and that the gentle voice of Eva and the manly generosity of St. Clare might be allowed to say those things of the system which would be invidious in any other form.

At first the book seemed to go by acclamation; the South did not condemn, and the North was loud and unanimous in praise; not a dissenting voice was raised; to my astonishment everybody praised. But when the book circulated so widely and began to penetrate the Southern States, when it began to be perceived how powerfully it affected every mind that read it, there came on a reaction.

Answers, pamphlets, newspaper attacks came thick and fast, and certain Northern papers, religious,—so called,— turned and began to denounce the work as unchristian, heretical, etc. The reason of all this is that it has been seen that the book has a direct tendency to do what it was written for,— to awaken conscience in the slaveholding States and lead to emancipation.

Now there is nothing that Southern political leaders and capitalists so dread as anti-slavery feeling among themselves. All the force of lynch law is employed to smother discussion and blind conscience on this question. The question is not allowed to be discussed, and he who sells a book or publishes a tract makes himself liable to fine and imprisonment.

My book is, therefore, as much under an interdict in some parts of the South as the Bible is in Italy. It is not allowed in the bookstores, and the greater part of the people hear of it and me only through grossly caricatured representations in the papers, with garbled extracts from the book.

A cousin residing in Georgia this winter says that the prejudice against my name is so strong that she dares not have it appear on the outside of her letters, and that very amiable and excellent people have asked her if such as I could be received into reputable society at the North.

Under these circumstances, it is a matter of particular regret that the "New York Observer," an old and long-established religious paper in the United States, extensively read at the South, should have come out in such a bitter and unscrupulous style of attack as even to induce some Southern papers, with a generosity one often finds at the South, to protest against it.

That they should use their Christian character and the sacred name of Christ still further to blind the minds and strengthen the prejudices of their Southern brethren is to me a matter of deepest sorrow. All those things, of course, cannot touch me in my private capacity, sheltered as I am by a happy home and very warm friends. I only grieve for it as a dishonor to Christ and a real injustice to many noble-minded people at the South, who, if they were allowed quietly and dispassionately to hear and judge, might be led to the best results.

But, my lord, all this only shows us how strong is the interest we touch. *All the wealth of America* may be said to be interested in it. And, if I may judge from the furious and bitter tone of some English papers, they also have some sensitive connection with the evil.

I trust that those noble and gentle ladies of England who have in so good a spirit expressed their views of the question will not be discouraged by the strong abuse that will follow. England is doing us good. We need the vitality of a disinterested country to warm our torpid and benumbed public sentiment.

Nay, the storm of feeling which the book raises in Italy, Germany, and France is all good, though truly 'tis painful for us Americans to bear. The fact is, we have become used to this frightful evil, and we need the public sentiment of the world to help us.

I am now writing a work to be called "Key to Uncle Tom's Cabin." It contains, in an undeniable form, the facts which corroborate all that I have said. One third of it is taken up with judicial records of trials and decisions, and with statute law. It is a most fearful story, my lord,—I can truly say that I write with life-blood, but as called of God. I give in my evidence, and I hope that England may so fix the attention of the world on the facts of which I am the unwilling publisher, that the Southern States may be compelled to notice what hitherto they have denied and ignored. If they call the fiction dreadful, what will they say of the fact, where I cannot deny, suppress, or color? But it is God's will that it must be told, and I am the unwilling agent.

This coming month of April, my husband and myself expect to sail for England on the invitation of the Anti-Slavery Society of the Ladies and Gentlemen of Glasgow, to confer with friends there.

There are points where English people can do much good; there are also points where what they seek to do may be made more efficient by a little communion with those who know the feelings and habits of our countrymen: but I am persuaded that England can do much for us.

My lord, they greatly mistake who see, in this movement of English Christians for the abolition of slavery, signs of disunion between the nations. It is the purest and best proof of friendship England has ever shown us, and will, I am confident, be so received. I earnestly trust that all who have begun to take in hand the cause will be in nothing daunted, but persevere to the end; for though everything else be against us, *Christ* is certainly on our side and He *must at last prevail,* and it will be done, "not by might, nor by power, but by His Spirit."

Yours in Christian sincerity,
H. B. STOWE.

Mrs. Stowe also received a letter from Arthur Helps accompanying a review of her work written by himself and published in "Fraser's Magazine." In his letter Mr. Helps took exception to the comparison instituted in "Uncle Tom's Cabin" between the working-classes of England and the slaves of America. In her answer to this criticism and complaint Mrs. Stowe says:—

MR. ARTHUR HELPS:

My dear Sir,—I cannot but say I am greatly obliged to you for the kind opinions expressed in your letter. On one point, however, it appears that my book has not faithfully represented to you the feelings of my heart. I mean in relation to the English nation as a nation. You will notice that the remarks on that subject occur in the *dramatic* part of the book, in the mouth of an intelligent Southerner. As a fair-minded person, bound to state for both sides all that could be said in the person of St. Clare, the best that could be said on that point, and what I know *is* in fact constantly reiterated, namely, that the laboring class of the South are in many respects, as to physical comfort, in a better condition than the poor of England.

This is the slaveholder's stereotyped apology,—a defense it cannot be, unless two wrongs make one right.

It is generally supposed among us that this estimate of the relative condition of the slaves and the poor of England is correct, and we base our ideas on reports made in Parliament and various documentary evidence; also such sketches as "London Labor and London Poor," which have been widely circulated among us. The inference, however, which *we* of the freedom party draw from it, is *not* that the slave is, on the whole, in the best condition because of this striking difference; that in America the slave has not a recognized *human* character *in law, has not even an existence*, whereas in England the law recognizes and protects the meanest subject, in theory *always*, and in *fact* to a certain extent. A prince of the blood could not strike the meanest laborer without a liability to prosecution, in *theory* at least, and that is something. In America any man may strike any slave he meets, and if the master does not choose to notice it, he has no redress.

I do not suppose *human nature* to be widely different in England and America. In both countries, when any class holds power and wealth by institutions which in the long run bring misery on lower classes, they are very unwilling still to part with that wealth and power. They are unwilling to be convinced that it is their duty, and unwilling to do it if they are. It is always so everywhere; it is not English nature or American nature, but human nature. We have seen in England the battle for popular rights fought step by step with as determined a resistance from parties in possession as the slaveholder offers in America.

There was the same kind of resistance in certain quarters there to the laws restricting the employing of young children eighteen hours a day in factories, as there is here to the anti-slavery effort.

Again, in England as in America, there are, in those very classes whose interests are most invaded by what are called popular rights, some of the most determined supporters of them, and here I think that the balance preponderates in favor of England. I think there are more of the high nobility of England who are friends of the common people and willing to help the cause of human progress, irrespective of its influence on their own interests, than there are those of a similar class among slaveholding aristocracy, though even that class is not without such men. But I am far from having any of that senseless prejudice against the English nation as a nation which, greatly to my regret, I observe sometimes in America. It is a relic of barbarism for two such nations as England and America to cherish any such unworthy prejudice.

For my own part, I am proud to be of English blood; and though I do not think England's national course faultless, and though I think many of her institutions and arrangements capable of much revision and improvement, yet my heart warms to her as, *on the whole*, the strongest, greatest, and best nation on earth. Have not England and America one blood, one language, one literature, and a glorious literature it is! Are not Milton and Shakespeare, and all the wise and brave and good of old, common to us both, and should there be anything but cordiality between countries that have so glorious an inheritance in common? If there is, it will be elsewhere than in hearts like mine.

Sincerely yours,
H. B. STOWE.

CHAPTER VIII

FIRST TRIP TO EUROPE, 1853.

THE EDMONDSONS.—BUYING SLAVES TO SET THEM FREE.—JENNY LIND.—PROFESSOR STOWE IS CALLED TO ANDOVER.—FITTING UP THE NEW HOME.—THE "KEY TO UNCLE TOM'S CABIN."—"UNCLE TOM" ABROAD.— HOW IT WAS PUBLISHED IN ENGLAND.—PREFACE TO THE EUROPEAN EDITION.—THE BOOK IN FRANCE.—IN GERMANY.—A GREETING FROM CHARLES KINGSLEY.— PREPARING TO VISIT SCOTLAND.—LETTER TO MRS. FOLLEN.

VERY soon after the publication of "Uncle Tom's Cabin" Mrs. Stowe visited her brother Henry in Brooklyn, and while there became intensely interested in the case of the Edmondsons, a slave family of Washington, D. C. Emily and Mary two of the daughters of Paul (a free colored man) and Milly (a slave) Edmondson, had, for trying to escape from bondage, been sold to a trader for the New Orleans market. While they were lying in jail in Alexandria awaiting the making up of a gang for the South, their heartbroken father determined to visit the North and try to beg from a freedom-loving people the money with which to purchase his daughters' liberty. The sum asked by the trader was $2,250, but its magnitude did not appall the brave old man, and he set forth upon his quest full of faith that in some way he would secure it.

Reaching New York, he went to the anti-slavery bureau and related his pitiful story. The sum demanded was such a large one and seemed so exorbitant that even those who took the greatest interest in the case were disheartened over the prospect of raising it. The old man was finally advised to go to Henry Ward Beecher and ask his aid. He made his way to the door of the great Brooklyn preacher's house, but, overcome by many disappointments and fearing to meet with another rebuff, hesitated to ring the bell, and sat down on the steps with tears streaming from his eyes.

There Mr. Beecher found him, learned his story, and promised to do what he could. There was a great meeting in Plymouth Church that evening, and, taking the old colored man with him to it, Mrs. Stowe's brother made such an eloquent and touching appeal on behalf of the slave girls as to rouse his audience to profound indignation and pity. The entire sum of $2,250 was raised then and there, and the old man, hardly able to realize his great joy, was sent back to his despairing children with their freedom money in his hand.

All this had happened in the latter part of 1848, and Mrs. Stowe had first known of the liberated girls in 1851, when she had been appealed to for aid in educating them. From that time forward she became personally responsible for all their expenses while they remained in school, and until the death of one of them in 1853.

Now during her visit to New York in the spring of 1852 she met their old mother, Milly Edmondson, who had come North in the hope of saving her two remaining slave children, a girl and a young man, from falling into the trader's clutches. Twelve hundred dollars was the sum to be raised, and by hard work the father had laid by one hundred of it when a severe illness put an end to his efforts. After many prayers and much consideration of the matter, his feeble old wife said to him one day, "Paul, I'm a gwine up to New York myself to see if I can't get that money."

Her husband objected that she was too feeble, that she would be unable to find her way, and that Northern people had got tired of buying slaves to set them free, but the resolute old woman clung to her purpose and finally set forth. Reaching New York she made her way to Mr. Beecher's house, where she was so fortunate as to find Mrs. Stowe. Now her troubles were at an end, for this champion of the oppressed at once made the slave woman's cause her own and promised that her children should be redeemed. She at once set herself to the task of raising the purchase-money, not only for Milly's children, but for giving freedom to the old slave woman herself. On May 29, she writes to her husband in Brunswick:—

"The mother of the Edmondson girls, now aged and feeble, is in the city. I did not actually know when I wrote 'Uncle Tom' of a living example in which Christianity had reached its fullest development under the crushing wrongs of slavery, but in this woman I see it. I never knew before what I could feel till, with her sorrowful, patient eyes upon me, she told me her history and begged my aid. The expression of her face as she spoke, and the depth of patient sorrow in her eyes, was beyond anything I ever saw.

"'Well,' said I, when she had finished, 'set your heart at rest; you and your children shall be redeemed. If I can't raise the money otherwise, I will pay it myself.' You should have seen the wonderfully sweet, solemn look she gave me as she said, 'The Lord bless you, my child!'

"Well, I have received a sweet note from Jenny Lind, with her name and her husband's with which to head my subscription list. They give a hundred dollars. Another hundred is subscribed by Mr. Bowen in his wife's name, and I have put my own name down for an equal amount. A lady has given me twenty-five dollars, and Mr. Storrs has pledged me fifty dollars. Milly and I are to meet the ladies of Henry's and Dr. Cox's churches to-morrow, and she is to tell them her story. I have written to Drs. Bacon and Dutton in New Haven to secure a similar meeting of ladies there. I mean to have one in Boston, and another in Portland. It will do good to the givers as well as to the receivers.

"But all this time I have been so longing to get your letter from New Haven, for I heard it was there. It is not fame nor praise that contents me. I seem never to have needed love so much as now. I long to hear you say how much you love me. Dear one, if this effort impedes my journey home, and wastes some of my strength, you will not murmur. When I see this Christlike soul standing so patiently bleeding, yet forgiving, I feel a sacred call to be the helper of the helpless, and it is better that my own family do without me for a while longer than that this mother lose all. *I must redeem her.*

"*New Haven, June 2.* My old woman's case progresses gloriously. I am to see the ladies of this place to-morrow. Four hundred dollars were contributed by individuals in Brooklyn, and the ladies who took subscription papers at the meeting will undoubtedly raise two hundred dollars more."

Before leaving New York, Mrs. Stowe gave Milly Edmondson her check for the entire sum necessary to purchase her own freedom and that of her children, and sent her home rejoicing. That this sum was made up to her by the generous contributions of those to whom she appealed is shown by a note written to her husband and dated July, 1852, in which she says:—

"Had a very kind note from A. Lawrence inclosing a twenty-dollar gold-piece for the Edmondsons. Isabella's ladies gave me twenty-five dollars, so you see our check is more than paid already."

Although during her visit in New York Mrs. Stowe made many new friends, and was overwhelmed with congratulations and praise of her book, the most pleasing incident of this time seems to have been an epistolatory interview with Jenny Lind (Goldschmidt). In writing of it to her husband she says:—

"Well, we have heard Jenny Lind, and the affair was a bewildering dream of sweetness and beauty. Her face and movements are full of poetry and feeling. She has the artless grace of a little child, the poetic effect of a wood-nymph, is airy, light, and graceful.

"We had first-rate seats, and how do you think we got them? When Mr. Howard went early in the morning for tickets, Mr. Goldschmidt told him it was impossible to get any good ones, as they were all sold. Mr. Howard said he regretted that, on Mrs. Stowe's account, as she was very desirous of hearing Jenny Lind. 'Mrs. Stowe!' exclaimed Mr. Goldschmidt, 'the author of "Uncle Tom's Cabin"? Indeed, she shall have a seat whatever happens!'

"Thereupon he took his hat and went out, returning shortly with tickets for two of the best seats in the house, inclosed in an envelope directed to me in his wife's handwriting. Mr. Howard said he could have sold those tickets at any time during the day for ten dollars each.

"To-day I sent a note of acknowledgment with a copy of my book. I am most happy to have seen her, for she is a noble creature."

To this note the great singer wrote in answer:—

MY DEAR MADAM,—Allow me to express my sincere thanks for your very kind letter, which I was very happy to receive.

You must feel and know what a deep impression "Uncle Tom's Cabin" has made upon every heart that can feel for the dignity of human existence: so I with my miserable English would not even try to say a word about the great excellency of that most beautiful book, but I must thank you for the great joy I have felt over that book.

Forgive me, my dear madam: it is a great liberty I take in thus addressing you, I know, but I have so wished to find an opportunity to pour out my thankfulness in a few words to you that I cannot help this intruding. I have the feeling about "Uncle Tom's Cabin" that great changes will take place by and by, from the impression people receive out of it, and that the writer of that book can fall asleep to-day or to-morrow with the bright, sweet conscience of having been a strong means in the Creator's hand of operating essential good in one of the most important questions for the welfare of our black brethren. God bless and protect you and yours, dear madam, and certainly God's hand will remain with a blessing over your head.

Once more forgive my bad English and the liberty I have taken, and believe me to be, dear madam,

> Yours most truly,
> JENNY GOLDSCHMIDT, *née* LIND.

In answer to Mrs. Stowe's appeal on behalf of the Edmonsons, Jenny Lind wrote:—

MY DEAR MRS. STOWE,—I have with great interest read your statement of the black family at Washington. It is with pleasure also that I and my husband are placing our humble names on the list you sent.

The time is short. I am very, very sorry that I shall not be able to *see* you. I must say farewell to you in this way. Hoping that in the length of time you may live to witness the progression of the good sake for which you so nobly have fought, my best wishes go with you.

Yours in friendship,
JENNY GOLDSCHMIDT.

While Mrs. Stowe was thus absent from home, her husband received and accepted a most urgent call to the Professorship of Sacred Literature in the Theological Seminary at Andover, Mass.

In regard to leaving Brunswick and her many friends there, Mrs. Stowe wrote: "For my part, if I *must* leave Brunswick, I would rather leave at once. I can tear away with a sudden pull more easily than to linger there knowing that I am to leave at last. I shall never find people whom I shall like better than those of Brunswick."

As Professor Stowe's engagements necessitated his spending much of the summer in Brunswick, and also making a journey to Cincinnati, it devolved upon his wife to remain in Andover, and superintend the preparation of the house they were to occupy. This was known as the old stone workshop, on the west side of the Common, and it had a year or two before been fitted up by Charles Munroe and Jonathan Edwards as the Seminary gymnasium. Beneath Mrs. Stowe's watchful care and by the judicious expenditure of money, it was transformed by the first of November into the charming abode which under the name of "The Cabin" became noted as one of the pleasantest literary centres of the country. Here for many years were received, and entertained in a modest way, many of the most distinguished people of this and other lands, and here were planned innumerable philanthropic undertakings in which Mrs. Stowe and her scholarly husband were the prime movers.

The summer spent in preparing this home was one of great pleasure as well as literary activity. In July Mrs. Stowe writes to her husband: "I had no idea this place was so beautiful. Our family circle is charming. All the young men are so gentlemanly and so agreeable, as well as Christian in spirit. Mr. Dexter, his wife, and sister are delightful. Last evening a party of us went to ride on horseback down to Pomp's Pond. What a beautiful place it is! There is everything here that there is at Brunswick except the sea,—a great exception. Yesterday I was out all the forenoon sketching elms. There is no end to the beauty of these trees. I shall fill my book with them before I get through. We had a levee at

Professor Park's last week,—quite a brilliant affair. To-day there is to be a fishing party to go to Salem beach and have a chowder.

THE ANDOVER HOME

"It seems almost too good to be true that we are going to have such a house in such a beautiful place, and to live here among all these agreeable people, where everybody seems to love you so much and to think so much of you. I am almost afraid to accept it, and should not, did I not see the Hand that gives it all and know that it is both firm and true. He knows if it is best for us, and His blessing addeth no sorrow therewith. I cannot describe to you the constant undercurrent of love and joy and peace ever flowing through my soul. I am so happy—so blessed!"

The literary work of this summer was directed toward preparing articles on many subjects for the "New York Independent" and the "National Era," as well as collecting material for future books. That the "Pearl of Orr's Island," which afterward appeared as a serial in the "Independent," was already contemplated, is shown by a letter written July 29th, in which Mrs. Stowe says: "What a lovely place Andover is! So many beautiful walks! Last evening a number of us climbed Prospect Hill, and had a most charming walk. Since I came here we have taken up hymn-singing to quite an extent, and while we were all up on the hill we sang 'When I can read my title clear.' It went finely.

"I seem to have so much to fill my time, and yet there is my Maine story waiting. However, I am composing it every day, only I greatly need living studies for the filling in of my sketches. There is 'old Jonas,' my 'fish father,' a sturdy, independent fisherman farmer, who in his youth sailed all over the world and made up his mind about everything. In his old age he attends prayer-meetings and reads the 'Missionary Herald.' He also has plenty of money in an old brown sea-chest. He is a great heart with an inflexible will and iron muscles. I must go to Orr's Island and see him again. I am now writing an article for the 'Era' on Maine and its scenery, which I think is even better than the 'Independent' letter. In it I took up Longfellow. Next I shall write one on Hawthorne and his surroundings.

"To-day Mrs. Jewett sent out a most solemnly savage attack upon me from the 'Alabama Planter.' Among other things it says: 'The plan for assaulting the best institutions in the world may be made just as rational as it is by the wicked (perhaps unconsciously so) authoress of this book. The woman who wrote it must be either a very bad or a very fanatical person. For her own domestic peace we trust no enemy will ever penetrate into her household to pervert the scenes he may find there with as little logic or kindness as she has used in her "Uncle Tom's Cabin."' There's for you! Can you wonder now that such a wicked woman should be gone from you a full month instead of the week I intended? Ah, welladay!"

At last the house was finished, the removal from Brunswick effected, and the reunited family was comfortably settled in its Andover home. The plans for the winter's literary work were, however, altered by force of circumstances. Instead of proceeding quietly and happily with her charming Maine story, Mrs. Stowe found it necessary to take notice in some manner of the cruel and incessant attacks made upon her as the author of "Uncle Tom's

Cabin," and to fortify herself against them by a published statement of incontrovertible facts. It was claimed on all sides that she had in her famous book made such ignorant or malicious misrepresentations that it was nothing short of a tissue of falsehoods, and to refute this she was compelled to write a "Key to Uncle Tom's Cabin," in which should appear the sources from which she had obtained her knowledge. Late in the winter Mrs. Stowe wrote:—

"I am now very much driven. I am preparing a Key to unlock 'Uncle Tom's Cabin.' It will contain all the original facts, anecdotes, and documents on which the story is founded, with some very interesting and affecting stories parallel to those told of Uncle Tom. Now I want you to write for me just what you heard that slave-buyer say, exactly as he said it, that people may compare it with what I have written. My Key will be stronger than the Cabin."

In regard to this "Key" Mrs. Stowe also wrote to the Duchess of Sutherland upon hearing that she had headed an address from the women of England to those of America:—

It is made up of the facts, the documents, the things which my own eyes have looked upon and my hands have handled, that attest this awful indictment upon my country. I write it in the anguish of my soul, with tears and prayer, with sleepless nights and weary days. I bear my testimony with a heavy heart, as one who in court is forced by an awful oath to disclose the sins of those dearest.

So I am called to draw up this fearful witness against my country and send it into all countries, that the general voice of humanity may quicken our paralyzed vitality, that all Christians may pray for us, and that shame, honor, love of country, and love of Christ may be roused to give us strength to cast out this mighty evil.

Yours for the oppressed,
H. B. STOWE.

This harassing, brain-wearying, and heart-sickening labor was continued until the first of April, 1853, when, upon invitation of the Anti-Slavery Society of Glasgow, Scotland, Mrs. Stowe, accompanied by her husband and her brother, Charles Beecher, sailed for Europe.

In the mean time the success of "Uncle Tom's Cabin" abroad was already phenomenal and unprecedented. From the pen of Mr. Sampson Low, the well-known London publisher, we have the following interesting statement regarding it:—

"The first edition printed in London was in April, 1852, by Henry Vizetelly, in a neat volume at ten and sixpence, of which he issued 7,000 copies. He received the first copy imported, through a friend who had bought it in Boston the day the steamer sailed, for his own reading. He gave it to Mr. V., who took it to the late Mr. David Bogue, well known for his general shrewdness and enterprise. He had the book to read and consider over night, and in the morning returned it, declining to take it at the very moderate price of five pounds.

"Vizetelly at once put the volume into the hands of a friendly printer and brought it out on his own account, through the nominal agency of Clarke & Co. The 7,000 copies sold, other editions followed, and Mr. Vizetelly disposed of his interest in the book to the printer and agent, who joined with Mr. Beeton and at once began to issue monster editions. The demand called for fresh supplies, and these created an increased demand. The discovery was soon made that any one was at liberty to reprint the book, and the initiative was thus given to a new era in cheap literature, founded on American reprints. A shilling edition followed the one-and-sixpence, and this in turn became the precursor of one 'complete for sixpence.' From April to December, 1852, twelve different editions (not reissues) were published, and within the twelve months of its first appearance eighteen different London publishing houses were engaged in supplying the great demand that had set in, the total number of editions being forty, varying from fine art-illustrated editions at 15s., 10s., and 7s. 6d., to the cheap popular editions of 1s., 9d., and 6d.

"After carefully analyzing these editions and weighing probabilities with ascertained facts, I am able pretty confidently to say that the aggregate number of copies circulated in Great Britain and the colonies exceeds one and a half millions."

A similar statement made by Clarke & Co. in October, 1852, reveals the following facts. It says: "An early copy was sent from America the latter end of April to Mr. Bogue, the publisher, and was offered by him to Mr. Gilpin, late of Bishopsgate Street. Being declined by Mr. Gilpin, Mr. Bogue offered it to Mr. Henry Vizetelly, and by the latter gentleman it was eventually purchased for us. Before printing it, however, as there was one night allowed for decision, one volume was taken home to be read by Mr. Vizetelly, and the other by Mr. Salisbury, the printer, of Bouverie Street. The report of the latter gentleman the following morning, to quote his own words, was: 'I sat up till four in the morning reading the book, and the interest I felt was expressed one moment by laughter, another by tears. Thinking it might be weakness and not the power of the author that affected me, I resolved to try the effect upon my wife (a rather strong-minded woman). I accordingly woke her and read a few chapters to her. Finding that the interest in the story kept her awake, and that she, too, laughed and cried, I settled in my mind that it was a book that ought to, and might with safety, be printed.'

"Mr. Vizetelly's opinion coincided with that of Mr. Salisbury, and to the latter gentleman it was confided to be brought out immediately. The week following the book was produced and one edition of 7,000 copies worked off. It made no stir until the middle of June, although we advertised it very extensively. From June it began to make its way, and it sold at the rate of 1,000 per week during July. In August the demand became very great, and went on increasing to the 20th, by which time it was perfectly overwhelming. We have now about 400 people employed in getting out the book, and seventeen printing machines besides hand presses. Already about 150,000 copies of the book are in the hands of the people, and still the returns of sales show no decline."

The story was dramatized in the United States in August, 1852, without the consent or knowledge of the author, who had neglected to reserve her rights for this purpose. In September of the same year we find it announced as the attraction at two London theatres, namely, the Royal Victoria and the Great National Standard. In 1853 Professor Stowe writes: "The drama of 'Uncle Tom' has been going on in the National Theatre of New York all summer with most unparalleled success. Everybody goes night after night, and nothing can stop it. The enthusiasm beats that of the run in the Boston Museum out and out. The 'Tribune' is full of it. The 'Observer,' the 'Journal of Commerce,' and all that sort of fellows, are astonished and nonplussed. They do not know what to say or do about it."

While the English editions of the story were rapidly multiplying, and being issued with illustrations by Cruikshank, introductions by Elihu Burritt, Lord Carlisle, etc., it was also making its way over the Continent. For the authorized French edition, translated by Madame Belloc, and published by Charpentier of Paris, Mrs. Stowe wrote the following:—

PREFACE TO THE EUROPEAN EDITION.

In authorizing the circulation of this work on the Continent of Europe, the author has only this apology, that the love of *man* is higher than the love of country.

The great mystery which all Christian nations hold in common, the union of God with man through the humanity of Jesus Christ, invests human existence with an awful sacredness; and in the eye of the true believer in Jesus, he who tramples on the rights of his meanest fellow-man is not only inhuman but sacrilegious, and the worst form of this sacrilege is the institution of *slavery*.

It has been said that the representations of this book are exaggerations! and oh, *would* that this were true! Would that this book were indeed a fiction, and not a close mosaic of facts! But that it is not a fiction the proofs lie bleeding in thousands of hearts; they have been attested by surrounding voices from almost every slave State, and from slave-owners themselves. Since so it must be, thanks be to God that this mighty cry, this wail of an unutterable anguish, has at last been heard!

It has been said, and not in utter despair but in solemn hope and assurance may we regard the struggle that now convulses America,—the outcry of the demon of slavery, which has heard the voice of Jesus of Nazareth, and is rending and convulsing the noble nation from which at last it must depart.

It cannot be that so monstrous a solecism can long exist in the bosom of a nation which in all respects is the best exponent of the great principle of universal brotherhood. In America the Frenchman, the German, the Italian, the Swede, and the Irish all mingle on terms of equal right; all nations there display their characteristic excellences and are admitted by her liberal laws to equal privileges: everything is tending to liberalize, humanize, and elevate, and for that very reason it is that the contest with slavery there grows every year more terrible.

The stream of human progress, widening, deepening, strengthening from the confluent forces of all nations, meets this barrier, behind which is concentrated all the ignorance, cruelty, and oppression of the dark ages, and it roars and foams and shakes the barrier, and anon it must bear it down.

In its commencement slavery overspread every State in the Union: the progress of society has now emancipated the North from its yoke. In Kentucky, Tennessee, Virginia, and Maryland, at different times, strong movements have been made for emancipation,—movements enforced by a comparison of the progressive march of the adjoining free States with the poverty and sterility and ignorance produced by a system which in a few years wastes and exhausts all the resources of the soil without the power of renewal.

The time cannot be distant when these States will emancipate for self-preservation; and if no new slave territory be added, the increase of slave population in the remainder will enforce measures of emancipation.

Here, then, is the point of the battle. Unless more slave territory is gained, slavery dies; if it is gained, it lives. Around this point political parties fight and manœuvre, and every year the battle wages hotter.

The internal struggles of no other nation in the world are so interesting to Europeans as those of America; for America is fast filling up from Europe, and every European has almost immediately his vote in her councils.

If, therefore, the oppressed of other nations desire to find in America an asylum of permanent freedom, let them come prepared, heart and hand, and vote against the institution of slavery; for they who enslave man cannot themselves remain free.

True are the great words of Kossuth: "No nation can remain free with whom freedom is a *privilege* and not a principle."

This preface was more or less widely copied in the twenty translations of the book that quickly followed its first appearance. These, arranged in the alphabetical order of their languages, are as follows: Armenian, Bohemian, Danish, Dutch, Finnish, Flemish, French, German, Hungarian, Illyrian, Italian, Polish, Portuguese, Romaic or modern Greek, Russian, Servian, Spanish, Wallachian, and Welsh.

In Germany it received the following flattering notice from one of the leading literary journals: "The abolitionists in the United States should vote the author of 'Uncle Tom's Cabin' a civic crown, for a more powerful ally than Mrs. Harriet Beecher Stowe and her romance they could not have. We confess that in the whole modern romance literature of Germany, England, and France, we know of no novel to be called equal to this. In comparison with its glowing eloquence that never fails of its purpose, its wonderful truth to nature, the largeness of its ideas, and the artistic faultlessness of the machinery in this book, George Sand, with her Spiridion and Claudie, appears to us untrue and artificial; Dickens, with his but too faithful pictures from the popular life of London, petty; Bulwer, hectic and self-conscious. It is like a sign of warning from the New World to the Old."

Madame George Sand reviewed the book, and spoke of Mrs. Stowe herself in words at once appreciative and discriminating: "Mrs. Stowe is all instinct; it is the very reason she appears to some not to have talent. Has she not talent? What is talent? Nothing, doubtless, compared to genius; but has she genius? She has genius as humanity feels the need of genius,—the genius of goodness, not that of the man of letters, but that of the saint."

Charles Sumner wrote from the senate chamber at Washington to Professor Stowe: "All that I hear and read bears testimony to the good Mrs. Stowe has done. The article of George Sand is a most remarkable tribute, such as was hardly ever offered by such a genius to any living mortal. Should Mrs. Stowe conclude to visit Europe she will have a triumph."

From Eversley parsonage Charles Kingsley wrote to Mrs. Stowe:—

A thousand thanks for your delightful letter. As for your progress and ovation here in England, I have no fear for you. You will be flattered and worshiped. You deserve it and you must bear it. I am sure that you have seen and suffered too much and too long to be injured by the foolish yet honest and heartfelt lionizing which you must go through.

I have many a story to tell you when we meet about the effects of the great book upon the most unexpected people.

Yours ever faithfully,
C. KINGSLEY.

March 28, 1853, Professor Stowe sent the following communication to the Committee of Examination of the Theological Seminary at Andover: "As I shall not be present at the examinations this term, I think it proper to make to you a statement of the reasons of my absence. During the last winter I have not enjoyed my usual health. Mrs. Stowe also became sick and very much exhausted. At this time we had the offer of a voyage to Great Britain and back free of expense."

This offer, coming as it did from the friends of the cause of emancipation in the United Kingdom, was gladly accepted by Mr. and Mrs. Stowe, and they sailed immediately.

The preceding month Mrs. Stowe had received a letter from Mrs. Follen in London, asking for information with regard to herself, her family, and the circumstances of her writing "Uncle Tom's Cabin."

In reply Mrs. Stowe sent the following very characteristic letter, which may be safely given at the risk of some repetition:—

ANDOVER, *February 16, 1853.*

MY DEAR MADAM,—I hasten to reply to your letter, to me the more interesting that I have long been acquainted with you, and during all the nursery part of my life made daily use of your poems for children.

I used to think sometimes in those days that I would write to you, and tell you how much I was obliged to you for the pleasure which they gave us all.

So you want to know something about what sort of a woman I am! Well, if this is any object, you shall have statistics free of charge. To begin, then, I am a little bit of a woman,— somewhat more than forty, about as thin and dry as a pinch of snuff; never very much to look at in my best days, and looking like a used-up article now.

I was married when I was twenty-five years old to a man rich in Greek and Hebrew, Latin and Arabic, and, alas! rich in nothing else. When I went to housekeeping, my entire stock of china for parlor and kitchen was bought for eleven dollars. That lasted very well for two years, till my brother was married and brought his bride to visit me. I then found, on review, that I had neither plates nor teacups to set a table for my father's family; wherefore I thought it best to reinforce the establishment by getting me a tea-set that cost ten dollars more, and this, I believe, formed my whole stock in trade for some years.

But then I was abundantly enriched with wealth of another sort.

I had two little, curly-headed twin daughters to begin with, and my stock in this line has gradually increased, till I have been the mother of seven children, the most beautiful and the most loved of whom lies buried near my Cincinnati residence. It was at his dying bed and at his grave that I learned what a poor slave mother may feel when her child is torn away from her. In those depths of sorrow which seemed to me immeasurable, it was my only prayer to God that such anguish might not be suffered in vain. There were circumstances about his death of such peculiar bitterness, of what seemed almost cruel suffering, that I felt that I could never be consoled for it, unless this crushing of my own heart might enable me to work out some great good to others. . . .

I allude to this here because I have often felt that much that is in that book ("Uncle Tom") had its root in the awful scenes and bitter sorrows of that summer. It has left now, I trust, no trace on my mind, except a deep compassion for the sorrowful, especially for mothers who are separated from their children.

During long years of struggling with poverty and sickness, and a hot, debilitating climate, my children grew up around me. The nursery and the kitchen were my principal fields of labor. Some of my friends, pitying my trials, copied and sent a number of little sketches from my pen to certain liberally paying "Annuals" with my name. With the first money that I earned in this way I bought a feather-bed! for as I had married into poverty and without a dowry, and as my husband had only a large library of books and a great deal of learning, the bed and pillows were thought the most profitable investment. After this I thought that I had discovered the philosopher's stone. So when a new carpet or mattress was going to be needed, or when, at the close of the year, it began to be evident that my family accounts, like poor Dora's, "wouldn't add up," then I used to say to my faithful friend and factotum Anna, who shared all my joys and sorrows, "Now, if you will keep the babies and attend to the things in the house for one day, I'll write a piece, and then we shall be out of the scrape." So I became an author,—very modest at first, I do assure you, and remonstrating very seriously with the friends who had thought it best to put my name to the pieces by way of getting up a reputation; and if you ever see a woodcut of me, with an immoderately long nose, on the cover of all the U. S. Almanacs, I wish you to take notice, that I have been forced into it contrary to my natural modesty by the imperative solicitations of my dear five thousand friends and the public generally. One thing I must say with regard to my life at the

West, which you will understand better than many English women could.

I lived two miles from the city of Cincinnati, in the country, and domestic service, not always you know to be found in the city, is next to an impossibility to obtain in the country, even by those who are willing to give the highest wages; so what was to be expected for poor me, who had very little of this world's goods to offer?

Had it not been for my inseparable friend Anna, a noble-hearted English girl, who landed on our shores in destitution and sorrow, and clave to me as Ruth to Naomi, I had never lived through all the trials which this uncertainty and want of domestic service imposed on both: you may imagine, therefore, how glad I was when, our seminary property being divided out into small lots which were rented at a low price, a number of poor families settled in our vicinity, from whom we could occasionally obtain domestic service. About a dozen families of liberated slaves were among the number, and they became my favorite resort in cases of emergency. If anybody wishes to have a black face look handsome, let them be left, as I have been, in feeble health in oppressive hot weather, with a sick baby in arms, and two or three other little ones in the nursery, and not a servant in the whole house to do a single turn. Then, if they could see my good old Aunt Frankie coming with her honest, bluff, black face, her long, strong arms, her chest as big and stout as a barrel, and her hilarious, hearty laugh, perfectly delighted to take one's washing and do it at a fair price, they would appreciate the beauty of black people.

My cook, poor Eliza Buck,—how she would stare to think of her name going to England!—was a regular epitome of slave life in herself; fat, gentle, easy, loving and lovable, always calling my very modest house and door-yard "The Place," as if it had been a plantation with seven hundred hands on it. She had lived through the whole sad story of a Virginia-raised slave's life. In her youth she must have been a very handsome mulatto girl. Her voice was sweet, and her manners refined and agreeable. She was raised in a good family as a nurse and seamstress. When the family became embarrassed, she was suddenly sold on to a plantation in Louisiana. She has often told me how, without any warning, she was suddenly forced into a carriage, and saw her little mistress screaming and stretching her arms from the window towards her as she was driven away. She has told me of scenes on the Louisiana plantation, and she has often been out at night by stealth ministering to poor slaves who had been mangled and lacerated by the lash. Hence she was sold into Kentucky, and her last master was the father of all her children. On this point she ever maintained a delicacy and reserve that always appeared to me remarkable. She always called him her husband; and it was not till after she had lived with me some years that I discovered the real nature of the connection. I shall never forget how sorry I felt for her, nor my feelings at her humble apology, "You know, Mrs. Stowe, slave women cannot help themselves." She had two very pretty quadroon daughters, with her beautiful hair and eyes, interesting children, whom I had instructed in the family school with my children. Time would fail to tell you all that I learned incidentally of the slave system in the history of various slaves who came into my family, and of the underground railroad which, I may say, ran through our house. But the letter is already too long.

You ask with regard to the remuneration which I have received for my work here in America. Having been poor all my life and expecting to be poor the rest of it, the idea of making money by a book which I wrote just because I could not help it, never occurred to me. It was therefore an agreeable surprise to receive ten thousand dollars as the first-fruits of three months' sale. I presume as much more is now due. Mr. Bosworth in England, the firm of Clarke & Co., and Mr. Bentley, have all offered me an interest in the sales of their editions in London. I am very glad of it, both on account of the value of what they offer, and the value of the example they set in this matter, wherein I think that justice has been too little regarded.

I have been invited to visit Scotland, and shall probably spend the summer there and in England.

I have very much at heart a design to erect in some of the Northern States a normal school, for the education of colored teachers in the United States and in Canada. I have very much wished that some permanent memorial of good to the colored race might be created out of the proceeds of a work which promises to have so unprecedented a sale. My own share of the profits will be less than that of the publishers', either English or American; but I am willing to give largely for this purpose, and I have no doubt that the publishers, both American and English, will unite with me; for nothing tends more immediately to the emancipation of the slave than the education and elevation of the free.

I am now writing a work which will contain, perhaps, an equal amount of matter with "Uncle Tom's Cabin." It will contain all the facts and documents on which that story was founded, and an immense body of facts, reports of trials, legal documents, and testimony of people now living South, which will more than confirm every statement in "Uncle Tom's Cabin."

I must confess that till I began the examination of facts in order to write this book, much as I thought I knew before, I had not begun to measure the depth of the abyss. The law records of courts and judicial proceedings are so incredible as to fill me with amazement whenever I think of them. It seems to me that the book cannot but be felt, and, coming upon the sensibility awaked by the other, do something.

I suffer exquisitely in writing these things. It may be truly said that I write with my heart's blood. Many times in writing "Uncle Tom's Cabin" I thought my health would fail utterly; but I prayed earnestly that God would help me till I got through, and still I am pressed beyond measure and above strength.

This horror, this nightmare abomination! can it be in my country! It lies like lead on my heart, it shadows my life with sorrow; the more so that I feel, as for my own brothers, for the South, and am pained by every horror I am obliged to write, as one who is forced by some awful oath to disclose in court some family disgrace. Many times I have thought that I must die, and yet I pray God that I may live to see something done. I shall in all probability be in London in May; shall I see you?

It seems to me so odd and dream-like that so many persons desire to see me, and now I cannot help thinking that they will think, when they do, that God hath chosen "the weak things of this world."

If I live till spring I shall hope to see Shakespeare's grave, and Milton's mulberry-tree, and the good land of my fathers,— old, old England! May that day come!

Yours affectionately,
H. B. STOWE.

CHAPTER IX

SUNNY MEMORIES, 1853

CROSSING THE ATLANTIC.—ARRIVAL IN ENGLAND.—
RECEPTION IN LIVERPOOL.—WELCOME TO SCOTLAND.—
A GLASGOW TEA-PARTY.—EDINBURGH HOSPITALITY.—
ABERDEEN.—DUNDEE AND BIRMINGHAM.—JOSEPH
STURGE.—ELIHU BURRITT.—LONDON.—THE LORD
MAYOR'S DINNER.—CHARLES DICKENS AND HIS WIFE.

THE journey undertaken by Mrs. Stowe with her husband and
brother through England and Scotland, and afterwards with her
brother alone over much of the Continent, was one of unusual
interest. No one was more surprised than Mrs. Stowe herself by
the demonstrations of respect and affection that everywhere
greeted her.

Fortunately an unbroken record of this memorable journey, in
Mrs. Stowe's own words, has been preserved, and we are thus able
to receive her own impressions of what she saw, heard, and did,
under circumstances that were at once pleasant, novel, and
embarrassing. Beginning with her voyage, she writes as follows:—

LIVERPOOL, *April 11, 1853.*

MY DEAR CHILDREN,—You wish, first of all, to hear of
the voyage. Let me assure you, my dears, in the very
commencement of the matter, that going to sea is not at all the
thing that we have taken it to be.

Let me warn you, if you ever go to sea, to omit all
preparations for amusement on shipboard. Don't leave so
much as the unlocking of a trunk to be done after sailing. In
the few precious minutes when the ship stands still, before she
weighs her anchor, set your house, that is to say your
stateroom, as much in order as if you were going to be hanged;
place everything in the most convenient position to be seized

without trouble at a moment's notice; for be sure that in half an hour after sailing, an infinite desperation will seize you, in which the grasshopper will be a burden. If anything is in your trunk, it might almost as well be in the sea, for any practical probability of your getting to it.

Our voyage out was called "a good run." It was voted unanimously to be "an extraordinary good passage," "a pleasant voyage;" yet the ship rocked the whole time from side to side with a steady, dizzy, continuous motion, like a great cradle. I had a new sympathy for babies, poor little things, who are rocked hours at a time without so much as a "by your leave" in the case. No wonder there are so many stupid people in the world!

We arrived on Sunday morning: the custom-house officers, very gentlemanly men, came on board; our luggage was all set out, and passed through a rapid examination, which in many cases amounted only to opening the trunk and shutting it, and all was over. The whole ceremony did not occupy two hours.

We were inquiring of some friends for the most convenient hotel, when we found the son of Mr. Cropper, of Dingle Bank, waiting in the cabin to take us with him to their hospitable abode. In a few moments after the baggage had been examined, we all bade adieu to the old ship, and went on board the little steam tender which carries passengers up to the city.

This Mersey River would be a very beautiful one, if it were not so dingy and muddy. As we are sailing up in the tender towards Liverpool, I deplore the circumstance feelingly.

"What does make this river so muddy?"

"Oh," says a by-stander, "don't you know that

"'The quality of mercy is not strained'?"

I had an early opportunity of making acquaintance with my English brethren; for, much to my astonishment, I found quite a crowd on the wharf, and we walked up to our carriage through a long lane of people, bowing, and looking very glad to see us.

When I came to get into the hack it was surrounded by more faces than I could count. They stood very quietly, and looked very kindly, though evidently very much determined to look. Something prevented the hack from moving on; so the interview was prolonged for some time.

Our carriage at last drove on, taking us through Liverpool and a mile or two out, and at length wound its way along the gravel paths of a beautiful little retreat, on the banks of the Mersey, called the "Dingle." It opened to my eyes like a paradise, all wearied as I was with the tossing of the sea. I have since become familiar with these beautiful little spots, which are so common in England; but now all was entirely new to me.

After a short season allotted to changing our ship garments and for rest, we found ourselves seated at the dinner table. While dining, the sister-in-law of our friends came in from the next door, to exchange a word or two of welcome, and invite us to breakfast with them the following morning.

The next morning we slept late and hurried to dress, remembering our engagement to breakfast with the brother of our host, whose cottage stands on the same ground, within a few steps of our own. I had not the slightest idea of what the English mean by a breakfast, and therefore went in all innocence, supposing I should see nobody but the family circle of my acquaintances. Quite to my astonishment, I found a party of between thirty and forty people; ladies sitting with their bonnets on, as in a morning call. It was impossible, however, to feel more than a momentary embarrassment in the friendly warmth and cordiality of the circle by whom we were surrounded.

In the evening I went into Liverpool to attend a party of friends of the anti-slavery cause. When I was going away, the lady of the house said that the servants were anxious to see me; so I came into the dressing-room to give them an opportunity.

The next day was appointed to leave Liverpool. A great number of friends accompanied us to the cars, and a beautiful bouquet of flowers was sent with a very affecting message from a sick gentleman, who, from the retirement of his chamber, felt a desire to testify his sympathy. We left Liverpool with hearts a little tremulous and excited by the vibration of an atmosphere of universal sympathy and kindness, and found ourselves, at length, shut from the warm adieu of our friends, in a snug compartment of the railroad car.

"Dear me!" said Mr. S.; "six Yankees shut up in a car together! Not one Englishman to tell us anything about the country! Just like the six old ladies that made their living by taking tea at each other's houses!"

What a bright lookout we kept for ruins and old houses! Mr. S., whose eyes are always in every place, allowed none of us to slumber, but looking out, first on his own side and then on ours, called our attention to every visible thing. If he had been appointed on a mission of inquiry, he could not have been more zealous and faithful, and I began to think that our desire for an English cicerone was quite superfluous.

Well, we are in Scotland at last, and now our pulse rises as the sun declines in the west. We catch glimpses of Solway Firth and talk about Redgauntlet. The sun went down and night drew on; still we were in Scotland. Scotch ballads, Scotch tunes, and Scotch literature were in the ascendant. We sang "Auld Lang Syne," "Scots wha hae," and "Bonnie Doon," and then, changing the key, sang "Dundee," "Elgin," and "Martyr."

"Take care," said Mr. S.; "don't get too much excited."

"Ah," said I, "this is a thing that comes only once in a lifetime; do let us have the comfort of it. We shall never come into Scotland for the *first time* again."

While we were thus at the fusion point of enthusiasm, the cars stopped at Lockerbie. All was dim and dark outside, but we soon became conscious that there was quite a number of people collected, peering into the window; and with a strange kind of thrill, I heard my name inquired for in the Scottish accent. I went to the window; there were men, women, and children gathered, and hand after hand was presented, with the words, "Ye're welcome to Scotland!"

Then they inquired for and shook hands with all the party, having in some mysterious manner got the knowledge of who they were, even down to little G., whom they took to be my son. Was it not pleasant, when I had a heart so warm for this old country? I shall never forget the thrill of those words, "Ye're welcome to Scotland," nor the "Gude night."

After that we found similar welcomes in many succeeding stopping-places; and though I did wave a towel out of the window, instead of a pocket handkerchief, and commit other awkwardnesses, from not knowing how to play my part, yet I fancied, after all, that Scotland and we were coming on well together. Who the good souls were that were thus watching for us through the night, I am sure I do not know; but that they were of the "one blood" which unites all the families of the earth, I felt.

At Glasgow, friends were waiting in the station-house. Earnest, eager, friendly faces, ever so many. Warm greetings, kindly words. A crowd parting in the middle, through which we were conducted into a carriage, and loud cheers of welcome, sent a throb, as the voice of living Scotland.

I looked out of the carriage, as we drove on, and saw, by the light of a lantern, Argyll Street. It was past twelve o'clock when I found myself in a warm, cosy parlor, with friends whom I have ever since been glad to remember. In a little time we were all safely housed in our hospitable apartments, and sleep fell on me for the first time in Scotland.

The next morning I awoke worn and weary, and scarce could the charms of the social Scotch breakfast restore me.

Our friend and host was Mr. Bailie Paton. I believe that it is to his suggestion in a public meeting that we owe the invitation which brought us to Scotland.

After breakfast the visiting began. First, a friend of the family, with three beautiful children, the youngest of whom was the bearer of a handsomely bound album, containing a pressed collection of the sea-mosses of the Scottish coast, very vivid and beautiful.

All this day is a confused dream to me of a dizzy and overwhelming kind. So many letters that it took brother Charles from nine in the morning till two in the afternoon to read and answer them in the shortest manner; letters from all classes of people, high and low, rich and poor, in all shades and styles of composition, poetry and prose; some mere outbursts of feeling; some invitations; some advice and suggestions; some requests and inquiries; some presenting books, or flowers, or fruit.

Then came, in their turn, deputations from Paisley, Greenock, Dundee, Aberdeen, Edinburgh, and Belfast in Ireland; calls of friendship, invitations of all descriptions to go everywhere, and to see everything, and to stay in so many places. One kind, venerable minister, with his lovely daughter, offered me a retreat in his quiet manse on the beautiful shores of the Clyde.

For all these kindnesses, what could I give in return? There was scarce time for even a grateful thought on each. People have often said to me that it must have been an exceeding bore. For my part, I could not think of regarding it so. It only oppressed me with an unutterable sadness.

In the afternoon I rode out with the lord provost to see the cathedral. The lord provost answers to the lord mayor in England. His title and office in both countries continue only a year, except in case of re-election.

As I saw the way to the cathedral blocked up by a throng of people who had come out to see me, I could not help saying, "What went ye out for to see? a reed shaken with the wind?" In fact I was so worn out that I could hardly walk through the building. The next morning I was so ill as to need a physician, unable to see any one that called, or to hear any of the letters. I passed most of the day in bed, but in the evening I had to get up, as I had engaged to drink tea with two thousand people. Our kind friends, Dr. and Mrs. Wardlaw, came after us, and Mr. S. and I went in the carriage with them. Our carriage stopped at last at the place. I have a dim remembrance of a way being made for us through a great crowd all round the house, and of going with Mrs. Wardlaw up into a dressing-room where I met and shook hands with many friendly people. Then we passed into a gallery, where a seat was reserved for our party, directly in front of the audience. Our friend Bailie Paton presided. Mrs. Wardlaw and I sat together, and around us many friends, chiefly ministers of the different churches, the ladies and gentlemen of the Glasgow Anti-Slavery Society and others. I told you it was a tea-party; but the arrangements were altogether different from any I had ever seen. There were narrow tables stretched up and down the whole extent of the great hall, and every person had an appointed seat. These tables were set out with cups and saucers, cakes, biscuit, etc., and when the proper time came, attendants passed along serving tea. The arrangements were so accurate and methodical that the whole multitude actually took tea together, without the least apparent inconvenience or disturbance.

There was a gentle, subdued murmur of conversation all over the house, the sociable clinking of teacups and teaspoons, while the entertainment was going on. It seemed to me such an odd idea, I could not help wondering what sort of a teapot that must be in which all this tea for two thousand people was made. Truly, as Hadji Baba says, I think they must have had the "father of all the tea-kettles" to boil it in. I could not help wondering if old mother Scotland had put two thousand teaspoonfuls of tea for the company, and one for the teapot, as is our good Yankee custom.

We had quite a sociable time up in our gallery. Our tea-table stretched quite across, and we drank tea in sight of all the people. By *we*, I mean a great number of ministers and their wives, and ladies of the Anti-Slavery Society, besides our party, and the friends whom I have mentioned before. All seemed to be enjoying themselves.

After tea they sang a few verses of the seventy-second psalm in the old Scotch version.

April 17. To-day a large party of us started on a small steamer to go down the Clyde. It was a trip full of pleasure and incident. Now we were shown the remains of old Cardross Castle, where it was said Robert Bruce breathed his last. And now we came near the beautiful grounds of Roseneath, a green, velvet-like peninsula, stretching out into the widening waters.

Somewhere about here I was presented, by his own request, to a broad-shouldered Scotch farmer, who stood some six feet two, and who paid me the compliment to say that he had read my book, and that he would walk six miles to see me any day. Such a flattering evidence of discriminating taste, of course, disposed my heart towards him; but when I went up and put my hand into his great prairie of a palm, I was as a grasshopper in my own eyes. I inquired who he was and was told he was one of the Duke of Argyll's farmers. I thought to myself if all the duke's farmers were of this pattern, that he might be able to speak to the enemy in the gates to some purpose.

It was concluded after we left Roseneath that, instead of returning by the boat, we should take carriage and ride home along the banks of the river. In our carriage were Mr. S. and myself, Dr. Robson, and Lady Anderson. About this time I commenced my first essay towards giving titles, and made, as you may suppose, rather an odd piece of work of it, generally saying "Mrs." first, and "Lady" afterwards, and then begging pardon. Lady Anderson laughed and said she would give me a general absolution. She is a truly genial, hearty Scotchwoman, and seemed to enter happily into the spirit of the hour.

As we rode on, we found that the news of our coming had spread through the village. People came and stood in their doors, beckoning, bowing, smiling, and waving their handkerchiefs, and the carriage was several times stopped by persons who came to offer flowers. I remember, in particular, a group of young girls bringing to the carriage two of the most beautiful children I ever saw, whose little hands literally deluged us with flowers.

At the village of Helensburgh we stopped a little while to call upon Mrs. Bell, the wife of Mr. Bell, the inventor of the steamboat. His invention in this country was at about the same time as that of Fulton in America. Mrs. Bell came to the carriage to speak to us. She is a venerable woman, far advanced in years. They had prepared a lunch for us, and quite a number of people had come together to meet us, but our friends said there was not time for us to stop.

We rode through several villages after this, and met everywhere a warm welcome. What pleased me was, that it was not mainly from the literary, nor the rich, nor the great, but the plain, common people. The butcher came out of his stall and the baker from his shop, the miller dusty with flour, the blooming, comely young mother, with her baby in her arms, all smiling and bowing, with that hearty, intelligent, friendly look, as if they knew we should be glad to see them.

Once, while we stopped to change horses, I, for the sake of seeing something more of the country, walked on. It seems the honest landlord and his wife were greatly disappointed at this; however, they got into the carriage and rode on to see me, and I shook hands with them with a right good will.

We saw several of the clergymen, who came out to meet us; and I remember stopping just to be introduced, one by one, to a most delightful family, a gray-headed father and mother, with comely brothers and fair sisters, all looking so kindly and homelike, that I should have been glad to accept the invitation they gave me to their dwelling.

This day has been a strange phenomenon to me. In the first place, I have seen in all these villages how universally the people read. I have seen how capable they are of a generous excitement and enthusiasm, and how much may be done by a work of fiction so written as to enlist those sympathies which are common to all classes. Certainly a great deal may be effected in this way, if God gives to any one the power, as I hope he will to many. The power of fictitious writing, for good as well as evil, is a thing which ought most seriously to be reflected on. No one can fail to see that in our day it is becoming a very great agency.

We came home quite tired, as you may well suppose. You will not be surprised that the next day I found myself more disposed to keep my bed than go out.

Two days later: We bade farewell to Glasgow, overwhelmed with kindness to the last, and only oppressed by the thought of how little that was satisfactory we were able to give in return. Again we were in the railroad car on our way to Edinburgh. A pleasant two hours' trip is this from Glasgow to Edinburgh. When the cars stopped at Linlithgow station, the name started us as out of a dream.

In Edinburgh the cars stopped amid a crowd of people who had assembled to meet us. The lord provost met us at the door of the car, and presented us to the magistracy of the city and the committees of the Edinburgh Anti-Slavery Societies. The drab dresses and pure white bonnets of many Friends were conspicuous among the dense moving crowd, as white doves seen against a dark cloud. Mr. S. and myself, and our future hostess, Mrs. Wigham, entered the carriage with the lord provost, and away we drove, the crowd following with their shouts and cheers. I was inexpressibly touched and affected by this. While we were passing the monument of Scott, I felt an oppressive melancholy. What a moment life seems in the presence of the noble dead! What a momentary thing is art, in all its beauty! Where are all those great souls that have created such an atmosphere of light about Edinburgh? and how little a space was given them to live and enjoy!

We drove all over Edinburgh, up to the castle, to the university, to Holyrood, to the hospitals, and through many of the principal streets, amid shouts, and smiles, and greetings. Some boys amused me very much by their pertinacious attempts to keep up with the carriage.

"Heck," says one of them, "that's her; see the *courls!*"

The various engravers who have amused themselves by diversifying my face for the public having all, with great unanimity, agreed in giving prominence to this point, I suppose the urchins thought they were on safe ground there. I certainly think I answered one good purpose that day, and that is of giving the much-oppressed and calumniated class called boys an opportunity to develop all the noise that was in them,—a thing for which I think they must bless me in their remembrances.

At last the carriage drove into a deep-graveled yard, and we alighted at a porch covered with green ivy, and found ourselves once more at home.

You may spare your anxieties about me, for I do assure you that if I were an old Sèvres china jar I could not have more careful handling than I do. Everybody is considerate; a great deal to say when there appears to be so much excitement. Everybody seems to understand how good-for-nothing I am; and yet, with all this consideration, I have been obliged to keep my room and bed for a good part of the time. Of the multitudes who have called, I have seen scarcely any.

To-morrow evening is to be the great tea-party here. How in the world I am ever to live through it I don't know.

The amount of letters we found waiting for us here in Edinburgh was, if possible, more appalling than in Glasgow. Among those from persons whom you would be interested in hearing of, I may mention a very kind and beautiful one from the Duchess of Sutherland, and one also from the Earl of Carlisle, both desiring to make appointments for meeting us as soon as we come to London. Also a very kind and interesting note from the Rev. Mr. Kingsley and lady. I look forward with a great deal of interest to passing a little time with them in their rectory.

As to all engagements, I am in a state of happy acquiescence, having resigned myself, as a very tame lion, into the hands of my keepers. Whenever the time comes for me to do anything, I try to behave as well as I can, which, as Dr. Young says, is all that an angel could do under the same circumstances.

April 26. Last night came off the *soirée*. The hall was handsomely decorated with flags in front. We went with the lord provost in his carriage. We went up as before into a dressing-room, where I was presented to many gentlemen and ladies. When we go in, the cheering, clapping, and stamping at first strikes one with a strange sensation; but then everybody looks so heartily pleased and delighted, and there is such an all-pervading atmosphere of geniality and sympathy, as makes me in a few moments feel quite at home. After all, I consider that these cheers and applauses are Scotland's voice to America, a recognition of the brotherhood of the countries.

The national penny offering, consisting of a thousand golden sovereigns on a magnificent silver salver, stood conspicuously in view of the audience. It has been an unsolicited offering, given in the smallest sums, often from the extreme poverty of the giver. The committee who collected it in Edinburgh and Glasgow bore witness to the willingness with which the very poorest contributed the offering of their sympathy. In one cottage they found a blind woman, and said, "Here, at least, is one who will feel no interest, as she cannot have read the book."

"Indeed," said the old lady, "if I cannot read, my son has read it to me, and I've got my penny saved to give."

It is to my mind extremely touching to see how the poor, in their poverty, can be moved to a generosity surpassing that of the rich. Nor do I mourn that they took it from their slender store, because I know that a penny given from a kindly impulse is a greater comfort and blessing to the poorest giver than even a penny received.

As in the case of the other meeting, we came out long before the speeches were ended. Well, of course I did not sleep all night, and the next day I felt quite miserable.

From Edinburgh we took cars for Aberdeen. I enjoyed this ride more than anything we had seen yet, the country was so wild and singular. In the afternoon we came in sight of the German Ocean. The free, bracing air from the sea, and the thought that it actually *was* the German Ocean, and that over the other side was Norway, within a day's sail of us, gave it a strange, romantic charm. It was towards the close of the afternoon that we found ourselves crossing the Dee, in view of Aberdeen. My spirits were wonderfully elated: the grand scenery and fine, bracing air; the noble, distant view of the city, rising with its harbor and shipping,—all filled me with delight. In this propitious state, disposed to be pleased with everything, our hearts responded warmly to the greetings of the many friends who were waiting for us at the station-house.

The lord provost received us into his carriage, and as we drove along pointed out to us the various objects of interest in the beautiful town. Among other things, a fine old bridge across the Dee attracted our particular attention. We were conducted to the house of Mr. Cruikshank, a Friend, and found waiting for us there the thoughtful hospitality which we had ever experienced in all our stopping-places. A snug little quiet supper was laid out upon the table, of which we partook in haste, as we were informed that the assembly at the hall were waiting to receive us.

There arrived, we found the hall crowded, and with difficulty made our way to the platform. Whether owing to the stimulating effect of the air from the ocean, or to the comparatively social aspect of the scene, or perhaps to both, certain it is that we enjoyed the meeting with great zest. I was surrounded on the stage with blooming young ladies, one of whom put into my hands a beautiful bouquet, some flowers of which I have now, dried, in my album. The refreshment tables were adorned with some exquisite wax flowers, the work, as I was afterwards told, of a young lady in the place. One of these designs especially interested me. It was a group of water-lilies resting on a mirror, which gave them the appearance of growing in the water.

We had some very animated speaking, in which the speakers contrived to blend enthusiastic admiration and love for America with detestation of slavery.

They presented an offering in a beautiful embroidered purse, and after much shaking of hands we went home, and sat down to the supper-table for a little more chat before going to bed. The next morning—as we had only till noon to stay in Aberdeen—our friends, the lord provost and Mr. Leslie, the architect, came immediately after breakfast to show us the place.

About two o'clock we started from Aberdeen, among crowds of friends, to whom we bade farewell with real regret.

At Stonehaven station, where we stopped a few minutes, there was quite a gathering of the inhabitants to exchange greetings, and afterwards, at successive stations along the road, many a kindly face and voice made our journey a pleasant one.

When we got into Dundee it seemed all alive with welcome. We went in the carriage with the lord provost, Mr. Thoms, to his residence, where a party had been waiting dinner for us for some time.

The meeting in the evening was in a large church, densely crowded, and conducted much as the others had been. When they came to sing the closing hymn, I hoped they would sing Dundee; but they did not, and I fear in Scotland, as elsewhere, the characteristic national melodies are giving way before more modern ones.

We left Dundee at two o'clock, by cars, for Edinburgh again, and in the evening attended another *soirée* of the workingmen of Edinburgh. We have received letters from the workingmen, both in Dundee and Glasgow, desiring our return to attend *soirées* in those cities. Nothing could give us greater pleasure, had we time or strength. The next day we had a few calls to make, and an invitation from Lady Drummond to visit classic Hawthornden, which, however, we had not time to accept. In the forenoon, Mr. S. and I called on Lord and Lady Gainsborough. Though she is one of the queen's household, she is staying here at Edinburgh while the queen is at Osborne. I infer, therefore, that the appointment includes no very onerous duties. The Earl of Gainsborough is the eldest brother of the Rev. Baptist W. Noel.

It was a rainy, misty morning when I left my kind retreat and friends in Edinburgh. Considerate as everybody had been about imposing on my time or strength, still you may well believe that I was much exhausted. We left Edinburgh, therefore, with the determination to plunge at once into some hidden and unknown spot, where we might spend two or three days quietly by ourselves; and remembering your Sunday at Stratford-on-Avon, I proposed that we should go there. As Stratford, however, is off the railroad line, we determined to accept the invitation, which was lying by us, from our friend, Joseph Sturge, of Birmingham, and take sanctuary with him. So we wrote on, intrusting him with the secret, and charging him on no account to let any one know of our arrival.

About night our cars whizzed into the depot at Birmingham; but just before we came in a difficulty was started in the company. "Mr. Sturge is to be there waiting for us, but he does not know us and we don't know him; what is to be done?" C. insisted that he should know him by instinct; and so, after we reached the depot, we told him to sally out and try. Sure enough, in a few moments he pitched upon a cheerful, middle-aged gentleman, with a moderate but not decisive broad brim to his hat, and challenged him as Mr. Sturge. The result verified the truth that "instinct is a great matter." In a few moments our new friend and ourselves were snugly encased in a fly, trotting off as briskly as ever we could to his place at Edgbaston, nobody a whit the wiser. You do not know how pleased we felt to think we had done it so nicely.

As we were drinking tea that evening, Elihu Burritt came in. It was the first time I had ever seen him, though I had heard a great deal of him from our friends in Edinburgh. He is a man in middle life, tall and slender, with fair complexion, blue eyes, an air of delicacy and refinement, and manners of great gentleness. My ideas of the "learned blacksmith" had been of something altogether more ponderous and peremptory. Elihu has been for some years operating, in England and on the Continent, in a movement which many in our half-Christianized times regard with as much incredulity as the grim, old warlike barons did the suspicious imbecilities of reading and writing. The sword now, as then, seems so much more direct a way to terminate controversies, that many Christian men, even, cannot conceive how the world is to get along without it.

We spent the evening in talking over various topics relating to the anti-slavery movement. Mr. Sturge was very confident that something more was to be done than had ever been done yet, by combinations for the encouragement of free in the place of slave grown produce; a question which has, ever since the days of Clarkson, more or less deeply occupied the minds of abolitionists in England. I should say that Mr. Sturge in his family has for many years conscientiously forborne the use of any article produced by slave labor. I could scarcely believe it possible that there could be such an abundance and variety of all that is comfortable and desirable in the various departments of household living within these limits. Mr. Sturge presents the subject with very great force, the more so from the consistency of his example.

The next morning, as we were sitting down to breakfast, our friends sent in to me a plate of the largest, finest strawberries I have ever seen, which, considering that it was only the latter part of April, seemed to me quite an astonishing luxury.

Before we left, we had agreed to meet a circle of friends from Birmingham, consisting of the Abolition Society there, which is of long standing, extending back in its memories to the very commencement of the agitation under Clarkson and Wilberforce. The windows of the parlor were opened to the ground; and the company invited filled not only the room, but stood in a crowd on the grass around the window. Among the peaceable company present was an admiral in the navy, a fine, cheerful old gentleman, who entered with hearty interest into the scene.

A throng of friends accompanied us to the depot, while from Birmingham we had the pleasure of the company of Elihu Burritt, and enjoyed a delightful run to London, where we arrived towards evening.

At the station-house in London we found the Rev. Messrs. Binney and Sherman waiting for us with carriages. C. went with Mr. Sherman, and Mr. S. and I soon found ourselves in a charming retreat called Rose Cottage, in Walworth, about which I will tell you more anon. Mrs. B. received us with every attention which the most thoughtful hospitality could suggest. One of the first things she said to me after we got into our room was, "Oh, we are so glad you have come! for we are all going to the lord mayor's dinner to-night, and you are invited." So, though I was tired, I hurried to dress in all the glee of meeting an adventure. As soon as Mr. and Mrs. B. and the rest of the party were ready, crack went the whip, round went the wheels, and away we drove.

We found a considerable throng, and I was glad to accept a seat which was offered me in the agreeable vicinity of the lady mayoress, so that I might see what would be interesting to me of the ceremonial.

A very dignified gentleman, dressed in black velvet, with a fine head, made his way through the throng, and sat down by me, introducing himself as Lord Chief Baron Pollock. He told me he had just been reading the legal part of the "Key to Uncle Tom's Cabin," and remarked especially on the opinion of Judge Ruffin, in the case of *State* v. *Mann*, as having made a deep impression on his mind.

Dinner was announced between nine and ten o'clock, and we were conducted into a splendid hall, where the tables were laid.

Directly opposite me was Mr. Dickens, whom I now beheld for the first time, and was surprised to see looking so young. Mr. Justice Talfourd, known as the author of "Ion," was also there with his lady. She had a beautiful, antique cast of head. The lord mayor was simply dressed in black, without any other adornment than a massive gold chain. We rose from table between eleven and twelve o'clock—that is, we ladies—and went into the drawing-room, where I was presented to Mrs. Dickens and several other ladies. Mrs. Dickens is a good specimen of a truly English woman; tall, large, and well developed, with fine, healthy color, and an air of frankness, cheerfulness, and reliability. A friend whispered to me that she was as observing and fond of humor as her husband.

After a while the gentlemen came back to the drawing-room, and I had a few moments of very pleasant, friendly conversation with Mr. Dickens. They are both people that one could not know a little of without desiring to know more.

After a little we began to talk of separating; the lord mayor to take his seat in the House of Commons, and the rest of the party to any other engagement that might be upon their list.

"Come, let us go to the House of Commons," said one of my friends, "and make a night of it." "With all my heart," replied I, "if I only had another body to go into to-morrow."

What a convenience in sight-seeing it would be if one could have a relay of bodies as of clothes, and slip from one into the other! But we, not used to the London style of turning night into day, are full weary already. So good-night to you all.

CHAPTER X

FROM OVER THE SEA, 1853

THE EARL OF CARLISLE.—ARTHUR HELPS.—THE
DUKE AND DUCHESS OF ARGYLL.—MARTIN FARQUHAR
TUPPER.—A MEMORABLE MEETING AT STAFFORD
HOUSE.—MACAULAY AND DEAN MILMAN.—WINDSOR
CASTLE.—PROFESSOR STOWE RETURNS TO AMERICA.—
MRS. STOWE ON THE CONTINENT.—IMPRESSIONS OF
PARIS.—EN ROUTE TO SWITZERLAND AND GERMANY.—
BACK TO ENGLAND.—HOMEWARD BOUND.

ROSE COTTAGE, WALWORTH, LONDON, *May 2,*
1856.

MY DEAR,—This morning Mrs. Follen called and we had
quite a chat. We are separated by the whole city. She lives at
the West End, while I am down here in Walworth, which is
one of the postscripts of London, for this place has as many
postscripts as a lady's letter. This evening we dined with the
Earl of Carlisle. There was no company but ourselves, for he,
with great consideration, said in his note that he thought a little
quiet would be the best thing he could offer.

Lord Carlisle is a great friend to America, and so is his
sister, the Duchess of Sutherland. He is the only English
traveler who ever wrote notes on our country in a real spirit of
appreciation.

We went about seven o'clock, the dinner hour being here
somewhere between eight and nine. We were shown into an
ante-room adjoining the entrance hall, and from that into an
adjacent apartment, where we met Lord Carlisle. The room
had a pleasant, social air, warmed and enlivened by the blaze of
a coal fire and wax candles.

We had never, any of us, met Lord Carlisle before; but the considerateness and cordiality of our reception obviated whatever embarrassment there might have been in this circumstance. In a few moments after we were all seated, a servant announced the Duchess of Sutherland, and Lord Carlisle presented me. She is tall and stately, with a most noble bearing. Her fair complexion, blonde hair, and full lips speak of Saxon blood.

The only person present not of the family connection was my quondam correspondent in America, Arthur Helps. Somehow or other I had formed the impression from his writings that he was a venerable sage of very advanced years, who contemplated life as an aged hermit from the door of his cell. Conceive my surprise to find a genial young gentleman of about twenty-five, who looked as if he might enjoy a joke as well as another man.

After the ladies left the table, the conversation turned on the Maine law, which seems to be considered over here as a phenomenon in legislation, and many of the gentlemen present inquired about it with great curiosity.

After the gentlemen rejoined us, the Duke and Duchess of Argyll came in, and Lord and Lady Blantyre. These ladies are the daughters of the Duchess of Sutherland. The Duchess of Argyll is of slight and fairy-like figure, with flaxen hair and blue eyes, answering well enough to the description of Annot Lyle in the Legend of Montrose. Lady Blantyre was somewhat taller, of fuller figure, with a very brilliant bloom. Lord Blantyre is of the Stuart blood, a tall and slender young man with very graceful manners.

As to the Duke of Argyll, we found that the picture drawn of him by his countrymen in Scotland was in every way correct. Though slight of figure, with fair complexion and blue eyes, his whole appearance is indicative of energy and vivacity. His talents and efficiency have made him a member of the British Cabinet at a much earlier age than is usual; and he has distinguished himself not only in political life, but as a writer, having given to the world a work on Presbyterianism, embracing an analysis of the ecclesiastical history of Scotland since the Reformation, which is spoken of as written with great ability, and in a most liberal spirit. He made many inquiries about our distinguished men, particularly of Emerson, Longfellow, and Hawthorne; also of Prescott, who appears to be a general favorite here. I felt at the moment that we never value our own literary men so much as when we are placed in a circle of intelligent foreigners.

The following evening we went to dine with our old friends of the Dingle, Mr. and Mrs. Edward Cropper, who are now spending a little time in London. We were delighted to meet them once more and to hear from our Liverpool friends. Mrs. Cropper's father, Lord Denman, has returned to England, though with no sensible improvement in his health.

At dinner we were introduced to Lord and Lady Hatherton. Lady Hatherton is a person of great cultivation and intelligence, warmly interested in all the progressive movements of the day; and I gained much information in her society. There were also present Sir Charles and Lady Trevelyan; the former holds an appointment at the treasury, and Lady Trevelyan is a sister of Macaulay.

In the evening quite a circle came in, among others Lady Emma Campbell, sister of the Duke of Argyll; the daughters of the Archbishop of Canterbury, who very kindly invited me to visit them at Lambeth; and Mr. Arthur Helps, besides many others whose names I need not mention.

May 7. This evening our house was opened in a general way for callers, who were coming and going all the evening. I think there must have been over two hundred people, among them Martin Farquhar Tupper, a little man with fresh, rosy complexion and cheery, joyous manners; and Mary Howitt, just such a cheerful, sensible, fireside companion as we find her in her books,—winning love and trust the very first moment of the interview.

The general topic of remark on meeting me seems to be, that I am not so bad-looking as they were afraid I was; and I do assure you that when I have seen the things that are put up in the shop windows here with my name under them, I have been in wondering admiration at the boundless loving-kindness of my English and Scottish friends in keeping up such a warm heart for such a Gorgon. I should think that the Sphinx in the London Museum might have sat for most of them. I am going to make a collection of these portraits to bring home to you. There is a great variety of them, and they will be useful, like the Irishman's guide-board, which showed where the road did not go.

Before the evening was through I was talked out and worn out; there was hardly a chip of me left. To-morrow at eleven o'clock comes the meeting at Stafford House. What it will amount to I do not know; but I take no thought for the morrow.

May 8.

MY DEAR C.,—In fulfillment of my agreement I will tell you, as nearly as I can remember, all the details of the meeting at Stafford House. At about eleven o'clock we drove under the arched carriage-way of a mansion externally not very showy in appearance.

When the duchess appeared, I thought she looked handsomer by daylight than in the evening. She received us with the same warm and simple kindness which she had shown before. We were presented to the Duke of Sutherland. He is a tall, slender man, with rather a thin face, light-brown hair, and a mild blue eye, with an air of gentleness and dignity.

Among the first that entered were the members of the family, the Duke and Duchess of Argyll, Lord and Lady Blantyre, the Marquis and Marchioness of Stafford, and Lady Emma Campbell. Then followed Lord Shaftesbury with his beautiful lady, and her father and mother, Lord and Lady Palmerston. Lord Palmerston is of middle height, with a keen dark eye and black hair streaked with gray. There is something peculiarly alert and vivacious about all his movements; in short, his appearance perfectly answers to what we know of him from his public life. One has a strange, mythological feeling about the existence of people of whom one hears for many years without ever seeing them. While talking with Lord Palmerston I could but remember how often I had heard father and Mr. S. exulting over his foreign dispatches by our own fireside. There were present, also, Lord John Russell, Mr. Gladstone, and Lord Granville. The latter we all thought very strikingly resembled in his appearance the poet Longfellow.

After lunch the whole party ascended to the picture-gallery, passing on our way the grand staircase and hall, said to be the most magnificent in Europe. The company now began to assemble and throng the gallery, and very soon the vast room was crowded. Among the throng I remember many presentations, but of course must have forgotten many more. Archbishop Whateley was there, with Mrs. and Miss Whateley; Macaulay, with two of his sisters; Milman, the poet and historian; the Bishop of Oxford, Chevalier Bunsen and lady, and many more.

When all the company were together, Lord Shaftesbury read a very short, kind, and considerate address in behalf of the ladies of England, expressive of their cordial welcome.

This Stafford House meeting, in any view of it, is a most remarkable fact. Kind and gratifying as its arrangements have been to me, I am far from appropriating it to myself individually as a personal honor. I rather regard it as the most public expression possible of the feelings of the women of England on one of the most important questions of our day, that of individual liberty considered in its religious bearings.

On this occasion the Duchess of Sutherland presented Mrs. Stowe with a superb gold bracelet, made in the form of a slave's shackle, bearing the inscription: "We trust it is a memorial of a chain that is soon to be broken." On two of the links were inscribed the dates of the abolition of the slave-trade and of slavery in English territory. Years after its presentation to her, Mrs. Stowe was able to have engraved on the clasp of this bracelet, "Constitutional Amendment (forever abolishing slavery in the United States)."

Continuing her interesting journal, Mrs. Stowe writes, May 9th:—

DEAR E.,—This letter I consecrate to you, because I know that the persons and things to be introduced into it will most particularly be appreciated by you.

In your evening reading circles, Macaulay, Sydney Smith, and Milman have long been such familiar names that you will be glad to go with me over all the scenes of my morning breakfast at Sir Charles Trevelyan's yesterday. Lady Trevelyan, I believe I have said before, is a sister of Macaulay.

We were set down at Westbourne Terrace somewhere, I believe, about eleven o'clock, and found quite a number already in the drawing-room. I had met Macaulay before, but being seated between him and Dean Milman, I must confess I was a little embarrassed at times, because I wanted to hear what they were both saying at the same time. However, by the use of the faculty by which you play a piano with both hands, I got on very comfortably.

There were several other persons of note present at this breakfast, whose conversation I had not an opportunity of hearing, as they sat at a distance from me. There was Lord Glenelg, brother of Sir Robert Grant, governor of Bombay, whose beautiful hymns have rendered him familiar in America. The favorite one, commencing

"When gathering clouds around I view,"

was from his pen.

The historian Hallam was also present, and I think it very likely there may have been other celebrities whom I did not know. I am always finding out, a day or two after, that I have been with somebody very remarkable and did not know it at the time.

Under date of May 18th she writes to her sister Mary:—

DEAR M.,—I can compare the embarrassment of our London life, with its multiplied solicitations and infinite stimulants to curiosity and desire, only to that annual perplexity which used to beset us in our childhood on Thanksgiving Day. Like Miss Edgeworth's philosophic little Frank, we are obliged to make out a list of what man *must* want, and of what he *may* want; and in our list of the former we set down, in large and decisive characters, one quiet day for the exploration and enjoyment of Windsor.

The ride was done all too soon. About eleven o'clock we found ourselves going up the old stone steps to the castle. We went first through the state apartments. The principal thing that interested me was the ball-room, which was a perfect gallery of Vandyke's paintings. After leaving the ball-room we filed off to the proper quarter to show our orders for the private rooms. The state apartments, which we had been looking at, are open at all times, but the private apartments can only be seen in the Queen's absence and by a special permission, which had been procured for us on that occasion by the kindness of the Duchess of Sutherland.

One of the first objects that attracted my attention upon entering the vestibule was a baby's wicker wagon, standing in one corner. It was much such a carriage as all mothers are familiar with; such as figures largely in the history of almost every family. It had neat curtains and cushions of green merino, and was not royal, only maternal. I mused over the little thing with a good deal of interest.

We went for our dinner to the White Hart, the very inn which Shakespeare celebrates in his "Merry Wives," and had a most overflowing merry time of it. After dinner we had a beautiful drive.

We were bent upon looking up the church which gave rise to Gray's "Elegy in a Country Churchyard," intending when we got there to have a little scene over it; Mr. S., in all the conscious importance of having been there before, assuring us that he knew exactly where it was. So, after some difficulty with our coachman, and being stopped at one church which would not answer our purpose in any respect, we were at last set down by one which looked authentic; embowered in mossy elms, with a most ancient and goblin yew-tree, an ivy-mantled tower, all perfect as could be. Here, leaning on the old fence, we repeated the Elegy, which certainly applies here as beautifully as language could apply.

Imagine our chagrin, on returning to London, at being informed that we had not been to the genuine churchyard after all. The gentleman who wept over the scenes of his early days on the wrong doorstep was not more grievously disappointed.

However, he and we could both console ourselves with the reflection that the emotion was admirable, and wanted only the right place to make it the most appropriate in the world.

The evening after our return from Windsor was spent with our kind friends, Mr. and Mrs. Gurney. After breakfast the next day, Mr. S., C., and I drove out to call upon Kossuth. We found him in an obscure lodging on the outskirts of London. I would that some of the editors in America, who have thrown out insinuations about his living in luxury, could have seen the utter bareness and plainness of the reception room, which had nothing in it beyond the simplest necessaries. He entered into conversation with us with cheerfulness, speaking English well, though with the idioms of foreign languages. When we parted he took my hand kindly and said, "God bless you, my child!"

I have been quite amused with something which has happened lately. This week the "Times" has informed the United Kingdom that Mrs. Stowe is getting a new dress made! It wants to know if Mrs. Stowe is aware what sort of a place her dress is being made in; and there is a letter from a dressmaker's apprentice stating that it is being made up piecemeal, in the most shockingly distressed dens of London, by poor, miserable white slaves, worse treated than the plantation slaves of America!

Now Mrs. Stowe did not know anything of this, but simply gave the silk into the hands of a friend, and was in due time waited on in her own apartment by a very respectable-appearing woman, who offered to make the dress, and lo, this is the result! Since the publication of this piece, I have received earnest missives, from various parts of the country, begging me to interfere, hoping that I was not going to patronize the white slavery of England, and that I would employ my talents equally against oppression in every form. Could these people only know in what sweet simplicity I had been living in the State of Maine, where the only dressmaker of our circle was an intelligent, refined, well-educated woman who was considered as the equal of us all, and whose spring and fall ministrations to our wardrobe were regarded a double pleasure,—a friendly visit as well as a domestic assistance,—I say, could they know all this, they would see how guiltless I was in the matter. I verily never thought but that the nice, pleasant person who came to measure me for my silk dress was going to take it home and make it herself; it never occurred to me that she was the head of an establishment.

May 22, she writes to her husband, whose duties had obliged him to return to America: "To-day we went to hear a sermon in behalf of the ragged schools by the Archbishop of Canterbury. My thoughts have been much saddened by the news which I received of the death of Mary Edmonson."

"*May 30.* The next day from my last letter came off Miss Greenfield's concert, of which I send a card. You see in what company they have put your poor little wife. Funny!—isn't it? Well, the Hons. and Right Hons. all were there. I sat by Lord Carlisle.

"After the concert the duchess asked Lady Hatherton and me to come round to Stafford House and take tea, which was not a thing to be despised, either on account of the tea or the duchess. A lovelier time we never had,—present, the Duchess of Argyll, Lady Caroline Campbell, Lady Hatherton, and myself. We had the nicest cup of tea, with such cream, and grapes and apricots, with some Italian bread, etc.

"When we were going the duchess got me, on some pretext, into another room, and came up and put her arms round me, with her noble face all full of feeling.

"'Oh, Mrs. Stowe, I have been reading that last chapter in the "Key"; Argyll read it aloud to us. Oh, surely, surely you will succeed,—God surely will bless you!'

"I said then that I thanked her for all her love and feeling for us, told her how earnestly all the women of England sympathized with her, and many in America. She looked really radiant and inspired. Had those who hang back from our cause seen her face, it might have put a soul into them as she said again, 'It will be done—it will be done—oh, I trust and pray it may!'

"So we kissed each other, and vowed friendship and fidelity— so I came away.

"To-day I am going with Lord Shaftesbury to St. Paul's to see the charity children, after which lunch with Dean Milman.

"*May 31.* We went to lunch with Miss R. at Oxford Terrace, where, among a number of distinguished guests, was Lady Byron, with whom I had a few moments of deeply interesting conversation. No engravings that ever have been circulated in America do any justice to her appearance. She is of slight figure, formed with exceeding delicacy, and her whole form, face, dress, and air unite to make an impression of a character singularly dignified, gentle, pure, and yet strong. No words addressed to me in any conversation hitherto have made their way to my inner soul with such force as a few remarks dropped by her on the present religious aspect of England,—remarks of such quality as one seldom hears.

"According to request, I will endeavor to keep you informed of all our goings-on after you left, up to the time of our departure for Paris.

"We have borne in mind your advice to hasten away to the Continent. Charles wrote, a day or two since, to Mrs. C. at Paris to secure very private lodgings, and by no means let any one know that we were coming. She has replied urging us to come to her house, and promising entire seclusion and rest. So, since you departed, we have been passing with a kind of comprehensive skip and jump over remaining engagements. And just the evening after you left came off the presentation of the inkstand by the ladies of Surrey Chapel.

"It is a beautiful specimen of silver-work, eighteen inches long, with a group of silver figures on it representing Religion, with the Bible in her hand, giving liberty to the slave. The slave is a masterly piece of work. He stands with his hands clasped, looking up to Heaven, while a white man is knocking the shackles from his feet. But the prettiest part of the scene was the presentation of a *gold pen* by a band of beautiful children, one of whom made a very pretty speech. I called the little things to come and stand around me, and talked with them a few minutes, and this was all the speaking that fell to my share.

"To-morrow we go—go to quiet, to obscurity, to peace—to Paris, to Switzerland; there we shall find the loveliest glen, and, as the Bible says, 'fall on sleep.'

"*Paris, June 4.* Here we are in Paris, in a most charming family. I have been out all the morning exploring shops, streets, boulevards, and seeing and hearing life in Paris. When one has a pleasant home and friends to return to, this gay, bustling, vivacious, graceful city is one of the most charming things in the world; and we *have* a most charming home.

"I wish the children could see these Tuileries with their statues and fountains, men, women, and children seated in family groups under the trees, chatting, reading aloud, working muslin,—children driving hoop, playing ball, all alive and chattering French. Such fresh, pretty girls as are in the shops here! *Je suis ravé,* as they say. In short I am decidedly in a French humor, and am taking things quite *couleur de rose.*

"*Monday, June 13.* We went this morning to the studio of M. Belloc, who is to paint my portrait. The first question which he proposed, with a genuine French air, was the question of 'pose' or position. It was concluded that, as other pictures had taken me looking at the spectator, this should take me looking away. M. Belloc remarked that M. Charpentier said I appeared always with the air of an observer,—was always looking around on everything. Hence M. Belloc would take me '*en observatrice, mais pas en curieuse,*'— with the air of observation, but not of curiosity. By and by M. Charpentier came in. He began panegyrizing 'Uncle Tom,' and this led to a discussion of the ground of its unprecedented success. In his thirty-five years' experience as a bookseller, he had known nothing like it. It surpassed all modern writings! At first he would not read it; his taste was for old masters of a century or two ago. 'Like M. Belloc in painting,' said I. At length he found his friend M., the first intelligence of the age, reading it.

"'What, you, too?' said he.

"'Ah, ah!' replied the friend; 'say nothing about this book! There is nothing like it. This leaves us all behind,—all, all, miles behind!'

"M. Belloc said the reason was because there was in it more *genuine faith* than in any book, and we branched off into florid eloquence touching paganism, Christianity, and art.

"*Wednesday, June 22*. Adieu to Paris! Ho for Chalons-sur-Saône! After affectionate farewells of our kind friends, by eleven o'clock we were rushing, in the pleasantest of cars, over the smoothest of rails, through Burgundy. We arrived at Chalons at nine P. M.

"*Thursday, 23*, eight o'clock A. M. Since five we have had a fine bustle on the quay below our windows. There lay three steamers, shaped for all the world like our last night's rolls. One would think Ichabod Crane might sit astride one of them and dip his feet in the water. They ought to be swift. L'Hirondelle (The Swallow) flew at five; another at six. We leave at nine.

"*Lyons*. There was a scene of indescribable confusion upon our arrival here. Out of the hold of our steamer a man with a rope and hook began hauling baggage up a smooth board. Three hundred people were sorting their goods without checks. Porters were shouldering immense loads, four or five heavy trunks at once, corded together, and stalking off Atlantean. Hat-boxes, bandboxes, and valises burst like a meteoric shower out of a crater. '*A moi, à moi!*' was the cry, from old men, young women, soldiers, shopkeepers, and *frères*, scuffling and shoving together.

"*Saturday, June 25*. Lyons to Genève. As this was our first experience in the diligence line, we noticed particularly every peculiarity. I had had the idea that a diligence was a ricketty, slow-moulded antediluvian nondescript, toiling patiently along over impassable roads at a snail's pace. Judge of my astonishment at finding it a full-blooded, vigorous monster, of unscrupulous railway momentum and imperturbable equipoise of mind. Down the macadamized slopes we thundered at a prodigious pace; up the hills we trotted, with six horses, three abreast; madly through the little towns we burst, like a whirlwind, crashing across the pebbled streets, and out upon the broad, smooth road again. Before we had well considered the fact that we were out of Lyons we stopped to change horses. Done in a jiffy; and whoop, crick, crack, whack, rumble, bump, whirr, whisk, away we blazed, till, ere we knew it, another change and another.

"As evening drew on, a wind sprang up and a storm seemed gathering on the Jura. The rain dashed against the panes of the berlin as we rode past the grim-faced monarch of the 'misty shroud.' It was night as we drove into Geneva and stopped at the Messagerie. I heard with joy a voice demanding if this were *Madame Besshare*. I replied, not without some scruples of conscience, '*Oui, Monsieur, c'est moi,*' though the name did not sound exactly like the one to which I had been wont to respond. In half an hour we were at home in the mansion of Monsieur Fazy."

From Geneva the party made a tour of the Swiss Alps, spending some weeks among them. While there Charles Beecher wrote from a small hotel at the foot of the Jura:—

"The people of the neighborhood, having discovered who Harriet was, were very kind, and full of delight at seeing her. It was Scotland over again. We have had to be unflinching to prevent her being overwhelmed, both in Paris and Geneva, by the same demonstrations of regard. To this we were driven, as a matter of life and death. It was touching to listen to the talk of these secluded mountaineers. The good hostess, even the servant maids, hung about Harriet, expressing such tender interest for the slave. All had read 'Uncle Tom;' and it had apparently been an era in their life's monotony, for they said, 'Oh, madam, do write another! Remember, our winter nights here are very long!'"

Upon their return to Geneva they visited the Castle of Chillon, of which, in describing the dungeons, Mrs. Stowe writes:—

"One of the pillars in this vault is covered with names. I think it is Bonnevard's Pillar. There are the names of Byron, Hunt, Schiller, and ever so many more celebrities. As we were going from the cell our conductress seemed to have a sudden light upon her mind. She asked a question or two of some of our party, and fell upon me vehemently to put my name also there. Charley scratched it on the soft freestone, and there it is for future ages. The lady could scarce repress her enthusiasm; she shook my hand over and over again, and said she had read 'Uncle Tom.' 'It is beautiful,' she said, 'but it is cruel.'

"*Monday, July 18.* Weather suspicious. Stowed ourselves and our baggage into our *voiture*, and bade adieu to our friends and to Geneva. Ah, how regretfully! From the market-place we carried away a basket of cherries and fruit as a consolation. Dined at Lausanne, and visited the cathedral and picture-gallery, where was an exquisite *Eva*. Slept at Meudon.

"*Tuesday, July 19*. Rode through Payerne to Freyburg. Stopped at the Zähringer Hof,—most romantic of inns.

"*Wednesday, July 20*. Examined, not the lions, but the bears of Berne. Engaged a *voiture* and drove to Thun. Dined and drove by the shore of the lake to Interlachen, arriving just after a brilliant sunset.

"We crossed the Wengern Alps to Grindelwald. The Jungfrau is right over against us,—her glaciers purer, tenderer, more dazzlingly beautiful, if possible, than those of Mont Blanc. Slept at Grindelwald."

From Rosenlaui, on this journey, Charles Beecher writes:—

"*Friday, July 22*. Grindelwald to Meyringen. On we came, to the top of the Great Schiedeck, where H. and W. botanized, while I slept. Thence we rode down the mountain till we reached Rosenlaui, where, I am free to say, a dinner was to me a more interesting object than a glacier. Therefore, while H. and W. went to the latter, I turned off to the inn, amid their cries and reproaches.

"Here, then, I am, writing these notes in the *salle à manger* of the inn, where other voyagers are eating and drinking, and there is H. feeding on the green moonshine of an emerald ice cave. One would almost think her incapable of fatigue. How she skips up and down high places and steep places, to the manifest perplexity of the honest guide Kienholz, *père*, who tries to take care of her, but does not exactly know how! She gets on a pyramid of débris, which the edge of the glacier is plowing and grinding up, sits down, and falls—not asleep exactly, but into a trance. W. and I are ready to go on: we shout; our voice is lost in the roar of the torrent. We send the guide. He goes down, and stands doubtfully. He does not know exactly what to do. She hears him, and starts to her feet, pointing with one hand to yonder peak, and with the other to that knife-like edge that seems cleaving heaven with its keen and glistening cimeter of snow, reminding one of Isaiah's sublime imagery, 'For my sword is bathed in heaven.' She points at the grizzly rocks, with their jags and spear-points. Evidently she is beside herself, and thinks she can remember the names of those monsters, born of earthquake and storm, which cannot be named nor known but by sight, and then are known at once perfectly and forever."

After traveling through Germany, Belgium, and Holland, the party returned to Paris toward the end of August, from which place Mrs. Stowe writes:—

"I am seated in a snug little room at M. Belloc's. The weather is overpoweringly hot, but these Parisian houses seem to have seized and imprisoned coolness. French household ways are delightful. I like their seclusion from the street by these deep-paned quadrangles.

"Madame Belloc was the translator of Maria Edgeworth, by that lady's desire; corresponded with her for years, and still has many of her letters. Her translation of 'Uncle Tom' has to me all the merit and all the interest of an original composition. In perusing it, I enjoy the pleasure of reading the story with scarce any consciousness of its ever having been mine."

The next letter is from London *en route* for America, to which passage had been engaged on the Collins steamer Arctic. In it Mrs. Stowe writes:—

"*London, August 28.* Our last letters from home changed all our plans. We concluded to hurry away by the next steamer, if at that late hour we could get a passage. We were all in a bustle. The last shoppings for aunts, cousins, and little folks were to be done by us all. The Palais Royal was to be rummaged; bronzes, vases, statuettes, bonbons, playthings,—all that the endless fertility of France could show,—was to be looked over for the 'folks at home.'

"How we sped across the Channel C. relates. We are spending a few very pleasant days with our kind friends the L.'s, in London.

"*On board the Arctic, September 7.* On Thursday, September 1, we reached York, and visited the beautiful ruins of St. Mary's Abbey, and the magnificent cathedral. It rained with inflexible pertinacity during all the time we were there, and the next day it rained still, when we took the cars for Castle Howard station.

"Lady Carlisle welcomed us most affectionately, and we learned that, had we not been so reserved at the York station in concealing our names, we should have received a note from her. However, as we were safely arrived, it was of no consequence.

"Our friends spoke much of Sumner and Prescott, who had visited there; also of Mr. Lawrence, our former ambassador, who had visited them just before his return. After a very pleasant day, we left with regret the warmth of this hospitable circle, thus breaking one more of the links that bind us to the English shore.

"Nine o'clock in the evening found us sitting by a cheerful fire in the parlor of Mr. E. Baines at Leeds. The next day the house was filled with company, and the Leeds offering was presented.

"Tuesday we parted from our excellent friends in Leeds, and soon found ourselves once more in the beautiful "Dingle," our first and last resting-place on English shores.

"A deputation from Belfast, Ireland, here met me, presenting a beautiful bog-oak casket, lined with gold, and carved with appropriate national symbols, containing an offering for the cause of the oppressed. They read a beautiful address, and touched upon the importance of inspiring with the principles of emancipation the Irish nation, whose influence in our land is becoming so great. Had time and strength permitted, it had been my purpose to visit Ireland, to revisit Scotland, and to see more of England. But it is not in man that walketh to direct his steps. And now came parting, leave-taking, last letters, notes, and messages.

"Thus, almost sadly as a child might leave its home, I left the shores of kind, strong Old England,—the mother of us all."

CHAPTER XI

HOME AGAIN, 1853-1856

ANTI-SLAVERY WORK.—STIRRING TIMES IN THE UNITED STATES.—ADDRESS TO THE LADIES OF GLASGOW.—APPEAL TO THE WOMEN OF AMERICA.— CORRESPONDENCE WITH WILLIAM LLOYD GARRISON.— THE WRITING OF "DRED."—FAREWELL LETTER FROM GEORGIANA MAY.—SECOND VOYAGE TO ENGLAND.

AFTER her return in the autumn of 1853 from her European tour, Mrs. Stowe threw herself heart and soul into the great struggle with slavery. Much of her time was occupied in distributing over a wide area of country the English gold with which she had been intrusted for the advancement of the cause. With this money she assisted in the redemption of slaves whose cases were those of peculiar hardship, and helped establish them as free men. She supported anti-slavery lectures wherever they were most needed, aided in establishing and maintaining anti-slavery publications, founded and assisted in supporting schools in which colored people might be taught how to avail themselves of the blessings of freedom. She arranged public meetings, and prepared many of the addresses that should be delivered at them. She maintained such an extensive correspondence with persons of all shades of opinion in all parts of the world, that the letters received and answered by her between 1853 and 1856 would fill volumes. With all these multifarious interests, her children received a full share of her attention, nor were her literary activities relaxed.

Immediately upon the completion of her European tour, her experiences were published in the form of a journal, both in this country and England, under the title of "Sunny Memories." She also revised and elaborated the collection of sketches which had been published by the Harpers in 1843, under title of "The Mayflower," and having purchased the plates caused them to be republished in 1855 by Phillips & Sampson, the successors of John

P. Jewett & Co., in this country, and by Sampson Low & Co. in London.

Soon after her return to America, feeling that she owed a debt of gratitude to her friends in Scotland, which her feeble health had not permitted her adequately to express while with them, Mrs. Stowe wrote the following open letter:—

TO THE LADIES' ANTI-SLAVERY SOCIETY OF GLASGOW:

Dear Friends,—I have had many things in my mind to say to you, which it was my hope to have said personally, but which I am now obliged to say by letter.

I have had many fears that you must have thought our intercourse, during the short time that I was in Glasgow, quite unsatisfactory.

At the time that I accepted your very kind invitation, I was in tolerable health, and supposed that I should be in a situation to enjoy society, and mingle as much in your social circles as you might desire.

When the time came for me to fulfil my engagement with you, I was, as you know, confined to my bed with a sickness brought on by the exertion of getting the "Key to Uncle Tom's Cabin" through the press during the winter.

In every part of the world the story of "Uncle Tom" had awakened sympathy for the American slave, and consequently in every part of the world the story of his wrongs had been denied; it had been asserted to be a mere work of romance, and I was charged with being the slanderer of the institutions of my own country. I knew that if I shrank from supporting my position, the sympathy which the work had excited would gradually die out, and the whole thing would be looked upon as a mere romantic excitement of the passions.

When I came abroad, I had not the slightest idea of the kind of reception which was to meet me in England and Scotland. I had thought of something involving considerable warmth, perhaps, and a good deal of cordiality and feeling on the part of friends; but of the general extent of feeling through society, and of the degree to which it would be publicly expressed, I had, I may say, no conception.

As through your society I was invited to your country, it may seem proper that what communication I have to make to friends in England and Scotland should be made through you.

In the first place, then, the question will probably arise in your minds, Have the recent demonstrations in Great Britain done good to the anti-slavery cause in America?

The first result of those demonstrations, as might have been expected, was an intense reaction. Every kind of false, evil, and malignant report has been circulated by malicious and partisan papers; and if there is any blessing in having all manner of evil said against us falsely, we have seemed to be in a fair way to come in possession of it.

The sanction which was given in this matter to the voice of the people, by the nobility of England and Scotland, has been regarded and treated with special rancor; and yet, in its place, it has been particularly important. Without it great advantages would have been taken to depreciate the value of the national testimony. The value of this testimony in particular will appear from the fact that the anti-slavery cause has been treated with especial contempt by the leaders of society in this country, and every attempt made to brand it with ridicule.

The effect of making a cause generally unfashionable is much greater in this world than it ought to be. It operates very powerfully with the young and impressible portion of the community; therefore Cassius M. Clay very well said with regard to the demonstration at Stafford House: "It will help our cause by rendering it fashionable."

With regard to the present state of the anti-slavery cause in America, I think, for many reasons, that it has never been more encouraging. It is encouraging in this respect, that the subject is now fairly up for inquiry before the public mind. And that systematic effort which has been made for years to prevent its being discussed is proving wholly ineffectual.

The "Key to Uncle Tom's Cabin" has sold extensively at the South, following in the wake of "Uncle Tom." Not one fact or statement in it has been disproved as yet. I have yet to learn of even an *attempt* to disprove.

The "North American Review," a periodical which has never been favorable to the discussion of the slavery question, has come out with a review of "Uncle Tom's Cabin," in which, while rating the book very low as a work of art, they account for its great circulation and success by the fact of its being a true picture of slavery. They go on to say that the system is one so inherently abominable that, unless slaveholders shall rouse themselves and abolish the principle of chattel ownership, they can no longer sustain themselves under the contempt and indignation of the whole civilized world. What are the slaveholders to do when this is the best their friends and supporters can say for them?

I regret to say that the movements of Christian denominations on this subject are yet greatly behind what they should be. Some movements have been made by religious bodies, of which I will not now speak; but as a general thing the professed Christian church is pushed up to its duty by the world, rather than the world urged on by the church.

The colored people in this country are rapidly rising in every respect. I shall request Frederick Douglass to send you the printed account of the recent colored convention. It would do credit to any set of men whatever, and I hope you will get some notice taken of it in the papers of the United Kingdom. It is time that the slanders against this unhappy race should be refuted, and it should be seen how, in spite of every social and political oppression, they are rising in the scale of humanity. In my opinion they advance quite as fast as any of the foreign races which have found an asylum among us.

May God so guide us in all things that our good be not evil spoken of, and that we be left to defend nothing which is opposed to his glory and the good of man!

Yours in all sympathy,
H. B. STOWE.

During the Kansas and Nebraska agitation (1853-54), Mrs. Stowe, in common with the abolitionists of the North, was deeply impressed with a solemn sense that it was a desperate crisis in the nation's history. She was in constant correspondence with Charles Sumner and other distinguished statesmen of the time, and kept herself informed as to the minutest details of the struggle. At this time she wrote and caused to be circulated broadcast the following appeal to the women of America:—

"The Providence of God has brought our nation to a crisis of most solemn interest.

"A question is now pending in our national legislature which is most vitally to affect the temporal and eternal interests, not only of ourselves, but of our children and our children's children for ages yet unborn. Through our nation it is to affect the interests of liberty and Christianity throughout the world.

"Of the woes, the injustice, and the misery of slavery it is not needful to speak. There is but one feeling and one opinion upon this subject among us all. I do not think there is a mother who clasps her child to her breast who would ever be made to feel it right that that child should be a slave, not a mother among us who would not rather lay that child in its grave.

"Nor can I believe that there is a woman so unchristian as to think it right to inflict upon her neighbor's child what she would consider worse than death were it inflicted upon her own. I do not believe there is a wife who would think it right that *her* husband should be sold to a trader to be worked all his life without wages or a recognition of rights. I do not believe there is a husband who would consider it right that his wife should be regarded by law the property of another man. I do not believe there is a father or mother who would consider it right were they forbidden by law to teach their children to read. I do not believe there is a brother who would think it right to have his sister held as property, with no legal defense for her personal honor, by any man living.

"All this is inherent in slavery. It is not the abuse of slavery, but its legal nature. And there is not a woman in the United States, where the question is fairly put to her, who thinks these things are right.

"But though our hearts have bled over this wrong, there have been many things tending to fetter our hands, to perplex our efforts, and to silence our voice. We have been told that to speak of it was an invasion of the rights of states. We have heard of promises and compacts, and the natural expression of feeling has in many cases been repressed by an appeal to those honorable sentiments which respect the keeping of engagements.

"But a time has now come when the subject is arising under quite a different aspect.

"The question is not now, shall the wrongs of slavery exist as they have within their own territories, but shall we permit them to be extended all over the free territories of the United States? Shall the woes and the miseries of slavery be extended over a region of fair, free, unoccupied territory nearly equal in extent to the whole of the free States?

"Nor is this all! This is not the last thing that is expected or intended. Should this movement be submitted to in silence, should the North consent to this solemn breach of contract on the part of the South, there yet remains one more step to be apprehended, namely, the legalizing of slavery throughout the free States. By a decision of the supreme court in the Lemmon case, it may be declared lawful for slave property to be held in the Northern States. Should this come to pass, it is no more improbable that there may be four years hence slave depots in New York city than it was four years ago that the South would propose a repeal of the Missouri Compromise.

"Women of the free States! the question is not shall we remonstrate with slavery on its own soil, but are we willing to receive slavery into the free States and Territories of this Union? Shall the whole power of these United States go into the hands of slavery? Shall every State in the Union be thrown open to slavery? This is the possible result and issue of the question now pending. This is the fearful crisis at which we stand.

"And now you ask, What can the *women* of a country do?

"O women of the free States! what did your brave mothers do in the days of our Revolution? Did not liberty in those days feel the strong impulse of woman's heart?

"There was never a great interest agitating a community where woman's influence was not felt for good or for evil. At the time when the abolition of the slave-trade was convulsing England, women contributed more than any other laborers to that great triumph of humanity. The women of England refused to receive into their houses the sugar raised by slaves. Seventy thousand families thus refused the use of sugar in testimony of their abhorrence of the manner in which it was produced. At that time women were unwearied in going from house to house distributing books and tracts upon the subject, and presenting it clearly and forcibly to thousands of families who would otherwise have disregarded it.

"The women all over England were associated in corresponding circles for prayer and labor. Petitions to the government were prepared and signed by women of every station in all parts of the kingdom.

"Women of America! we do not know with what thrilling earnestness the hopes and the eyes of the world are fastened upon our country, and how intense is the desire that we should take a stand for universal liberty. When I was in England, although I distinctly stated that the raising of money was no part of my object there, it was actually forced upon me by those who could not resist the impulse to do something for this great cause. Nor did it come from the well-to-do alone; but hundreds of most affecting letters were received from poor working men and women, who inclosed small sums in postage-stamps to be devoted to freeing slaves.

"Nor is this deep feeling confined to England alone. I found it in France, Switzerland, and Germany. Why do foreign lands regard us with this intensity of interest? Is it not because the whole world looks hopefully toward America as a nation especially raised by God to advance the cause of human liberty and religion?

"There has been a universal expectation that the next step taken by America would surely be one that should have a tendency to right this great wrong. Those who are struggling for civil and religious liberty in Europe speak this word 'slavery' in sad whispers, as one names a fault of a revered friend. They can scarce believe the advertisements in American papers of slave sales of men, women, and children, traded like cattle. Scarcely can they trust their eyes when they read the laws of the slave States, and the decisions of their courts. The advocates of despotism hold these things up to them and say: 'See what comes of republican liberty!' Hitherto the answer has been, 'America is more than half free, and she certainly will in time repudiate slavery altogether.'

"But what can they say now if, just as the great struggle for human rights is commencing throughout Europe, America opens all her Territories to the most unmitigated despotism?

"While all the nations of Europe are thus moved on the subject of American slavery, shall we alone remain unmoved? Shall we, the wives, mothers, and sisters of America, remain content with inaction in such a crisis as this?

"The first duty of every American woman at this time is to thoroughly understand the subject for herself, and to feel that she is bound to use her influence for the right. Then they can obtain signatures to petitions to our national legislature. They can spread information upon this vital topic throughout their neighborhoods. They can employ lecturers to lay the subject before the people. They can circulate the speeches of their members of Congress that bear upon the subject, and in many other ways they can secure to all a full understanding of the present position of our country.

"Above all, it seems to be necessary and desirable that we should make this subject a matter of earnest prayer. A conflict is now begun between the forces of liberty and despotism throughout the whole world. We who are Christians, and believe in the sure word of prophecy, know that fearful convulsions and overturnings are predicted before the coming of Him who is to rule the earth in righteousness. How important, then, in this crisis, that all who believe in prayer should retreat beneath the shadow of the Almighty!

"It is a melancholy but unavoidable result of such great encounters of principle that they tend to degenerate into sectional and personal bitterness. It is this liability that forms one of the most solemn and affecting features of the crisis now presented. We are on the eve of a conflict which will try men's souls, and strain to the utmost the bonds of brotherly union that bind this nation together.

"Let us, then, pray that in the agitation of this question between the North and the South the war of principle may not become a mere sectional conflict, degenerating into the encounter of physical force. Let us raise our hearts to Him who has the power to restrain the wrath of men, that He will avert the consequences that our sins as a nation so justly deserve.

"There are many noble minds in the South who do not participate in the machinations of their political leaders, and whose sense of honor and justice is outraged by this proposition equally with our own. While, then, we seek to sustain the cause of freedom unwaveringly, let us also hold it to be our office as true women to moderate the acrimony of political contest, remembering that the slaveholder and the slave are alike our brethren, whom the law of God commands us to love as ourselves.

"For the sake, then, of our dear children, for the sake of our common country, for the sake of outraged and struggling liberty throughout the world, let every woman of America now do her duty."

At this same time Mrs. Stowe found herself engaged in an active correspondence with William Lloyd Garrison, much of which appeared in the columns of his paper, the "Liberator." Late in 1853 she writes to him:—

"In regard to you, your paper, and in some measure your party, I am in an honest embarrassment. I sympathize with you fully in many of your positions. Others I consider erroneous, hurtful to liberty and the progress of humanity. Nevertheless, I believe you and those who support them to be honest and conscientious in your course and opinions. What I fear is that your paper will take from poor Uncle Tom his Bible, and give him nothing in its place."

To this Mr. Garrison answers: "I do not understand why the imputation is thrown upon the 'Liberator' as tending to rob Uncle Tom of his Bible. I know of no writer in its pages who wishes to deprive him of it, or of any comfort he may derive from it. It is for him to place whatever estimate he can upon it, and for you and me to do the same; but for neither of us to accept any more of it than we sincerely believe to be in accordance with reason, truth, and eternal right. How much of it is true and obligatory, each one can determine only for himself; for on Protestant ground there is no room for papal infallibility. All Christendom professes to believe in the inspiration of the volume, and at the same time all Christendom is by the ears as to its real teachings. Surely you would not have me disloyal to my conscience. How do you prove that you are not trammeled by educational or traditional notions as to the entire sanctity of the book? Indeed, it seems to me very evident that you are not free in spirit, in view of the apprehension and sorrow you feel because you find your conceptions of the Bible controverted in the 'Liberator,' else why such disquietude of mind? 'Thrice is he armed who hath his quarrel just.'"

In answer to this Mrs. Stowe writes:—

I did not reply to your letter immediately, because I did not wish to speak on so important a subject unadvisedly, or without proper thought and reflection. The greater the interest involved in a truth the more careful, self-distrustful, and patient should be the inquiry.

I would not attack the faith of a heathen without being sure I had a better one to put in its place, because, such as it is, it is better than nothing. I notice in Mr. Parker's sermons a very eloquent passage on the uses and influences of the Bible. He considers it to embody absolute and perfect religion, and that no better mode for securing present and eternal happiness can be found than in the obedience to certain religious precepts therein recorded. He would have it read and circulated, and considers it, as I infer, a Christian duty to send it to the heathen, the slave, etc. I presume you agree with him.

These things being supposed about the Bible would certainly make it appear that, if any man deems it his duty to lessen its standing in the eyes of the community, he ought at least to do so in a cautious and reverential spirit, with humility and prayer.

My objection to the mode in which these things are handled in the "Liberator" is that the general tone and spirit seem to me the reverse of this. If your paper circulated only among those of disciplined and cultivated minds, skilled to separate truth from falsehood, knowing where to go for evidence and how to satisfy the doubts you raise, I should feel less regret. But your name and benevolent labors have given your paper a circulation among the poor and lowly. They have no means of investigating, no habits of reasoning. The Bible, as they at present understand it, is doing them great good, and is a blessing to them and their families. The whole tendency of your mode of proceeding is to lessen their respect and reverence for the Bible, without giving them anything in its place.

I have no fear of discussion as to its final results on the Bible; my only regrets are for those human beings whose present and immortal interests I think compromised by this manner of discussion. Discussion of the evidence of the authenticity and inspiration of the Bible and of all theology will come more and more, and I rejoice that they will. But I think they must come, as all successful inquiries into truth must, in a calm, thoughtful, and humble spirit; not with bold assertions, hasty generalizations, or passionate appeals.

I appreciate your good qualities none the less though you differ with me on this point. I believe you to be honest and sincere. In Mr. Parker's works I have found much to increase my respect and esteem for him as a man. He comes to results, it is true, to which it would be death and utter despair for me to arrive at. Did I believe as he does about the Bible and Jesus, I were of all creatures most miserable, because I could not love God. I could find no God to love. I would far rather never have been born.

As to you, my dear friend, you must own that my frankness to you is the best expression of my confidence in your honor and nobleness. Did I not believe that "an excellent spirit" is in you, I would not take the trouble to write all this. If in any points in this note I appear to have misapprehended or done you injustice, I hope you will candidly let me know where and how.

Truly your friend,
H. B. STOWE.

In addition to these letters the following extracts from a subsequent letter to Mr. Garrison are given to show in what respect their fields of labor differed, and to present an idea of what Mrs. Stowe was doing for the cause of freedom besides writing against slavery:—

ANDOVER, MASS., *February 18, 1854.*

DEAR FRIEND,—I see and sincerely rejoice in the result of your lecture in New York. I am increasingly anxious that all who hate slavery be united, if not in form, at least in fact,—a unity in difference. *Our* field lies in the church, and as yet I differ from you as to what may be done and hoped there. Brother Edward (Beecher) has written a sermon that goes to the very root of the decline of moral feeling in the church. As soon as it can be got ready for the press I shall have it printed, and shall send a copy to every minister in the country.

Our lectures have been somewhat embarrassed by a pressure of new business brought upon us by the urgency of the Kansas-Nebraska question. Since we began, however, brother Edward has devoted his whole time to visiting, consultation, and efforts the result of which will shortly be given to the public. We are trying to secure a universal arousing of the pulpit.

Dr. Bacon's letter is noble. You must think so. It has been sent to every member of Congress. Dr. Kirk's sermon is an advance, and his congregation warmly seconded it. Now, my good friend, be willing to see that the church is better than you have thought it. Be not unwilling to see some good symptoms, and hope that even those who see not at all at first will gain as they go on. I am acting on the conviction that you love the cause better than self. If anything can be done now advantageously by the aid of money, let me know. God has given me some power in this way, though I am too feeble to do much otherwise.

Yours for the cause,
H. B. STOWE.

Although the demand was very great upon Mrs. Stowe for magazine and newspaper articles, many of which she managed to write in 1854-55, she had in her mind at this time a new book which should be in many respects the complement of "Uncle Tom's Cabin." In preparing her Key to the latter work, she had collected much new material. In 1855, therefore, and during the spring of 1856, she found time to weave these hitherto unused facts into the story of "Dred." In her preface to the English edition of this book she writes:—

"The author's object in this book is to show the general effect of slavery on society; the various social disadvantages which it brings, even to its most favored advocates; the shiftlessness and misery and backward tendency of all the economical arrangements of slave States; the retrograding of good families into poverty; the deterioration of land; the worse demoralization of all classes, from the aristocratic, tyrannical planter to the oppressed and poor white, which is the result of the introduction of slave labor.

"It is also an object to display the corruption of Christianity which arises from the same source; a corruption that has gradually lowered the standard of the church, North and South, and been productive of more infidelity than the works of all the encyclopædists put together."

The story of "Dred" was suggested by the famous negro insurrection, led by Nat Turner, in Eastern Virginia in 1831. In this affair one of the principal participators was named "Dred." An interesting incident connected with the writing of "Dred" is vividly remembered by Mrs. Stowe's daughters.

One sultry summer night there arose a terrific thunder-storm, with continuous flashes of lightning and incessant rumbling and muttering of thunder, every now and then breaking out into sharp, crashing reports followed by torrents of rain.

The two young girls, trembling with fear, groped their way down-stairs to their mother's room, and on entering found her lying quietly in bed awake, and calmly watching the storm from the windows, the shades being up. She expressed no surprise on seeing them, but said that she had not been herself in the least frightened, though intensely interested in watching the storm. "I have been writing a description of a thunder-storm for my book, and I am watching to see if I need to correct it in any particular." Our readers will be interested to know that she had so well described a storm from memory that even this vivid object-lesson brought with it no new suggestions. This scene is to be found in the twenty-fourth chapter of "Dred,"—"Life in the Swamps."

"The day had been sultry and it was now an hour or two past midnight, when a thunder-storm, which had long been gathering and muttering in the distant sky, began to develop its forces. A low, shivering sigh crept through the woods, and swayed in weird whistlings the tops of the pines; and sharp arrows of lightning came glittering down among the branches, as if sent from the bow of some warlike angel. An army of heavy clouds swept in a moment across the moon; then came a broad, dazzling, blinding sheet of flame."

What particularly impressed Mrs. Stowe's daughters at the time was their mother's perfect calmness, and the minute study of the storm. She was on the alert to detect anything which might lead her to correct her description.

Of this new story Charles Summer wrote from the senate chamber:—

MY DEAR MRS. STOWE,—I am rejoiced to learn, from your excellent sister here, that you are occupied with another tale exposing slavery. I feel that it will act directly upon pending questions, and help us in our struggle for Kansas, and also to overthrow the slave-oligarchy in the coming Presidential election. We need your help at once in our struggle.

Ever sincerely yours,
CHARLES SUMNER.

Having finished this second great story of slavery, in the early summer of 1856 Mrs. Stowe decided to visit Europe again, in search of a much-needed rest. She also found it necessary to do so in order to secure the English right to her book, which she had failed to do on "Uncle Tom's Cabin."

Just before sailing she received the following touching letter from her life-long friend, Georgiana May. It is the last one of a series that extended without interruption over a period of thirty years, and as such has been carefully cherished:—

OCEAN HOUSE, GROTON POINT, *July 26, 1856.*

DEAR HATTIE,—Very likely it is too late for me to come with my modest knock to your study door, and ask to be taken in for a moment, but I do so want to *bless* you before you go, and I have not been well enough to write until to-day. It seems just as if I *could* not let you go till I have seen once more your face in the flesh, for great uncertainties hang over my future. One thing, however, is certain: whichever of us two gets first to the farther shore of the great ocean between us and the unseen will be pretty sure to be at hand to welcome the other. It is not poetry, but solemn verity between us that we *shall* meet again.

But there is nothing *morbid* or *morbific* going into these few lines. I have made "Old Tiff's" acquaintance. *He* is a verity,— will stand up with Uncle Tom and Topsy, pieces of negro property you will be guilty of holding after you are dead. Very likely your children may be selling them.

Hattie, I rejoice over this completed work. Another work for God and your generation. I am glad that you have come out of it alive, that you have pleasure in prospect, that you "walk at liberty" and have done with "fits of languishing." Perhaps some day I shall be set free, but the prospect does not look promising, except as I have full faith that "the Good Man above is looking on, and will bring it all round right." Still "heart and flesh" both "fail me." He will be the "strength of my heart," and I never seem to doubt "my portion forever."

If I never speak to you again, this is the farewell utterance.

Yours truly,
GEORGIANA.

Mrs. Stowe was accompanied on this second trip to Europe by her husband, her two eldest daughters, her son Henry, and her sister Mary (Mrs. Perkins). It was a pleasant summer voyage, and was safely accomplished without special incident.

CHAPTER XII

DRED, 1856

SECOND VISIT TO ENGLAND.—A GLIMPSE AT THE QUEEN.—THE DUKE OF ARGYLL AND INVERARY.— EARLY CORRESPONDENCE WITH LADY BYRON.— DUNROBIN CASTLE AND ITS INMATES.—A VISIT TO STOKE PARK.—LORD DUFFERIN.—CHARLES KINGSLEY AT HOME.—PARIS REVISITED.—MADAME MOHL'S RECEPTIONS.

AFTER reaching England, about the middle of August, 1856, Mrs. Stowe and her husband spent some days in London completing arrangements to have an English edition of "Dred" published by Sampson Low & Co. Professor Stowe's duties in America being very pressing, he had intended returning at once, but was detained for a short time, as will be seen in the following letter written by him from Glasgow, August 29, to a friend in America:—

DEAR FRIEND,—I finished my business in London on Wednesday, and intended to return by the Liverpool steamer of to-morrow, but find that every berth on that line is engaged until the 3d of October. We therefore came here yesterday, and I shall take passage in the steamer New York from this port next Tuesday. We have received a special invitation to visit Inverary Castle, the seat of the Duke of Argyll, and yesterday we had just the very pleasantest little interview with the Queen that ever was. None of the formal, drawing-room, breathless receptions, but just an accidental, done-on-purpose meeting at a railway station, while on our way to Scotland.

The Queen seemed really delighted to see my wife, and remarkably glad to see me for her sake. She pointed us out to Prince Albert, who made two most gracious bows to my wife and two to me, while the four royal children stared their big blue eyes almost out looking at the little authoress of "Uncle Tom's Cabin." Colonel Grey handed the Queen, with my wife's compliments, a copy of the new book ("Dred"). She took one volume herself and handed the other to Prince Albert, and they were soon both very busy reading. She is a real nice little body with exceedingly pleasant, kindly manners.

I expect to be in Natick the last week in September. God bless you all.

C. E. STOWE.

After her husband's departure for the United States, Mrs. Stowe, with her son Henry, her two eldest daughters, and her sister Mary (Mrs. Perkins), accepted the Duke of Argyll's invitation to visit the Highlands. Of this visit we catch a pleasant glimpse from a letter written to Professor Stowe during its continuance, which is as follows:—

INVERARY CASTLE, *September 6, 1856.*

MY DEAR HUSBAND,—We have been now a week in this delicious place, enjoying the finest skies and scenery, the utmost of kind hospitality. From Loch Goil we took the coach for Inverary, a beautiful drive of about two hours. We had seats on the outside, and the driver John, like some of the White Mountain guides, was full of song and story, and local tradition. He spoke Scotch and Gaelic, recited ballads, and sung songs with great gusto. Mary and the girls stopped in a little inn at St. Catherine's, on the shores of Loch Fine, while Henry and I took steamboat for Inverary, where we found the duchess waiting in a carriage for us, with Lady Emma Campbell. . . .

The common routine of the day here is as follows: We rise about half past eight. About half past nine we all meet in the dining-hall, where the servants are standing in a line down one side, and a row of chairs for guests and visitors occupies the other. The duchess with her nine children, a perfectly beautiful little flock, sit together. The duke reads the Bible and a prayer, and pronounces the benediction. After that, breakfast is served,—a very hearty, informal, cheerful meal,—and after that come walks, or drives, or fishing parties, till lunch time, and then more drives, or anything else: everybody, in short, doing what he likes till half past seven, which is the dinner hour. After that we have coffee and tea in the evening.

The first morning, the duke took me to see his mine of nickel silver. We had a long and beautiful drive, and talked about everything in literature, religion, morals, and the temperance movement, about which last he is in some state of doubt and uncertainty, not inclining, I think, to have it pressed yet, though feeling there is need of doing something.

If "Dred" has as good a sale in America as it is likely to have in England, we shall do well. There is such a demand that they had to placard the shop windows in Glasgow with,—

> "To prevent disappointment,
> 'Dred'
> Not to be had till," etc.

> Everybody is after it, and the prospect is of an enormous sale.

God, to whom I prayed night and day while I was writing the book, has heard me, and given us of worldly goods more *than* I asked. I feel, therefore, a desire to "walk softly," and inquire, for what has He so trusted us?

Every day I am more charmed with the duke and duchess; they are simple-hearted, frank, natural, full of feeling, of piety, and good sense. They certainly are, apart from any considerations of rank or position, most interesting and noble people. The duke laughed heartily at many things I told him of our Andover theological tactics, of your preaching, etc.; but I think he is a sincere, earnest Christian.

Our American politics form the daily topic of interest. The late movements in Congress are discussed with great warmth, and every morning the papers are watched for new details.

I must stop now, as it is late and we are to leave here early to-morrow morning. We are going to Staffa, Iona, the Pass of Glencoe, and finally through the Caledonian Canal up to Dunrobin Castle, where a large party of all sorts of interesting people are gathered around the Duchess of Sutherland.

Affectionately yours,
HARRIET.

From Dunrobin Castle one of his daughters writes to Professor Stowe: "We spent five most delightful days at Inverary, and were so sorry you could not be there with us. From there we went to Oban, and spent several days sight-seeing, finally reaching Inverness by way of the Caledonian Canal. Here, to our surprise, we found our rooms at the hotel all prepared for us. The next morning we left by post for Dunrobin, which is fifty-nine miles from Inverness. At the borders of the duke's estate we found a delightfully comfortable carriage awaiting us, and before we had gone much farther the postilion announced that the duchess was coming to meet us. Sure enough, as we looked up the road we saw a fine cavalcade approaching. It consisted of a splendid coach-and-four (in which sat the duchess) with liveried postilions, and a number of outriders, one of whom rode in front to clear the way. The duchess seemed perfectly delighted to see mamma, and taking her into her own carriage dashed off towards the castle, we following on behind."

At Dunrobin Mrs. Stowe found awaiting her the following note from her friend, Lady Byron:—

LONDON, *September 10, 1856.*

Your book, dear Mrs. Stowe, is of the "little leaven" kind, and must prove a great moral force,—perhaps not manifestly so much as secretly, and yet I can hardly conceive so much power without immediate and sensible effects; only there will be a strong disposition to resist on the part of all the hollow-hearted professors of religion, whose heathenisms you so unsparingly expose. They have a class feeling like others. To the young, and to those who do not reflect much on what is offered to their belief, you will do great good by showing how spiritual food is adulterated. The Bread from Heaven is in the same case as baker's bread. I feel that one perusal is not enough. It is a "mine," to use your own simile. If there is truth in what I heard Lord Byron say, that works of fiction *lived* only by the amount of *truth* which they contained, your story is sure of long life. . . .

I know now, more than before, how to value communion with you.

> With kind regards to your family,
> Yours affectionately,
> A. T. NOEL BYRON.

From this pleasant abiding-place Mrs. Stowe writes to her husband:—

DUNROBIN CASTLE, *September 15, 1856.*

MY DEAR HUSBAND,—Everything here is like a fairy story. The place is beautiful! It is the most perfect combination of architectural and poetic romance, with home comfort. The people, too, are charming. We have here Mr. Labouchere, a cabinet minister, and Lady Mary his wife,—I like him very much, and her, too,—Kingsley's brother, a very entertaining man, and to-morrow Lord Ellsmere is expected. I wish you could be here, for I am sure you would like it. Life is so quiet and sincere and friendly, that you would feel more as if you had come at the hearts of these people than in London.

The Sutherland estate looks like a garden. We stopped at the town of Frain, four miles before we reached Sutherlandshire, where a crowd of well-to-do, nice-looking people gathered around the carriage, and as we drove off gave three cheers. This was better than I expected, and looks well for their opinion of my views.

"Dred" is selling over here wonderfully. Low says, with all the means at his command, he has not been able to meet the demand. He sold fifty thousand in two weeks, and probably will sell as many more.

I am showered with letters, private and printed, in which the only difficulty is to know what the writers would be at. I see evidently happiness and prosperity all through the line of this estate. I see the duke giving his thought and time, and spending the whole income of this estate in improvements upon it. I see the duke and duchess evidently beloved wherever they move. I see them most amiable, most Christian, most considerate to everybody. The writers of the letters admit the goodness of the duke, but denounce the system, and beg me to observe its effects for myself. I do observe that, compared with any other part of the Highlands, Sutherland is a garden. I observe well-clothed people, thriving lands, healthy children, fine schoolhouses, and all that.

Henry was invited to the tenants' dinner, where he excited much amusement by pledging every toast in fair water, as he has done invariably on all occasions since he has been here.

The duchess, last night, showed me her copy of "Dred," in which she has marked what most struck or pleased her. I begged it, and am going to send it to you. She said to me this morning at breakfast, "The Queen says that she began 'Dred' the very minute she got it, and is deeply interested in it."

She bought a copy of Lowell's poems, and begged me to mark the best ones for her; so if you see him, tell him that we have been reading him together. She is, taking her all in all, one of the noblest-appointed women I ever saw; real old, genuine English, such as one reads of in history; full of nobility, courage, tenderness, and zeal. It does me good to hear her read prayers daily, as she does, in the midst of her servants and guests, with a manner full of grand and noble feeling.

Thursday Morning, September 25. We were obliged to get up at half past five the morning we left Dunrobin, an effort when one doesn't go to bed till one o'clock. We found breakfast laid for us in the library, and before we had quite finished the duchess came in. Our starting off was quite an imposing sight. First came the duke's landau, in which were Mary, the duke, and myself; then a carriage in which were Eliza and Hatty, and finally the carriage which we had hired, with Henry, our baggage, and Mr. Jackson (the duke's secretary). The gardener sent a fresh bouquet for each of us, and there was such a leave-taking, as if we were old and dear friends. We did really love them, and had no doubt of their love for us.

The duke rode with us as far as Dornach, where he showed us the cathedral beneath which his ancestors are buried, and where is a statue of his father, similar to one the tenants have erected on top of the highest hill in the neighborhood.

We also saw the prison, which had but two inmates, and the old castle. Here the duke took leave of us, and taking our own carriage we crossed the ferry and continued on our way. After a very bad night's rest at Inverness, in consequence of the town's being so full of people attending some Highland games that we could have no places at the hotel, and after a weary ride in the rain, we came into Aberdeen Friday night.

To-morrow we go on to Edinburgh, where I hope to meet a letter from you. The last I heard from Low, he had sold sixty thousand of "Dred," and it was still selling well. I have not yet heard from America how it goes. The critics scold, and whiffle, and dispute about it, but on the whole it is a success, so the "Times" says, with much coughing, hemming, and standing first on one foot and then on the other. If the "Times" were sure we should beat in the next election, "Dred" would go up in the scale; but as long as there is that uncertainty, it has first one line of praise, and then one of blame.

Henry Stowe returned to America in October to enter Dartmouth College, while the rest of the party pursued their way southward, as will be seen by the following letters:—

CITY OF YORK, *October 10, 1856.*

DEAR HUSBAND,—Henry will tell you all about our journey, and at present I have but little time for details. I received your first letter with great joy, relief, and gratitude, first to God for restoring your health and strength, and then to you for so good, long, and refreshing a letter.

Henry, I hope, comes home with a serious determination to do well and be a comfort. Seldom has a young man seen what he has in this journey, or made more valuable friends.

Since we left Aberdeen, from which place my last was mailed, we have visited in Edinburgh with abounding delight; thence yesterday to Newcastle. Last night attended service in Durham Cathedral, and after that came to York, whence we send Henry to Liverpool.

I send you letters, etc., by him. One hundred thousand copies of "Dred" sold in four weeks! After that who cares what critics say? Its success in England has been complete, so far as sale is concerned. It is very bitterly attacked, both from a literary and a religious point of view. The "Record" is down upon it with a cartload of solemnity; the "Athenæum" with waspish spite; the "Edinburgh" goes out of its way to say that the author knows nothing of the society she describes; but yet it goes everywhere, is read everywhere, and Mr. Low says that he puts the hundred and twenty-fifth thousand to press confidently. The fact that so many good judges like it better than "Uncle Tom" is success enough.

In my journal to Henry, which you may look for next week, you will learn how I have been very near the Queen, and formed acquaintance with divers of her lords and ladies, and heard all she has said about "Dred;" how she prefers it to "Uncle Tom," how she inquired for you, and other matters.

Till then, I am, as ever, your affectionate wife,

H. B. STOWE.

After leaving York, Mrs. Stowe and her party spent a day or two at Carlton Rectory, on the edge of Sherwood Forest, in which they enjoyed a most delightful picnic. From there they were to travel to London by way of Warwick and Oxford, and of this journey Mrs. Stowe writes as follows to her son Henry:—

"The next morning we were induced to send our things to London, being assured by Mr. G. that he would dispatch them immediately with some things of his own that were going, and that they should certainly await us upon our arrival. In one respect it was well for us that we thus rid ourselves of the trouble of looking after them, for I never saw such blind, confusing arrangements as these English railroads have.

"When we were set down at the place where we were to change for Warwick, we were informed that probably the train had gone. At any rate it could only be found on the other side of the station. You might naturally think we had nothing to do but walk across to the other side. No, indeed! We had to ascend a flight of stairs, go through a sort of tubular bridge, and down another pair of stairs. When we got there the guard said the train was just about to start, and yet the ticket office was closed. We tried the door in vain. 'You must hurry,' said the guard. 'How can we?' said I, 'when we can't get tickets.' He went and thumped, and at last roused the dormant intelligence inside. We got our tickets, ran for dear life, got in, and then *waited ten minutes*! Arrived at Warwick we had a very charming time, and after seeing all there was to see we took cars for Oxford.

"The next day we tried to see Oxford. You can have no idea of it. Call it a college! it is a city of colleges,—a mountain of museums, colleges, halls, courts, parks, chapels, lecture-rooms. Out of twenty-four colleges we saw only three. We saw enough, however, to show us that to explore the colleges of Oxford would take a week. Then we came away, and about eleven o'clock at night found ourselves in London.

"It was dripping and raining here, for all the world, just as it did when we left; but we found a cosy little parlor, papered with cheerful crimson paper, lighted by a coal-fire, a neat little supper laid out, and the Misses Low waiting; for us. Wasn't it nice?

"We are expecting our baggage to-night. Called at Sampson Low's store to-day and found it full everywhere of red 'Dreds.'"

Upon reaching London Mrs. Stowe found the following note from Lady Byron awaiting her:—

OXFORD HOUSE, *October 15, 1856.*

DEAR MRS. STOWE,—The newspapers represent you as returning to London, but I cannot wait for the chance, slender I fear, of seeing you there, for I wish to consult you on a point admitting but of little delay. Feeling that the sufferers in Kansas have a claim not only to sympathy, but to the expression of it, I wish to send them a donation. It is, however, necessary to know what is the best application of money and what the safest channel. Presuming that you will approve the object, I ask you to tell me. Perhaps you would undertake the transmission of my £50. My present residence, two miles beyond Richmond, is opposite. I have watched for instructions of your course with warm interest. The sale of your book will go on increasing. It is beginning to be understood.

Believe me, with kind regards to your daughters,

Your faithful and affectionate

A. T. NOEL BYRON.

To this note the following answer was promptly returned:—

GROVE TERRACE, KENTISH TOWN, *October 16, 1856.*

DEAR LADY BYRON,—How glad I was to see your handwriting once more! how more than glad I should be to see *you!* I do long to see you. I have so much to say,—so much to ask, and need to be refreshed with a sense of a congenial and sympathetic soul.

Thank you, my dear friend, for your sympathy with our poor sufferers in Kansas. May God bless you for it! By doing this you will step to my side; perhaps you may share something of that abuse which they who "know not what they do" heap upon all who so feel for the right. I assure you, dear friend, I am *not* insensible to the fiery darts which thus fly around me. . . .

Direct as usual to my publishers, and believe me, as ever, with all my heart,

Affectionately yours, H. B. S.

Having dispatched this note, Mrs. Stowe wrote to her husband concerning their surroundings and plans as follows:—

"*Friday, 16th.* Confusion in the camp! no baggage come, nobody knows why; running to stations, inquiries, messages, and no baggage. Meanwhile we have not even a clean collar, nothing but very soiled traveling dresses; while Lady Mary Labouchere writes that her carriage will wait for us at Slough Station this afternoon, and we must be off at two. What's to be done? Luckily I did not carry all my dresses to Dunrobin; so I, of all the party, have a dress that can be worn. We go out and buy collars and handkerchiefs, and two o'clock beholds us at the station house.

"*Stoke Park.* I arrived here alone, the baggage not having yet been heard from. Mr. G., being found in London, confessed that he delayed sending it by the proper train. In short, Mr. G. is what is called an easy man, and one whose easiness makes everybody else uneasy. So because he was easy and thought it was no great matter, and things would turn out well enough, without any great care, *we* have had all this discomfort.

"I arrived alone at the Slough Station and found Lady Mary's carriage waiting. Away we drove through a beautiful park full of deer, who were so tame as to stand and look at us as we passed. The house is in the Italian style, with a dome on top, and wide terraces with stone balustrades around it.

"Lady Mary met me at the door, and seemed quite concerned to learn of our ill-fortune. We went through a splendid suite of rooms to a drawing-room, where a little tea-table was standing.

"After tea Lady Mary showed me my room. It had that delightful, homelike air of repose and comfort they succeed so well in giving to rooms here. There was a cheerful fire burning, an arm-chair drawn up beside it, a sofa on the other side with a neatly arranged sofa-table on which were writing materials. One of the little girls had put a pot of pretty greenhouse moss in a silver basket on this table, and my toilet cushion was made with a place in the centre to hold a little vase of flowers. Here Lady Mary left me to rest before dressing for dinner. I sat down in an easy-chair before the fire, and formed hospitable resolutions as to how I would try to make rooms always look homelike and pleasant to tired guests. Then came the maid to know if I wanted hot water,— if I wanted anything,—and by and by it was time for dinner. Going down into the parlor I met Mr. Labouchere and we all went in to dinner. It was not quite as large a party as at Dunrobin, but much in the same way. No company, but several ladies who were all family connections.

"The following morning Lord Dufferin and Lord Alfred Paget, two gentlemen of the Queen's household, rode over from Windsor to lunch with us. They brought news of the goings-on there. Do you remember one night the Duchess of S. read us a letter from Lady Dufferin, describing the exploits of her son, who went yachting with Prince Napoleon up by Spitzbergen, and when Prince Napoleon and all the rest gave up and went back, still persevered and discovered a new island? Well, this was the same man. A thin, slender person, not at all the man you would fancy as a Mr. Great Heart,—lively, cheery, and conversational.

"Lord Alfred is also very pleasant.

"Lady Mary prevailed on Lord Dufferin to stay and drive with us after lunch, and we went over to Clifden, the duchess's villa, of which we saw the photograph at Dunrobin. For grace and beauty some of the rooms in this place exceed any I have yet seen in England.

"When we came back my first thought was whether Aunt Mary and the girls had come. Just as we were all going up to dress for dinner they appeared. Meanwhile, the Queen had sent over from Windsor for Lady Mary and her husband to dine with her that evening, and such invitations are understood as commands.

"So, although they themselves had invited four or five people to dinner, they had to go and leave us to entertain ourselves. Lady Mary was dressed very prettily in a flounced white silk dress with a pattern of roses woven round the bottom of each flounce, and looked very elegant. Mr. Labouchere wore breeches, with knee and shoe buckles sparkling with diamonds.

"They got home soon after we had left the drawing-room, as the Queen always retires at eleven. No late hours for her.

"The next day Lady Mary told me that the Queen had talked to her all about 'Dred,' and how she preferred it to 'Uncle Tom's Cabin,' how interested she was in Nina, how provoked when she died, and how she was angry that something dreadful did not happen to Tom Gordon. She inquired for papa, and the rest of the family, all of whom she seemed to be well informed about.

"The next morning we had Lord Dufferin again to breakfast. He is one of the most entertaining young men I have seen in England, full of real thought and noble feeling, and has a wide range of reading. He had read all our American literature, and was very flattering in his remarks on Hawthorne, Poe, and Longfellow. I find J. R. Lowell less known, however, than he deserves to be.

"Lord Dufferin says that his mother wrote him some verses on his coming of age, and that he built a tower for them and inscribed them on a brass plate. I recommend the example to you, Henry; make yourself the tower and your memory the brass plate.

"This morning came also, to call, Lady Augusta Bruce, Lord Elgin's daughter, one of the Duchess of Kent's ladies-in-waiting; a very excellent, sensible girl, who is a strong anti-slavery body.

"After lunch we drove over to Eton, and went in to see the provost's house. After this, as we were passing by Windsor the coachman suddenly stopped and said, 'The Queen is coming, my lady.' We stood still and the royal cortége passed. I only saw the Queen, who bowed graciously.

"Lady Mary stayed at our car door till it left the station, and handed in a beautiful bouquet as we parted. This is one of the loveliest visits I have made."

After filling a number of other pleasant engagements in England, among which was a visit in the family of Charles Kingsley, Mrs. Stowe and her party crossed the Channel and settled down for some months in Paris for the express purpose of studying French. From the French capital she writes to her husband in Andover as follows:—

PARIS, *November 7, 1856.*

MY DEAR HUSBAND,—On the 28th, when your last was written, I was at Charles Kingsley's. It seemed odd enough to Mary and me to find ourselves, long after dark, alone in a hack, driving towards the house of a man whom we never had seen (nor his wife either).

My heart fluttered as, after rumbling a long way through the dark, we turned into a yard. We knocked at a door and were met in the hall by a man who stammers a little in his speech, and whose inquiry, "Is this Mrs. Stowe?" was our first positive introduction. Ushered into a large, pleasant parlor lighted by a coal fire, which flickered on comfortable chairs, lounges, pictures, statuettes, and book-cases, we took a good view of him. He is tall, slender, with blue eyes, brown hair, and a hale, well-browned face, and somewhat loose-jointed withal. His wife is a real Spanish beauty.

How we did talk and go on for three days! I guess he is tired. I'm sure we were. He is a nervous, excitable being, and talks with head, shoulders, arms, and hands, while his hesitance makes it the harder. Of his theology I will say more some other time. He, also, has been through the great distress, the "Conflict of Ages," but has come out at a different end from Edward, and stands with John Foster, though with more positiveness than he.

He laughed a good deal at many stories I told him of father, and seemed delighted to hear about him. But he is, what I did not expect, a zealous Churchman; insists that the Church of England is the finest and broadest platform a man can stand on, and that the thirty-nine articles are the only ones he could subscribe to. I told him you thought them the best summary (of doctrine) you knew, which pleased him greatly.

Well, I got your letter to-night in Paris, at No. 19 Rue de Clichy, where you may as well direct your future letters.

We reached Paris about eleven o'clock last night and took a carriage for 17 Rue de Clichy, but when we got there, no ringing or pounding could rouse anybody. Finally, in despair, we remembered a card that had been handed into the cars by some hotel-runner, and finding it was of an English and French hotel, we drove there, and secured very comfortable accommodations. We did not get to bed until after two o'clock. The next morning I sent a messenger to find Mme. Borione, and discovered that we had mistaken the number, and should have gone to No. 19, which was the next door; so we took a carriage and soon found ourselves established here, where we have a nice parlor and two bedrooms.

There are twenty-one in the family, mostly Americans, like ourselves, come to learn to speak French. One of them is a tall, handsome, young English lady, Miss Durant, who is a sculptress, studying with Baron de Triqueti. She took me to his studio, and he immediately remarked that she ought to get me to sit. I said I would, "only my French lessons." "Oh," said he, smiling, "we will give you French lessons while you sit." So I go to-morrow morning.

As usual, my horrid pictures do me a service, and people seem relieved when they see me; think me even handsome "in a manner." Kingsley, in his relief, expressed as much to his wife, and as beauty has never been one of my strong points I am open to flattery upon it.

We had a most agreeable call from Arthur Helps before we left London. He, Kingsley, and all the good people are full of the deepest anxiety for our American affairs. They really do feel very deeply, seeing the peril so much plainer than we do in America.

Sunday night. I fear I have delayed your letter too long. The fact is, that of the ten days I have been here I have been laid up three with severe neuralgia, viz., *toothache in the backbone*, and since then have sat all day to be modeled for my bust.

We spent the other evening with Baron de Triqueti, the sculptor. He has an English wife, and a charming daughter about the age of our girls. Life in Paris is altogether more simple and natural than in England. They give you a plate of cake and a cup of tea in the most informal, social way,—the tea-kettle sings at the fire, and the son and daughter busy themselves gayly together making and handing tea. When tea was over, M. de Triqueti showed us a manuscript copy of the Gospels, written by his mother, to console herself in a season of great ill-health, and which he had illustrated all along with exquisite pen-drawings, resembling the most perfect line engravings. I can't describe the beauty, grace, delicacy, and fullness of devotional feeling in these people. He is one of the loveliest men I ever saw.

We have already three evenings in the week in which we can visit and meet friends if we choose, namely, at Madame Mohl's, Madame Lanziel's, and Madame Belloc's. All these salôns are informal, social gatherings, with no fuss of refreshments, no nonsense of any kind. Just the cheeriest, heartiest, kindest little receptions you ever saw.

A kiss to dear little Charley. If he could see all the things that I see every day in the Tuileries and Champs Elysées, he would go wild. All Paris is a general whirligig out of doors, but indoors people seem steady, quiet, and sober as anybody.

November 30. This is Sunday evening, and a Sunday in Paris always puts me in mind of your story about somebody who said, "Bless you! they make such a noise that the Devil couldn't meditate." All the extra work and odd jobs of life are put into Sunday. Your washerwoman comes Sunday, with her innocent, good-humored face, and would be infinitely at a loss to know why she shouldn't. Your bonnet, cloak, shoes, and everything are sent home Sunday morning, and all the way to church there is such whirligiging and pirouetting along the boulevards as almost takes one's breath away. To-day we went to the Oratoire to hear M. Grand Pierre. I could not understand much; my French ear is not quick enough to follow. I could only perceive that the subject was "La Charité," and that the speaker was fluent, graceful, and earnest, the audience serious and attentive.

Last night we were at Baron de Triqueti's again, with a party invited to celebrate the birthday of their eldest daughter, Blanche, a lovely girl of nineteen. There were some good ladies there who had come eighty leagues to meet me, and who were so delighted with my miserable French that it was quite encouraging. I believe I am getting over the sandbar at last, and conversation is beginning to come easy to me.

There were three French gentlemen who had just been reading "Dred" in English, and who were as excited and full of it as could be, and I talked with them to a degree that astonished myself. There is a review of "Dred" in the "Revue des Deux Mondes" which has long extracts from the book, and is written in a very appreciative and favorable spirit. Generally speaking, French critics seem to have a finer appreciation of my subtle shades of meaning than English. I am curious to hear what Professor Park has to say about it. There has been another review in "La Presse" equally favorable. All seem to see the truth about American slavery much plainer than people can who are in it. If American ministers and Christians could see through their sophistical spider-webs, with what wonder, pity, and contempt they would regard their own vacillating condition!

We visit once a week at Madame Mohl's, where we meet all sorts of agreeable people. Lady Elgin doesn't go into society now, having been struck with paralysis, but sits at home and receives her friends as usual. This notion of sitting always in the open air is one of her peculiarities.

I must say, life in Paris is arranged more sensibly than with us. Visiting involves no trouble in the feeding line. People don't go to eat. A cup of tea and plate of biscuit is all,—just enough to break up the stiffness.

It is wonderful that the people here do not seem to have got over "Uncle Tom" a bit. The impression seems fresh as if just published. How often have they said, That book has revived the Gospel among the poor of France; it has done more than all the books we have published put together. It has gone among the *les ouvriers*, among the poor of Faubourg St. Antoine, and nobody knows how many have been led to Christ by it. Is not this blessed, my dear husband? Is it not worth all the suffering of writing it?

I went the other evening to M. Grand Pierre's, where there were three rooms full of people, all as eager and loving as ever we met in England or Scotland. Oh, if Christians in Boston could only see the earnestness of feeling with which Christians here regard slavery, and their surprise and horror at the lukewarmness, to say the least, of our American church! About eleven o'clock we all joined in singing a hymn, then M. Grand Pierre made an address, in which I was named in the most affectionate and cordial manner. Then followed a beautiful prayer for our country, for America, on which hang so many of the hopes of Protestantism. One and all then came up, and there was great shaking of hands and much effusion.

Under date of December 28, Mrs. Perkins writes: "On Sunday we went with Mr. and Mrs. (Jacob) Abbott to the Hôtel des Invalides, and I think I was never more interested and affected. Three or four thousand old and disabled soldiers have here a beautiful and comfortable home. We went to the morning service. The church is very large, and the colors taken in battle are hung on the walls. Some of them are so old as to be moth-eaten. The service is performed, as near as possible, in imitation of the service before a battle. The drum beats the call to assemble, and the common soldiers march up and station themselves in the centre of the church, under the commander. All the services are regulated by the beat of the drum. Only one priest officiates, and soldiers are stationed around to protect him. The music is from a brass band, and is very magnificent.

"In the afternoon I went to vespers in the Madeleine, where the music was exquisite. They have two fine organs at opposite ends of the church. The 'Adeste Fidelis' was sung by a single voice, accompanied by the organ, and after every verse it was taken up by male voices and the other organ and repeated. The effect was wonderfully fine. I have always found in our small churches at home that the organ was too powerful and pained my head, but in these large cathedrals the effect is different. The volume of sound rolls over, full but soft, and I feel as though it must come from another sphere.

"In the evening Mr. and Mrs. Bunsen called. He is a son of Chevalier Bunsen, and she a niece of Elizabeth Fry,—very intelligent and agreeable people."

Under date of January 25, Mrs. Stowe writes from Paris:—

"Here is a story for Charley. The boys in the Faubourg St. Antoine are the children of *ouvriers*, and every day their mothers give them two sous to buy a dinner. When they heard I was coming to the school, of their own accord they subscribed half their dinner money to give to me for the poor slaves. This five-franc piece I have now; I have bought it of the cause for five dollars, and am going to make a hole in it and hang it round Charley's neck as a medal.

"I have just completed arrangements for leaving the girls at a Protestant boarding-school while I go to Rome.

"We expect to start the 1st of February, and my direction will be, E. Bartholimeu, 108 Via Margaretta."

CHAPTER XIII

OLD SCENES REVISITED, 1856

En Route to Rome.—Trials of Travel.—A
Midnight Arrival and an Inhospitable
Reception.—Glories of the Eternal City.—Naples
and Vesuvius.—Venice.—Holy Week in Rome.—
Return to England.—Letter from Harriet
Martineau on "Dred."—A Word from Mr. Prescott
on "Dred."—Farewell to Lady Byron.

AFTER leaving Paris Mrs. Stowe and her sister, Mrs. Perkins, traveled leisurely through the South of France toward Italy, stopping at Amiens, Lyons, and Marseilles. At this place they took steamer for Genoa, Leghorn, and Civita Vecchia. During their last night on shipboard they met with an accident, of which, and their subsequent trials in reaching Rome, Mrs. Stowe writes as follows:—

About eleven o'clock, as I had just tranquilly laid down in my berth, I was roused by a grating crash, accompanied by a shock that shook the whole ship, and followed by the sound of a general rush on deck, trampling, scuffling, and cries. I rushed to the door and saw all the gentlemen hurrying on their clothes and getting confusedly towards the stairway. I went back to Mary, and we put on our things in silence, and, as soon as we could, got into the upper saloon. It was an hour before we could learn anything certainly, except that we had run into another vessel. The fate of the Arctic came to us both, but we did not mention it to each other; indeed, a quieter, more silent company you would not often see. Had I had any confidence in the administration of the boat, it would have been better, but as I had not, I sat in momentary uncertainty. Had we then known, as we have since, the fate of a boat recently sunk in the Mediterranean by a similar carelessness, it would have increased our fears. By a singular chance an officer, whose wife and children were lost on board that boat, was on board ours, and happened to be on the forward part of the boat when the accident occurred. The captain and mate were both below; there was nobody looking out, and had not this officer himself called out to stop the boat, we should have struck her with such force as to have sunk us. As it was, we turned aside and the shock came on a paddle-wheel, which was broken by it, for when, after two hours' delay, we tried to start and had gone a little way, there was another crash and the paddle-wheel fell down. You may be sure we did little sleeping that night. It was an inexpressible desolation to think that we might never again see those we loved. No one knows how much one thinks, and how rapidly, in such hours.

In the Naples boat that was sunk a short time ago, the women perished in a dreadful way. The shock threw the chimney directly across the egress from below, so that they could not get on deck, and they were all drowned in the cabin.

We went limping along with one broken limb till the next day about eleven, when we reached Civita Vecchia, where there were two hours more of delay about passports. Then we, that is, Mary and I, and a Dr. Edison from Philadelphia, with his son Alfred, took a carriage to Rome, but they gave us a miserable thing that looked as if it had been made soon after the deluge. About eight o'clock at night, on a lonely stretch of road, the wheel came off. We got out, and our postilions stood silently regarding matters. None of us could speak Italian, they could not speak French; but the driver at last conveyed the idea that for five francs he could get a man to come and mend the wheel. The five francs were promised, and he untackled a horse and rode off. Mary and I walked up and down the dark, desolate road, occasionally reminding each other that we were on classic ground, and laughing at the oddity of our lonely, starlight promenade. After a while our driver came back, Tag, Rag, and Bobtail at his heels. I don't think I can do greater justice to Italian costumes than by this respectable form of words.

Then there was another consultation. They put a bit of rotten timber under to pry the carriage up. Fortunately, it did not break, as we all expected it would, till after the wheel was on. Then a new train of thought was suggested. How was it to be kept on? Evidently they had not thought far in that direction, for they had brought neither hammer nor nail, nor tool of any kind, and therefore they looked first at the wheel, then at each other, and then at us. The doctor now produced a little gimlet, with the help of which the broken fragments of the former linchpin were pushed out, and the way was cleared for a new one. Then they began knocking a fence to pieces to get out nails, but none could be found to fit. At last another ambassador was sent back for nails. While we were thus waiting, the diligence, in which many of our ship's company were jogging on to Rome, came up. They had plenty of room inside, and one of the party, seeing our distress, tried hard to make the driver stop, but he doggedly persisted in going on, and declared if anybody got down to help us he would leave him behind.

An interesting little episode here occurred. It was raining, and Mary and I proposed, as the wheel was now on, to take our seats. We had no sooner done so than the horses were taken with a sudden fit of animation and ran off with us in the most vivacious manner, Tag, Rag, and Co. shouting in the rear. Some heaps of stone a little in advance presented an interesting prospect by way of a terminus. However, the horses were lucidly captured before the wheel was off again; and our ambassador being now returned, we were set right and again proceeded.

I must not forget to remark that at every post where we changed horses and drivers, we had a pitched battle with the driver for more money than we had been told was the regular rate, and the carriage was surrounded with a perfect mob of ragged, shock-headed, black-eyed people, whose words all ended in "ino," and who raved and ranted at us till finally we paid much more than we ought, to get rid of them.

At the gates of Rome the official, after looking at our passports, coolly told the doctor that if he had a mind to pay him five francs he could go in without further disturbance, but if not he would keep the baggage till morning. This form of statement had the recommendation of such precision and neatness of expression that we paid him forthwith, and into

Rome we dashed at two o'clock in the morning of the 9th of February, 1857, in a drizzling rain.

We drove to the Hotel d'Angleterre,—it was full,—and ditto to four or five others, and in the last effort our refractory wheel came off again, and we all got out into the street. About a dozen lean, ragged "corbies," who are called porters and who are always lying in wait for travelers, pounced upon us. They took down our baggage in a twinkling, and putting it all into the street surrounded it, and chattered over it, while M. and I stood in the rain and received first lessons in Italian. How we did try to say something! but they couldn't talk anything but in "ino" as aforesaid. The doctor finally found a man who could speak a word or two of French, and leaving Mary, Alfred, and me to keep watch over our pile of trunks, he went off with him to apply for lodgings. I have heard many flowery accounts of first impressions of Rome. I must say ours was somewhat sombre.

A young man came by and addressed us in English. How cheering! We almost flew upon him. We begged him, at least, to lend us his Italian to call another carriage, and he did so. A carriage which was passing was luckily secured, and Mary and I, with all our store of boxes and little parcels, were placed in it out of the rain, at least. Here we sat while the doctor from time to time returned from his wanderings to tell us he could find no place. "Can it be," said I, "that we are to be obliged to spend a night in the streets?" What made it seem more odd was the knowledge that, could we only find them, we had friends enough in Rome who would be glad to entertain us. We began to speculate on lodgings. Who knows what we may get entrapped into? Alfred suggested stories he had read of beds placed on trap-doors,—of testers which screwed down on people and smothered them; and so, when at last the doctor announced lodgings found, we followed in rather an uncertain frame of mind.

We alighted at a dirty stone passage, smelling of cats and onions, damp, cold, and earthy, we went up stone stairways, and at last were ushered into two very decent chambers, where we might lay our heads. The "corbies" all followed us,—black-haired, black-browed, ragged, and clamorous as ever. They insisted that we should pay the pretty little sum of twenty francs, or four dollars, for bringing our trunks about twenty steps. The doctor modestly but firmly declined to be thus imposed upon, and then ensued a general "chatteration;" one and all fell into attitudes, and the "inos" and "issimos" rolled freely. "For pity's sake get them off," we said; so we made a truce for ten francs, but still they clamored, forced their way even into our bedroom, and were only repulsed by a loud and combined volley of "No, no, noes!" which we all set up at once, upon which they retreated.

Our hostess was a little French woman, and that reassured us. I examined the room, and seeing no trace of treacherous testers, or trap-doors, resolved to avail myself without fear of the invitation of a very clean, white bed, where I slept till morning without dreaming.

The next day we sent our cards to M. Bartholimeu, and before we had finished breakfast he was on the spot. We then learned that he had been watching the diligence office for over a week, and that he had the pleasant set of apartments we are now occupying all ready and waiting for us.

March 1.

MY DEAR HUSBAND,—Every day is opening to me a new world of wonders here in Italy. I have been in the Catacombs, where I was shown many memorials of the primitive Christians, and to-day we are going to the Vatican. The weather is sunny and beautiful beyond measure, and flowers are springing in the fields on every side. Oh, my dear, how I do long to have you here to enjoy what you are so much better fitted to appreciate than I,—this wonderful combination of the past and the present, of what has been and what is!

Think of strolling leisurely through the Forum, of seeing the very stones that were laid in the time of the Republic, of rambling over the ruined Palace of the Cæsars, of walking under the Arch of Titus, of seeing the Dying Gladiator, and whole ranges of rooms filled with wonders of art, all in one morning! All this I did on Saturday, and only wanted you. You know so much more and could appreciate so much better. At the Palace of the Cæsars, where the very dust is a *mélange* of exquisite marbles, I saw for the first time an acanthus growing, and picked my first leaf.

Our little *ménage* moves on prosperously; the doctor takes excellent care of us and we of him. One sees everybody here at Rome, John Bright, Mrs. Hemans' son, Mrs. Gaskell, etc., etc. Over five thousand English travelers are said to be here. Jacob Abbot and wife are coming. Rome is a world! Rome is an astonishment! Papal Rome is an enchantress! Old as she is, she is like Niñon d'Enclos,—the young fall in love with her.

You will hear next from us at Naples.

Affectionately yours,
H. B. S.

From Rome the travelers went to Naples, and after visiting Pompeii and Herculaneum made the ascent of Vesuvius, a graphic account of which is contained in a letter written at this time by Mrs. Stowe to her daughters in Paris. After describing the preparations and start, she says:—

"Gradually the ascent became steeper and steeper, till at length it was all our horses could do to pull us up. The treatment of horses in Naples is a thing that takes away much from the pleasure and comfort of such travelers as have the least feeling for animals. The people seem absolutely to have no consideration for them. You often see vehicles drawn by one horse carrying fourteen or fifteen great, stout men and women. This is the worse as the streets are paved with flat stones which are exceedingly slippery. On going up hill the drivers invariably race their horses, urging them on with a constant storm of blows.

"As the ascent of the mountain became steeper, the horses panted and trembled in a way that made us feel that we could not sit in the carriage, yet the guide and driver never made the slightest motion to leave the box. At last three of us got out and walked, and invited our guide to do the same, yet with all this relief the last part of the ascent was terrible, and the rascally fellows actually forced the horses to it by beating them with long poles on the back of their legs. No Englishman or American would ever allow a horse to be treated so.

"The Hermitage is a small cabin, where one can buy a little wine or any other refreshment one may need. There is a species of wine made of the grapes of Vesuvius, called 'Lachryma Christi,' that has a great reputation. Here was a miscellaneous collection of beggars, ragged boys, men playing guitars, bawling donkey drivers, and people wanting to sell sticks or minerals, the former to assist in the ascent, and the latter as specimens of the place. In the midst of the commotion we were placed on our donkeys, and the serious, pensive brutes moved away. At last we reached the top of the mountain, and I gladly sprang on firm land. The whole top of the mountain was covered with wavering wreaths of smoke, from the shadows of which emerged two English gentlemen, who congratulated us on our safe arrival, and assured us that we were fortunate in our day, as the mountain was very active. We could hear a hollow, roaring sound, like the burning of a great furnace, but saw nothing. 'Is this all?' I said. 'Oh, no. Wait till the guide comes up with the rest of the party,' and soon one after another came up, and we then followed the guide up a cloudy, rocky path, the noise of the fire constantly becoming nearer. Finally we stood on the verge of a vast, circular pit about forty feet deep, the floor of which is of black, ropy waves of congealed lava.

"The sides are sulphur cliffs, stained in every brilliant shade, from lightest yellow to deepest orange and brown. In the midst of the lava floor rises a black cone, the chimney of the great furnace. This was burning and flaming like the furnace of a glass-house, and every few moments throwing up showers of cinders and melted lava which fell with a rattling sound on the black floor of the pit. One small bit of the lava came over and fell at our feet, and a gentleman lighted his cigar at it.

"All around where we stood the smoke was issuing from every chance rent and fissure of the rock, and the Neapolitans who crowded round us were every moment soliciting us to let them cook us an egg in one of these rifts, and, overcome by persuasion, I did so, and found it very nicely boiled, or rather steamed, though the shell tasted of Glauber's salt and sulphur.

"The whole place recalled to my mind so vividly Milton's description of the infernal regions, that I could not but believe that he had drawn the imagery from this source. Milton, as we all know, was some time in Italy, and, although I do not recollect any account of his visiting Vesuvius, I cannot think how he should have shaped his language so coincidently to the phenomena if he had not.

"On the way down the mountain our ladies astonished the natives by making an express stipulation that our donkeys were not to be beaten,—why, they could not conjecture. The idea of any feeling of compassion for an animal is so foreign to a Neapolitan's thoughts that they supposed it must be some want of courage on our part. When, once in a while, the old habit so prevailed that the boy felt that he must strike the donkey, and when I forbade him, he would say, 'Courage, signora, courage.'

"Time would fail me to tell the whole of our adventures in Southern Italy. We left it with regret, and I will tell you some time by word of mouth what else we saw.

"We went by water from Naples to Leghorn, and were gloriously seasick, all of us. From Leghorn we went to Florence, where we abode two weeks nearly. Two days ago we left Florence and started for Venice, stopping one day and two nights *en route* at Bologna. Here we saw the great university, now used as a library, the walls of which are literally covered with the emblazoned names and coats of arms of distinguished men who were educated there.

"*Venice*. The great trouble of traveling in Europe, or indeed of traveling anywhere, is that you can never *catch* romance. No sooner are you in any place than being there seems the most natural, matter-of-fact occurrence in the world. Nothing looks foreign or strange to you. You take your tea and your dinner, eat, drink, and sleep as aforetime, and scarcely realize where you are or what you are seeing. But Venice is an exception to this state of things; it is all romance from beginning to end, and never ceases to seem strange and picturesque.

"It was a rainy evening when our cars rumbled over the long railroad bridge across the lagoon that leads to the station. Nothing but flat, dreary swamps, and then the wide expanse of sea on either side. The cars stopped, and the train, being a long one, left us a little out of the station. We got out in a driving rain, in company with flocks of Austrian soldiers, with whom the third-class cars were filled. We went through a long passage, and emerged into a room where all nations seemed commingling; Italians, Germans, French, Austrians, Orientals, all in wet weather trim.

"Soon, however, the news was brought that our baggage was looked out and our gondolas ready.

"The first plunge under the low, black hood of a gondola, especially of a rainy night, has something funereal in it. Four of us sat cowering together, and looked, out of the rain-dropped little windows at the sides, at the scene. Gondolas of all sizes were gliding up and down, with their sharp, fishy-looking prows of steel pushing their ways silently among each other, while gondoliers shouted and jabbered, and made as much confusion in their way as terrestrial hackmen on dry land. Soon, however, trunks and carpet-bags being adjusted, we pushed off, and went gliding away up the Grand Canal, with a motion so calm that we could scarce discern it except by the moving of objects on shore. Venice, *la belle*, appeared to as much disadvantage as a beautiful woman bedraggled in a thunder-storm."

"*Lake Como.* We stayed in Venice five days, and during that time saw all the sights that it could enter the head of a *valet-de-place* to afflict us with. It is an affliction, however, for which there is no remedy, because you want to see the things, and would be very sorry if you went home without having done so. From Venice we went to Milan to see the cathedral and Leonardo da Vinci's 'Last Supper.' The former is superb, and of the latter I am convinced, from the little that remains of it, that it *was* the greatest picture the world ever saw. We shall run back to Rome for Holy Week, and then to Paris.

"*Rome.* From Lake Como we came back here for Holy Week, and now it is over.

"'What do you think of it?'

"Certainly no thoughtful or sensitive person, no person impressible either through the senses or the religious feelings, can fail to feel it deeply.

"In the first place, the mere fact of the different nations of the earth moving, so many of them, with one accord, to so old and venerable a city, to celebrate the death and resurrection of Jesus, is something in itself affecting. Whatever dispute there may be about the other commemorative feasts of Christendom, the time of this epoch is fixed unerringly by the Jews' Passover. That great and solemn feast, therefore, stands as an historical monument to mark the date of the most important and thrilling events which this world ever witnessed.

"When one sees the city filling with strangers, pilgrims arriving on foot, the very shops decorating themselves in expectancy, every church arranging its services, the prices even of temporal matters raised by the crowd and its demands, he naturally thinks, Wherefore, why is all this? and he must be very careless indeed if it do not bring to mind, in a more real way than before, that at this very time, so many years ago, Christ and his apostles were living actors in the scenes thus celebrated to-day."

As the spring was now well advanced, it was deemed advisable to bring this pleasant journey to a close, and for Mrs. Stowe at least it was imperative that she return to America. Therefore, leaving Rome with many regrets and lingering, backward glances, the two sisters hurried to Paris, where they found their brother-in-law, Mr. John Hooker, awaiting them. Under date of May 3 Mrs. Stowe writes from Paris to her husband: "Here I am once more, safe in Paris after a fatiguing journey. I found the girls well, and greatly improved in their studies. As to bringing them home with me now, I have come to the conclusion that it would not be expedient. A few months more of study here will do them a world of good. I have, therefore, arranged that they shall come in November in the Arago, with a party of friends who are going at that time.

"John Hooker is here, so Mary is going with him and some others for a few weeks into Switzerland. I have some business affairs to settle in England, and shall sail from Liverpool in the Europa on the sixth of June. I am *so* homesick to-day, and long with a great longing to be with you once more. I am impatient to go, and yet dread the voyage. Still, to reach you I must commit myself once more to the ocean, of which at times I have a nervous horror, as to the arms of my Father. 'The sea is his, and He made it.' It is a rude, noisy old servant, but it is always obedient to his will, and cannot carry me beyond his power and love, wherever or to whatever it bears me."

Having established her daughters in a Protestant boarding-school in Paris, Mrs. Stowe proceeded to London. While there she received the following letter from Harriet Martineau:—

DEAR MRS. STOWE,—I have been at my wits' end to learn how to reach you, as your note bore no direction but "London." Arnolds, Croppers, and others could give no light, and the newspapers tell only where you *had* been. So I commit this to your publishers, trusting that it will find you somewhere, and in time, perhaps, bring you here. *Can't* you come? You are aware that we shall never meet if you don't come soon. I see no strangers at all, but I hope to have breath and strength enough for a little talk with you, if you could come. You could have perfect freedom at the times when I am laid up, and we could seize my "capability seasons" for our talk.

The weather and scenery are usually splendid just now. Did I see you (in white frock and black silk apron) when I was in Ohio in 1835? Your sister I knew well, and I have a clear recollection of your father. I believe and hope you were the young lady in the black silk apron.

Do you know I rather dreaded reading your book! Sick people *are* weak: and one of my chief weaknesses is dislike of novels,—(except some old ones which I almost know by heart). I knew that with you I should be safe from the cobweb-spinning of our modern subjective novelists and the jaunty vulgarity of our "funny philosophers"—the Dickens sort, who have tired us out. But I dreaded the alternative,—the too strong interest. But oh! the delight I have had in "Dred!" The genius carries all before it, and drowns everything in glorious pleasure. So marked a work of genius claims exemption from every sort of comparison; but, *as you ask for my opinion of the book*, you may like to know that I think it far superior to "Uncle Tom." I have no doubt that a multitude of people will say it is a falling off, because they made up their minds that any new book of yours must be inferior to that, and because it is so rare a thing for a prodigious fame to be sustained by a second book; but, in my own mind I am entirely convinced that the second book is by far the best. Such faults as you have are in the artistic department, and there is less defect in "Dred" than in "Uncle Tom," and the whole material and treatment seem to me richer and more substantial. I have had critiques of "Dred" from the two very wisest people I know—perfectly unlike each other (the critics, I mean), and they delight me by thinking exactly like each other and like me. They distinctly prefer it to "Uncle Tom." To say the plain truth, it seems to me so splendid a work of genius that nothing that I can say can give you an idea of the intensity of admiration with which I read it. It seemed to me, as I told my nieces, that our English fiction writers had better shut up altogether and have done with it, for one will have no patience with any but didactic writing after yours. My nieces (and you may have heard that Maria, my nurse, is very, very clever) are thoroughly possessed with the book, and Maria says she feels as if a fresh department of human life had been opened to her since this day week. I feel the freshness no less, while, from my travels, I can be even more assured of the truthfulness of your wonderful representation. I see no limit to the good it may do by suddenly splitting open Southern life, for everybody to look into. It is precisely the thing that is most wanted,—just as "Uncle Tom" was wanted, three years since, to show what negro slavery in your republic was like. It is plantation-life, particularly in the present case, that I mean. As for your exposure of the weakness and helplessness of the churches, I deeply honor you for the courage with which you have made the exposure; but I don't suppose that any amendment is to be looked for in that direction. You have unburdened your own soul in that matter, and if they had been corrigible, you would have helped a good many more. But I don't expect that result. The Southern railing at you will be something unequaled, I suppose. I hear that three of us have the honor of being abused from day to day already, as most portentous and shocking women, you, Mrs. Chapman, and myself (as the traveler of twenty years ago). Not only newspapers, but pamphlets of such denunciation are circulated, I'm told. I'm afraid now I, and even Mrs. Chapman, must lose our fame, and all the railing will be engrossed by you. My little function is to keep English people tolerably right, by means of a London daily paper, while the danger of misinformation and misreading from the "Times" continues. I can't conceive how such a paper as the "Times" can fail to be *better informed* than it is. At times it seems as if its New York correspondent was making game of it. The able and excellent editor of the "Daily News" gives me complete liberty on American subjects, and Mrs. Chapman's and other friends' constant supply of information enables me to use this liberty for making the cause better understood. I hope I shall hear that you are coming. It is like a great impertinence—my having written so freely about your book: but you asked my opinion,—that is all I can say. Thank you much for sending the book to me. If you come you will write our names in it, and this will make it a valuable legacy to a nephew or niece.

Believe me gratefully and affectionately yours,

HARRIET MARTINEAU.

In London Mrs. Stowe also received the following letter from Prescott, the historian, which after long wandering had finally rested quietly at her English publishers awaiting her coming.

PEPPERELL, *October 4, 1856.*

MY DEAR MRS. STOWE,—I am much obliged to you for the copy of "Dred" which Mr. Phillips put into my hands. It has furnished us our evening's amusement since we have been in the country, where we spend the brilliant month of October.

The African race are much indebted to you for showing up the good sides of their characters, their cheerfulness, and especially their powers of humor, which are admirably set off by their peculiar *patois*, in the same manner as the expression of the Scottish sentiment is by the peculiar Scottish dialect. People differ; but I was most struck among your characters with Uncle Tiff and Nina. The former a variation of good old Uncle Tom, though conceived in a merrier vein than belonged to that sedate personage; the difference of their tempers in this respect being well suited to the difference of the circumstances in which they were placed. But Nina, to my mind, is the true *hero* of the book, which I should have named after her instead of "Dred." She is indeed a charming conception, full of what is called character, and what is masculine in her nature is toned down by such a delightful sweetness and kindness of disposition as makes her perfectly fascinating. I cannot forgive you for smothering her so prematurely. No *dramatis personæ* could afford the loss of such a character. But I will not bore you with criticism, of which you have had quite enough. I must thank you, however, for giving Tom Gordon a guttapercha cane to perform his flagellations with.

I congratulate you on the brilliant success of the work, unexampled even in this age of authorship; and, as Mr. Phillips informs me, greater even in the old country than in ours. I am glad you are likely to settle the question and show that a Yankee writer can get a copyright in England—little thanks to our own government, which compels him to go there in order to get it.

> With sincere regard, believe me, dear Mrs. Stowe,
>
> > Very truly yours,
> > WM. H. PRESCOTT.

From Liverpool, on the eve of her departure for America, Mrs. Stowe wrote to her daughters in Paris:—

I spent the day before leaving London with Lady Byron. She is lovelier than ever, and inquired kindly about you both. I left London to go to Manchester, and reaching there found the Rev. Mr. Gaskell waiting to welcome me in the station. Mrs. Gaskell seems lovely at home, where besides being a writer she proves herself to be a first-class housekeeper, and performs all the duties of a minister's wife. After spending a delightful day with her I came here to the beautiful "Dingle," which is more enchanting than ever. I am staying with Mrs. Edward Cropper, Lord Denman's daughter.

I want you to tell Aunt Mary that Mr. Ruskin lives with his father at a place called Denmark Hill, Camberwell. He has told me that the gallery of Turner pictures there is open to me or my friends at any time of the day or night. Both young and old Mr. Ruskin are fine fellows, sociable and hearty, and will cordially welcome any of my friends who desire to look at their pictures.

I write in haste, as I must be aboard the ship to-morrow at eight o'clock. So good-by, my dear girls, from your ever affectionate mother.

Her last letter written before sailing was to Lady Byron, and serves to show how warm an intimacy had sprung up between them. It was as follows:—

June 5, 1857.

DEAR FRIEND,—I left you with a strange sort of yearning, throbbing feeling—you make me feel quite as I did years ago, a sort of girlishness quite odd for me. I have felt a strange longing to send you something. Don't smile when you see what it turns out to be. I have a weakness for your pretty Parian things; it is one of my own home peculiarities to have strong passions for pretty tea-cups and other little matters for my own quiet meals, when, as often happens, I am too unwell to join the family. So I send you a cup made of primroses, a funny little pitcher, quite large enough for cream, and a little vase for violets and primroses—which will be lovely together—and when you use it think of me and that I love you more than I can say.

I often think how strange it is that I should *know* you—you who were a sort of legend of my early days—that I should love you is only a natural result. You seem to me to stand on the confines of that land where the poor formalities which separate hearts here pass like mist before the sun, and therefore it is that I feel the language of love must not startle you as strange or unfamiliar. You are so nearly there in spirit that I fear with every adieu that it may be the last; yet did you pass within the veil I should not feel you lost.

I have got past the time when I feel that my heavenly friends are *lost* by going there. I feel them *nearer*, rather than farther off.

So good-by, dear, dear friend, and if you see morning in our Father's house before I do, carry my love to those that wait for me, and if I pass first, you will find me there, and we shall love each other *forever.*

Ever yours,
H. B. STOWE.

The homeward voyage proved a prosperous one, and it was followed by a joyous welcome to the "Cabin" in Andover. The world seemed very bright, and amid all her happiness came no intimation of the terrible blow about to descend upon the head of the devoted mother.

CHAPTER XIV

THE MINISTER'S WOOING, 1857-1859

DEATH OF MRS. STOWE'S OLDEST SON.—LETTER TO
THE DUCHESS OF SUTHERLAND.—LETTER TO HER
DAUGHTERS IN PARIS.—LETTER TO HER SISTER
CATHERINE.—VISIT TO BRUNSWICK AND ORR'S
ISLAND.—WRITES "THE MINISTER'S WOOING" AND
"THE PEARL OF ORR'S ISLAND."—MR. WHITTIER'S
COMMENTS.—MR. LOWELL ON THE "MINISTER'S
WOOING."—LETTER TO MRS. STOWE FROM MR.
LOWELL.—JOHN RUSKIN ON THE "MINISTER'S
WOOING."—A YEAR OF SADNESS.—LETTER TO LADY
BYRON.—LETTER TO HER DAUGHTER.—DEPARTURE
FOR EUROPE.

IMMEDIATELY after Mrs. Stowe's return from England in June,
1857, a crushing sorrow came upon her in the death of her oldest
son, Henry Ellis, who was drowned while bathing in the
Connecticut River at Hanover, N. H., where he was pursuing his
studies as a member of the Freshman class in Dartmouth College.
This melancholy event took place the 9th of July, 1857, and the 3d
of August Mrs. Stowe wrote to the Duchess of Sutherland:—

> DEAR FRIEND,—Before this reaches you you will have
> perhaps learned from other sources of the sad blow which has
> fallen upon us,—our darling, our good, beautiful boy, snatched
> away in the moment of health and happiness. Alas! could I
> know that when I parted from my Henry on English shores
> that I should never see him more? I returned to my home, and,
> amid the jubilee of meeting the rest, was fain to be satisfied
> with only a letter from him, saying that his college
> examinations were coming on, and he must defer seeing me a
> week or two till they were over. I thought then of taking his
> younger brother and going up to visit him; but the health of
> the latter seeming unfavorably affected by the seacoast air, I

turned back with him to a water-cure establishment. Before I had been two weeks absent a fatal telegram hurried me home, and when I arrived there it was to find the house filled with his weeping classmates, who had just come bringing his remains. There he lay so calm, so placid, so peaceful, that I could not believe that he would not smile upon me, and that my voice which always had such power over him could not recall him. There had always been such a peculiar union, such a tenderness between us. I had had such power always to call up answering feelings to my own, that it seemed impossible that he could be silent and unmoved at my grief. But yet, dear friend, I am sensible that in this last sad scene I had an alleviation that was not granted to you. I recollect, in the mournful letter you wrote me about that time, you said that you mourned that you had never told your own dear one how much you loved him. That sentence touched me at the time. I laid it to heart, and from that time lost no occasion of expressing to my children those feelings that we too often defer to express to our dearest friends till it is forever too late.

He did fully know how I loved him, and some of the last loving words he spoke were of me. The very day that he was taken from us, and when he was just rising from the table of his boarding-house to go whence he never returned, some one noticed the seal ring, which you may remember to have seen on his finger, and said, How beautiful that ring is! Yes, he said, and best of all, it was my mother's gift to me. That ring, taken from the lifeless hand a few hours later, was sent to me. Singularly enough, it is broken right across the name from a fall a little time previous. . . .

It is a great comfort to me, dear friend, that I took Henry with me to Dunrobin. I hesitated about keeping him so long from his studies, but still I thought a mind so observing and appreciative might learn from such a tour more than through books, and so it was. He returned from England full of high resolves and manly purposes. "I may not be what the world calls a Christian," he wrote, "but I will live such a life as a Christian ought to live, such a life as every true man ought to live." Henceforth he became remarkable for a strict order and energy, and a vigilant temperance and care of his bodily health, docility and deference to his parents and teachers, and perseverance in every duty. . . . Well, from the hard battle of this life he is excused, and the will is taken for the deed, and whatever comes his heart will not be pierced as mine is. But I am glad that I can connect him with all my choicest remembrances of the Old World.

Dunrobin will always be dearer to me now, and I have felt towards you and the duke a turning of spirit, because I remember how kindly you always looked on and spoke to him. I knew then it was the angel of your lost one that stirred your hearts with tenderness when you looked on another so near his age. The plaid that the duke gave him, and which he valued as one of the chief of his boyish treasures, will hang in his room—for still we have a room that we call his.

You will understand, you will feel, this sorrow with us as few can. My poor husband is much prostrated. I need not say more: you know what this must be to a father's heart. But still

I repeat what I said when I saw you last. Our dead are ministering angels; they teach us to love, they fill us with tenderness for all that can suffer. These weary hours when sorrow makes us for the time blind and deaf and dumb, have their promise. These hours come in answer to our prayers for nearness to God. It is always our treasure that the lightning strikes. . . . I have poured out my heart to you because you can understand. While I was visiting in Hanover, where Henry died, a poor, deaf old slave woman, who has still five children in bondage, came to comfort me. "Bear up, dear soul, she said; you must bear it, for the Lord loves ye." She said further, "Sunday is a heavy day to me, 'cause I can't work, and can't hear preaching, and can't read, so I can't keep my mind off my poor children. Some on 'em the blessed Master's got, and they's safe; but, oh, there are five that I don't know where they are."

What are our mother sorrows to this! I shall try to search out and redeem these children, though, from the ill success of efforts already made, I fear it will be hopeless. Every sorrow I have, every lesson on the sacredness of family love, makes me the more determined to resist to the last this dreadful evil that makes so many mothers so much deeper mourners than I ever can be. . . .

Affectionately yours,
H. B. STOWE.

About this same time she writes to her daughters in Paris: "Can anybody tell what sorrows are locked up with our best affections, or what pain may be associated with every pleasure? As I walk the house, the pictures he used to love, the presents I brought him, and the photographs I meant to show him, all pierce my heart. I have had a dreadful faintness of sorrow come over me at times. I have felt so crushed, so bleeding, so helpless, that I could only call on my Saviour with groanings that could not be uttered. Your papa justly said, 'Every child that dies is for the time being an only one; yes—his individuality no time, no change, can ever replace.'

"'Two days after the funeral your father and I went to Hanover. We saw Henry's friends, and his room, which was just as it was the day he left it.

"'There is not another such room in the college as his,' said one of his classmates with tears. I could not help loving the dear boys as they would come and look sadly in, and tell us one thing and another that they remembered of him. 'He was always talking of his home and his sisters,' said one. The very day he died he was so happy because I had returned, and he was expecting soon to go home and meet me. He died with that dear thought in his heart.

"There was a beautiful lane leading down through a charming glen to the river. It had been for years the bathing-place of the students, and into the pure, clear water he plunged, little dreaming that he was never to come out alive.

"In the evening we went down to see the boating club of which he was a member. He was so happy in this boating club. They had a beautiful boat called the Una, and a uniform, and he enjoyed it so much.

"This evening all the different crews were out; but Henry's had their flag furled, and tied with black crape. I felt such love to the dear boys, all of them, because they loved Henry, that it did not pain me as it otherwise would. They were glad to see us there, and I was glad that we could be there. Yet right above where their boats were gliding in the evening light lay the bend in the river, clear, still, beautiful, fringed with overhanging pines, from whence our boy went upward to heaven. To heaven—if earnest, manly purpose, if sincere, deliberate strife with besetting sin is accepted of God, as I firmly believe it is. Our dear boy was but a beginner in the right way. Had he lived, we had hoped to see all wrong gradually fall from his soul as the worn-out calyx drops from the perfected flower. But Christ has taken him into his own teaching.

"'And one view of Jesus as He is,
Will strike all sin forever dead.'

"Since I wrote to you last we have had anniversary meetings, and with all the usual bustle and care, our house full of company. Tuesday we received a beautiful portrait of our dear Henry, life-size, and as perfect almost as life. It has just that half-roguish, half-loving expression with which he would look at me sometimes, when I would come and brush back his hair and look into his eyes. Every time I go in or out of the room, it seems to give so bright a smile that I almost think that a spirit dwells within it.

"When I am so heavy, so weary, and go about as if I were wearing an arrow that had pierced my heart, I sometimes look up, and this smile seems to say, 'Mother, patience, I am happy. In our Father's house are many mansions.' Sometimes I think I am like a gardener who has planted the seed of some rare exotic. He watches as the two little points of green leaf first spring above the soil. He shifts it from soil to soil, from pot to pot. He watches it, waters it, saves it through thousands of mischiefs and accidents. He counts every leaf, and marks the strengthening of the stem, till at last the blossom bud was fully formed. What curiosity, what eagerness,— what expectation—what longing now to see the mystery unfold in the new flower.

"Just as the calyx begins to divide and a faint streak of color becomes visible,—lo! in one night the owner of the greenhouse sends and takes it away. He does, not consult me, he gives me no warning; he silently takes it and I look, but it is no more. What, then? Do I suppose he has destroyed the flower? Far from it; I know that he has taken it to his own garden. What Henry might have been I could guess better than any one. What Henry is, is known to Jesus only."

Shortly after this time Mrs. Stowe wrote to her sister Catherine:—

If ever I was conscious of an attack of the Devil trying to separate me from the love of Christ, it was for some days after the terrible news came. I was in a state of great physical weakness, most agonizing, and unable to control my thoughts. Distressing doubts as to Henry's spiritual state were rudely thrust upon my soul. It was as if a voice had said to me: "You trusted in God, did you? You believed that He loved you! You had perfect confidence that he would never take your child till the work of grace was mature! Now He has hurried him into eternity without a moment's warning, without preparation, and where is he?"

I saw at last that these thoughts were irrational, and contradicted the calm, settled belief of my better moments, and that they were dishonorable to God, and that it was my duty to resist them, and to assume and steadily maintain that Jesus in love had taken my dear one to his bosom. Since then the Enemy has left me in peace.

It is our duty to assume that a thing which would be in its very nature unkind, ungenerous, and unfair has not been done. What should we think of the crime of that human being who should take a young mind from circumstances where it was progressing in virtue, and throw it recklessly into corrupting and depraving society? Particularly if it were the child of one who had trusted and confided in Him for years. No! no such slander as this shall the Devil ever fix in my mind against my Lord and my God! He who made me capable of such an absorbing, unselfish devotion for my children, so that I would sacrifice my eternal salvation for them, He certainly did not make me capable of more love, more disinterestedness than He has himself. He invented mothers' hearts, and He certainly has the pattern in his own, and my poor, weak rush-light of love is enough to show me that some things can and some things cannot be done. Mr. Stowe said in his sermon last Sunday that the mysteries of God's ways with us must be swallowed up by the greater mystery of the love of Christ, even as Aaron's rod swallowed up the rods of the magicians.

Papa and mamma are here, and we have been reading over the "Autobiography and Correspondence." It is glorious, beautiful; but more of this anon.

Your affectionate sister,
HATTIE.

ANDOVER, *August 24, 1857.*

DEAR CHILDREN,—Since anniversary papa and I have been living at home; Grandpa and Grandma Beecher are here also, and we have had much comfort in their society. . . . To-night the last sad duty is before us. The body is to be removed from the receiving tomb in the Old South Churchyard, and laid in the graveyard near by. Pearson has been at work for a week on a lot that is to be thenceforth ours.

"Our just inheritance consecrated by his grave."

How little he thought, wandering there as he often has with us, that his mortal form would so soon be resting there. Yet that was written for him. It was as certain then as now, and the hour and place of our death is equally certain, though we know it not.

It seems selfish that I should yearn to lie down by his side, but I never knew how much I loved him till now.

The one lost piece of silver seems more than all the rest,— the one lost sheep dearer than all the fold, and I so long for one word, one look, one last embrace. . . .

ANDOVER, *September 1, 1857.*

MY DARLING CHILDREN,—I must not allow a week to pass without sending a line to you. . . . Our home never looked lovelier. I never saw Andover look so beautiful; the trees so green, the foliage so rich. Papa and I are just starting to spend a week in Brunswick, for I am so miserable;—so weak—the least exertion fatigues me, and much of my time I feel a heavy languor, indifferent to everything. I know nothing is so likely to bring me up as the air of the seaside. . . . I have set many flowers around Henry's grave, which are blossoming; pansies, white immortelle, white petunia, and verbenas. Papa walks there every day, often twice or three times. The lot has been rolled and planted with fine grass, which is already up and looks green and soft as velvet, and the little birds gather about it. To-night as I sat there the sky was so beautiful, all rosy, with the silver moon looking out of it. Papa said with a deep sigh, "I am submissive, but not reconciled."

BRUNSWICK, *September 6, 1857.*

MY DEAR GIRLS,—Papa and I have been here for four or five days past. We both of us felt so unwell that we thought we would try the sea air and the dear old scenes of Brunswick. Everything here is just as we left it. We are staying with Mrs. Upham, whose house is as wide, cool, and hospitable as ever.

The trees in the yard have grown finely, and Mrs. Upham has cultivated flowers so successfully that the house is all surrounded by them. Everything about the town is the same, even to Miss Gidding's old shop, which is as disorderly as ever, presenting the same medley of tracts, sewing-silk, darning-cotton, and unimaginable old bonnets, which existed there of yore. She has been heard to complain that she can't find things as easily as once. Day before yesterday papa, Charley, and I went down to Harpswell about seven o'clock in the morning. The old spruces and firs look lovely as ever, and I was delighted, as I always used to be, with every step of the way. Old Getchell's mill stands as forlorn as ever in its sandy wastes, and More Brook creeps on glassy and clear beyond. Arriving at Harpswell a glorious hot day, with scarce a breeze to ruffle the water, papa and Charley went to fish for cunners, who soon proved too *cun*ning for them, for they ate every morsel of bait off the hooks, so that out of twenty bites they only secured two or three. What they did get were fried for our dinner, reinforced by a fine clam-chowder. The evening was one of the most glorious I ever saw—a calm sea and round, full moon; Mrs. Upham and I sat out on the rocks between the mainland and the island until ten o'clock. I never did see a more perfect and glorious scene, and to add to it there was a splendid northern light dancing like spirits in the sky. Had it not been for a terrible attack of mosquitoes in our sleeping-rooms, that kept us up and fighting all night, we should have called it a perfect success.

We went into the sea to bathe twice, once the day we came, and about eight o'clock in the morning before we went back. Besides this we have been to Middle Bay, where Charley, standing where you all stood before him, actually caught a flounder with his own hand, whereat he screamed loud enough to scare all the folks on Eagle Island. We have also been to Maquoit. We have visited the old pond, and, if I mistake not, the relics of your old raft yet float there; at all events, one or two fragments of a raft are there, caught among rushes.

I do not realize that one of the busiest and happiest of the train who once played there shall play there no more. "He shall return to his house no more, neither shall his place know him any more." I think I have felt the healing touch of Jesus of Nazareth on the deep wound in my heart, for I have golden hours of calm when I say: "Even so, Father, for so it seemed good in thy sight." So sure am I that the most generous love has ordered all, that I can now take pleasure to give this little proof of my unquestioning confidence in resigning one of my dearest comforts to Him. I feel very near the spirit land, and the words, "I shall go to him, but he shall not return to me," are very sweet.

Oh, if God would give to you, my dear children, a view of the infinite beauty of Eternal Love,—if He would unite us in himself, then even on earth all tears might be wiped away.

Papa has preached twice to-day, and is preaching again to-night. He told me to be sure to write and send you his love. I hope his health is getting better. Mrs. Upham sends you her best love, and hopes you will make her a visit some time.

Good-by, my darlings. Come soon to your affectionate mother.

H. B. S.

The winter of 1857 was passed quietly and uneventfully at Andover. In November Mrs. Stowe contributed to the "Atlantic Monthly" a touching little allegory, "The Mourning Veil."

In December, 1858, the first chapter of "The Minister's Wooing" appeared in the same magazine. Simultaneously with this story was written "The Pearl of Orr's Island," published first as a serial in the "Independent."

She dictated a large part of "The Minister's Wooing" under a great pressure of mental excitement, and it was a relief to her to turn to the quiet story of the coast of Maine, which she loved so well.

In February, 1874, Mrs. Stowe received the following words from Mr. Whittier, which are very interesting in this connection: "When I am in the mood for thinking deeply I read 'The Minister's Wooing.' But 'The Pearl of Orr's Island' is my favorite. It is the most charming New England idyl ever written."

"The Minister's Wooing" was received with universal commendation from the first, and called forth the following appreciative words from the pen of Mr. James Russell Lowell:—

"It has always seemed to us that the anti-slavery element in the two former novels by Mrs. Stowe stood in the way of a full appreciation of her remarkable genius, at least in her own country. It was so easy to account for the unexampled popularity of 'Uncle Tom' by attributing it to a cheap sympathy with sentimental philanthropy! As people began to recover from the first enchantment, they began also to resent it and to complain that a dose of that insane Garrison-root which takes the reason prisoner had been palmed upon them without their knowing it, and that their ordinary water-gruel of fiction, thinned with sentiment and thickened with moral, had been hocussed with the bewildering hasheesh of Abolition. We had the advantage of reading that truly extraordinary book for the first time in Paris, long after the whirl of excitement produced by its publication had subsided, in the seclusion of distance, and with a judgment unbiased by those political sympathies which it is impossible, perhaps unwise, to avoid at home. We felt then, and we believe now, that the secret of Mrs. Stowe's power lay in that same genius by which the great successes in creative literature have always been achieved,—the genius that instinctively goes right to the organic elements of human nature, whether under a white skin or a black, and which disregards as trivial the conventional and factitious notions which make so large a part both of our thinking and feeling. Works of imagination written with an aim to immediate impression are commonly ephemeral, like Miss Martineau's 'Tales,' and Elliott's 'Corn-law Rhymes;' but the creative faculty of Mrs. Stowe, like that of Cervantes in 'Don Quixote' and of Fielding in 'Joseph Andrews,' overpowered the narrow specialty of her design, and expanded a local and temporary theme with the cosmopolitanism of genius.

"It is a proverb that 'There is a great deal of human nature in men,' but it is equally and sadly true that there is amazingly little of it in books. Fielding is the only English novelist who deals with life in its broadest sense. Thackeray, his disciple and congener, and Dickens, the congener of Smollett, do not so much treat of life as of the strata of society; the one studying nature from the club-room window, the other from the reporters' box in the police court. It may be that the general obliteration of distinctions of rank in this country, which is generally considered a detriment to the novelist, will in the end turn to his advantage by compelling him to depend for his effects on the contrasts and collisions of innate character, rather than on those shallower traits superinduced by particular social arrangements, or by hereditary associations. Shakespeare drew ideal, and Fielding natural men and women; Thackeray draws either gentlemen or snobs, and Dickens either unnatural men or the oddities natural only in the lowest grades of a highly artificial system of society. The first two knew human nature; of the two latter, one knows what is called the world, and the other the streets of London. Is it possible that the very social democracy which here robs the novelist of so much romance, so much costume, so much antithesis of caste, so much in short that is purely external, will give him a set-off in making it easier for him to get at that element of universal humanity which neither of the two extremes of an aristocratic system, nor the salient and picturesque points of contrast between the two, can alone lay open to him?

"We hope to see this problem solved by Mrs. Stowe. That kind of romantic interest which Scott evolved from the relations of lord and vassal, of thief and clansman, from the social more than the moral contrast of Roundhead and Cavalier, of far-descended pauper and *nouveau riche* which Cooper found in the clash of savagery with civilization, and the shaggy virtue bred on the border-land between the two, Indian by habit, white by tradition, Mrs. Stowe seems in her former novels to have sought in a form of society alien to her sympathies, and too remote for exact study, or for the acquirement of that local truth which is the slow result of unconscious observation. There can be no stronger proof of the greatness of her genius, of her possessing that conceptive faculty which belongs to the higher order of imagination, than the avidity with which 'Uncle Tom' was read at the South. It settled the point that this book was true to human nature, even if not minutely so to plantation life.

"If capable of so great a triumph where success must so largely depend on the sympathetic insight of her mere creative power, have we not a right to expect something far more in keeping with the requirements of art, now that her wonderful eye is to be the mirror of familiar scenes, and of a society in which she was bred, of which she has seen so many varieties, and that, too, in the country, where it is most *naïve* and original? It is a great satisfaction to us that in 'The Minister's Wooing' she has chosen her time and laid her scene amid New England habits and traditions. There is no other writer who is so capable of perpetuating for us, in a work of art, a style of thought and manners which railways and newspapers will soon render as palæozoic as the mastodon or the megalosaurians. Thus far the story has fully justified our hopes. The leading characters are all fresh and individual creations. Mrs. Kate Scudder, the notable Yankee housewife; Mary, in whom Cupid is to try conclusions with Calvin; James Marvyn, the adventurous boy of the coast, in whose heart the wild religion of nature swells till the strait swathings of Puritanism are burst; Dr. Hopkins, the conscientious minister come upon a time when the social *prestige* of the clergy is waning, and whose independence will test the voluntary system of ministerial support; Simeon Brown, the man of theological dialectics, in whom the utmost perfection of creed is shown to be not inconsistent with the most contradictory imperfection of life,—all these are characters new to literature. And the scene is laid just far enough away in point of time to give proper tone and perspective.

"We think we find in the story, so far as it has proceeded, the promise of an interest as unhackneyed as it will be intense. There is room for the play of all the passions and interests that make up the great tragi-comedy of life, while all the scenery and accessories will be those which familiarity has made dear to us. We are a little afraid of Colonel Burr, to be sure, it is so hard to make a historical personage fulfill the conditions demanded by the novel of every-day life. He is almost sure either to fall below our traditional conception of him, or to rise above the natural and easy level of character, into the vague or the melodramatic. Moreover, we do not want a novel of society from Mrs. Stowe; she is quite too good to be wasted in that way, and her tread is much more firm on the turf of the "door-yard" or the pasture, and the sanded floor of the farmhouse, than on the velvet of the *salôn*. We have no notion how she is to develop her plot, but we think we foresee chances for her best power in the struggle which seems foreshadowed between Mary's conscientious admiration of the doctor and her half-conscious passion for James, before she discovers that one of these conflicting feelings means simply moral liking and approval, and the other that she is a woman and that she loves. And is not the value of dogmatic theology as a rule of life to be thoroughly tested for the doctor by his slave-trading parishioners? Is he not to learn the bitter difference between intellectual acceptance of a creed and that true partaking of the sacrament of love and faith and sorrow that makes Christ the very life-blood of our being and doing? And has not James Marvyn also his lesson to be taught? We foresee him drawn gradually back by Mary from his recoil against Puritan formalism to a perception of how every creed is pliant and plastic to a beautiful nature, of how much charm there may be in an hereditary faith, even if it have become almost conventional.

"In the materials of character already present in the story, there is scope for Mrs. Stowe's humor, pathos, clear moral sense, and quick eye for the scenery of life. We do not believe that there is any one who, by birth, breeding, and natural capacity, has had the opportunity to know New England so well as she, or who has the peculiar genius so to profit by the knowledge. Already there have been scenes in 'The Minister's Wooing' that, in their lowness of tone and quiet truth, contrast as charmingly with the humid vagueness of the modern school of novel-writers as 'The Vicar of Wakefield' itself, and we are greatly mistaken if it do not prove to be the most characteristic of Mrs. Stowe's works, and therefore that on which her fame will chiefly rest with posterity."

"The Minister's Wooing" was not completed as a serial till December, 1859. Long before its completion Mrs. Stowe received letters from many interested readers, who were as much concerned for the future of her "spiritual children," as George Eliot would call them, as if they had been flesh and blood.

The following letter from Mr. Lowell is given as the most valuable received by Mrs. Stowe at this time:—

CAMBRIDGE, *February 4, 1859.*

MY DEAR MRS. STOWE,—I certainly did mean to write you about your story, but only to cry *bravissima!* with the rest of the world. I intended no kind of criticism; deeming it wholly out of place, and in the nature of a wet-blanket, so long as a story is unfinished. When I got the first number in MS., I said to Mr. Phillips that I thought it would be the best thing you had done, and what followed has only confirmed my first judgment. From long habit, and from the tendency of my studies, I cannot help looking at things purely from an æsthetic point of view, and what *I* valued in "Uncle Tom" was the genius, and not the moral. That is saying a good deal, for I never use the word *genius* at haphazard, and always (perhaps, too) sparingly. I am going to be as frank as I ought to be with one whom I value so highly. What especially charmed me in the new story was, that you had taken your stand on New England ground. You are one of the few persons lucky enough to be born with eyes in your head,—that is, with something behind the eyes which makes them of value. To most people the seeing apparatus is as useless as the great telescope at the observatory is to me,—something to stare through with no intelligent result. Nothing could be better than the conception of your plot (so far as I divine it), and the painting-in of your figures. As for "theology," it is as much a part of daily life in New England as in Scotland, and all I should have to say about it is this: let it crop out when it naturally comes to the surface, only don't dig down to it. A moral aim is a fine thing, but in making a story an artist is a traitor who does not sacrifice everything to art. Remember the lesson that Christ gave us twice over. First, he preferred the useless Mary to the dish-washing Martha, and next, when that exemplary moralist and friend of humanity, Judas, objected to the sinful waste of the Magdalen's ointment, the great Teacher would rather it should be wasted in an act of simple beauty than utilized for the benefit of the poor. Cleopatra was an artist when she dissolved her biggest pearl to captivate her Antony-public. May I, a critic by profession, say the whole truth to a woman of genius? Yes? And never be forgiven? I shall try, and try to be forgiven, too. In the first place, pay no regard to the advice of anybody. In the second place, pay a great deal to mine! A Kilkenny-cattish style of advice? Not at all. My advice is to follow your own instincts,— to stick to nature, and to avoid what people commonly call the "Ideal;" for that, and beauty, and pathos, and success, all lie in the simply natural. We all preach it, from Wordsworth down, and we all, from Wordsworth down, don't practice it. Don't I feel it every day in this weary editorial mill of mine, that there are ten thousand people who can write "ideal" things for one who can see, and feel, and reproduce nature and character? Ten thousand, did I say? Nay, ten million What made Shakespeare so great? Nothing but eyes and—faith in them. The same is true of Thackeray. I see nowhere more often than in authors the truth that men love their opposites. Dickens insists on being tragic and makes shipwreck.

I always thought (forgive me) that the Hebrew parts of "Dred" were a mistake. Do not think me impertinent; I am only honestly anxious that what I consider a very remarkable genius should have faith in itself. Let your moral take care of itself, and remember that an author's writing-desk is something infinitely higher than a pulpit. What I call "care of itself" is shown in that noble passage in the February number about the ladder up to heaven. That is grand preaching and in the right way. I am sure that "The Minister's Wooing" is going to be the best of your products hitherto, and I am sure of it because you show so thorough a mastery of your material, so true a perception of realities, without which the ideality is impossible.

As for "orthodoxy," be at ease. Whatever is well done the world finds orthodox at last, in spite of all the Fakir journals, whose only notion of orthodoxy seems to be the power of standing in one position till you lose all the use of your limbs. If, with your heart and brain, *you* are not orthodox, in Heaven's name who is? If you mean "Calvinistic," no woman could ever be such, for Calvinism is logic, and no woman worth the name could ever live by syllogisms. Woman charms a higher faculty in us than reason, God be praised, and nothing has delighted me more in your new story than the happy instinct with which you develop this incapacity of the lovers' logic in your female characters. Go on just as you have begun, and make it appear in as many ways as you like,—that, whatever creed may be true, it is *not* true and never will be that man can be saved by machinery. I can speak with some chance of being right, for I confess a strong sympathy with many parts of Calvinistic theology, and, for one thing, believe in hell with all my might, and in the goodness of God for all that.

I have not said anything. What could I say? One might almost as well advise a mother about the child she still bears under her heart, and say, give it these and those qualities, as an author about a work yet in the brain.

Only this I will say, that I am honestly delighted with "The Minister's Wooing;" that reading it has been one of my few editorial pleasures; that no one appreciates your genius more highly than I, or hopes more fervently that you will let yourself go without regard to this, that, or t'other. Don't read any criticisms on your story: believe that you know better than any of us, and be sure that everybody likes it. That I know. There is not, and never was, anybody so competent to write a true New England poem as yourself, and have no doubt that you are doing it. The native sod sends up the best inspiration to the brain, and you are as sure of immortality as we all are of dying,—if you only go on with entire faith in yourself.

Faithfully and admiringly yours,
J. R. LOWELL.

After the book was published in England, Mr. Ruskin wrote to Mrs. Stowe:—

"Well, I have read the book now, and I think nothing can be nobler than the noble parts of it (Mary's great speech to Colonel Burr, for instance), nothing wiser than the wise parts of it (the author's parenthetical and under-breath remarks), nothing more delightful than the delightful parts (all that Virginie says and does), nothing more edged than the edged parts (Candace's sayings and doings, to wit); but I do not like the plan of the whole, because the simplicity of the minister seems to diminish the probability of Mary's reverence for him. I cannot fancy even so good a girl who would not have laughed at him. Nor can I fancy a man of real intellect reaching such a period of life without understanding his own feelings better, or penetrating those of another more quickly.

"Then I am provoked at nothing happening to Mrs. Scudder, whom I think as entirely unendurable a creature as ever defied poetical justice at the end of a novel meant to irritate people. And finally, I think you are too disdainful of what ordinary readers seek in a novel, under the name of 'interest,'—that gradually developing wonder, expectation, and curiosity which makes people who have no self-command sit up till three in the morning to get to the crisis, and people who have self-command lay the book down with a resolute sigh, and think of it all the next day through till the time comes for taking it up again. Still, I know well that in many respects it was impossible for you to treat this story merely as a work of literary art. There must have been many facts which you could not dwell upon, and which no one may judge by common rules.

"It is also true, as you say once or twice in the course of the work, that we have not among us here the peculiar religious earnestness you have mainly to describe.

"We have little earnest formalism, and our formalists are for the most part hollow, feeble, uninteresting, mere stumbling-blocks. We have the Simeon Brown species, indeed; and among readers even of his kind the book may do some good, and more among the weaker, truer people, whom it will shake like mattresses,—making the dust fly, and perhaps with it some of the sticks and quill-ends, which often make that kind of person an objectionable mattress. I write too lightly of the book,—far too lightly,—but your letter made me gay, and I have been lighter-hearted ever since; only I kept this after beginning it, because I was ashamed to send it without a line to Mrs. Browning as well. I do not understand why you should apprehend (or rather anticipate without apprehension) any absurd criticism on it. It is sure to be a popular book,—not as 'Uncle Tom' was, for that owed part of its popularity to its dramatic effect (the flight on the ice, etc.), which I did not like; but as a true picture of human life is always popular. Nor, I should think, would any critics venture at all to carp at it.

"The Candace and Virginie bits appear to me, as far as I have yet seen, the best. I am very glad there is this nice French lady in it: the French are the least appreciated in general, of all nations, by other nations. . . . My father says the book is worth its weight in gold, and he knows good work."

When we turn from these criticisms and commendations to the inner history of this period, we find that the work was done in deep sadness of heart, and the undertone of pathos that forms the dark background of the brightest and most humorous parts of "The Minister's Wooing" was the unconscious revelation of one of sorrowful spirit, who, weary of life, would have been glad to lie down with her arms "round the wayside cross, and sleep away into a brighter scene."

Just before beginning the writing of "The Minister's Wooing" she sent the following letter to Lady Byron:—

ANDOVER, *June 30, 1858.*

MY DEAR FRIEND,—I did long to hear from you at a time when few knew how to speak, because I knew that you did know everything that sorrow can teach,—you whose whole life has been a crucifixion, a long ordeal. But I believe that the "Lamb," who stands forever in the midst of the throne "as it had been slain," has everywhere his followers, those who are sent into the world, as he was, to suffer for the redemption of others, and like him they must look to the joy set before them of redeeming others.

I often think that God called you to this beautiful and terrible ministry when He suffered you to link your destiny with one so strangely gifted, so fearfully tempted, and that the reward which is to meet you, when you enter within the veil, where you must soon pass, will be to see the angel, once chained and defiled within him, set free from sin and glorified, and so know that to you it has been given, by your life of love and faith, to accomplish this glorious change.

I think very much on the subject on which you conversed with me once,—the future state of retribution. It is evident to me that the spirit of Christianity has produced in the human spirit a tenderness of love which wholly revolts from the old doctrine on the subject, and I observe the more Christ-like any one becomes, the more impossible it seems for him to accept it; and yet, on the contrary, it was Christ who said, "Fear Him that is able to destroy soul and body in hell," and the most appalling language on this subject is that of Christ himself. Certain ideas once prevalent certainly must be thrown off. An endless infliction for past sins was once the doctrine that we now generally reject. The doctrine as now taught is that of an eternal persistence in evil necessitating eternal punishment, since evil induces misery by an eternal nature of things, and this, I fear, is inferable from the analogies of nature, and confirmed by the whole implication of the Bible.

Is there any fair way of disposing of the current of assertion, and the still deeper undercurrent of implication, on this subject, without one which loosens all faith in revelation, and throws us on pure naturalism? But of one thing I am sure,—probation does not end with this life, and the number of the redeemed may therefore be infinitely greater than the world's history leads us to suppose.

The views expressed in this letter certainly throw light on many passages in "The Minister's Wooing."

The following letter, written to her daughter Georgiana, is introduced as revealing the spirit in which much of "The Minister's Wooing" was written:—

February 12, 1859.

MY DEAR GEORGIE,—Why haven't I written? Because, dear Georgie, I am like the dry, dead, leafless tree, and have only cold, dead, slumbering buds of hope on the end of stiff, hard, frozen twigs of thought, but no leaves, no blossoms; nothing to send to a little girl who doesn't know what to do with herself any more than a kitten. I am cold, weary, dead; everything is a burden to me.

I let my plants die by inches before my eyes, and do not water them, and I dread everything I do, and wish it was not to be done, and so when I get a letter from my little girl I smile and say, "Dear little puss, I will answer it;" and I sit hour after hour with folded hands, looking at the inkstand and dreading to begin. The fact is, pussy, mamma is tired. Life to you is gay and joyous, but to mamma it has been a battle in which the spirit is willing but the flesh weak, and she would be glad, like the woman in the St. Bernard, to lie down with her arms around the wayside cross, and sleep away into a brighter scene. Henry's fair, sweet face looks down upon me now and then from out a cloud, and I feel again all the bitterness of the eternal "No" which says I must never, never, in this life, see that face, lean on that arm, hear that voice. Not that my faith in God in the least fails, and that I do not believe that all this is for good. I do, and though not happy, I am blessed. Weak, weary as I am, I rest on Jesus in the innermost depth of my soul, and am quite sure that there is coming an inconceivable hour of beauty and glory when I shall regain Jesus, and he will give me back my beloved one, whom he is educating in a far higher sphere than I proposed. So do not mistake me,—only know that mamma is sitting weary by the wayside, feeling weak and worn, but in no sense discouraged.

Your affectionate mother,
H. B. S.

So is it ever: when with bold step we press our way into the holy place where genius hath wrought, we find it to be a place of sorrows. Art has its Gethsemane and its Calvary as well as religion. Our best loved books and sweetest songs are those "that tell of saddest thought."

The summer of 1859 found Mrs. Stowe again on her way to Europe, this time accompanied by all her children except the youngest.

CHAPTER XV

THE THIRD TRIP TO EUROPE, 1859

THIRD VISIT TO EUROPE.—LADY BYRON ON "THE
MINISTER'S WOOING."—SOME FOREIGN PEOPLE AND
THINGS AS THEY APPEARED TO PROFESSOR STOWE.—A
WINTER IN ITALY.—THINGS UNSEEN AND
UNREVEALED.—SPECULATIONS CONCERNING
SPIRITUALISM.—JOHN RUSKIN.—MRS. BROWNING.—THE
RETURN TO AMERICA.—LETTERS TO DR. HOLMES.

MRS. STOWE'S third and last trip to Europe was undertaken in the summer of 1859. In writing to Lady Byron in May of that year, she says: "I am at present writing something that interests me greatly, and may interest you, as an attempt to portray the heart and life of New England, its religion, theology, and manners. Sampson Low & Son are issuing it in numbers, and I should be glad to know how they strike you. It is to publish this work complete that I intend to visit England this summer."

The story thus referred to was "The Minister's Wooing," and Lady Byron's answer to the above, which is appended, leaves no room for doubt as to her appreciation of it. She writes:—

LONDON, *May 31, 1859.*

DEAR FRIEND,—I have found, particularly as to yourself, that if I did not answer from the first impulse, all had evaporated. Your letter came by the Niagara, which brought Fanny Kemble, to learn the loss of her *best* friend, that Miss Fitzhugh whom you saw at my house.

I have an intense interest in your new novel. More power in these few numbers than in any of your former writings, relatively, at least to my own mind. More power than in "Adam Bede," which is *the* book of the season, and well deserves a high place. Whether Mrs. Scudder will rival Mrs. Poyser, we shall see.

It would amuse you to hear my granddaughter and myself attempting to foresee the future of the "love story," being quite persuaded for the moment that James is at sea, and the minister about to ruin himself. We think that she will labor to be in love with the self-devoting man, under her mother's influence, and from that hyper-conscientiousness so common with good girls,—but we don't wish her to succeed. Then what is to become of her older lover? He—Time will show. I have just missed Dale Owen, with whom I wished to have conversed about the "Spiritualism." Harris is lecturing here on religion. I do not hear him praised. People are looking for helps to believe everywhere but in life,—in music, in architecture, in antiquity, in ceremony,—and upon all is written, "Thou shalt *not* believe." At least, if this be faith, happier the unbeliever. I am willing to see *through* that materialism, but if I am to rest there, I would rend the veil.

June 1. The day of the packet's sailing. I shall hope to be visited by you here. The best flowers sent me have been placed in your little vases, giving life, as it were, to the remembrance of you, though not to pass away like them.

Ever yours,
A. T. NOEL BYRON.

The entire family, with the exception of the youngest son, was abroad at this time. The two eldest daughters were in Paris, having previously sailed for Havre in March, in company with their cousin, Miss Beecher. On their arrival in Paris, they went directly to the house of their old friend, Madame Borione, and soon afterwards entered a Protestant school. The rest of the family, including Mrs. Stowe, her husband and youngest daughter, sailed for Liverpool early in August. At about the same time, Fred Stowe, in company with his friend Samuel Scoville, took passage for the same port in a sailing vessel. A comprehensive outline of the earlier portion of this foreign tour is given in the following letter written by Professor Stowe to the sole member of the family remaining in America:

CASTLE CHILLON, SWITZERLAND, *September 1, 1859.*

DEAR LITTLE CHARLEY,—We are all here except Fred, and all well. We have had a most interesting journey, of which I must give a brief account.

We sailed from New York in the steamer Asia, on the 3d of August [1859], a very hot day, and for ten days it was the hottest weather I ever knew at sea. We had a splendid ship's company, mostly foreigners, Italians, Spaniards, with a sprinkling of Scotch and Irish. We passed one big iceberg in the night close to, and as the iceberg wouldn't turn out for us we turned out for the iceberg, and were very glad to come off so. This was the night of the 9th of August, and after that we had cooler weather, and on the morning of the 13th the wind blew like all possessed, and so continued till afternoon. Sunday morning, the 14th, we got safe into Liverpool, landed, and went to the Adelphi Hotel. Mamma and Georgie were only a little sick on the way over, and that was the morning of the 13th.

As it was court time, the high sheriff of Lancashire, Sir Robert Gerauld, a fine, stout, old, gray-haired John Bull, came thundering up to the hotel at noon in his grand coach with six beautiful horses with outriders, and two trumpeters, and twelve men with javelins for a guard, all dressed in the gayest manner, and rushing along like Time in the primer, the trumpeters too-ti-toot-tooing like a house a-fire, and how I wished my little Charley had been there to see it!

Monday we wanted to go and see the court, so we went over to St. George's Hall, a most magnificent structure, that beats the Boston State House all hollow, and Sir Robert Gerauld himself met us, and said he would get us a good place. So he took us away round a narrow, crooked passage, and opened a little door, where we saw nothing but a great, crimson curtain, which he told us to put aside and go straight on; and where do you think we all found ourselves?

Right on the platform with the judges in their big wigs and long robes, and facing the whole crowded court! It was enough to frighten a body into fits, but we took it quietly as we could, and your mamma looked as meek as Moses in her little, battered straw hat and gray cloak, seeming to say, "I didn't come here o' purpose."

That same night we arrived in London, and Tuesday (August 16th), riding over the city, we called at Stafford House, and inquired if the Duchess of Sutherland was there. A servant came out and said the duchess was in and would be very glad to see us; so your mamma, Georgie, and I went walking up the magnificent staircase in the entrance hall, and the great, noble, brilliant duchess came sailing down the stairs to meet us, in her white morning dress (for it was only four o'clock in the afternoon, and she was not yet dressed for dinner), took your mamma into her great bosom, and folded her up till the little Yankee woman looked like a small gray kitten half covered in a snowbank, and kissed and kissed her, and then she took up little Georgie and kissed her, and then she took my hand, and didn't kiss me.

Next day we went to the duchess's villa, near Windsor Castle, and had a grand time riding round the park, sailing on the Thames, and eating the very best dinner that was ever set on a table.

We stayed in London till the 25th of August, and then went to Paris and found H. and E. and H. B. all well and happy; and on the 30th of August we all went to Geneva together, and to-day, the 1st of September, we all took a sail up the beautiful Lake Leman here in the midst of the Alps, close by the old castle of Chillon, about which Lord Byron has written a poem. In a day or two we shall go to Chamouni, and then Georgie and I will go back to Paris and London, and so home at the time appointed. Until then I remain as ever,

Your loving father,
C. E. STOWE.

Mrs. Stowe accompanied her husband and daughter to England, where, after traveling and visiting for two weeks, she bade them good-by and returned to her daughters in Switzerland. From Lausanne she writes under date of October 9th:—

MY DEAR HUSBAND,—Here we are at Lausanne, in the Hotel Gibbon, occupying the very parlor that the Ruskins had when we were here before. The day I left you I progressed prosperously to Paris. Reached there about one o'clock at night; could get no carriage, and finally had to turn in at a little hotel close by the station, where I slept till morning. I could not but think what if anything should happen to me there? Nobody knew me or where I was, but the bed was clean, the room respectable; so I locked my door and slept, then took a carriage in the morning, and found Madame Borione at breakfast. I write to-night, that you may get a letter from me at the earliest possible date after your return.

Instead of coming to Geneva in one day, I stopped over one night at Macon, got to Geneva the next day about four o'clock, and to Lausanne at eight. Coming up-stairs and opening the door, I found the whole party seated with their books and embroidery about a centre-table, and looking as homelike and cosy as possible. You may imagine the greetings, the kissing, laughing, and good times generally.

From Lausanne the merry party traveled toward Florence by easy stages, stopping at Lake Como, Milan, Verona, Venice, Genoa, and Leghorn. At Florence, where they arrived early in November, they met Fred Stowe and his friend, Samuel Scoville, and here they were also joined by their Brooklyn friends, the Howards. Thus it was a large and thoroughly congenial party that settled down in the old Italian city to spend the winter. From here Mrs. Stowe wrote weekly letters to her husband in Andover, and among them are the following, that not only throw light upon their mode of life, but illustrate a marked tendency of her mind:—

FLORENCE, *Christmas Day, 1859.*

MY DEAR HUSBAND,—I wish you all a Merry Christmas, hoping to spend the next one with you.

For us, we are expecting to spend this evening with quite a circle of American friends. With Scoville and Fred came L. Bacon (son of Dr. Bacon); a Mr. Porter, who is to study theology at Andover, and is now making the tour of Europe; Mr. Clarke, formerly minister at Cornwall; Mr. Jenkyns, of Lowell; Mr. and Mrs. Howard, John and Annie Howard, who came in most unexpectedly upon us last night. So we shall have quite a New England party, and shall sing Millais'

Christmas hymn in great force. Hope you will all do the same in the old stone cabin.

Our parlor is all trimmed with laurel and myrtle, looking like a great bower, and our mantel and table are redolent with bouquets of orange blossoms and pinks.

January 16, 1860.

MY DEAR HUSBAND,—Your letter received to-day has raised quite a weight from my mind, for it shows that at last you have received all mine, and that thus the chain of communication between us is unbroken. What you said about your spiritual experiences in feeling the presence of dear Henry with you, and, above all, the vibration of that mysterious guitar, was very pleasant to me. Since I have been in Florence, I have been distressed by inexpressible yearnings after him,— such sighings and outreachings, with a sense of utter darkness and separation, not only from him but from all spiritual communion with my God. But I have become acquainted with a friend through whom I receive consoling impressions of these things,—a Mrs. E., of Boston, a very pious, accomplished, and interesting woman, who has had a history much like yours in relation to spiritual manifestations.

Without doubt she is what the spiritualists would regard as a very powerful medium, but being a very earnest Christian, and afraid of getting led astray, she has kept carefully aloof from all circles and things of that nature. She came and opened her mind to me in the first place, to ask my advice as to what she had better do; relating experiences very similar to many of yours.

My advice was substantially to try the spirits whether they were of God,—to keep close to the Bible and prayer, and then accept whatever came. But I have found that when I am with her I receive very strong impressions from the spiritual world, so that I feel often sustained and comforted, as if I had been near to my Henry and other departed friends. This has been at times so strong as greatly to soothe and support me. I told her your experiences, in which she was greatly interested. She said it was so rare to hear of Christian and reliable people with such peculiarities.

I cannot, however, think that Henry strikes the guitar,—that must be Eliza. Her spirit has ever seemed to cling to that mode of manifestation, and if you would keep it in your sleeping-room, no doubt you would hear from it oftener. I have been reading lately a curious work from an old German in Paris who has been making experiments in spirit-writing. He purports to describe a series of meetings held in the presence of fifty witnesses, whose names he gives, in which writing has come on paper, without the apparition of hands or any pen or pencil, from various historical people.

He seems a devout believer in inspiration, and the book is curious for its mixture of all the phenomena, Pagan and Christian, going over Hindoo, Chinese, Greek, and Italian literature for examples, and then bringing similar ones from the Bible.

One thing I am convinced of,—that spiritualism is a reaction from the intense materialism of the present age. Luther, when he recognized a personal devil, was much nearer right. We ought to enter fully, at least, into the spiritualism of the Bible. Circles and spiritual jugglery I regard as the lying signs and wonders, with all deceivableness of unrighteousness; but there is a real scriptural spiritualism which has fallen into disuse, and must be revived, and there are, doubtless, people who, from some constitutional formation, can more readily receive the impressions of the surrounding spiritual world. Such were apostles, prophets, and workers of miracles.

Sunday evening. To-day I went down to sit with Mrs. E. in her quiet parlor. We read in Revelation together, and talked of the saints and spirits of the just made perfect, till it seemed, as it always does when with her, as if Henry were close by me. Then a curious thing happened. She has a little Florentine guitar which hangs in her parlor, quite out of reach. She and I were talking, and her sister, a very matter-of-fact, practical body, who attends to temporals for her, was arranging a little lunch for us, when suddenly the bass string of the guitar was struck loudly and distinctly.

"Who struck that guitar?" said the sister. We both looked up and saw that no body or thing was on that side of the room. After the sister had gone out, Mrs. E. said, "Now, that is strange! I asked last night that if any spirit was present with us after you came to-day, that it would try to touch that guitar." A little while after her husband came in, and as we were talking we were all stopped by a peculiar sound, as if somebody had drawn a hand across all the strings at once. We marveled, and I remembered the guitar at home.

What think you? Have you had any more manifestations, any truths from the spirit world?

About the end of February the pleasant Florentine circle broke up, and Mrs. Stowe and her party journeyed to Rome, where they remained until the middle of April. We next find them in Naples, starting on a six days' trip to Castellamare, Sorrento, Salerno, Pæstum, and Amalfi; then up Vesuvius, and to the Blue Grotto of Capri, and afterwards back to Rome by diligence. Leaving Rome on May 9th, they traveled leisurely towards Paris, which they reached on the 27th. From there Mrs. Stowe wrote to her husband on May 28th:—

Since my last letter a great change has taken place in our plans, in consequence of which our passage for America is engaged by the Europa, which sails the 16th of June; so, if all goes well, we are due in Boston four weeks from this date. I long for home, for my husband and children, for my room, my yard and garden, for the beautiful trees of Andover. We will make a very happy home, and our children will help us.

Affectionately yours,
HATTY.

This extended and pleasant tour was ended with an equally pleasant homeward voyage, for on the Europa were found Nathaniel Hawthorne and James T. Fields, who proved most delightful traveling companions.

While Mrs. Stowe fully enjoyed her foreign experiences, she was so thoroughly American in every fibre of her being that she was always thankful to return to her own land and people. She could not, therefore, in any degree reciprocate the views of Mr.

Ruskin on this subject, as expressed in the following letter, received soon after her return to Andover:—

GENEVA, *June 18, 1860.*

DEAR MRS. STOWE,—It takes a great deal, when I am at Geneva, to make me wish myself anywhere else, and, of all places else, in London; nevertheless, I very heartily wish at this moment that I were looking out on the Norwood Hills, and were expecting you and the children to breakfast to-morrow.

I had very serious thoughts, when I received your note, of running home; but I expected that very day an American friend, Mr. S., who I thought would miss me more here than you would in London; so I stayed.

What a dreadful thing it is that people should have to go to America again, after coming to Europe! It seems to me an inversion of the order of nature. I think America is a sort of "United" States of Probation, out of which all wise people, being once delivered, and having obtained entrance into this better world, should never be expected to return (sentence irremediably ungrammatical), particularly when they have been making themselves cruelly pleasant to friends here. My friend Norton, whom I met first on this very blue lake water, had no business to go back to Boston again, any more than you.

I was waiting for S. at the railroad station on Thursday, and thinking of you, naturally enough,—it seemed so short a while since we were there together. I managed to get hold of Georgie as she was crossing the rails, and packed her in opposite my mother and beside me, and was thinking myself so clever, when you sent that rascally courier for her! I never forgave him any of his behavior after his imperativeness on that occasion.

And so she is getting nice and strong? Ask her, please, when you write, with my love, whether, when she stands now behind the great stick, one can see much of her on each side?

So you have been seeing the Pope and all his Easter performances? I congratulate you, for I suppose it is something like "Positively the last appearance on any stage." What was the use of thinking about *him*? You should have had

- 268 -

your own thoughts about what was to come after him. I don't mean that Roman Catholicism will die out so quickly. It will last pretty nearly as long as Protestantism, which keeps it up; but I wonder what is to come next. That is the main question just now for everybody.

So you are coming round to Venice, after all? We shall all have to come to it, depend upon it, some way or another. There never has been anything in any other part of the world like Venetian strength well developed.

I've no heart to write about anything in Europe to you now. When are you coming back again? Please send me a line as soon as you get safe over, to say you are all—wrong, but not lost in the Atlantic.

I don't know if you will ever get this letter, but I hope you will think it worth while to glance again at the Denmark Hill pictures; so I send this to my father, who, I hope, will be able to give it you.

I really am very sorry you are going,—you and yours; and that is absolute fact, and I shall not enjoy my Swiss journey at all so much as I might. It was a shame of you not to give me warning before. I could have stopped at Paris so easily for you! All good be with you! Remember me devotedly to the young ladies, and believe me ever affectionately yours,

J. RUSKIN.

In Rome Mrs. Stowe had formed a warm friendship with the Brownings, with whom she afterwards maintained a correspondence. The following letter from Mrs. Browning was written a year after their first meeting.

ROME, 126 VIA FELICE, *14 March, 1861.*

MY DEAR MRS. STOWE,—Let me say one word first. Your letter, which would have given me pleasure if I had been in the midst of pleasures, came to me when little beside could have pleased. Dear friend, let me say it, I had had a great blow and loss in England, and you wrote things in that letter which seemed meant for me, meant to do me good, and which did me good,—the first good any letter or any talk did me; and it struck me as strange, as more than a coincidence, that your first word since we parted in Rome last spring should come to me in Rome, and bear so directly on an experience which you did not know of. I thank you very much.

The earnest stanzas I sent to England for one who wanted them even more than I. I don't know how people can keep up their prejudices against spiritualism with tears in their eyes,— how they are not, at least, thrown on the "wish that it might be true," and the investigation of the phenomena, by that abrupt shutting in their faces of the door of death, which shuts them out from the sight of their beloved. My tendency is to beat up against it like a crying child. Not that this emotional impulse is the best for turning the key and obtaining safe conclusions,— no. I did not write before because I always do shrink from touching my own griefs, one feels at first so sore that nothing but stillness is borne. It is only after, when one is better, that one can express one's self at all. This is so with me, at least, though perhaps it ought not to be so with a poet.

If you saw my "De Profundis" you must understand that it was written nearly twenty years ago, and referred to what went before. Mr. Howard's affliction made me think of the MS. (in reference to a sermon of Dr. Beecher's in the "Independent"), and I pulled it out of a secret place and sent it to America, not thinking that the publication would fall in so nearly with a new grief of mine as to lead to misconceptions. In fact the poem would have been an exaggeration in that case, and unsuitable in other respects.

It refers to the greatest affliction of my life,—the only time when I felt *despair*,—written a year after or more. Forgive all these reticences. My husband calls me "peculiar" in some things,—peculiarly *lâche*, perhaps. I can't articulate some names, or speak of certain afflictions;—no, not to *him*,—not after all these years! It's a sort of *dumbness* of the soul. Blessed are those who can speak, I say. But don't you see from this how I must want "spiritualism" above most persons?

Now let me be ashamed of this egotism, together with the rest of the weakness obtruded on you here, when I should rather have congratulated you, my dear friend, on the great crisis you are passing through in America. If the North is found noble enough to stand fast on the moral question, whatever the loss or diminution of territory, God and just men will see you greater and more glorious as a nation.

I had much anxiety for you after the Seward and Adams speeches, but the danger seems averted by that fine madness of the South which seems judicial. The tariff movement we should regret deeply (and do, some of us), only I am told it was wanted in order to persuade those who were less accessible to moral argument. It's eking out the holy water with ditch water. If the Devil flees before it, even so, let us be content. How you must feel, *you* who have done so much to set this accursed slavery in the glare of the world, convicting it of hideousness! They should raise a statue to you in America and elsewhere.

Meanwhile I am reading you in the "Independent," sent to me by Mr. Tilton, with the greatest interest. Your new novel opens beautifully.

Do write to me and tell me of yourself and the subjects which interest us both. It seems to me that our Roman affairs may linger a little (while the Papacy bleeds slowly to death in its finances) on account of this violent clerical opposition in France. Otherwise we were prepared for the fall of the house any morning. Prince Napoleon's speech represents, with whatever slight discrepancy, the inner mind of the emperor. It occupied seventeen columns of the "Moniteur" and was magnificent. Victor Emmanuel wrote to thank him for it in the name of Italy, and even the English papers praised it as "a masterly exposition of the policy of France." It is settled that we shall wait for Venice. It will not be for long. Hungary is *only* waiting, and even in the ashes of Poland there are flickering sparks. Is it the beginning of the restitution of all things?

Here in Rome there are fewer English than usual, and more empty houses. There is a new story every morning, and nobody to cut off the head of the Scheherazade. Yesterday the Pope was going to Venice directly, and, the day before, fixed the hour for Victor Emmanuel's coming, and the day before *that* brought a letter from Cavour to Antonelli about sweeping the streets clean for the feet of the king. The poor Romans live on these stories, while the Holy Father and king of Naples meet holding one another's hands, and cannot speak for sobs. The little queen, however, is a heroine in her way and from her point of view, and when she drives about in a common fiacre, looking very pretty under her only crown left of golden hair, one must feel sorry that she was not born and married nearer to holy ground. My husband prays you to remember him, and I ask your daughters to remember both of us. Our boy rides his pony and studies under his abbé, and keeps a pair of red cheeks, thank God.

I ought to send you more about the society in Rome, but I have lived much alone this winter, and have little to tell you. Dr. Manning and Mr. De Vere stay away, not bearing, perhaps, to see the Pope in his agony.

Your ever affectionate friend,
ELIZABETH B. BROWNING.

Soon after her return to America Mrs. Stowe began a correspondence with Dr. Oliver Wendell Holmes, which opened the way for the warm friendship that has stood the test of years. Of this correspondence the two following letters, written about this time, are of attention.

ANDOVER, *September 9, 1860.*

DEAR DR. HOLMES,—I have had an impulse upon me for a long time to write you a line of recognition and sympathy, in response to those that reached me monthly in your late story in the "Atlantic" ("Elsie Venner").

I know not what others may think of it, since I have seen nobody since my return; but to me it is of deeper and broader interest than anything you have done yet, and I feel an intense curiosity concerning that underworld of thought from which like bubbles your incidents and remarks often seem to burst up. The foundations of moral responsibility, the interlacing laws of nature and spirit, and their relations to us here and hereafter, are topics which I ponder more and more, and on which only one medically educated can write *well*. I think a course of medical study ought to be required of all ministers.

How I should like to talk with you upon the strange list of topics suggested in the schoolmaster's letter! They are bound to agitate the public mind more and more, and it is of the chiefest importance to learn, if we can, to think soundly and wisely of them. Nobody can be a sound theologian who has not had his mind drawn to think with reverential fear on these topics.

Allow me to hint that the monthly numbers are not long enough. Get us along a little faster. You must work this well out. Elaborate and give us all the particulars. Old Sophie is a jewel; give us more of her. I have seen her. Could you ever come out and spend a day with us? The professor and I would so like to have a talk on some of these matters with you!

Very truly yours,
H. B. STOWE.

ANDOVER, *February 18, 1861.*

DEAR DOCTOR,—I was quite indignant to hear yesterday of the very unjust and stupid attack upon you in the ———. Mr. Stowe has written to them a remonstrance which I hope they will allow to appear as he wrote it, and over his name. He was well acquainted with your father and feels the impropriety of the thing.

But, my dear friend, in being shocked, surprised, or displeased personally with such things, we must consider other people's natures. A man or woman may wound us to the quick without knowing it, or meaning to do so, simply through difference of fibre. As Cowper hath somewhere happily said:—

"Oh, why are farmers made so coarse,
Or clergy made so fine?
A kick that scarce might move a horse
Might kill a sound divine."

When once people get ticketed, and it is known that one is a hammer, another a saw, and so on, if we happen to get a taste of their quality we cannot help being hurt, to be sure, but we shall not take it ill of them. There be pious, well-intending beetles, wedges, hammers, saws, and all other kinds of implements, good—except where they come in the way of our fingers—and from a beetle you can have only a beetle's gospel.

I have suffered in my day from this sort of handling, which is worse for us women, who must never answer, and once when I wrote to Lady Byron, feeling just as you do about some very stupid and unkind things that had invaded my personality, she answered me, "Words do not kill, my dear, or I should have been dead long ago."

There is much true religion and kindness in the world, after all, and as a general thing he who has struck a nerve would be very sorry for it if he only knew what he had done.

I would say nothing, if I were you. There is eternal virtue in silence.

I must express my pleasure with the closing chapters of "Elsie." They are nobly and beautifully done, and quite come up to what I wanted to complete my idea of her character. I am quite satisfied with it now. It is an artistic creation, original and beautiful.

Believe me to be your true friend,
H. B. STOWE.

CHAPTER XVI

THE CIVIL WAR, 1860-1865

THE OUTBREAK OF CIVIL WAR.—MRS. STOWE'S SON
ENLISTS.—THANKSGIVING DAY IN WASHINGTON.—THE
PROCLAMATION OF EMANCIPATION.—REJOICINGS IN
BOSTON.—FRED STOWE AT GETTYSBURG.—LEAVING
ANDOVER AND SETTLING IN HARTFORD.—A REPLY TO
THE WOMEN OF ENGLAND.—LETTERS FROM JOHN
BRIGHT, ARCHBISHOP WHATELY, AND NATHANIEL
HAWTHORNE.

IMMEDIATELY after Mrs. Stowe's return from Europe, it
became only too evident that the nation was rapidly and inevitably
drifting into all the horrors of civil war. To use her own words: "It
was God's will that this nation—the North as well as the South—
should deeply and terribly suffer for the sin of consenting to and
encouraging the great oppressions of the South; that the ill-gotten
wealth, which had arisen from striking hands with oppression and
robbery, should be paid back in the taxes of war; that the blood of
the poor slave, that had cried so many years from the ground in
vain, should be answered by the blood of the sons from the best
hearthstones through all the free States; that the slave mothers,
whose tears nobody regarded, should have with them a great
company of weepers, North and South,—Rachels weeping for
their children and refusing to be comforted; that the free States,
who refused to listen when they were told of lingering starvation,
cold, privation, and barbarous cruelty, as perpetrated on the slave,
should have lingering starvation, cold, hunger, and cruelty doing its
work among their own sons, at the hands of these slave-masters,
with whose sins our nation had connived."

Mrs. Stowe spoke from personal experience, having seen her
own son go forth in the ranks of those who first responded to the
President's call for volunteers. He was one of the first to place his
name on the muster-roll of Company A of the First Massachusetts

Volunteers. While his regiment was still at the camp in Cambridge, Mrs. Stowe was called to Brooklyn on important business, from which place she writes to her husband under the date June 11, 1861:—

"Yesterday noon Henry (Ward Beecher) came in, saying that the Commonwealth, with the First (Massachusetts) Regiment on board, had just sailed by. Immediately I was of course eager to get to Jersey City to see Fred. Sister Eunice said she would go with me, and in a few minutes she, Hatty, Sam Scoville, and I were in a carriage, driving towards the Fulton Ferry. Upon reaching Jersey City we found that the boys were dining in the depot, an immense building with many tracks and platforms. It has a great cast-iron gallery just under the roof, apparently placed there with prophetic instinct of these times. There was a crowd of people pressing against the grated doors, which were locked, but through which we could see the soldiers. It was with great difficulty that we were at last permitted to go inside, and that object seemed to be greatly aided by a bit of printed satin that some man gave Mr. Scoville.

"When we were in, a vast area of gray caps and blue overcoats was presented. The boys were eating, drinking, smoking, talking, singing, and laughing. Company A was reported to be here, there, and everywhere. At last S. spied Fred in the distance, and went leaping across the tracks towards him. Immediately afterwards a blue-overcoated figure bristling with knapsack and haversack, and looking like an assortment of packages, came rushing towards us.

"Fred was overjoyed, you may be sure, and my first impulse was to wipe his face with my handkerchief before I kissed him. He was in high spirits, in spite of the weight of blue overcoat, knapsack, etc., etc., that he would formerly have declared intolerable for half an hour. I gave him my handkerchief and Eunice gave him hers, with a sheer motherly instinct that is so strong within her, and then we filled his haversack with oranges.

"We stayed with Fred about two hours, during which time the gallery was filled with people, cheering and waving their handkerchiefs. Every now and then the band played inspiriting airs, in which the soldiers joined with hearty voices. While some of the companies sang, others were drilled, and all seemed to be having a general jollification. The meal that had been provided was plentiful, and consisted of coffee, lemonade, sandwiches, etc.

"On our way out we were introduced to the Rev. Mr. Cudworth, chaplain of the regiment. He is a fine-looking man, with black eyes and hair, set off by a white havelock. He wore a sword, and Fred, touching it, asked, 'Is this for use or ornament, sir?'

"'Let me see you in danger,' answered the chaplain, 'and you'll find out.'

"I said to him I supposed he had had many an one confided to his kind offices, but I could not forbear adding one more to the number. He answered, 'You may rest assured, Mrs. Stowe, I will do all in my power.'

"We parted from Fred at the door. He said he felt lonesome enough Saturday evening on the Common in Boston, where everybody was taking leave of somebody, and he seemed to be the only one without a friend, but that this interview made up for it all.

"I also saw young Henry. Like Fred he is mysteriously changed, and wears an expression of gravity and care. So our boys come to manhood in a day. Now I am watching anxiously for the evening paper to tell me that the regiment has reached Washington in safety."

In November, 1862, Mrs. Stowe was invited to visit Washington, to be present at a great thanksgiving dinner provided for the thousands of fugitive slaves who had flocked to the city. She accepted the invitation the more gladly because her son's regiment was encamped near the city, and she should once more see him. He was now Lieutenant Stowe, having honestly won his promotion by bravery on more than one hard-fought field. She writes of this visit:—

Imagine a quiet little parlor with a bright coal fire, and the gaslight burning above a centre-table, about which Hatty, Fred, and I are seated. Fred is as happy as happy can be to be with mother and sister once more. All day yesterday we spent in getting him. First we had to procure a permit to go to camp, then we went to the fort where the colonel is, and then to another where the brigadier-general is stationed. I was so afraid they would not let him come with us, and was never happier than when at last he sprang into the carriage free to go with us for forty-eight hours. "Oh!" he exclaimed in a sort of rapture, "this pays for a year and a half of fighting and hard work!"

We tried hard to get the five o'clock train out to Laurel, where J.'s regiment is stationed, as we wanted to spend Sunday all together; but could not catch it, and so had to content ourselves with what we could have. I have managed to secure a room for Fred next ours, and feel as though I had my boy at home once more. He is looking very well, has grown in thickness, and is as loving and affectionate as a boy can be.

I have just been writing a pathetic appeal to the brigadier-general to let him stay with us a week. I have also written to General Buckingham in regard to changing him from the infantry, in which there seems to be no prospect of anything but garrison duty, to the cavalry, which is full of constant activity.

General B. called on us last evening. He seemed to think the prospect before us was, at best, of a long war. He was the officer deputed to carry the order to General McClellan relieving him of command of the army. He carried it to him in his tent about twelve o'clock at night. Burnside was there. McClellan said it was very unexpected, but immediately turned over the command. I said I thought he ought to have expected it after having so disregarded the President's order. General B. smiled and said he supposed McClellan had done that so often before that he had no idea any notice would be taken of it this time.

Now, as I am very tired, I must close, and remain as always, lovingly yours,

HATTY.

During the darkest and most bitter period of the Civil War, Mrs. Stowe penned the following letter to the Duchess of Argyll:—

ANDOVER, *July 31, 1863.*

MY DEAR FRIEND,—Your lovely, generous letter was a real comfort to me, and reminded me that a year—and, alas! a whole year—had passed since I wrote to your dear mother, of whom I think so often as one of God's noblest creatures, and one whom it comforts me to think is still in our world.

So many, good and noble, have passed away whose friendship was such a pride, such a comfort to me! Your noble father, Lady Byron, Mrs. Browning,—their spirits are as perfect as ever passed to the world of light. I grieve about your dear mother's eyes. I have thought about you all, many a sad, long, quiet hour, as I have lain on my bed and looked at the pictures on my wall; one, in particular, of the moment before the Crucifixion, which is the first thing I look at when I wake in the morning. I think how suffering is, and must be, the portion of noble spirits, and no lot so brilliant that must not first or last dip into the shadow of that eclipse. Prince Albert, too, the ideal knight, the *Prince Arthur* of our times, the good, wise, steady head and heart we—that is, our world, we Anglo-Saxons—need so much. And the Queen! yes, I have thought of and prayed for her, too. But could a woman hope to have *always* such a heart, and yet ever be weaned from earth "all this and heaven, too"?

Under my picture I have inscribed, "Forasmuch as Christ also hath suffered for us in the flesh, arm yourselves with the same mind."

This year has been one long sigh, one smothering sob, to me. And I thank God that we have as yet one or two generous friends in England who understand and feel for our cause.

The utter failure of Christian, anti-slavery England, in those *instincts* of a right heart which always can see where the cause of liberty lies, has been as bitter a grief to me as was the similar prostration of all our American religious people in the day of the Fugitive Slave Law. Exeter Hall is a humbug, a pious humbug, like the rest. Lord Shaftesbury. Well, let him go; he is a Tory, and has, after all, the instincts of his class. But I saw *your* duke's speech to his tenants! That was grand! If *he* can see these things, they are to be seen, and why cannot Exeter Hall see them? It is simply the want of the honest heart.

Why do the horrible barbarities of *Southern* soldiers cause no comment? Why is the sympathy of the British Parliament reserved for the poor women of New Orleans, deprived of their elegant amusement of throwing vitriol into soldiers' faces, and practicing indecencies inconceivable in any other state of society? Why is *all* expression of sympathy on the *Southern* side? There is a class of women in New Orleans whom Butler protects from horrible barbarities, that up to his day have been practiced on them by these so-called New Orleans ladies, but British sympathy has ceased to notice *them*. You see I am bitter. I am. You wonder at my brother. He is a man, and feels a thousand times more than I can, and deeper than all he ever has expressed, the spirit of these things. You must not wonder, therefore. Remember it is the moment when every nerve is vital; it is our agony; we tread the winepress alone, and they whose cheap rhetoric has been for years pushing us into it now desert *en masse*. I thank my God I always loved and trusted most those who now *do* stand true,—your family, your duke, yourself, your noble mother. I have lost Lady Byron. Her great heart, her eloquent letters, would have been such a joy to me! And Mrs. Browning, oh such a heroic woman! None of her poems can express what *she* was,—so grand, so comprehending, so strong, with such inspired insight! She stood by Italy through its crisis. Her heart was with all good through the world. Your prophecy that we shall come out better, truer, stronger, will, I am confident, be true, and it was worthy of yourself and your good lineage.

Slavery will be sent out by this agony. We are only in the throes and ravings of the exorcism. The roots of the cancer have gone everywhere, but they must die—will. Already the Confiscation Bill is its natural destruction. Lincoln has been too slow. He should have done it sooner, and with an impulse, but come it must, come it will. Your mother will live to see slavery abolished, *unless* England forms an alliance to hold it up. England is the great reliance of the slave-power to-day, and next to England the faltering weakness of the North, which palters and dare not fire the great broadside for fear of hitting friends. These things *must* be done, and sudden, sharp remedies are *mercy*. Just now we are in a dark hour; but whether God be with us or not, I know He is with the slave, and with his redemption will come the solution of our question. I have long known *what* and who we had to deal with in this, for when I wrote "Uncle Tom's Cabin" I had letters addressed to me showing a state of society perfectly *inconceivable*. That they violate graves, make drinking-cups of skulls, that *ladies* wear cameos cut from bones, and treasure scalps, is no surprise to me. If I had written what I knew of the obscenity, brutality, and cruelty of that society down there, society would have cast out the books; and it is for their interest, the interest of the whole race in the South, that we should succeed. I wish *them* no ill, feel no bitterness; they have had a Dahomian education which makes them savage. We don't expect any more of *them*, but if slavery is destroyed, one generation of education and liberty will efface these stains. They will come to themselves, these States, and be glad it is over.

I am using up my paper to little purpose. Please give my best love to your dear mother. I am going to write to her. If I only could have written the things I have often thought! I am going to put on her bracelet, with the other dates, that of the abolition of slavery in the District of Columbia. Remember me to the duke and to your dear children. My husband desires his best regards, my daughters also.

I am lovingly ever yours,
H. B. STOWE.

Later in the year we hear again from her son in the army, and this time the news comes in a chaplain's letter from the terrible field of Gettysburg. He writes:—

GETTYSBURG, PA., *Saturday, July 11*, 9.30 P. M.

MRS. H. B. STOWE:

Dear Madam,—Among the thousands of wounded and dying men on this war-scarred field, I have just met with your son, Captain Stowe. If you have not already heard from him, it may cheer your heart to know that he is in the hands of good, kind friends. He was struck by a fragment of a shell, which entered his right ear. He is quiet and cheerful, longs to see some member of his family, and is, above all, anxious that they should hear from him as soon as possible. I assured him I would write at once, and though I am wearied by a week's labor here among scenes of terrible suffering, I know that, to a mother's anxious heart, even a hasty scrawl about her boy will be more than welcome.

May God bless and sustain you in this troubled time!

Yours with sincere sympathy,
J. M. CROWELL.

The wound in the head was not fatal, and after weary months of intense suffering it imperfectly healed; but the cruel iron had too nearly touched the brain of the young officer, and never again was he what he had been. Soon after the war his mother bought a plantation in Florida, largely in the hope that the out-of-door life connected with its management might be beneficial to her afflicted son. He remained on it for several years, and then, being possessed with the idea that a long sea voyage would do him more good than anything else, sailed from New York to San Francisco around the Horn. That he reached the latter city in safety is known; but that is all. No word from him or concerning him has ever reached the loving hearts that have waited so anxiously for it, and of his ultimate fate nothing is known.

Meantime, the year 1863 was proving eventful in many other ways to Mrs. Stowe. In the first place, the long and pleasant Andover connection of Professor Stowe was about to be severed, and the family were to remove to Hartford, Conn. They were to occupy a house that Mrs. Stowe was building on the bank of Park River. It was erected in a grove of oaks that had in her girlhood been one of Mrs. Stowe's favorite resorts. Here, with her friend Georgiana May, she had passed many happy hours, and had often declared that if she were ever able to build a house, it should stand in that very place. Here, then, it was built in 1863, and as the location was at that time beyond the city limits, it formed, with its extensive, beautiful groves, a particularly charming place of residence. Beautiful as it was, however, it was occupied by the family for only a few years. The needs of the growing city caused factories to spring up in the neighborhood, and to escape their encroachments the Stowes in 1873 bought and moved into the house on Forest Street that has ever since been their Northern home. Thus the only house Mrs. Stowe ever planned and built for herself has been appropriated to the use of factory hands, and is now a tenement occupied by several families.

Another important event of 1863 was the publishing of that charming story of Italy, "Agnes of Sorrento," which had been begun nearly four years before. This story suggested itself to Mrs. Stowe while she was abroad during the winter of 1859-60. The origin of the story is as follows: One evening, at a hotel in Florence, it was proposed that the various members of the party should write short stories and read them for the amusement of the company. Mrs. Stowe took part in this literary contest, and the result was the first rough sketch of "Agnes of Sorrento." From this beginning was afterwards elaborated "Agnes of Sorrento," with a dedication to Annie Howard, who was one of the party.

THE OLD HOME AT HARTFORD

Not the least important event of the year to Mrs. Stowe, and the world at large through her instrumentality, was the publication in the "Atlantic Monthly" of her reply to the address of the women of England. The "reply" is substantially as follows:—

January, 1863.

A REPLY

To "The affectionate and Christian Address of many thousands of Women of Great Britain and Ireland to their Sisters, the Women of the United States of America," (signed by)

- ANNA MARIA BEDFORD (Duchess of Bedford).

- OLIVIA CECILIA COWLEY (Countess Cowley).

- CONSTANCE GROSVENOR (Countess Grosvenor).

- HARRIET SUTHERLAND (Duchess of Sutherland).

- ELIZABETH ARGYLL (Duchess of Argyll).

- ELIZABETH FORTESCUE (Countess Fortescue).

- EMILY SHAFTESBURY (Countess of Shaftesbury).

- MARY RUTHVEN (Baroness Ruthven).

- M. A. MILMAN (wife of Dean of St. Paul).

- R. BUXTON (daughter of Sir Thomas Fowell Buxton).

- CAROLINE AMELIA OWEN (wife of Professor Owen).

- MRS. CHARLES WINDHAM.

- C. A. HATHERTON (Baroness Hatherton).

- ELIZABETH DUCIE (Countess Dowager of Ducie).

- CECILIA PARKE (wife of Baron Parke).

- MARY ANN CHALLIS (wife of the Lord Mayor of London).

- E. GORDON (Duchess Dowager of Gordon).

- ANNA M. L. MELVILLE (daughter of Earl of Leven and Melville).

- GEORGIANA EBRINGTON (Lady Ebrington).

- A. HILL (Viscountess Hill).

- MRS. GOBAT (wife of Bishop Gobat of Jerusalem).

- E. PALMERSTON (Viscountess Palmerston).

- (And others).

SISTERS,—More than eight years ago you sent to us in America a document with the above heading. It is as follows:—

"A common origin, a common faith, and, we sincerely believe, a common cause, urge us, at the present moment, to address you on the subject of that system of negro slavery which still prevails so extensively, and, even under kindly disposed masters, with such frightful results, in many of the vast regions of the Western world.

"We will not dwell on the ordinary topics,—on the progress of civilization, on the advance of freedom everywhere, on the rights and requirements of the nineteenth century; but we appeal to you very seriously to reflect, and to ask counsel of God, how far such a state of things is in accordance with his Holy Word, the inalienable rights of immortal souls, and the pure and merciful spirit of the Christian religion. We do not shut our eyes to the difficulties, nay, the dangers, that might beset the immediate abolition of that long-established system. We see and admit the necessity of preparation for so great an event; but, in speaking of indispensable preliminaries, we cannot be silent on those laws of your country which, in direct contravention of God's own law, 'instituted in the time of man's innocency,' deny in effect to the slave the sanctity of marriage, with all its joys, rights, and obligations; which separate, at the will of the master, the wife from the husband, and the children from the parents. Nor can we be silent on that awful system which, either by statute or by custom, interdicts to any race of men, or any portion of the human family, education in the truths of the gospel and the ordinances of Christianity. A remedy applied to these two evils alone would commence the amelioration of their sad condition. We appeal to you then, as sisters, as wives, and as mothers, to raise your voices to your fellow-citizens, and your prayers to God, for the removal of this affliction and disgrace from the Christian world.

"We do not say these things in a spirit of self-complacency, as though our nation were free from the guilt it perceives in others.

"We acknowledge with grief and shame our heavy share in this great sin. We acknowledge that our forefathers introduced, nay compelled the adoption, of slavery in those mighty colonies. We humbly confess it before Almighty God; and it is because we so deeply feel and unfeignedly avow our own complicity, that we now venture to implore your aid to wipe away our common crime and our common dishonor."

This address, splendidly illuminated on vellum, was sent to our shores at the head of twenty-six folio volumes, containing considerably more than half a million of signatures of British women. It was forwarded to me with a letter from a British nobleman, now occupying one of the highest official positions in England, with a request on behalf of these ladies that it should be in any possible way presented to the attention of my countrywomen.

This memorial, as it now stands in its solid oaken case, with its heavy folios, each bearing on its back the imprint of the American eagle, forms a most unique library, a singular monument of an international expression of a moral idea. No right-thinking person can find aught to be objected against the substance or form of this memorial. It is temperate, just, and kindly; and on the high ground of Christian equality, where it places itself, may be regarded as a perfectly proper expression of sentiment, as between blood relations and equals in two different nations. The signatures to this appeal are not the least remarkable part of it; for, beginning at the very steps of the throne, they go down to the names of women in the very humblest conditions in life, and represent all that Great Britain possesses, not only of highest and wisest, but of plain, homely common sense and good feeling. Names of wives of cabinet ministers appear on the same page with the names of wives of humble labourers,—names of duchesses and countesses, of wives of generals, ambassadors, savants, and men of letters, mingled with names traced in trembling characters by hands evidently unused to hold the pen, and stiffened by lowly toil. Nay, so deep and expansive was the feeling, that British subjects in foreign lands had their representation. Among the signatures are those of foreign residents, from Paris to Jerusalem. Autographs so diverse, and collected from sources so various, have seldom been found in juxtaposition. They remain at this day a silent witness of a most singular tide of feeling which at that time swept over the British community and *made* for itself an expression, even at the risk of offending the sensibilities of an equal and powerful nation.

No reply to that address, in any such tangible and monumental form, has ever been possible. It was impossible to canvass our vast territories with the zealous and indefatigable industry with which England was canvassed for signatures. In America, those possessed of the spirit which led to this efficient action had no leisure for it. All their time and energies were already absorbed in direct efforts to remove the great evil, concerning which the minds of their English sisters had been newly aroused, and their only answer was the silent continuance of these efforts.

From the slaveholding States, however, as was to be expected, came a flood of indignant recrimination and rebuke. No one act, perhaps, ever produced more frantic irritation, or called out more unsparing abuse. It came with the whole united weight of the British aristocracy and commonalty on the most diseased and sensitive part of our national life; and it stimulated that fierce excitement which was working before, and has worked since, till it has broken out into open war.

The time has come, however, when such an astonishing page has been turned, in the anti-slavery history of America, that the women of our country, feeling that the great anti-slavery work to which their English sisters exhorted them is almost done, may properly and naturally feel moved to reply to their appeal, and lay before them the history of what has occurred since the receipt of their affectionate and Christian address.

Your address reached us just as a great moral conflict was coming to its intensest point. The agitation kept up by the anti-slavery portion of America, by England, and by the general sentiment of humanity in Europe, had made the situation of the slaveholding aristocracy intolerable. As one of them at the time expressed it, they felt themselves under the ban of the civilized world. Two courses only were open to them: to abandon slave institutions, the sources of their wealth and political power, or to assert them with such an overwhelming national force as to compel the respect and assent of mankind. They chose the latter.

To this end they determined to seize on and control all the resources of the Federal Government, and to spread their institutions through new States and Territories until the balance of power should fall into their hands and they should be able to force slavery into all the free States.

A leading Southern senator boasted that he would yet call the roll of his slaves on Bunker Hill; and for a while the political successes of the slave-power were such as to suggest to New England that this was no impossible event.

They repealed the Missouri Compromise, which had hitherto stood like the Chinese wall, between our Northwestern Territories and the irruptions of slaveholding barbarians.

Then came the struggle between freedom and slavery in the new territory; the battle for Kansas and Nebraska, fought with fire and sword and blood, where a race of men, of whom John Brown was the immortal type, acted over again the courage, the perseverance, and the military-religious ardor of the old Covenanters of Scotland, and like them redeemed the ark of liberty at the price of their own blood, and blood dearer than their own.

The time of the Presidential canvass which elected Mr. Lincoln was the crisis of this great battle. The conflict had become narrowed down to the one point of the extension of slave territory. If the slaveholders could get States enough, they could control and rule; if they were outnumbered by free States, their institutions, by the very law of their nature, would die of suffocation. Therefore Fugitive Slave Law, District of Columbia, Inter-State Slave-trade, and what not, were all thrown out of sight for a grand rally on this vital point. A President was elected pledged to opposition to this one thing alone,—a man known to be in favor of the Fugitive Slave Law and other so-called compromises of the Constitution, but honest and faithful in his determination on this one subject. That this was indeed the vital point was shown by the result. The moment Lincoln's election was ascertained, the slaveholders resolved to destroy the Union they could no longer control.

They met and organized a Confederacy which they openly declared to be the first republic founded on the right and determination of the white man to enslave the black man, and, spreading their banners, declared themselves to the Christian world of the nineteenth century as a nation organized with the full purpose and intent of perpetuating slavery.

But in the course of the struggle that followed, it became important for the new confederation to secure the assistance of foreign powers, and infinite pains were then taken to blind and bewilder the mind of England as to the real issues of the conflict in America.

It has been often and earnestly asserted that slavery had nothing to do with this conflict; that it was a mere struggle for power; that the only object was to restore the Union as it was, with all its abuses. It is to be admitted that expressions have proceeded from the national administration which naturally gave rise to misapprehension, and therefore we beg to speak to you on this subject more fully.

And first the declaration of the Confederate States themselves is proof enough, that, whatever may be declared on the other side, the maintenance of slavery is regarded by them as the vital object of their movement.

We ask your attention under this head to the declaration of their Vice-President, Stephens, in that remarkable speech delivered on the 21st of March, 1861, at Savannah, Georgia, wherein he declares the object and purposes of the new Confederacy. It is one of the most extraordinary papers which our century has produced. I quote from the *verbatim* report in the "Savannah Republican" of the address as it was delivered in the Athenæum of that city, on which occasion, says the newspaper from which I copy, "Mr. Stephens took his seat amid a burst of enthusiasm and applause such as the Athenæum has never had displayed within its walls within the recollection 'of the oldest inhabitant.'"

Last, not least, the new Constitution has put at rest *forever* all the agitating questions relating to our peculiar institution,— African slavery as it exists among us, the proper *status* of the negro in our form of civilization. *This was the immediate cause of the late rupture and present revolution.* Jefferson, in his forecast, had anticipated this as the "rock upon which the old Union would split." He was right. What was a conjecture with him is now a realized fact. But whether he fully comprehended the great truth upon which that rock *stood* and *stands* may be doubted.

The prevailing ideas entertained by him and most of the leading statesmen at the time of the formation of the old Constitution were, that the enslavement of the African was in violation of the laws of nature; that it was wrong in principle, socially, morally, and politically.

In the mean while, during the past year, the Republican administration, with all the unwonted care of organizing an army and navy, and conducting military operations on an immense scale, have proceeded to demonstrate the feasibility of overthrowing slavery by purely constitutional measures. To this end they have instituted a series of movements which have made this year more fruitful in anti-slavery triumphs than any other since the emancipation of the British West Indies. The District of Columbia, as belonging strictly to the national government and to no separate State, has furnished a fruitful subject of remonstrance from British Christians with America. We have abolished slavery there, and thus wiped out the only blot of territorial responsibility on our escutcheon.

By another act, equally grand in principle, and far more important in its results, slavery is forever excluded from the Territories of the United States.

By another act, America has consummated the long-delayed treaty with Great Britain for the suppression of the slave-trade. In ports whence slave vessels formerly sailed with the connivance of the port officers, the administration has placed men who stand up to their duty, and for the first time in our history the slave-trader is convicted and hung as a pirate. This abominable secret traffic has been wholly demolished by the energy of the Federal Government.

Lastly, and more significant still, the United States government has in its highest official capacity taken distinct anti-slavery ground, and presented to the country a plan of peaceable emancipation with suitable compensation. This noble-spirited and generous offer has been urged on the slaveholding States by the chief executive with earnestness and sincerity. But this is but half the story of the anti-slavery triumphs of this year. We have shown you what has been done for freedom by the simple use of the ordinary constitutional forces of the Union. We are now to show you what has been done to the same end by the constitutional war-power of the nation.

By this power it has been this year decreed that every slave of a rebel who reaches the lines of our army becomes a free man; that all slaves found deserted by their masters become free men; that every slave employed in any service for the United States thereby obtains his liberty; and that every slave employed against the United States in any capacity obtains his liberty; and lest the army should contain officers disposed to remand slaves to their masters, the power of judging and delivering up slaves is denied to army officers, and all such acts are made penal.

By this act the Fugitive Slave Law is for all present purposes practically repealed. With this understanding and provision, wherever our armies march they carry liberty with them. For be it remembered that our army is almost entirely a volunteer one, and that the most zealous and ardent volunteers are those who have been for years fighting, with tongue and pen, the abolition battle. So marked is the character of our soldiers in this respect, that they are now familiarly designated in the official military dispatches of the Confederate States as "the Abolitionists." Conceive the results when an army so empowered by national law marches through a slave territory. One regiment alone has to our certain knowledge liberated two thousand slaves during the past year, and this regiment is but one out of hundreds.

Lastly, the great decisive measure of the war has appeared,—*the President's Proclamation of Emancipation.*

This also has been much misunderstood and misrepresented in England. It has been said to mean virtually this: Be loyal and you shall keep your slaves; rebel and they shall be free. But let us remember what we have just seen of the purpose and meaning of the Union to which the rebellious States are invited back. It is to a Union which has abolished slavery in the District of Columbia, and interdicted slavery in the Territories; which vigorously represses the slave-trade, and hangs the convicted slaver as a pirate; which necessitates emancipation by denying expansion to slavery, and facilitates it by the offer of compensation. Any slaveholding States which should return to such a Union might fairly be supposed to return with the purpose of peaceable emancipation. The President's Proclamation simply means this: Come in and emancipate peaceably with compensation; stay out and I emancipate, nor will I protect you from the consequences.

Will our sisters in England feel no heartbeat at that event? Is it not one of the predicted voices of the latter day, saying under the whole heavens, "It is done; the kingdoms of this world are become the kingdoms of our Lord and of His Christ"?

And now, sisters of England, in this solemn, expectant hour, let us speak to you of one thing which fills our hearts with pain and solicitude. It is an unaccountable fact, and one which we entreat you seriously to ponder, that the party which has brought the cause of freedom thus far on its way, during the past eventful year, has found little or no support in England. Sadder than this, the party which makes slavery the chief corner-stone of its edifice finds in England its strongest defenders.

The voices that have spoken for us who contend for liberty have been few and scattering. God forbid that we should forget those few noble voices, so sadly exceptional in the general outcry against us! They are, alas! too few to be easily forgotten. False statements have blinded the minds of your community, and turned the most generous sentiments of the British heart against us. The North are fighting for supremacy and the South for independence, has been the voice. Independence? for what? to do what? To prove the doctrine that all men are *not* equal; to establish the doctrine that the white may enslave the negro!

In the beginning of our struggle, the voices that reached us across the water said: "If we were only sure you were fighting for the abolition of slavery, we should not dare to say whither our sympathies for your cause might not carry us." Such, as we heard, were the words of the honored and religious nobleman who draughted this very letter which you signed and sent us, and to which we are now replying.

When these words reached us we said: "We can wait; our friends in England will soon see whither this conflict is tending." A year and a half have passed; step after step has been taken for liberty; chain after chain has fallen, till the march of our armies is choked and clogged by the glad flocking of emancipated slaves; the day of final emancipation is set; the border States begin to move in voluntary consent; universal freedom for all dawns like the sun in the distant horizon, and still no voice from England. No voice? Yes, we have heard on the high seas the voice of a war-steamer, built for a man-stealing Confederacy, with English gold, in an English dockyard, going out of an English harbor, manned by English sailors, with the full knowledge of English government officers, in defiance of the Queen's proclamation of neutrality! So far has English sympathy overflowed. We have heard of other steamers, iron-clad, designed to furnish to a slavery-defending Confederacy their only lack,—a navy for the high seas. We have heard that the British Evangelical Alliance refuses to express sympathy with the liberating party, when requested to do so by the French Evangelical Alliance. We find in English religious newspapers all those sad degrees in the downward-sliding scale of defending and apologizing for slaveholders and slaveholding, with which we have so many years contended in our own country. We find the President's Proclamation of Emancipation spoken of in those papers only as an incitement to servile insurrection. Nay, more,—we find in your papers, from thoughtful men, the admission of the rapid decline of anti-slavery sentiments in England.

This very day the writer of this has been present at a solemn religious festival in the national capital, given at the home of a portion of those fugitive slaves who have fled to our lines for protection,—who, under the shadow of our flag, find sympathy and succor. The national day of thanksgiving was there kept by over a thousand redeemed slaves, and for whom Christian charity had spread an ample repast. Our sisters, we wish *you* could have witnessed the scene. We wish you could have heard the prayer of a blind old negro, called among his fellows John the Baptist, when in touching broken English he poured forth his thanksgivings. We wish you could have heard the sound of that strange rhythmical chant which is now forbidden to be sung on Southern plantations,—the psalm of this modern exodus,—which combines the barbaric fire of the Marseillaise with the religious fervor of the old Hebrew prophet:—

> "Oh, go down, Moses,
> Way down into Egypt's land!
> Tell King Pharaoh
> To let my people go!
> Stand away dere,
> Stand away dere,
> And let my people go!"

As we were leaving, an aged woman came and lifted up her hands in blessing. "Bressed be de Lord dat brought me to see dis first happy day of my life! Bressed be de Lord!" In all England is there no Amen?

We have been shocked and saddened by the question asked in an association of Congregational ministers in England, the very blood relations of the liberty-loving Puritans,—"Why does not the North let the South go?"

What! give up the point of emancipation for these four million slaves? Turn our backs on them, and leave them to their fate? What! leave our white brothers to run a career of oppression and robbery, that, as sure as there is a God that ruleth in the armies of heaven, will bring down a day of wrath and doom? Remember that wishing success to this slavery-establishing effort is only wishing to the sons and daughters of the South all the curses that God has written against oppression. *Mark our words!* If we succeed, the children of these very men who are now fighting us will rise up to call us blessed. Just as surely as there is a God who governs in the world, so surely all the laws of national prosperity follow in the train of equity; and if we succeed, we shall have delivered the children's children of our misguided brethren from the wages of sin, which is always and everywhere death.

And now, sisters of England, think it not strange if we bring back the words of your letter, not in bitterness, but in deepest sadness, and lay them down at your door. We say to you, Sisters, you have spoken well; we have heard you; we have heeded; we have striven in the cause, even unto death. We have sealed our devotion by desolate hearth and darkened homestead,—by the blood of sons, husbands, and brothers. In many of our dwellings the very light of our lives has gone out; and yet we accept the life-long darkness as our own part in this great and awful expiation, by which the bonds of wickedness shall be loosed, and abiding peace established on the foundation of righteousness. Sisters, what have *you* done, and what do you mean to do?

We appeal to you as sisters, as wives, and as mothers, to raise your voices to your fellow-citizens, and your prayers to God for the removal of this affliction and disgrace from the Christian world.

In behalf of many thousands of American women.

HARRIET BEECHER STOWE.

- 295 -

The publication of this reply elicited the following interesting letter from John Bright:—

ROCHDALE, *March 9, 1863.*

DEAR MRS. STOWE,—I received your kind note with real pleasure, and felt it very good of you to send me a copy of the "Atlantic Monthly" with your noble letter to the women of England. I read every word of it with an intense interest, and I am quite sure that its effect upon opinion here has been marked and beneficial. It has covered some with shame, and it has compelled many to think, and it has stimulated not a few to act. Before this reaches you, you will have seen what large and earnest meetings have been held in all our towns in favor of abolition and the North. No town has a building large enough to contain those who come to listen, to applaud, and to vote in favor of freedom and the Union. The effect of this is evident on our newspapers and on the tone of Parliament, where now nobody says a word in favor of recognition, or mediation, or any such thing.

The need and duty of England is admitted to be a strict neutrality, but the feeling of the millions of her people is one of friendliness to the United States and its government. It would cause universal rejoicing, among all but a limited circle of aristocracy and commercially rich and corrupt, to hear that the Northern forces had taken Vicksburg on the great river, and Charleston on the Atlantic, and that the neck of the conspiracy was utterly broken.

I hope your people may have strength and virtue to win the great cause intrusted to them, but it is fearful to contemplate the amount of the depravity in the North engendered by the long power of slavery. New England is far ahead of the States as a whole,—too instructed and too moral; but still I will hope that she will bear the nation through this appalling danger.

I well remember the evening at Rome and our conversation. You lamented the election of Buchanan. You judged him with a more unfriendly but a more correct eye than mine. He turned out more incapable and less honest than I hoped for. And I think I was right in saying that your party was not then sufficiently consolidated to enable it to maintain its policy in the execution, even had Frémont been elected. As it is now, six years later, the North but falteringly supports the policy of the government, though impelled by the force of events which then you did not dream of. President Lincoln has lived half his troubled reign. In the coming half I hope he may see land; surely slavery will be so broken up that nothing can restore and renew it; and, slavery once fairly gone, I know not how all your States can long be kept asunder.

Believe me very sincerely yours,
JOHN BRIGHT.

It also called forth from Archbishop Whately the following letter:—

PALACE, DUBLIN, *January, 1863.*

DEAR MADAM,—In acknowledging your letter and pamphlet, I take the opportunity of laying before you what I collect to be the prevailing sentiments here on American affairs. Of course there is a great variety of opinion, as may be expected in a country like ours. Some few sympathize with the Northerns, and some few with the Southerns, but far the greater portion sympathize with neither completely, but lament that each party should be making so much greater an expenditure of life and property than can be compensated for by any advantage they can dream of obtaining.

Those who are the least favorable to the Northerns are not so from any approbation of slavery, but from not understanding that the war is waged in the cause of abolition. "It was waged," they say, "ostensibly for the restoration of the Union," and in attestation of this, they refer to the proclamation which announced the confiscation of slaves that were the property of secessionists, while those who adhered to the Federal cause should be exempt from such confiscation, which, they say, did not savor much of zeal for abolition. And if the other object—the restoration of the Union—could be accomplished, which they all regard as hopeless, they do not understand how it will tend to the abolition of slavery. On the contrary, "if," say they, "the separation had been allowed to take place peaceably, the Northerns might, as we do, have proclaimed freedom to every slave who set foot on their territory; which would have been a great check to slavery, and especially to any cruel treatment of slaves." Many who have a great dislike to slavery yet hold that the Southerns had at least as much right to secede as the Americans had originally to revolt from Great Britain. And there are many who think that, considering the dreadful distress we have suffered from the cotton famine, we have shown great forbearance in withstanding the temptation of recognizing the Southern States and to break the blockade.

Then, again, there are some who are provoked at the incessant railing at England, and threats of an invasion of Canada, which are poured forth in some of the American papers.

There are many, also, who consider that the present state of things cannot continue much longer if the Confederates continue to hold their own, as they have done hitherto; and that a people who shall have maintained their independence for two or three years will be recognized by the principal European powers. Such appears to have been the procedure of the European powers in all similar cases, such as the revolt of the Anglo-American and Spanish-American colonies, of the Haytians and the Belgians. In these and other like cases, the rule practically adopted seems to have been to recognize the revolters, not at once, but after a reasonable time had been allowed to see whether they could maintain their independence; and this without being understood to have pronounced any decision either way as to the justice of the cause.

Moreover, there are many who say that the negroes and people of color are far from being kindly or justly treated in the Northern States. An emancipated slave, at any rate, has not received good training for earning his bread by the wages of labor; and if, in addition to this and his being treated as an outcast, he is excluded, as it is said, from many employments, by the refusal of white laborers to work along with him, he will have gained little by taking refuge in the Northern States.

I have now laid before you the views which I conceive to be most prevalent among us, and for which I am not myself responsible.

For the safe and effectual emancipation of slaves, I myself consider there is no plan so good as the gradual one which was long ago suggested by Bishop Hinds. What he recommended was an *ad valorem tax* upon slaves,—the value to be fixed by the owner, with an option to government to purchase at that price. Thus the slaves would be a burden to the master, and those the most so who should be the most valuable, as being the most intelligent and steady, and therefore the best qualified for freedom; and it would be his interest to train his slaves to be free laborers, and to emancipate them, one by one, as speedily as he could with safety. I fear, however, that the time is gone by for trying this experiment in America.

With best wishes for the new year, believe me

> Yours faithfully,
> RD. WHATELY.

Among the many letters written from this side of the Atlantic regarding the reply, was one from Nathaniel Hawthorne, in which he says:—

I read with great pleasure your article in the last "Atlantic." If anything could make John Bull blush, I should think it might be that; but he is a hardened and villainous hypocrite. I always felt that he cared nothing for or against slavery, except as it gave him a vantage-ground on which to parade his own virtue and sneer at our iniquity.

> With best regards from Mrs. Hawthorne and myself to yourself and family, sincerely yours,
>
> NATH'L HAWTHORNE.

CHAPTER XVII

FLORIDA, 1865-1869

LETTER TO DUCHESS OF ARGYLL.—MRS. STOWE
DESIRES TO HAVE A HOME AT THE SOUTH.—FLORIDA
THE BEST FIELD FOR DOING GOOD.—SHE BUYS A PLACE
AT MANDARIN.—A CHARMING WINTER RESIDENCE.—
"PALMETTO   LEAVES."—EASTER   SUNDAY   AT
MANDARIN.—CORRESPONDENCE WITH DR. HOLMES.—
"POGANUC PEOPLE."—RECEPTIONS IN NEW ORLEANS
AND TALLAHASSEE.—LAST WINTER AT MANDARIN.

IN 1866, the terrible conflict between the North and
South having ended, Mrs. Stowe wrote the following letter
to the Duchess of Argyll:—

HARTFORD, *February 19, 1866.*

MY DEAR FRIEND,—Your letter was a real spring of
comfort to me, bringing refreshingly the pleasant library at
Inverary and the lovely days I spent there.

I am grieved at what you say of your dear mother's health. I
showed your letter to Mrs. Perkins, and we both agreed in
saying that *we* should like for a time to fill the place of maid to
her, as doubtless you all feel, too. I should so love to be with
her, to read to her, and talk to her! and oh, there is so much
that would cheer and comfort a noble heart like hers that we
could talk about. Oh, my friend, when I think of what has
been done these last few years, and of what is now doing, I am
lost in amazement. I have just, by way of realizing it to myself,
been reading "Uncle Tom's Cabin" again, and when I read that
book, scarred and seared and burned into with the memories
of an anguish and horror that can never be forgotten, and
think it is all over now, all past, and that now the questions
debated are simply of more or less time before granting legal
suffrage to those who so lately were held only as articles of

merchandise,—when this comes over me I think no private or individual sorrow can ever make me wholly without comfort. If my faith in God's presence and real, living power in the affairs of men ever grows dim, this makes it impossible to doubt.

I have just had a sweet and lovely Christian letter from Garrison, whose beautiful composure and thankfulness in his hour of victory are as remarkable as his wonderful courage in the day of moral battle. His note ends with the words, "And who but God is to be glorified?" Garrison's attitude is far more exalted than that of Wendell Phillips. He acknowledges the great deed done. He suspends his "Liberator" with words of devout thanksgiving, and devotes himself unobtrusively to the work yet to be accomplished for the freedmen; while Phillips seems resolved to ignore the mighty work that has been done, because of the inevitable shortcomings and imperfections that beset it still. We have a Congress of splendid men,—men of stalwart principle and determination. We have a President honestly seeking to do right; and if he fails in knowing just what right is, it is because he is a man born and reared in a slave State, and acted on by many influences which we cannot rightly estimate unless we were in his place. My brother Henry has talked with him earnestly and confidentially, and has faith in him as an earnest, good man seeking to do right. Henry takes the ground that it is unwise and impolitic to endeavor to force negro suffrage on the South at the point of the bayonet. His policy would be, to hold over the negro the protection of our Freedman's Bureau until the great laws of free labor shall begin to draw the master and servant together; to endeavor to soothe and conciliate, and win to act with us, a party composed of the really good men at the South.

For this reason he has always advocated lenity of measures towards them. He wants to get them into a state in which the moral influence of the North can act upon them beneficially, and to get such a state of things that there will be a party *at the South* to protect the negro.

Charles Sumner is looking simply at the abstract *right* of the thing. Henry looks at actual probabilities. We all know that the state of society at the South is such that laws are a very inadequate protection even to white men. Southern elections always have been scenes of mob violence *when only white men voted*.

Multitudes of lives have been lost at the polls in this way, and if against their will negro suffrage was forced upon them, I do not see how any one in their senses can expect anything less than an immediate war of races.

If negro suffrage were required as a condition of acquiring political position, there is no doubt the slave States would grant it; grant it nominally, because they would know that the grant never could or would become an actual realization. And what would then be gained for the negro?

I am sorry that people cannot differ on such great and perplexing public questions without impugning each other's motives. Henry has been called a back-slider because of the lenity of his counsels, but I cannot but think it is the Spirit of Christ that influences him. Garrison has been in the same way spoken of as a deserter, because he says that a work that is done shall be called done, and because he would not keep up an anti-slavery society when slavery is abolished; and I think our President is much injured by the abuse that is heaped on him, and the selfish and unworthy motives that are ascribed to him by those who seem determined to allow to nobody an honest, unselfish difference in judgment from their own.

Henry has often spoken of you and your duke as pleasant memories in a scene of almost superhuman labor and excitement. He often said to me: "When this is all over,— when we have won the victory,—*then* I will write to the duchess." But when it was over and the flag raised again at Sumter his arm was smitten down with the news of our President's death! We all appreciate your noble and true sympathy through the dark hour of our national trial. You and yours are almost the only friends we now have left in England. You cannot know what it was, unless you could imagine your own country to be in danger of death, extinction of nationality. *That*, dear friend, is an experience which shows us what we are and what we can feel. I am glad to hear that we may hope to see your son in this country. I fear so many pleasant calls will beset his path that we cannot hope for a moment, but it would give us *all* the greatest pleasure to see him here. Our dull, prosy, commonplace, though good old Hartford could offer few attractions compared with Boston or New York, and yet I hope he will not leave us out altogether if he comes among us. God bless him! You are very happy indeed in being permitted to keep all your dear ones and see them growing up.

I want to ask a favor. Do you have, as we do, *cartes de visite?* If you have, and could send me one of yourself and the duke and of Lady Edith and your eldest son, I should be so very glad to see how you are looking now; and the dear mother, too, I should so like to see how she looks. It seems almost like a dream to look back to those pleasant days. I am glad to see you still keep some memories of our goings on. Georgie's marriage is a very happy one to us. They live in Stockbridge, the loveliest part of Massachusetts, and her husband is a most devoted pastor, and gives all his time and property to the great work which he has embraced, purely for the love of it. My other daughters are with me, and my son, Captain Stowe, who has come with weakened health through our struggle, suffering constantly from the effects of a wound in his head received at Gettysburg, which makes his returning to his studies a hard struggle. My husband is in better health since he resigned his professorship, and desires his most sincere regards to yourself and the duke, and his profound veneration to your mother. Sister Mary also desires to be remembered to you, as do also my daughters. Please tell me a little in your next of Lady Edith; she must be very lovely now.

I am, with sincerest affection, ever yours,

H. B. STOWE.

Soon after the close of the war Mrs. Stowe conceived the idea of making for herself and her family a winter home in the South, where she might escape the rigors of Northern winters, and where her afflicted son Frederick might enjoy an out-of-door life throughout the year. She was also most anxious to do her share towards educating and leading to a higher life those colored people whom she had helped so largely to set free, and who were still in the state of profound ignorance imposed by slavery. In writing of her hopes and plans to her brother Charles Beecher, in 1866, she says:—

"My plan of going to Florida, as it lies in my mind, is not in any sense a mere worldly enterprise. I have for many years had a longing to be more immediately doing Christ's work on earth. My heart is with that poor people whose cause in words I have tried to plead, and who now, ignorant and docile, are just in that formative stage in which whoever seizes has them.

"Corrupt politicians are already beginning to speculate on them as possible capital for their schemes, and to fill their poor heads with all sorts of vagaries. Florida is the State into which they have, more than anywhere else, been pouring. Emigration is positively and decidedly setting that way; but as yet it is mere worldly emigration, with the hope of making money, nothing more.

"The Episcopal Church is, however, undertaking, under direction of the future Bishop of Florida, a wide-embracing scheme of Christian activity for the whole State. In this work I desire to be associated, and my plan is to locate at some salient point on the St. John's River, where I can form the nucleus of a Christian neighborhood, whose influence shall be felt far beyond its own limits."

During this year Mrs. Stowe partially carried her plan into execution by hiring an old plantation called "Laurel Grove," on the west side of the St. John's River, near the present village of Orange Park. Here she established her son Frederick as a cotton planter, and here he remained for two years. This location did not, however, prove entirely satisfactory, nor did the raising of cotton prove to be, under the circumstances, a profitable business. After visiting Florida during the winter of 1866-67, at which time her attention was drawn to the beauties and superior advantages of Mandarin on the east side of the river, Mrs. Stowe writes from Hartford, May 29, 1867, to Rev. Charles Beecher:—

MY DEAR BROTHER,—We are now thinking seriously of a place in Mandarin much more beautiful than any other in the vicinity. It has on it five large date palms, an olive tree in full bearing, besides a fine orange grove which this year will yield about seventy-five thousand oranges. If we get that, then I want you to consider the expediency of buying the one next to it. It contains about two hundred acres of land, on which is a fine orange grove, the fruit from which last year brought in two thousand dollars as sold at the wharf. It is right on the river, and four steamboats pass it each week, on their way to Savannah and Charleston. There is on the place a very comfortable cottage, as houses go out there, where they do not need to be built as substantially as with us.

THE HOME AT MANDARIN, FLORIDA.

I am now in correspondence with the Bishop of Florida, with a view to establishing a line of churches along the St. John's River, and if I settle at Mandarin, it will be one of my stations. Will you consent to enter the Episcopal Church and be our clergyman? You are just the man we want. If my tasks and feelings did not incline me toward the Church, I should still choose it as the best system for training immature minds such as those of our negroes. The system was composed with reference to the wants of the laboring class of England, at a time when they were as ignorant as our negroes now are.

I long to be at this work, and cannot think of it without my heart burning within me. Still I leave all with my God, and only hope He will open the way for me to do all that I want to for this poor people.

Affectionately yours,
H. B. STOWE.

Mrs. Stowe had some years before this joined the Episcopal Church, for the sake of attending the same communion as her daughters, who were Episcopalians. Her brother Charles did not, however, see fit to change his creed, and though he went to Florida he settled a hundred and sixty miles west from the St. John's River, at Newport, near St. Marks, on the Gulf coast, and about twenty miles from Tallahassee. Here he lived every winter and several summers for fifteen years, and here he left the impress of his own remarkably sweet and lovely character upon the scattered population of the entire region.

Mrs. Stowe in the mean time purchased the property, with its orange grove and comfortable cottage, that she had recommended to him, and thus Mandarin became her winter home. No one who has ever seen it can forget the peaceful beauty of this Florida home and its surroundings. The house, a story and a half cottage of many gables, stands on a bluff overlooking the broad St. John's, which is five miles wide at this point. It nestles in the shade of a grove of superb, moss-hung live-oaks, around one of which the front piazza is built. Several fine old orange trees also stand near the cottage, scenting the air with the sweet perfume of their blossoms in the early spring, and offering their golden fruit to whoever may choose to pluck it during the winter months. Back of the house stretches the well-tended orange grove in which Mrs. Stowe took such genuine pride and pleasure. Everywhere about the dwelling and within it were flowers and singing birds, while the rose garden in front, at the foot of the bluff, was the admiration of all who saw it.

Here, on the front piazza, beneath the grand oaks, looking out on the calm sunlit river, Professor Stowe enjoyed that absolute peace and restful quiet for which his scholarly nature had always longed, but which had been forbidden to the greater part of his active life. At almost any hour of the day the well-known figure, with snow-white, patriarchal beard and kindly face, might be seen sitting there, with a basket of books, many of them in dead and nearly forgotten languages, close at hand. An amusing incident of family life was as follows: Some Northern visitors seemed to think that the family had no rights which were worthy of a a moment's consideration. They would land at the wharf, roam about the place, pick flowers, peer into the house through the windows and doors, and act with that disregard of all the proprieties of life which characterizes ill-bred people when on a journey. The professor had been driven well-nigh distracted by these migratory bipeds. One day, when one of them broke a branch from an orange tree directly before his eyes, and was bearing it off in triumph with all its load of golden fruit, he leaped from his chair, and addressed the astonished individual on those fundamental principles of common honesty, which he deemed outraged by this act. The address was vigorous and truthful, but of a kind which will not bear repeating. "Why," said the horror-stricken culprit, "I thought that this was Mrs. Stowe's place!" "You thought it was Mrs. Stowe's place!" Then, in a voice of thunder, "I would have you understand, sir, that I am the proprietor and protector of Mrs. Stowe and of this place, and if you commit any more such shameful depredations I will have you punished as you deserve!" Thus this predatory Yankee was taught to realize that there is a God in Israel.

In April, 1869, Mrs. Stowe was obliged to hurry North in order to visit Canada in time to protect her English rights in "Oldtown Folks," which she had just finished.

About this time she secured a plot of land, and made arrangements for the erection on it of a building that should be used as a schoolhouse through the week, and as a church on Sunday. For several years Professor Stowe preached during the winter in this little schoolhouse, and Mrs. Stowe conducted Sunday-school, sewing classes, singing classes, and various other gatherings for instruction and amusement, all of which were well attended and highly appreciated by both the white and colored residents of the neighborhood.

Upon one occasion, having just arrived at her Mandarin home, Mrs. Stowe writes:—

"At last, after waiting a day and a half in Charleston, we arrived here about ten o'clock Saturday morning, just a week from the day we sailed. The house looked so pretty, and quiet, and restful, the day was so calm and lovely, it seemed as though I had passed away from all trouble, and was looking back upon you all from a secure resting-place. Mr. Stowe is very happy here, and is constantly saying how pleasant it is, and how glad he is that he is here. He is so much improved in health that already he is able to take a considerable walk every day.

"We are all well, contented, and happy, and we have six birds, two dogs, and a pony. Do write more and oftener. Tell me all the little nothings and nowheres. You can't imagine how they are magnified by the time they have reached into this remote corner."

In 1872 she wrote a series of Florida sketches, which were published in book form, the following year, by J. R. Osgood & Co., under the title of "Palmetto Leaves." May 19, 1873, she writes to her brother Charles at Newport, Fla.:—

"Although you have not answered my last letter, I cannot leave Florida without saying good-by. I send you the 'Palmetto Leaves' and my parting love. If I could either have brought or left my husband, I should have come to see you this winter. The account of your roses fills me with envy.

"We leave on the San Jacinto next Saturday, and I am making the most of the few charming hours yet left; for never did we have so delicious a spring. I never knew such altogether perfect weather. It is enough to make a saint out of the toughest old Calvinist that ever set his face as a flint. How do you think New England theology would have fared if our fathers had been landed here instead of on Plymouth Rock?

"The next you hear of me will be at the North, where our address is Forest Street, Hartford. We have bought a pretty cottage there, near to Belle, and shall spend the summer there."

In a letter written in May of the following year to her son Charles, at Harvard, Mrs. Stowe says: "I can hardly realize that this long, flowery summer, with its procession of blooms and fruit, has been running on at the same time with the snowbanks and sleet storms of the North. But so it is. It is now the first of May. Strawberries and blackberries are over with us; oranges are in a waning condition, few and far between. Now we are going North to begin another summer, and have roses, strawberries, blackberries, and green peas come again.

"I am glad to hear of your reading. The effect produced on you by Jonathan Edwards is very similar to that produced on me when I took the same mental bath. His was a mind whose grasp and intensity you cannot help feeling. He was a poet in the intensity of his conceptions, and some of his sermons are more terrible than Dante's 'Inferno.'"

In November, 1874, upon their return to Mandarin, she writes: "We have had heavenly weather, and we needed it; for our house was a cave of spider-webs, cockroaches, dirt, and all abominations, but less than a week has brought it into beautiful order. It now begins to put on that quaint, lively, pretty air that so fascinates me. Our weather is, as I said, heavenly, neither hot nor cold; cool, calm, bright, serene, and so tranquillizing. There is something indescribable about the best weather we have down here. It does not debilitate me like the soft October air in Hartford."

During the following February, she writes in reply to an invitation to visit a Northern watering place later in the season: "I shall be most happy to come, and know of nothing to prevent. I have, thank goodness, no serial story on hand for this summer, to hang like an Old Man of the Sea about my neck, and hope to enjoy a little season of being like other folks. It is a most lovely day to-day, most unfallen Eden-like."

In a letter written later in the same season, March 28, 1875, Mrs. Stowe gives us a pleasant glimpse at their preparations for the proper observance of Easter Sunday in the little Mandarin schoolhouse. She says: "It was the week before Easter, and we had on our minds the dressing of the church. There my two Gothic fireboards were to be turned into a pulpit for the occasion. I went to Jacksonville and got a five-inch moulding for a base, and then had one fireboard sawed in two, so that there was an arched panel for each end. Then came a rummage for something for a top, and to make a desk of, until it suddenly occurred to me that our old black walnut extension table had a set of leaves. They were exactly the thing. The whole was trimmed with a beading of yellow pine, and rubbed, and pumice-stoned, and oiled, and I got out my tubes of paint and painted the nail-holes with Vandyke brown. By Saturday morning it was a lovely little Gothic pulpit, and Anthony carried it over to the schoolhouse and took away the old desk which I gave him for his meeting-house. That afternoon we drove out into the woods and gathered a quantity of superb Easter lilies, papaw, sparkleberry, great fern-leaves, and cedar. In the evening the girls went over to the Meads to practice Easter hymns; but I sat at home and made a cross, eighteen inches long, of cedar and white lilies. This Southern cedar is the most exquisite thing; it is so feathery and delicate.

"Sunday morning was cool and bright, a most perfect Easter. Our little church was full, and everybody seemed delighted with the decorations. Mr. Stowe preached a sermon to show that Christ is going to put everything right at last, which is comforting. So the day was one of real pleasure, and also I trust of real benefit, to the poor souls who learned from it that Christ is indeed risen for them."

During this winter the following characteristic letters passed between Mrs. Stowe and her valued friend, Dr. Oliver Wendell Holmes, called forth by the sending to the latter of a volume of Mrs. Stowe's latest stories:—

BOSTON, *January 8, 1876.*

MY DEAR MRS. STOWE,—I would not write to thank you for your most welcome "Christmas Box,"

"A box whose sweets compacted lie,"

before I had read it, and every word of it. I have been very much taken up with antics of one kind and another, and have only finished it this afternoon. The last of the papers was of less comparative value to me than to a great fraction of your immense parish of readers, because I am so familiar with every movement of the Pilgrims in their own chronicles.

"Deacon Pitkin's Farm" is full of those thoroughly truthful touches of New England in which, if you are not unrivaled, I do not know who your rival may be. I wiped the tears from one eye in reading "Deacon Pitkin's Farm."

I wiped the tears, and plenty of them, from both eyes, in reading "Betty's Bright Idea." It is a most charming and touching story, and nobody can read who has not a heart like a pebble, without being melted into tenderness.

How much you have done and are doing to make our New England life wholesome and happy! If there is any one who can look back over a literary life which has pictured our old and helped our new civilization, it is yourself. Of course your later books have harder work cut out for them than those of any other writer. They have had "Uncle Tom's Cabin" for a rival. The brightest torch casts a shadow in the blaze of a light, and any transcendent success affords the easiest handle for that class of critics whose method is the one that Dogberry held to be "odious."

I think it grows pleasanter to us to be remembered by the friends we still have, as with each year they grow fewer. We have lost Agassiz and Sumner from our circle, and I found Motley stricken with threatening illness (which I hope is gradually yielding to treatment), in the profoundest grief at the loss of his wife, another old and dear friend of mine. So you may be assured that I feel most sensibly your kind attention, and send you my heartfelt thanks for remembering me.

Always, dear Mrs. Stowe, faithfully yours,
O. W. HOLMES.

To this letter Mrs. Stowe replied as follows:—

MANDARIN, *February 23, 1876.*

DEAR DOCTOR,—How kind it was of you to write me that very beautiful note! and how I wish you were just where I am, to see the trees laden at the same time with golden oranges and white blossoms! I should so like to cut off a golden cluster, leaves and all, for you. Well, Boston seems very far away and dreamy, like some previous state of existence, as I sit on the veranda and gaze on the receding shores of the St. John's, which at this point is five miles wide.

Dear doctor, how time slips by! I remember when Sumner seemed to me a young man, and now he has gone. And Wilson has gone, and Chase, whom I knew as a young man in society in Cincinnati, has gone, and Stanton has gone, and Seward has gone, and yet how lively the world races on! A few air-bubbles of praise or lamentation, and away sails the great ship of life, no matter over whose grave!

Well, one cannot but feel it! To me, also, a whole generation of friends has gone from the other side of the water since I was there and broke kindly bread with them. The Duchess of Sutherland, the good old duke, Lansdowne, Ellesmere, Lady Byron, Lord and Lady Amberly, Charles Kingsley, the good Quaker, Joseph Sturge, all are with the shadowy train that has moved on. Among them were as dear and true friends as I ever had, and as pure and noble specimens of human beings as God ever made. They are living somewhere in intense vitality, I must believe, and you, dear doctor, must not doubt.

I think about your writings a great deal, and one element in them always attracts me. It is their pitiful and sympathetic vein, the pity for poor, struggling human nature. In this I feel that you must be very near and dear to Him whose name is Love.

You wrote some verses once that have got into the hymn-books, and have often occurred to me in my most sacred hours as descriptive of the feelings with which I bear the sorrows and carry the cares of life. They begin,—

"Love Divine, that stooped to share."

I have not all your books down here, and am haunted by gaps in the verses that memory cannot make good; but it is that "Love Divine" which is my stay and comfort and hope, as one friend after another passes beyond sight and hearing. Please let me have it in your handwriting.

I remember a remark you once made on spiritualism. I cannot recall the words, but you spoke of it as modifying the sharp angles of Calvinistic belief, as a fog does those of a landscape. I would like to talk with you some time on spiritualism, and show you a collection of very curious facts that I have acquired through mediums *not* professional. Mr. Stowe has just been wading through eight volumes of "La Mystique," by Goerres, professor for forty years past in the University of Munich, first of physiology and latterly of philosophy. He examines the whole cycle of abnormal psychic, spiritual facts, trances, ecstasy, clairvoyance, witchcraft, spiritualism, etc., etc., as shown in the Romish miracles and the history of Europe.

I have long since come to the conclusion that the marvels of spiritualism are natural, and not supernatural, phenomena,—an uncommon working of natural laws. I believe that the door between those *in* the body and those *out* has never in any age been entirely closed, and that occasional perceptions within the veil are a part of the course of nature, and therefore not miraculous. Of course such a phase of human experience is very substantial ground for every kind of imposture and superstition, and I have no faith whatever in mediums who practice for money. In their case I think the law of Moses, that forbade consulting those who dealt with "familiar spirits," a very wise one.

Do write some more, dear doctor. You are too well off in your palace down there on the new land. Your Centennial Ballad was a charming little peep; now give us a full-fledged story. Mr. Stowe sends his best regards, and wishes you would read "Goerres." It is in French also, and he thinks the French translation better than the German.

Yours ever truly,
H. B. STOWE.

Writing in the autumn of 1876 to her son Charles, who was at that time abroad, studying at Bonn, Mrs. Stowe describes a most tempestuous passage between New York and Charleston, during which she and her husband and daughters suffered so much that they were ready to forswear the sea forever. The great waves as they rushed, boiling and seething, past would peer in at the little bull's-eye window of the state-room, as if eager to swallow up ship and passengers. From Charleston, however, they had a most delightful run to their journey's end. She writes: "We had a triumphal entrance into the St. John's, and a glorious sail up the river. Arriving at Mandarin, at four o'clock, we found all the neighbors, black as well as white, on the wharf to receive us. There was a great waving of handkerchiefs and flags, clapping of hands and cheering, as we drew near. The house was open and all ready for us, and we are delighted to be once more in our beautiful Florida home."

In the following December she writes to her son: "I am again entangled in writing a serial, a thing I never mean to do again, but the story, begun for a mere Christmas brochure, grew so under my hands that I thought I might as well fill it out and make a book of it. It is the last thing of the kind I ever expect to do. In it I condense my recollections of a bygone era, that in which I was brought up, the ways and manners of which are now as nearly obsolete as the Old England of Dickens's stories is.'

"I am so hampered by the necessity of writing this story, that I am obliged to give up company and visiting of all kinds and keep my strength for it. I hope I may be able to finish it, as I greatly desire to do so, but I begin to feel that I am not so strong as I used to be. Your mother is an old woman, Charley mine, and it is best she should give up writing before people are tired of reading her.

"I would much rather have written another such a book as 'Footsteps of the Master,' but all, even the religious papers, are gone mad on serials. Serials they demand and will have, and I thought, since this generation will listen to nothing but stories, why not tell them?"

The book thus referred to was "Poganuc People," that series of delightful reminiscences of the New England life of nearly a century ago, that has proved so fascinating to many thousands of readers. It was published in 1878, and, as Mrs. Stowe foresaw, was her last literary undertaking of any length, though for several years afterwards she wrote occasional short stories and articles.

In January, 1879, she wrote from Mandarin to Dr. Holmes:—

DEAR DOCTOR,—I wish I could give to you and Mrs. Holmes the exquisite charm of this morning. My window is wide open; it is a lovely, fresh, sunny day, and a great orange tree hung with golden balls closes the prospect from my window. The tree is about thirty feet high, and its leaves fairly glisten in the sunshine.

I sent "Poganuc People" to you and Mrs. Holmes as being among the few who know those old days. It is an extremely quiet story for these sensational days, when heaven and earth seem to be racked for a thrill; but as I get old I do love to think of those quiet, simple times when there was not a poor person in the parish, and the changing glories of the year were the only spectacle. We, that is the professor and myself, have been reading with much interest Motley's Memoir. That was a man to be proud of, a beauty, too (by your engraving). I never had the pleasure of a personal acquaintance.

I feel with you that we have come into the land of leave-taking. Hardly a paper but records the death of some of Mr. Stowe's associates. But the river is not so black as it seems, and there are clear days when the opposite shore is plainly visible, and now and then we catch a strain of music, perhaps even a gesture of recognition. They are thinking of us, without doubt, on the other side. My daughters and I have been reading "Elsie Venner" again. Elsie is one of my especial friends,—poor, dear child!—and all your theology in that book I subscribe to with both hands.

Does not the Bible plainly tell us of a time when there shall be no more pain? That is to be the end and crown of the Messiah's mission, when God shall wipe all tears away. My face is set that way, and yours, too, I trust and believe.

Mr. Stowe sends hearty and affectionate remembrance both to you and Mrs. Holmes, and I am, as ever, truly yours,

H. B. STOWE.

About this time Mrs. Stowe paid a visit to her brother Charles, at Newport, Fla., and, continuing her journey to New Orleans, was made to feel how little of bitterness towards her was felt by the best class of Southerners. In both New Orleans and Tallahassee she was warmly welcomed, and tendered public receptions that gave equal pleasure to her and to the throngs of cultivated people who attended them. She was also greeted everywhere with intense enthusiasm by the colored people, who, whenever they knew of her coming, thronged the railway stations in order to obtain a glimpse of her whom they venerated above all women.

The return to her Mandarin home each succeeding winter was always a source of intense pleasure to this true lover of nature in its brightest and tenderest moods. Each recurring season was filled with new delights. In December, 1879, she writes to her son, now married and settled as a minister in Saco, Me.:—

DEAR CHILDREN,—Well, we have stepped from December to June, and this morning is sunny and dewy, with a fresh sea-breeze giving life to the air. I have just been out to cut a great bunch of roses and lilies, though the garden is grown into such a jungle that I could hardly get about in it. The cannas, and dwarf bananas, and roses are all tangled together, so that I can hardly thread my way among them. I never in my life saw anything range and run rampant over the ground as cannas do. The ground is littered with fallen oranges, and the place looks shockingly untidy, but so beautiful that I am quite willing to forgive its disorder.

We got here Wednesday evening about nine o'clock, and found all the neighbors waiting to welcome us on the wharf. The Meads, and Cranes, and Webbs, and all the rest were there, while the black population was in a frenzy of joy. Your father is quite well. The sea had its usual exhilarating effect upon him. Before we left New York he was quite meek, and exhibited such signs of grace and submission that I had great hopes of him. He promised to do exactly as I told him, and stated that he had entire confidence in my guidance. What woman couldn't call such a spirit evidence of being prepared for speedy translation? I was almost afraid he could not be long for this world. But on the second day at sea his spirits rose, and his appetite reasserted itself. He declared in loud tones how well he felt, and quite resented my efforts to take care of him. I reminded him of his gracious vows and promises in the days of his low spirits, but to no effect. The fact is, his self-will has not left him yet, and I have now no fear of his immediate translation. He is going to preach for us this morning.

The last winter passed in this well-loved Southern home was that of 1883-84, for the following season Professor Stowe's health was in too precarious a state to permit him to undertake the long journey from Hartford. By this time one of Mrs. Stowe's fondest hopes had been realized; and, largely through her efforts, Mandarin had been provided with a pretty little Episcopal church, to which was attached a comfortable rectory, and over which was installed a regular clergyman.

In January, 1884, Mrs. Stowe writes:—

"Mandarin looks very gay and airy now with its new villas, and our new church and rectory. Our minister is perfect. I wish you could know him. He wants only physical strength. In everything else he is all one could ask.

"It is a bright, lovely morning, and four orange-pickers are busy gathering our fruit. Our trees on the bluff have done better than any in Florida.

"This winter I study nothing but Christ's life. First I read Farrar's account and went over it carefully. Now I am reading Geikie. It keeps my mind steady, and helps me to bear the languor and pain, of which I have more than usual this winter."

CHAPTER XVIII

OLDTOWN FOLKS, 1869

PROFESSOR STOWE THE ORIGINAL OF "HARRY" IN "OLDTOWN FOLKS."—PROFESSOR STOWE'S LETTER TO GEORGE ELIOT.—HER REMARKS ON THE SAME.— PROFESSOR STOWE'S NARRATIVE OF HIS YOUTHFUL ADVENTURES IN THE WORLD OF SPIRITS.—PROFESSOR STOWE'S INFLUENCE ON MRS. STOWE'S LITERARY LIFE.— GEORGE ELIOT ON "OLDTOWN FOLKS."

THIS biography would be signally incomplete without some mention of the birth, childhood, early associations, and very peculiar and abnormal psychological experiences of Professor Stowe. Aside from the fact of Dr. Stowe's being Mrs. Stowe's husband, and for this reason entitled to notice in any sketch of her life, however meagre, he is the original of the "visionary boy" in "Oldtown Folks;" and "Oldtown Fireside Stories" embody the experiences of his childhood and youth among the grotesque and original characters of his native town.

March 26, 1882, Professor Stowe wrote the following characteristic letter to Mrs. Lewes:—

MRS. LEWES,—I fully sympathize with you in your disgust with Hume and the professing mediums generally.

Hume spent his boyhood in my father's native town, among my relatives and acquaintances, and he was a disagreeable, nasty boy. But he certainly has qualities which science has not yet explained, and some of his doings are as real as they are strange. My interest in the subject of spiritualism arises from the fact of my own experience, more than sixty years ago, in my early childhood. I then never thought of questioning the objective reality of all I saw, and supposed that everybody else had the same experience. Of what this experience was you may gain some idea from certain passages in "Oldtown Folks."

The same experiences continue yet, but with serious doubts as to the objectivity of the scenes exhibited. I have noticed that people who have remarkable and minute answers to prayer, such as Stilling, Franke, Lavater, are for the most part of this peculiar temperament. Is it absurd to suppose that some peculiarity in the nervous system, in the connecting link between soul and body, may bring some, more than others, into an almost abnormal contact with the spirit-world (for example, Jacob Boehme and Swedenborg), and that, too, without correcting their faults, or making them morally better than others? Allow me to say that I have always admired the working of your mind, there is about it such a perfect uprightness and uncalculating honesty. I think you are a better Christian without church or theology than most people are with both, though I am, and always have been in the main, a Calvinist of the Jonathan Edwards school. God bless you! I have a warm side for Mr. Lewes on account of his Goethe labors.

Goethe has been my admiration for more than forty years. In 1830 I got hold of his "Faust," and for two gloomy, dreary November days, while riding through the woods of New Hampshire in an old-fashioned stagecoach, to enter upon a professorship in Dartmouth College, I was perfectly dissolved by it.

Sincerely yours,
C. E. STOWE.

In a letter to Mrs. Stowe, written June 24, 1872, Mrs. Lewes alludes to Professor Stowe's letter as follows: "Pray give my special thanks to the professor for his letter. His handwriting, which does really look like Arabic,—a very graceful character, surely,—happens to be remarkably legible to me, and I did not hesitate over a single word. Some of the words, as expressions of fellowship, were very precious to me, and I hold it very good of him to write to me that best sort of encouragement. I was much impressed with the fact—which you have told me—that he was the original of the "visionary boy" in "Oldtown Folks;" and it must be deeply interesting to talk with him on his experience. Perhaps I am inclined, under the influence of the facts, physiological and psychological, which have been gathered of late years, to give larger place to the interpretation of vision-seeing as subjective than the professor would approve. It seems difficult to limit—at least to limit with any precision—the possibility of confounding sense by impressions derived from inward conditions with those which are directly dependent on external stimulus. In fact, the division between within and without in this sense seems to become every year a more subtle and bewildering problem."

In 1834, while Mr. Stowe was a professor in Lane Theological Seminary at Cincinnati, Ohio, he wrote out a history of his youthful adventures in the spirit-world, from which the following extracts are taken:—

C. E. Stowe.

"I have often thought I would communicate to some scientific physician a particular account of a most singular delusion under which I lived from my earliest infancy till the fifteenth or sixteenth year of my age, and the effects of which remain very distinctly now that I am past thirty.

"The facts are of such a nature as to be indelibly impressed upon my mind they appear to me to be curious, and well worth the attention of the psychologist. I regard the occurrences in question as the more remarkable because I cannot discover that I possess either taste or talent for fiction or poetry. I have barely imagination enough to enjoy, with a high degree of relish, the works of others in this department of literature, but have never felt able or disposed to engage in that sort of writing myself. On the contrary, my style has always been remarkable for its dry, matter-of-fact plainness; my mind has been distinguished for its quickness and adaptedness to historical and literary investigations, for ardor and perseverance in pursuit of the knowledge of facts,—*eine verständige Richtung*, as the Germans would say,—rather than for any other quality; and the only talent of a higher kind which I am conscious of possessing is a turn for accurate observation of men and things, and a certain broad humor and drollery.

"From the hour of my birth I have been constitutionally feeble, as were my parents before me, and my nervous system easily excitable. With care, however, I have kept myself in tolerable health, and my life has been an industrious one, for my parents were poor and I have always been obliged to labor for my livelihood.

"With these preliminary remarks, I proceed to the curious details of my psychological history. As early as I can remember anything, I can remember observing a multitude of animated and active objects, which I could see with perfect distinctness, moving about me, and could sometimes, though seldom, hear them make a rustling noise, or other articulate sounds; but I could never touch them. They were in all respects independent of the sense of touch, and incapable of being obstructed in any way by the intervention of material objects; I could see them at any distance, and through any intervening object, with as much ease and distinctness as if they were in the room with me, and directly before my eyes. I could see them passing through the floors, and the ceilings, and the walls of the house, from one apartment to another, in all directions, without a door, or a keyhole, or crevice being open to admit them. I could follow them with my eyes to any distance, or directly through or just beneath the surface, or up and down, in the midst of boards and timbers and bricks, or whatever else would stop the motion or intercept the visibleness of all other objects. These appearances occasioned neither surprise nor alarm, except when they assumed some hideous and frightful form, or exhibited some menacing gesture, for I became acquainted with them as soon as with any of the objects of sense. As to the reality of their existence and the harmlessness of their character, I knew no difference between them and any other of the objects which met my eye. They were as familiar to me as the forms of my parents and my brother; they made up a part of my daily existence, and were as really the subjects of my consciousness as the little bench on which I sat in the corner by my mother's knee, or the wheels and sticks and strings with which I amused myself upon the floor. I indeed recognized a striking difference between them and the things which I could feel and handle, but to me this difference was no more a matter of surprise than that which I observed between my mother and the black woman who so often came to work for her; or between my infant brother and the little spotted dog Brutus of which I was so fond. There was no time, or place, or circumstance, in which they did not occasionally make their appearance. Solitude and silence, however, were more favorable to their appearance than company and conversation. They were more pleased with candle-light than the daylight. They were most numerous, distinct, and active when I was alone and in the dark, especially when my mother had laid me in bed and returned to her own room with the candle. At such times, I always expected the company of my ærial visitors, and counted upon it to amuse me till I dropped asleep. Whenever they failed to make their appearance, as was sometimes the case, I felt lonely and discontented. I kept up a lively conversation with them,—not by language or by signs, for the attempt on my part to speak or move would at once break the charm and drive them away in a fret, but by a peculiar sort of spiritual intercommunion.

"When their attention was directed towards me, I could feel and respond to all their thoughts and feelings, and was conscious that they could in the same manner feel and respond to mine. Sometimes they would take no notice of me, but carry on a brisk conversation among themselves, principally by looks and gestures, with now and then an audible word. In fact, there were but few with whom I was very familiar. These few were much more constant and uniform in their visits than the great multitude, who were frequently changing, and too much absorbed in their own concerns to think much of me. I scarcely know how I can give an idea of their form and general appearance, for there are no objects in the material world with which I can compare them, and no language adapted to an accurate description of their peculiarities. They exhibited all possible combinations of size, shape, proportion, and color, but their most usual appearance was with the human form and proportion, but under a shadowy outline that seemed just ready to melt into the invisible air, and sometimes liable to the most sudden and grotesque changes, and with a uniform darkly bluish color spotted with brown, or brownish white. This was the general appearance of the multitude; but there were many exceptions to this description, particularly among my more welcome and familiar visitors, as will be seen in the sequel.

"Besides these rational and generally harmless beings, there was another set of objects which never varied in their form or qualities, and were always mischievous and terrible. The fact of their appearance depended very much on the state of my health and feelings. If I was well and cheerful they seldom troubled me; but when sick or depressed they were sure to obtrude their hateful presence upon me. These were a sort of heavy clouds floating about overhead, of a black color, spotted with brown, in the shape of a very flaring inverted tunnel without a nozzle, and from ten to thirty or forty feet in diameter. They floated from place to place in great numbers, and in all directions, with a strong and steady progress, but with a tremulous, quivering, internal motion that agitated them in every part.

"Whenever they approached, the rational phantoms were thrown into great consternation; and well it might be, for if a cloud touched any part of one of the rational phantoms it immediately communicated its own color and tremulous motion to the part it touched.

"In spite of all the efforts and convulsive struggles of the unhappy victim, this color and motion slowly, but steadily and uninteruptedly, proceeded to diffuse itself over every part of the body, and as fast as it did so the body was drawn into the cloud and became a part of its substance. It was indeed a fearful sight to see the contortions, the agonizing efforts, of the poor creatures who had been touched by one of these awful clouds, and were dissolving and melting into it by inches without the possibility of escape or resistance.

"This was the only visible object that had the least power over the phantoms, and this was evidently composed of the same material as themselves. The forms and actions of all these phantoms varied very much with the state of my health and animal spirits, but I never could discover that the surrounding material objects had any influence upon them, except in this one particular, namely, if I saw them in a neat, well furnished room, there was a neatness and polish in their form and motions; and, on the contrary, if I was in an unfinished, rough apartment, there was a corresponding rudeness and roughness in my ærial visitors. A corresponding difference was visible when I saw them in the woods or in the meadows, upon the water or upon the ground, in the air or among the stars.

"Every different apartment which I occupied had a different set of phantoms, and they always had a degree of correspondence to the circumstances in which they were seen. (It should be noted, however, that it was not so much the place where the phantoms themselves appeared to me to be, that affected their forms and movements, as the place in which I myself actually was while observing them. The apparent locality of the phantoms, it is true, had some influence, but my own actual locality had much more.)

"Thus far I have attempted only a general outline of these curious experiences. I will now proceed to a detailed account of several particular incidents, for the sake of illustrating the general statements already made. I select a few from manifestations without number. I am able to ascertain dates from the following circumstances:—

"I was born in April, 1802, and my father died in July, 1808, after suffering for more than a year from a lingering organic disease. Between two and three years before his death he removed from the house in which I was born to another at a little distance from it. What occurred, therefore, before my father's last sickness, must have taken place during the first five years of my life, and whatever took place before the removal of the family must have taken place during the first three years of my life. Before the removal of the family I slept in a small upper chamber in the front part of the house, where I was generally alone for several hours in the evening and morning. Adjoining this room, and opening into it by a very small door, was a low, dark, narrow, unfinished closet, which was open on the other side into a ruinous, old chaise-house. This closet was a famous place for the gambols of the phantoms, but of their forms and actions I do not now retain any very distinct recollection. I only remember that I was very careful not to do anything that I thought would be likely to offend them; yet otherwise their presence caused me no uneasiness, and was not at all disagreeable to me.

"The first incident of which I have a distinct recollection was the following:—

"One night, as I was lying alone in my chamber with my little dog Brutus snoring beside my bed, there came out of the closet a very large Indian woman and a very small Indian man, with a huge bass-viol between them. The woman was dressed in a large, loose, black gown, secured around her waist by a belt of the same material, and on her head she wore a high, dark gray fur cap, shaped somewhat like a lady's muff, ornamented with a row of covered buttons in front, and open towards the bottom, showing a red lining. The man was dressed in a shabby, black-colored overcoat and a little round, black hat that fitted closely to his head. They took no notice of me, but were rather ill-natured towards each other, and seemed to be disputing for the possession of the bass-viol. The man snatched it away and struck upon it a few harsh, hollow notes, which I distinctly heard, and which seemed to vibrate through my whole body, with a strange, stinging sensation. The woman then took it and appeared to play very intently and much to her own satisfaction, but without producing any sound that was perceptible by me. They soon left the chamber, and I saw them go down into the back kitchen, where they sat and played and talked with my mother. It was only when the man took the bow that I could hear the harsh, abrupt, disagreeable sounds of the instrument. At length they arose, went out of the back door, and sprang upon a large heap of straw and unthreshed beans, and disappeared with a strange, rumbling sound. This vision was repeated night after night with scarcely any variation while we lived in that house, and once, and once only, after the family had removed to the other house. The only thing that seemed to me unaccountable and that excited my curiosity was that there should be such a large heap of straw and beans before the door every night, when I could see nothing of it in the daytime. I frequently crept out of bed and stole softly down into the kitchen, and peeped out of the door to see if it was there very early in the morning.

"I attempted to make some inquiries of my mother, but as I was not as yet very skillful in the use of language, I could get no satisfaction out of her answers, and could see that my questions seemed to distress her. At first she took little notice of what I said, regarding it no doubt as the meaningless prattle of a thoughtless child. My persistence, however, seemed to alarm her, and I suppose that she feared for my sanity. I soon desisted from asking anything further, and shut myself more and more within myself. One night, very soon after the removal, when the house was still, and all the family were in bed, these unearthly musicians once made their appearance in the kitchen of the new house, and after looking around peevishly, and sitting with a discontented frown and in silence, they arose and went out of the back door, and sprang on a pile of cornstalks, and I saw them no more.

"Our new dwelling was a low-studded house of only one story, and, instead of an upper chamber, I now occupied a bedroom that opened into the kitchen. Within this bedroom, directly on the left hand of the door as you entered from the kitchen, was the staircase which led to the garret; and, as the room was unfinished, some of the boards which inclosed the staircase were too short, and left a considerable space between them and the ceiling. One of these open spaces was directly in front of my bed, so that when I lay upon my pillow my face was opposite to it. Every night, after I had gone to bed and the candle was removed, a very pleasant-looking human face would peer at me over the top of that board, and gradually press forward his head, neck, shoulders, and finally his whole body as far as the waist, through the opening, and then, smiling upon me with great good-nature, would withdraw in the same manner in which he had entered. He was a great favorite of mine; for though we neither of us spoke, we perfectly understood, and were entirely devoted to, each other. It is a singular fact that the features of this favorite phantom bore a very close resemblance to those of a boy older than myself whom I feared and hated: still the resemblance was so strong that I called him by the same name, Harvey.

"Harvey's visits were always expected and always pleasant; but sometimes there were visitations of another sort, odious and frightful. One of these I will relate as a specimen of the rest.

"One night, after I had retired to bed and was looking for Harvey, I observed an unusual number of the tunnel-shaped tremulous clouds already described, and they seemed intensely black and strongly agitated. This alarmed me exceedingly, and I had a terrible feeling that something awful was going to happen. It was not long before I saw Harvey at his accustomed place, cautiously peeping at me through the aperture, with an expression of pain and terror on his countenance. He seemed to warn me to be on my guard, but was afraid to put his head into the room lest he should be touched by one of the clouds, which were every moment growing thicker and more numerous. Harvey soon withdrew and left me alone. On turning my eyes towards the left-hand wall of the room, I thought I saw at an immense distance below me the regions of the damned, as I had heard them pictured in sermons. From this awful world of horror the tunnel-shaped clouds were ascending, and I perceived that they were the principal instruments of torture in these gloomy abodes. These regions were at such an immense distance below me that I could obtain but a very indistinct view of the inhabitants, who were very numerous and exceedingly active. Near the surface of the earth, and as it seemed to me but a little distance from my bed, I saw four or five sturdy, resolute devils endeavoring to carry off an unprincipled and dissipated man in the neighborhood, by the name of Brown, of whom I had stood in terror for years. These devils I saw were very different from the common representations. They had neither red faces, nor horns, nor hoofs, nor tails. They were in all respects stoutly built and well-dressed gentlemen. The only peculiarity that I noted in their appearance was as to their heads. Their faces and necks were perfectly bare, without hair or flesh, and of a uniform sky-blue color, like the ashes of burnt paper before it falls to pieces, and of a certain glossy smoothness.

"As I looked on, full of eagerness, the devils struggled to force Brown down with them, and Brown struggled with the energy of desperation to save himself from their grip, and it seemed that the human was likely to prove too strong for the infernal. In this emergency one of the devils, panting for breath and covered with perspiration, beckoned to a strong, thick cloud that seemed to understand him perfectly, and, whirling up to Brown, touched his hand. Brown resisted stoutly, and struck out right and left at the cloud most furiously, but the usual effect was produced,—the hand grew black, quivered, and seemed to be melting into the cloud; then the arm, by slow degrees, and then the head and shoulders. At this instant Brown, collecting all his energies for one desperate effort, sprang at once into the centre of the cloud, tore it asunder, and descended to the ground, exclaiming, with a hoarse, furious voice that grated on my ear, 'There, I've got out; dam'me if I haven't!' This was the first word that had been spoken through the whole horrible scene. It was the first time I had ever seen a cloud fail to produce its appropriate result, and it terrified me so that I trembled from head to foot. The devils, however, did not seem to be in the least discouraged. One of them, who seemed to be the leader, went away and quickly returned bringing with him an enormous pair of rollers fixed in an iron frame, such as are used in iron-mills for the purpose of rolling out and slitting bars of iron, except instead of being turned by machinery, each roller was turned by an immense crank. Three of the devils now seized Brown and put his feet to the rollers, while two others stood, one at each crank, and began to roll him in with a steady strain that was entirely irresistible. Not a word was spoken, not a sound was heard; but the fearful struggles and terrified, agonizing looks of Brown were more than I could endure. I sprang from my bed and ran through the kitchen into the room where my parents slept, and entreated that they would permit me to spend the remainder of the night with them. After considerable parleying they assured me that nothing could hurt me, and advised me to go back to bed. I replied that I was not afraid of their hurting me, but I couldn't bear to see them acting so with C. Brown. 'Poh! poh! you foolish boy,' replied my father, sternly. 'You've only been dreaming; go right back to bed, or I shall have to whip you.' Knowing that there was no other alternative, I trudged back through the kitchen with all the courage I could muster, cautiously entered my room, where I found everything quiet, there being neither cloud, nor devil, nor anything of the kind to be seen, and getting into bed I slept quietly till morning. The next day I was rather sad and melancholy, but kept all my troubles to myself, through fear of Brown. This happened before my father's sickness, and consequently between the four and six years of my age.

"During my father's sickness and after his death I lived with my grandmother; and when I had removed to her house I forever lost sight of Harvey. I still continued to sleep alone for the most part, but in a neatly furnished upper chamber. Across the corner of the chamber, opposite to and at a little distance from the head of my bed, there was a closet in the form of an old-fashioned buffet. After going to bed, on looking at the door of this closet, I could see at a great distance from it a pleasant meadow, terminated by a beautiful little grove. Out of this grove, and across this meadow, a charming little female figure would advance, about eight inches high and exquisitely proportioned, dressed in a loose black silk robe, with long, smooth black hair parted up her head and hanging loose over her shoulders. She would come forward with a slow and regular step, becoming more distinctly visible as she approached nearer, till she came even with the surface of the closet door, when she would smile upon me, raise her hands to her head and draw them down on each side of her face, suddenly turn round, and go off at a rapid trot. The moment she turned I could see a good-looking mulatto man, rather smaller than herself, following directly in her wake and trotting off after her. This was generally repeated two or three times before I went to sleep. The features of the mulatto bore some resemblance to those of the Indian man with the bass-viol, but were much more mild and agreeable.

"I awoke one bright, moonlight night, and found a large, full-length human skeleton of an ashy-blue color in bed with me! I screamed out with fright, and soon summoned the family around me. I refused to tell the cause of my alarm, but begged permission to occupy another bed, which was granted.

"For the remainder of the night I slept but little; but I saw upon the window-stools companies of little fairies, about six inches high, in white robes, gamboling and dancing with incessant merriment. Two of them, a male and female, rather taller than the rest, were dignified with a crown and sceptre. They took the kindest notice of me, smiled upon me with great benignity, and seemed to assure me of their protection. I was soothed and cheered by their presence, though after all there was a sort of sinister and selfish expression in their countenances which prevented my placing implicit confidence in them.

"Up to this time I had never doubted the real existence of these phantoms, nor had I ever suspected that other people had not seen them as distinctly as myself. I now, however, began to discover with no little anxiety that my friends had little or no knowledge of the ærial beings among whom I have spent my whole life; that my allusions to them were not understood, and all complaints respecting them were laughed at. I had never been disposed to say much about them, and this discovery confirmed me in my silence. It did not, however, affect my own belief, or lead me to suspect that my imaginations were not realities.

"During the whole of this period I took great pleasure in walking out alone, particularly in the evening. The most lonely fields, the woods, and the banks of the river, and other places most completely secluded, were my favorite resorts, for there I could enjoy the sight of innumerable ærial beings of all sorts, without interruption. Every object, even every shaking leaf, seemed to me to be animated by some living soul, whose nature in some degree corresponded to its habitation. I spent much of my life in these solitary rambles; there were particular places to which I gave names, and visited them at regular intervals. Moonlight was particularly agreeable to me, but most of all I enjoyed a thick, foggy night. At times, during these walks, I would be excessively oppressed by an indefinite and deep feeling of melancholy. Without knowing why, I would be so unhappy as to wish myself annihilated, and suddenly it would occur to me that my friends at home were suffering some dreadful calamity, and so vivid would be the impression, that I would hasten home with all speed to see what had taken place. At such seasons I felt a morbid love for my friends that would almost burn up my soul, and yet, at the least provocation from them, I would fly into an uncontrollable passion and foam like a little fury. I was called a dreadful-tempered boy; but the Lord knows that I never occasioned pain to any animal, whether human or brutal, without suffering untold agonies in consequence of it. I cannot, even now, without feelings of deep sorrow, call to mind the alternate fits of corroding melancholy, irritation, and bitter remorse which I then endured. These fits of melancholy were most constant and oppressive during the autumnal months.

"I very early learned to read, and soon became immoderately attached to books. In the Bible I read the first chapters of Job, and parts of Ezekiel, Daniel, and Revelation, with most intense delight, and with such frequency that I could repeat large portions from memory long before the age at which boys in the country are usually able to read plain sentences. The first large book besides the Bible that I remember reading was Morse's 'History of New England,' which I devoured with insatiable greediness, particularly those parts which relate to Indian wars and witchcraft. I was in the habit of applying to my grandmother for explanations, and she would relate to me, while I listened with breathless attention, long stories from Mather's 'Magnalia' or (Mag-nilly, as she used to call it), a work which I earnestly longed to read, but of which I never got sight till after my twentieth year. Very early there fell into my hands an old school-book, called 'The Art of Speaking,' containing numerous extracts from Milton and Shakespeare. There was little else in the book that interested me, but these extracts from the two great English poets, though there were many things in them that I did not well understand, I read again and again, with increasing pleasure at every perusal, till I had nearly committed them to memory, and almost thumbed the old book into nonentity. But of all the books that I read at this period, there was none that went to my heart like Bunyan's 'Pilgrim's Progress.' I read it and re-read it night and day; I took it to bed with me and hugged it to my bosom while I slept; every different edition that I could find I seized upon and read with as eager a curiosity as if it had been a new story throughout; and I read with the unspeakable satisfaction of most devoutly believing that everything which 'Honest John' related was a real verity, an actual occurrence. Oh that I could read that most inimitable book once more with the same solemn conviction of its literal truth, that I might once more enjoy the same untold ecstacy!

"One other remark it seems proper to make before I proceed further to details. The appearance, and especially the motions, of my ærial visitors were intimately connected, either as cause or effect, I cannot determine which, with certain sensations of my own. Their countenances generally expressed pleasure or pain, complaisance or anger, according to the mood of my own mind: if they moved from place to place without moving their limbs, with that gliding motion appropriate to spirits, I felt in my stomach that peculiar tickling sensation which accompanies a rapid, progressive movement through the air; and if they went off with an uneasy trot, I felt an unpleasant jarring through my frame. Their appearance was always attended with considerable effort and fatigue on my part: the more distinct and vivid they were, the more would my fatigue be increased; and at such times my face was always pale, and my eyes unusually sparkling and wild. This continued to be the case after I became satisfied that it was all a delusion of the imagination, and it so continues to the present day."

It is not surprising that Mrs. Stowe should have felt herself impelled to give literary form to an experience so exceptional. Still more must this be the case when the early associations of this exceptional character were as amusing and interesting as they are shown forth in "Oldtown Fireside Stories."

None of the incidents or characters embodied in those sketches are ideal. The stories are told as they came from Mr. Stowe's lips, with little or no alteration. Sam Lawson was a real character. In 1874 Mr. Whittier wrote to Mrs. Stowe: "I am not able to write or study much, or read books that require thought, without suffering, but I have Sam Lawson lying at hand, and, as Corporal Trim said of Yorick's sermon, 'I like it hugely.'"

The power and literary value of these stories lie in the fact that they are true to nature. Professor Stowe was himself an inimitable mimic and story-teller. No small proportion of Mrs. Stowe's success as a literary woman is to be attributed to him. Not only was he possessed of a bright, quick mind, but wonderful retentiveness of memory. Mrs. Stowe was never at a loss for reliable information on any subject as long as the professor lived. He belonged to that extinct species, the "general scholar." His scholarship was not critical in the modern sense of the word, but in the main accurate, in spite of his love for the marvelous.

It is not out of place to give a little idea of his power in character-painting, as it shows how suggestive his conversation and letters must have been to a mind like that of Mrs. Stowe:—

I have had a real good time this week writing my oration. I have strolled over my old walking places, and found the same old stone walls, the same old foot-paths through the rye-fields, the same bends in the river, the same old bullfrogs with their green spectacles on, the same old terrapins sticking up their heads and bowing as I go by; and nothing was wanting but my wife to talk with to make all complete. . . . I have had some rare talks with old uncle "Jaw" Bacon, and other old characters, which you ought to have heard. The Curtises have been flooding Uncle "Jaw's" meadows, and he is in a great stew about it. He says: "I took and tell'd your Uncle Izic to tell them 'ere Curtises that if the Devil didn't git 'em far flowing my medder arter that sort, I didn't see no use o' havin' any Devil." "Have you talked with the Curtises yourself?" "Yes, hang the sarcy dogs! and they took and tell'd me that they'd take and flow clean up to my front door, and make me go out and in in a boat." "Why don't you go to law?" "Oh, they keep alterin' and er tinkerin'-up the laws so here in Massachusetts that a body can't git no damage fur flowing; they think cold water can't hurt nobody."

Mother and Aunt Nabby each keep separate establishments. First Aunt Nabby gets up in the morning and examines the sink, to see whether it leaks and rots the beam. She then makes a little fire, gets her little teapot of bright shining tin, and puts into it a teaspoonful of black tea, and so prepares her breakfast.

By this time mother comes creeping down-stairs, like an old tabby-cat out of the ash-hole; and she kind o' doubts and reckons whether or no she had better try to git any breakfast, bein' as she's not much appetite this mornin'; but she goes to the leg of bacon and cuts off a little slice, reckons sh'll broil it; then goes and looks at the coffee-pot and reckons sh'll have a little coffee; don't exactly know whether it's good for her, but she don't drink much. So while Aunt Nabby is sitting sipping her tea and munching her bread and butter with a matter-of-fact certainty and marvelous satisfaction, mother goes doubting and reckoning round, like Mrs. Diffidence in Doubting Castle, till you see rising up another little table in another corner of the room, with a good substantial structure of broiled ham and coffee, and a boiled egg or two, with various et ceteras, which Mrs. Diffidence, after many desponding ejaculations, finally sits down to, and in spite of all presentiments makes them fly as nimbly as Mr. Ready-to-Halt did Miss Much-afraid when he footed it so well with her on his crutches in the dance on the occasion of Giant Despair's overthrow.

I have thus far dined alternately with mother and Aunt Susan, not having yet been admitted to Aunt Nabby's establishment. There are now great talkings, and congresses and consultations of the allied powers, and already rumors are afloat that perhaps all will unite their forces and dine at one table, especially as Harriet and little Hattie are coming, and there is no knowing what might come out in the papers if there should be anything a little odd.

Mother is very well, thin as a hatchet and smart as a steel trap; Aunt Nabby, fat and easy as usual; for since the sink is mended, and no longer leaks and rots the beam, and she has nothing to do but watch it, and Uncle Bill has joined the Washingtonians and no longer drinks rum, she is quite at a loss for topics of worriment.

Uncle Ike has had a little touch of palsy and is rather feeble. He says that his legs and arms have rather gi'n out, but his head and pluck are as good as they ever were. I told him that our sister Kate was very much in the same fix, whereat he was considerably affected, and opened the crack in his great pumpkin of a face, displaying the same two rows of great white ivories which have been my admiration from my youth up. He is sixty-five years of age, and has never lost a tooth, and was never in his life more than fifteen miles from the spot where he was born, except once, in the ever-memorable year 1819, when I was at Bradford Academy.

In a sudden glow of adventurous rashness he undertook to go after me and bring me home for vacation; and he actually performed the whole journey of thirty miles with his horse and wagon, and slept at a tavern a whole night, a feat of bravery on which he has never since ceased to plume himself. I well remember that awful night in the tavern in the remote region of North Andover. We occupied a chamber in which were two beds. In the unsuspecting innocence of youth I undressed myself and got into bed as usual; but my brave and thoughtful uncle, merely divesting himself of his coat, put it under his pillow, and then threw himself on to the bed with his boots on his feet, and his two hands resting on the rim of his hat, which he had prudently placed on the apex of his stomach as he lay on his back. He wouldn't allow me to blow out the candle, but he lay there with his great white eyes fixed on the ceiling, in the cool, determined manner of a bold man who had made up his mind to face danger and meet whatever might befall him. We escaped, however, without injury, the doughty landlord and his relentless sons merely demanding pay for supper, lodging, horse-feed, and breakfast, which my valiant uncle, betraying no signs of fear, resolutely paid.

Mrs. Stowe has woven this incident into chapter thirty-two of "Oldtown Folks," where Uncle Ike figures as Uncle Jacob.

Mrs. Stowe had misgivings as to the reception which "Oldtown Folks" would meet in England, owing to its distinctively New England character. Shortly after the publication of the book she received the following words of encouragement from Mrs. Lewes (George Eliot), July 11, 1869:—

"I have received and read 'Oldtown Folks.' I think that few of your readers can have felt more interest than I have felt in that picture of an elder generation; for my interest in it has a double root,—one in my own love for our old-fashioned provincial life, which had its affinities with a contemporary life, even all across the Atlantic, and of which I have gathered glimpses in different phases from my father and mother, with their relations; the other is my experimental acquaintance with some shades of Calvinistic orthodoxy. I think your way of presenting the religious convictions which are not your own, except by the way of indirect fellowship, is a triumph of insight and true tolerance. . . . Both Mr. Lewes and I are deeply interested in the indications which the professor gives of his peculiar psychological experience, and we should feel it a great privilege to learn much more of it from his lips. It is a rare thing to have such an opportunity of studying exceptional experience in the testimony of a truthful and in every way distinguished mind."

"Oldtown Folks" is of interest as being undoubtedly the last of Mrs. Stowe's works which will outlive the generation for which it was written. Besides its intrinsic merit as a work of fiction, it has a certain historic value as being a faithful study of "New England life and character in that particular time of its history which may be called the seminal period."

Whether Mrs. Stowe was far enough away from the time and people she attempts to describe to "make (her) mind as still and passive as a looking-glass or a mountain lake, and to give merely the images reflected there," is something that will in great part determine the permanent value of this work. Its interest as a story merely is of course ephemeral.

CHAPTER XIX

THE BYRON CONTROVERSY, 1869-1870.

MRS. STOWE'S STATEMENT OF HER OWN CASE.—THE
CIRCUMSTANCES UNDER WHICH SHE FIRST MET LADY
BYRON.—LETTERS TO LADY BYRON.—LETTER TO DR.
HOLMES WHEN ABOUT TO PUBLISH "THE TRUE STORY OF
LADY BYRON'S LIFE" IN THE "ATLANTIC."—DR.
HOLMES'S REPLY.—THE CONCLUSION OF THE MATTER.

IT seems impossible to avoid the unpleasant episode in Mrs.
Stowe's life known as the "Byron Controversy." It will be our
effort to deal with the matter as colorlessly as is consistent with an
adequate setting forth of the motives which moved Mrs. Stowe to
awaken this unsavory discussion. In justification of her action in
this matter, Mrs. Stowe says:—

"What interest have you and I, my brother and my sister, in this
short life of ours, to utter anything but the truth? Is not truth
between man and man, and between man and woman, the
foundation on which all things rest? Have you not, every individual
of you, who must hereafter give an account yourself alone to God,
an interest to know the exact truth in this matter, and a duty to
perform as respects that truth? Hear me, then, while I tell you the
position in which I stood, and what was my course in relation to it.

"A shameless attack on my friend's memory had appeared in
the 'Blackwood' of July, 1869, branding Lady Byron as the vilest of
criminals, and recommending the Guiccioli book to a Christian
public as interesting from the very fact that it was the avowed
production of Lord Byron's mistress. No efficient protest was
made against this outrage in England, and Littell's 'Living Age'
reprinted the 'Blackwood' article, and the Harpers, the largest
publishing house in America, perhaps in the world, republished the
book.

"Its statements—with those of the 'Blackwood,' 'Pall Mall Gazette,' and other English periodicals—were being propagated through all the young reading and writing world of America. I was meeting them advertised in dailies, and made up into articles in magazines, and thus the generation of to-day, who had no means of judging Lady Byron but by these fables of her slanderers, were being foully deceived. The friends who knew her personally were a small, select circle in England, whom death is every day reducing. They were few in number compared with the great world, and were *silent*. I saw these foul slanders crystallizing into history, uncontradicted by friends who knew her personally, who, firm in their own knowledge of her virtues, and limited in view as aristocratic circles generally are, had no idea of the width of the world they were living in, and the exigency of the crisis. When time passed on and no voice was raised, I spoke."

It is hardly necessary to recapitulate, at any great length, facts already so familiar to the reading public; it may be sufficient simply to say that after the appearance in 1868 of the Countess Guiccioli's "Recollections of Lord Byron," Mrs. Stowe felt herself called upon to defend the memory of her friend from what she esteemed to be falsehoods and slanders. To accomplish this object, she prepared for the "Atlantic Monthly" of September, 1869, an article, "The True Story of Lady Byron's Life." Speaking of her first impressions of Lady Byron, Mrs. Stowe says:—

"I formed her acquaintance in the year 1853, during my first visit to England. I met her at a lunch party in the house of one of her friends. When I was introduced to her, I felt in a moment the words of her husband:—

"'There was awe in the homage that she drew;
Her spirit seemed as seated on a throne.'"

It was in the fall of 1856, on the occasion of Mrs. Stowe's second visit to England, as she and her sister were on their way to Eversley to visit the Rev. C. Kingsley, that they stopped by invitation to lunch with Lady Byron at her summer residence at Ham Common, near Richmond. At that time Lady Byron informed Mrs. Stowe that it was her earnest desire to receive a visit from her on her return, as there was a subject of great importance concerning which she desired her advice. Mrs. Stowe has thus described this interview with Lady Byron:—

"After lunch, I retired with Lady Byron, and my sister remained with her friends. I should here remark that the chief subject of the conversation which ensued was not entirely new to me.

"In the interval between my first and second visits to England, a lady who for many years had enjoyed Lady Byron's friendship and confidence had, with her consent, stated the case generally to me, giving some of the incidents, so that I was in a manner prepared for what followed.

"Those who accuse Lady Byron of being a person fond of talking upon this subject, and apt to make unconsidered confidences, can have known very little of her, of her reserve, and of the apparent difficulty she had in speaking on subjects nearest her heart. Her habitual calmness and composure of manner, her collected dignity on all occasions, are often mentioned by her husband, sometimes with bitterness, sometimes with admiration. He says: 'Though I accuse Lady Byron of an excess of self-respect, I must in candor admit that, if ever a person had excuse for an extraordinary portion of it, she has, as in all her thoughts, words, and deeds she is the most decorous woman that ever existed, and must appear, what few I fancy could, a perfectly refined gentlewoman, even to her *femme de chambre*.'

"This calmness and dignity were never more manifested than in this interview. In recalling the conversation at this distance of time, I cannot remember all the language used. Some particular words and forms of expression I do remember, and those I give; and in other cases I give my recollection of the substance of what was said.

"There was something awful to me in the intensity of repressed emotion which she showed as she proceeded. The great fact upon which all turned was stated in words that were unmistakable."

Mrs. Stowe goes on to give minutely Lady Byron's conversation, and concludes by saying:—

Of course I did not listen to this story as one who was investigating its worth. I received it as truth, and the purpose for which it was communicated was not to enable me to prove it to the world, but to ask my opinion whether she should show it to the world before leaving it. The whole consultation was upon the assumption that she had at her command such proofs as could not be questioned. Concerning what they were I did not minutely inquire, only, in answer to a general question, she said that she had letters and documents in proof of her story. Knowing Lady Byron's strength of mind, her clear-headedness, her accurate habits, and her perfect knowledge of the matter, I considered her judgment on this point decisive. I told her that I would take the subject into consideration and give my opinion in a few days. That night, after my sister and myself had retired to our own apartment, I related to her the whole history, and we spent the night in talking it over. I was powerfully impressed with the justice and propriety of an immediate disclosure; while she, on the contrary, represented the fatal consequences that would probably come upon Lady Byron from taking such a step.

Before we parted the next day, I requested Lady Byron to give me some memoranda of such dates and outlines of the general story as would enable me better to keep it in its connection, which she did. On giving me the paper, Lady Byron requested me to return it to her when it had ceased to be of use to me for the purpose intended. Accordingly, a day or two after, I inclosed it to her in a hasty note, as I was then leaving London for Paris, and had not yet had time fully to consider the subject. On reviewing my note I can recall that then the whole history appeared to me like one of those singular cases where unnatural impulses to vice are the result of a taint of constitutional insanity. This has always seemed to me the only way of accounting for instances of utterly motiveless and abnormal wickedness and cruelty. These, my first impressions, were expressed in the hasty note written at the time:

LONDON, *November 5, 1856.*

DEAREST FRIEND,—I return these. They have held mine eyes waking. How strange! How unaccountable! Have you ever subjected the facts to the judgment of a medical man, learned in nervous pathology? Is it not insanity?

"Great wits to madness nearly are allied,
And thin partitions do their bounds divide."

But my purpose to-night is not to write to you fully what I think of this matter. I am going to write to you from Paris more at leisure.

(The rest of the letter was taken up in the final details of a charity in which Lady Byron had been engaged with me in assisting an unfortunate artist. It concludes thus:)

I write now in all haste, *en route* for Paris. As to America, all is not lost yet. Farewell. I love you, my dear friend, as never before, with an intense feeling that I cannot easily express. God bless you.

H. B. S.

The next letter is as follows:—

PARIS, *December 17, 1856.*

DEAR LADY BYRON,—The Kansas Committee have written me a letter desiring me to express to Miss —— their gratitude for the five pounds she sent them. I am not personally acquainted with her, and must return these acknowledgments through you.

I wrote you a day or two since, inclosing the reply of the Kansas Committee to you.

On that subject on which you spoke to me the last time we were together, I have thought often and deeply. I have changed my mind somewhat. Considering the peculiar circumstances of the case, I could wish that the sacred veil of silence, so bravely thrown over the past, should never be withdrawn during the time that you remain with us. I would say then, leave all with some discreet friends, who, after both have passed from earth, shall say what was due to justice. I am led to think this by seeing how low, how unworthy, the judgments of this world are; and I would not that what I so much respect, love, and revere should be placed within reach of its harpy claw, which pollutes what it touches. The day will yet come which will bring to light every hidden thing. "There is nothing covered that shall not be revealed, neither hid that shall not be known;" and so justice will not fail.

Such, my dear friend, are my thoughts; different from what they were since first I heard that strange, sad history. Meanwhile I love you forever, whether we meet again on earth or not.

Affectionately yours,
H. B. S.

Before her article appeared in print, Mrs. Stowe addressed the following letter to Dr. Holmes in Boston:—

HARTFORD, <i>June 26, 1869.</i>

Dear Doctor,—I am going to ask help of you, and I feel that confidence in your friendship that leads me to be glad that I have a friend like you to ask advice of. In order that you may understand fully what it is, I must go back some years and tell you about it.

When I went to England the first time, I formed a friendship with Lady Byron which led to a somewhat interesting correspondence. When there the second time, after the publication of "Dred" in 1856, Lady Byron wrote to me that she wished to have some private confidential conversation with me, and invited me to come spend a day with her at her country-seat near London. I went, met her alone, and spent an afternoon with her. The object of the visit she then explained to me. She was in such a state of health that she considered she had very little time to live, and was engaged in those duties and reviews which every thoughtful person finds who is coming deliberately, and with their eyes open, to the boundaries of this mortal life.

Lady Byron, as you must perceive, has all her life lived under a weight of slanders and false imputations laid upon her by her husband. Her own side of the story has been told only to that small circle of confidential friends who needed to know it in order to assist her in meeting the exigencies which it imposed on her. Of course it has thrown the sympathy mostly on his side, since the world generally has more sympathy with impulsive incorrectness than with strict justice.

At that time there was a cheap edition of Byron's works in contemplation, meant to bring them into circulation among the masses, and the pathos arising from the story of his domestic misfortunes was one great means relied on for giving it currency.

Under these circumstances some of Lady Byron's friends had proposed the question to her whether she had not a responsibility to society for the truth; whether she did right to allow these persons to gain influence over the popular mind by a silent consent to an utter falsehood. As her whole life had been passed in the most heroic self-abnegation and self sacrifice, the question was now proposed to her whether one more act of self-denial was not required of her, namely, to declare the truth, no matter at what expense to her own feelings.

For this purpose she told me she wished to recount the whole story to a person in whom she had confidence,—a person of another country, and out of the whole sphere of personal and local feelings which might be supposed to influence those in the country and station in life where the events really happened,—in order that I might judge whether anything more was required of her in relation to this history.

The interview had almost the solemnity of a death-bed confession, and Lady Byron told me the history which I have embodied in an article to appear in the "Atlantic Monthly." I have been induced to prepare it by the run which the Guiccioli book is having, which is from first to last an unsparing attack on Lady Byron's memory by Lord Byron's mistress.

When you have read my article, I want, not your advice as to whether the main facts shall be told, for on this point I am so resolved that I frankly say advice would do me no good. But you might help me, with your delicacy and insight, to make the manner of telling more perfect, and I want to do it as wisely and well as such story can be told.

My post-office address after July 1st will be Westport Point, Bristol Co., Mass., care of Mrs. I. M. Soule. The proof-sheets will be sent you by the publisher.

Very truly yours,
H. B. STOWE.

In reply to the storm of controversy aroused by the publication of this article, Mrs. Stowe made a more extended effort to justify the charges which she had brought against Lord Byron, in a work published in 1869, "Lady Byron Vindicated." Immediately after the publication of this work, she mailed a copy to Dr. Oliver Wendell Holmes, accompanied by the following note:—

BOSTON, *May 19, 1869.*

DEAR DOCTOR,— . . . In writing this book, which I now take the liberty of sending to you, I have been in . . . a "critical place." It has been a strange, weird sort of experience, and I have had not a word to say to anybody, though often thinking of you and wishing I could have a little of your help and sympathy in getting out what I saw. I think of you very much, and rejoice to see the *hold* your works get on England as well as this country, and I would give more for your opinion than that of most folks. How often I have pondered your last letter to me, and sent it to many (friends)! God bless you. Please accept for yourself and your good wife, this copy.

From yours truly,
H. B. STOWE.

Mrs. Stowe also published in 1870, through Sampson Low & Son, of London, a volume for English readers, "The History of the Byron Controversy." These additional volumes, however, do not seem to have satisfied the public as a whole, and perhaps the expediency of the publication of Mrs. Stowe's first article is doubtful, even to her most ardent admirers. The most that can be hoped for, through the mention of the subject in this biography, is the vindication of Mrs. Stowe's purity of motive and nobility of intention in bringing this painful matter into notice.

While she was being on all hands effectively, and evidently in some quarters with rare satisfaction, roundly abused for the article, and her consequent responsibility in bringing this unsavory discussion so prominently before the public mind, she received the following letter from Dr. O. W. Holmes:—

BOSTON, *September 25, 1869.*

MY DEAR MRS. STOWE,—I have been meaning to write to you for some time, but in the midst of all the wild and virulent talk about the article in the "Atlantic," I felt as if there was little to say until the first fury of the storm had blown over.

I think that we all perceive now that the battle is not to be fought here, but in England. I have listened to a good deal of talk, always taking your side in a quiet way, backed very heartily on one occasion by one of my most intellectual friends, reading all that came in my way, and watching the course of opinion. And first, it was to be expected that the Guiccioli fanciers would resent any attack on Lord Byron, and would highly relish the opportunity of abusing one who, like yourself, had been identified with all those moral enterprises which elevate the standard of humanity at large, and of womanhood in particular. After this scum had worked itself off, there must necessarily follow a controversy, none the less sharp and bitter, but not depending essentially on abuse. The first point the recusants got hold of was the error of the two years which contrived to run the gauntlet of so many pairs of eyes. Some of them were made happy by mouthing and shaking this between their teeth, as a poodle tears round with a glove. This did not last long. No sensible person could believe for a moment you were mistaken in the essential character of a statement every word of which would fall on the ear of a listening friend like a drop of melted lead, and burn its scar deep into the memory. That Lady Byron believed and told you the story will not be questioned by any but fools and malignants. Whether her belief was well founded there may be positive evidence in existence to show affirmatively. The fact that her statement is not peremptorily contradicted by those most likely to be acquainted with the facts of the case, is the one result so far which is forcing itself into unwilling recognition. I have seen nothing, in the various hypotheses brought forward, which did not to me involve a greater improbability than the presumption of guilt. Take that, for witness, that Byron accused himself, through a spirit of perverse vanity, of crimes he had not committed. How preposterous! He would stain the name of a sister, whom, on the supposition of his innocence, he loved with angelic ardor as well as purity, by associating it with such an infamous accusation. Suppose there are some anomalies hard to explain in Lady Byron's conduct. Could a young and guileless woman, in the hands of such a man, be expected to act in any given way, or would she not be likely to waver, to doubt, to hope, to contradict herself, in the anomalous position in which, without experience, she found herself?

As to the intrinsic evidence contained in the poems, I think it confirms rather than contradicts the hypothesis of guilt. I do not think that Butler's argument, and all the other attempts at invalidation of the story, avail much in the face of the acknowledged fact that it was told to various competent and honest witnesses, and remains without a satisfactory answer from those most interested.

I know your firm self-reliance, and your courage to proclaim the truth when any good end is to be served by it. It is to be expected that public opinion will be more or less divided as to the expediency of this revelation. . . .

Hoping that you have recovered from your indisposition, I am

Faithfully yours,
O. W. HOLMES.

While undergoing the most unsparing and pitiless criticism and brutal insult, Mrs. Stowe received the following sympathetic words from Mrs. Lewes (George Eliot):—

THE PRIORY, 21 NORTH BANK, *December 10, 1869.*

MY DEAR FRIEND,— . . . In the midst of your trouble I was often thinking of you, for I feared that you were undergoing a considerable trial from the harsh and unfair judgments, partly the fruit of hostility glad to find an opportunity for venting itself, and partly of that unthinking cruelty which belongs to hasty anonymous journalism. For my own part, I should have preferred that the Byron question should never have been brought before the public, because I think the discussion of such subjects is injurious socially. But with regard to yourself, dear friend, I feel sure that, in acting on a different basis of impressions, you were impelled by pure, generous feeling. Do not think that I would have written to you of this point to express a judgment. I am anxious only to convey to you a sense of my sympathy and confidence, such as a kiss and a pressure of the hand could give if I were near you.

I trust that I shall hear a good account of Professor Stowe's health, as well as your own, whenever you have time to write me a word or two. I shall not be so unreasonable as to expect a long letter, for the hours of needful rest from writing become more and more precious as the years go on, but some brief news of you and yours will be especially welcome just now. Mr. Lewes unites with me in high regards to your husband and yourself, but in addition to that I have the sister woman's privilege of saying that I am always

Your affectionate friend,
M. H. LEWES.

CHAPTER XX

GEORGE ELIOT

CORRESPONDENCE WITH GEORGE ELIOT.—GEORGE ELIOT'S FIRST IMPRESSIONS OF MRS. STOWE.—MRS. STOWE'S LETTER TO MRS. FOLLEN.—GEORGE ELIOT'S LETTER TO MRS. STOWE.—MRS. STOWE'S REPLY.—LIFE IN FLORIDA.—ROBERT DALE OWEN AND MODERN SPIRITUALISM.—GEORGE ELIOT'S LETTER ON THE PHENOMENA OF SPIRITUALISM.—MRS. STOWE'S DESCRIPTION OF SCENERY IN FLORIDA.—MRS. STOWE CONCERNING "MIDDLEMARCH."—GEORGE ELIOT TO MRS. STOWE DURING REV. H. W. BEECHER'S TRIAL.— MRS. STOWE CONCERNING HER LIFE EXPERIENCE WITH HER BROTHER, H. W. BEECHER, AND HIS TRIAL.—MRS. LEWES' LAST LETTER TO MRS. STOWE.—DIVERSE MENTAL CHARACTERISTICS OF THESE TWO WOMEN.— MRS. STOWE'S FINAL ESTIMATE OF MODERN SPIRITUALISM.

IT is with a feeling of relief that we turn from one of the most disagreeable experiences of Mrs. Stowe's life to one of the most delightful, namely, the warm friendship of one of the most eminent women of this age, George Eliot.

There seems to have been some deep affinity of feeling that drew them closely together in spite of diversity of intellectual tastes.

George Eliot's attention was first personally attracted to Mrs. Stowe in 1853, by means of a letter which the latter had written to Mrs. Follen. Speaking of this incident she (George Eliot) writes: "Mrs. Follen showed me a delightful letter which she has just had from Mrs. Stowe, telling all about herself. She begins by saying, 'I am a little bit of a woman, rather more than forty, as withered and dry as a pinch of snuff; never very well worth looking at in my best days, and now a decidedly used-up article.' The whole letter is most fascinating, and makes one love her."

The correspondence between these two notable women was begun by Mrs. Stowe, and called forth the following extremely interesting letter from the distinguished English novelist:—

THE PRIORY, 21 NORTH BANK, *May 8, 1869.*

MY DEAR FRIEND,—I value very highly the warrant to call you friend which your letter has given me. It lay awaiting me on our return the other night from a nine weeks' absence in Italy, and it made me almost wish that you could have a momentary vision of the discouragement,—nay, paralyzing despondency—in which many days of my writing life have been passed, in order that you might fully understand the good I find in such sympathy as yours, in such an assurance as you give me that my work has been worth doing. But I will not dwell on any mental sickness of mine. The best joy your words give me is the sense of that sweet, generous feeling in you which dictated them. I shall always be the richer because you have in this way made me know you better. I must tell you that my first glimpse of you as a woman came through a letter of yours, and charmed me very much. The letter was addressed to Mrs. Follen, and one morning I called on her in London (how many years ago!); she was kind enough to read it to me, because it contained a little history of your life, and a sketch of your domestic circumstances. I remember thinking that it was very kind of you to write that long letter, in reply to inquiries of one who was personally unknown to you; and, looking back with my present experience, I think it was kinder than it then appeared, for at that time you must have been much oppressed with the immediate results of your fame. I remember, too, that you wrote of your husband as one who was richer in Hebrew and Greek than in pounds or shillings; and as an ardent scholar has always been a character of peculiar interest to me, I have rarely had your image in my mind without the accompanying image (more or less erroneous) of such a scholar by your side. I shall welcome the fruit of his Goethe studies, whenever it comes.

I have good hopes that your fears are groundless as to the obstacles your new book ("Oldtown Folks") may find here from its thorough American character. Most readers who are likely to be really influenced by writing above the common order will find that special aspect an added reason for interest and study; and I dare say you have long seen, as I am beginning to see with new clearness, that if a book which has any sort of exquisiteness happens also to be a popular, widely circulated book, the power over the social mind for any good is, after all, due to its reception by a few appreciative natures, and is the slow result of radiation from that narrow circle. I mean that you can affect a few souls, and that each of these in turn may affect a few more, but that no exquisite book tells properly and directly on a multitude, however largely it may be spread by type and paper. Witness the things the multitude will say about it, if one is so unhappy as to be obliged to hear their sayings. I do not write this cynically, but in pure sadness and pity. Both traveling abroad and staying at home among our English sights and sports, one must continually feel how slowly the centuries work toward the moral good of men, and that thought lies very close to what you say as to your wonder or conjecture concerning my religious point of view. I believe that religion, too, has to be modified according to the dominant phases; that a religion more perfect than any yet prevalent must express less care of personal consolation, and the more deeply awing sense of responsibility to man springing from sympathy with that which of all things is most certainly known to us,—the difficulty of the human lot. Letters are necessarily narrow and fragmentary, and when one writes on wide subjects, are likely to create more misunderstanding than illumination. But I have little anxiety in writing to you, dear friend and fellow-laborer; for you have had longer experience than I as a writer, and fuller experience as a woman, since you have borne children and known a mother's history from the beginning. I trust your quick and long-taught mind as an interpreter little liable to mistake me.

When you say, "We live in an orange grove, and are planting many more," and when I think you must have abundant family love to cheer you, it seems to me that you must have a paradise about you. But no list of circumstances will make a paradise. Nevertheless, I must believe that the joyous, tender humor of your books clings about your more immediate life, and makes some of that sunshine for yourself which you have given to us. I see the advertisement of "Oldtown Folks," and shall eagerly expect it. That and every other new link between us will be reverentially valued. With great devotion and regard,

Yours always,
M. L. LEWES.

Mrs. Stowe writes from Mandarin to George Eliot:—

MANDARIN, *February 8, 1872.*

DEAR FRIEND,—It is two years nearly since I had your last very kind letter, and I have never answered, because two years of constant and severe work have made it impossible to give a drop to anything beyond the needs of the hour. Yet I have always thought of you, loved you, trusted you all the same, and read every little scrap from your writing that came to hand.

One thing brings you back to me. I am now in Florida in my little hut in the orange orchard, with the broad expanse of the blue St. John's in front, and the waving of the live-oaks, with their long, gray mosses, overhead, and the bright gold of oranges looking through dusky leaves around. It is like Sorrento,—so like that I can quite dream of being there. And when I get here I enter another life. The world recedes; I am out of it; it ceases to influence; its bustle and noise die away in the far distance; and here is no winter, an open-air life,—a quaint, rude, wild wilderness sort of life, both rude and rich; but when I am here I write more letters to friends than ever I do elsewhere. The mail comes only twice a week, and then is the event of the day. My old rabbi and I here set up our tent, he with German, and Greek, and Hebrew, devouring all sorts of black-letter books, and I spinning ideal webs out of bits that he lets fall here and there.

I have long thought that I would write you again when I got here, and so I do. I have sent North to have them send me the "Harper's Weekly," in which your new story is appearing, and have promised myself leisurely to devour and absorb every word of it.

While I think of it I want to introduce to you a friend of mine, a most noble man, Mr. Owen, for some years our ambassador at Naples, now living a literary and scholar life in America. His father was Robert Dale Owen, the theorist and communist you may have heard of in England some years since.

Years ago, in Naples, I visited Mr. Owen for the first time, and found him directing his attention to the phenomena of spiritism. He had stumbled upon some singular instances of it accidentally, and he had forthwith instituted a series of researches and experiments on the subject, some of which he showed me. It was the first time I had ever seriously thought of the matter, and he invited my sister and myself to see some of the phenomena as exhibited by a medium friend of theirs who resided in their family. The result at the time was sufficiently curious, but I was interested in his account of the manner in which he proceeded, keeping records of every experiment with its results, in classified orders. As the result of his studies and observations, he has published two books, one "Footfalls on the Boundary of Another World," published in 1860, and latterly, "The Debatable Land Between this World and the Next." I regard Mr. Owen as one of the few men who are capable of entering into an inquiry of this kind without an utter drowning of common sense, and his books are both of them worth a fair reading. To me they present a great deal that is intensely curious and interesting, although I do not admit, of course, all his deductions, and think he often takes too much for granted. Still, with every abatement there remains a residuum of fact, which I think both curious and useful. In a late letter to me he says:—

"There is no writer of the present day whom I more esteem than Mrs. Lewes, nor any one whose opinion of my work I should more highly value."

I believe he intends sending them to you, and I hope you will read them. Lest some of the narratives should strike you, as such narratives did me once, as being a perfect Arabian

Nights' Entertainment, I want to say that I have accidentally been in the way of confirming some of the most remarkable by personal observation. . . . In regard to all this class of subjects, I am of the opinion of Goethe, that "it is just as absurd to deny the facts of spiritualism now as it was in the Middle Ages to ascribe them to the Devil." I think Mr. Owen attributes too much value to his facts. I do not think the things contributed from the ultra-mundane sphere are particularly valuable, apart from the evidence they give of continued existence after death.

I do not think there is yet any evidence to warrant the idea that they are a supplement or continuation of the revelations of Christianity, but I do regard them as an interesting and curious study in psychology, and every careful observer like Mr. Owen ought to be welcomed to bring in his facts. With this I shall send you my observations on Mr. Owen's books, from the "Christian Union." I am perfectly aware of the frivolity and worthlessness of much of the revealings purporting to come from spirits. In my view, the worth or worthlessness of them has nothing to do with the question of fact.

Do invisible spirits speak in any wise,—wise or foolish?—is the question *a priori*? I do not know of any reason why there should not be as many foolish virgins in the future state as in this. As I am a believer in the Bible and Christianity, I don't need these things as confirmations, and they are not likely to be a religion to me. I regard them simply as I do the phenomena of the Aurora Borealis, or Darwin's studies on natural selection, as curious studies into nature. Besides, I think some day we shall find a law by which all these facts will fall into their places.

I hope now this subject does not bore you: it certainly is one that seems increasingly to insist on getting itself heard. It is going on and on, making converts, who are many more than dare avow themselves, and for my part I wish it were all brought into the daylight of inquiry.

Let me hear from you if ever you feel like it. I know too well the possibilities and impossibilities of a nature like yours to ask more, but it can do you no harm to know that I still think of you and love you as ever.

Faithfully yours,
H. B. STOWE.

THE PRIORY, 21 NORTH BANK, REGENT'S PARK,
March 4, 1872.

DEAR FRIEND,—I can understand very easily that the two last years have been full for you of other and more imperative work than the writing of letters not absolutely demanded either by charity or business. The proof that you still think of me affectionately is very welcome now it has come, and more cheering because it enables me to think of you as enjoying your retreat in your orange orchard,—your western Sorrento—the beloved rabbi still beside you. I am sure it must be a great blessing to you to bathe in that quietude, as it always is to us when we go out of reach of London influences and have the large space of country days to study, walk, and talk in. . . .

When I am more at liberty I will certainly read Mr. Owen's books, if he is good enough to send them to me. I desire on all subjects to keep an open mind, but hitherto the various phenomena, reported or attested in connection with ideas of spirit intercourse and so on, have come before me here in the painful form of the lowest charlatanerie. . . .

But apart from personal contact with people who get money by public exhibitions as mediums, or with semi-idiots such as those who make a court for a Mrs. ——, or other feminine personages of that kind, I would not willingly place any barriers between my mind and any possible channel of truth affecting the human lot. The spirit in which you have written in the paper you kindly sent me is likely to touch others, and arouse them at least to attention in a case where you have been deeply impressed. . . .

Yours with sincere affection,
M. L. LEWES.

MANDARIN, FLORIDA, *May 11, 1872.*

MY DEAR FRIEND,—I was very glad to get your dear little note,—sorry to see by it that you are not in your full physical force. Owing to the awkwardness and misunderstanding of publishers, I am not reading "Middlemarch," as I expected to be, here in these orange shades: they don't send it, and I am too far out of the world to get it. I felt, when I read your letters, how glad I should be to have you here in our Florida cottage, in the wholly new, wild, woodland life. Though resembling Italy in climate, it is wholly different in the appearance of nature,—the plants, the birds, the animals, all different. The green tidiness and culture of England here gives way to a wild and rugged savageness of beauty. Every tree bursts forth with flowers; wild vines and creepers execute delirious gambols, and weave and interweave in interminable labyrinths. Yet here, in the great sandy plains back of our house, there is a constant wondering sense of beauty in the wild, wonderful growths of nature. First of all, the pines—high as the stone pines of Italy—with long leaves, eighteen inches long, through which there is a constant dreamy sound, as if of dashing waters. Then the live-oaks and the water-oaks, narrow-leaved evergreens, which grow to enormous size, and whose branches are draped with long festoons of the gray moss. There is a great, wild park of these trees back of us, which, with the dazzling, varnished green of the new spring leaves and the swaying drapery of moss, looks like a sort of enchanted grotto. Underneath grow up hollies and ornamental flowering shrubs, and the yellow jessamine climbs into and over everything with fragrant golden bells and buds, so that sometimes the foliage of a tree is wholly hidden in its embrace.

This wild, wonderful, bright and vivid growth, that is all new, strange, and unknown by name to me, has a charm for me. It is the place to forget the outside world, and live in one's self. And if you were here, we would go together and gather azaleas, and white lilies, and silver bells, and blue iris. These flowers keep me painting in a sort of madness. I have just finished a picture of white lilies that grow in the moist land by the watercourses. I am longing to begin on blue iris. Artist, poet, as you are by nature, you ought to see all these things, and if you would come here I would take you in heart and house, and you should have a little room in our cottage. The history of the cottage is this: I found a hut built close to a great live-oak twenty-five feet in girth, and with overarching boughs eighty feet up in the air, spreading like a firmament, and all swaying with mossy festoons. We began to live here, and gradually we improved the hut by lath, plaster, and paper. Then we threw out a wide veranda all round, for in these regions the veranda is the living-room of the house. Ours had to be built around the trunk of the tree, so that our cottage has a peculiar and original air, and seems as if it were half tree, or a something that had grown out of the tree. We added on parts, and have thrown out gables and chambers, as a tree throws out new branches, till our cottage is like nobody else's, and yet we settle into it with real enjoyment. There are all sorts of queer little rooms in it, and we are accommodating at this present a family of seventeen souls. In front, the beautiful, grand St. John's stretches five miles from shore to shore, and we watch the steamboats plying back and forth to the great world we are out of. On all sides, large orange trees, with their dense shade and ever-vivid green, shut out the sun so that we can sit, and walk, and live in the open air. Our winter here is only cool, bracing out-door weather, without snow. No month without flowers blooming in the open air, and lettuce and peas in the garden. The summer range is about 90°, but the sea-breezes keep the air delightfully fresh. Generally we go North, however, for three months of summer. Well, I did not mean to run on about Florida, but the subject runs away with me, and I want you to visit us in spirit if not personally.

My poor rabbi!—he sends you some Arabic, which I fear you cannot read: on diablerie he is up to his ears in knowledge, having read all things in all tongues, from the Talmud down. . . .

Ever lovingly yours,
H. B. STOWE.

BOSTON, *September 26, 1872.*

MY DEAR FRIEND,—I think when you see my name again
so soon, you will think it rains, hails, and snows notes from
this quarter. Just now, however, I am in this lovely, little nest
in Boston, where dear Mrs. Fields, like a dove, "sits brooding
on the charmed wave." We are both wishing we had you here
with us, and she has not received any answer from you as yet
in reply to the invitation you spoke of in your last letter to me.
It seems as if you must have written, and the letter somehow
gone astray, because I know, of course, you would write.
Yesterday we were both out of our senses with mingled pity
and indignation at that dreadful stick of a Casaubon,—and
think of poor Dorothea dashing like a warm, sunny wave
against so cold and repulsive a rock! He is a little too dreadful
for anything: there does not seem to be a drop of warm blood
in him, and so, as it is his misfortune and not his fault, to be
cold-blooded, one must not get angry with him. It is the scene
in the garden, after the interview with the doctor, that rests on

our mind at this present. There was such a man as he over in Boston, high in literary circles, but I fancy his wife wasn't like Dorothea, and a vastly proper time they had of it, treating each other with mutual reverence, like two Chinese mandarins.

My love, what I miss in this story is just what we would have if you would come to our tumble-down, jolly, improper, but joyous country,—namely, "jollitude." You write and live on so high a plane! It is all self-abnegation. We want to get you over here, and into this house, where, with closed doors, we sometimes make the rafters ring with fun, and say anything and everything, no matter what, and won't be any properer than we's a mind to be. I am wishing every day you could see our America,—travel, as I have been doing, from one bright, thriving, pretty, flowery town to another, and see so much wealth, ease, progress, culture, and all sorts of nice things. This dovecot where I now am is the sweetest little nest imaginable; fronting on a city street, with back windows opening on a sea view, with still, quiet rooms filled with books, pictures, and all sorts of things, such as you and Mr. Lewes would enjoy. Don't be afraid of the ocean, now! I've crossed it six times, and assure you it is an overrated item. Froude is coming here— why not you? Besides, we have the fountain of eternal youth here, that is, in Florida, where I live, and if you should come you would both of you take a new lease of life, and what glorious poems, and philosophies, and whatnot, we should have! My rabbi writes, in the seventh heaven, an account of your note to him. To think of his setting-off on his own account when I was away!

Come now, since your answer to dear Mrs. Fields is yet to come; let it be a glad yes, and we will clasp you to our heart of hearts.

Your ever loving,
H. B. S.

During the summer of 1874, while Mrs. Stowe's brother, the Rev. Henry Ward Beecher, was the victim of a most revolting, malicious, and groundless attack on his purity, Mrs. Lewes wrote the following words of sympathy:—

MY DEAR FRIEND, The other day I had a letter from Mrs. Fields, written to let me know something of you under that heavy trouble, of which such information as I have had has been quite untrustworthy, leaving me in entire incredulity in regard to it except on this point, that you and yours must be suffering deeply. Naturally I thought most of you in the matter (its public aspects being indeterminate), and many times before our friend's letter came I had said to Mr. Lewes: "What must Mrs. Stowe be feeling!" I remember Mrs. Fields once told me of the wonderful courage and cheerfulness which belonged to you, enabling you to bear up under exceptional trials, and I imagined you helping the sufferers with tenderness and counsel, but yet, nevertheless, I felt that there must be a bruising weight on your heart. Dear, honored friend, you who are so ready to give warm fellowship, is it any comfort to you to be told that those afar off are caring for you in spirit, and will be happier for all good issues that may bring you rest?

I cannot, dare not, write more in my ignorance, lest I should be using unreasonable words. But I trust in your not despising this scrap of paper which tells you, perhaps rather for my relief than yours, that I am always in grateful, sweet remembrance of your goodness to me and your energetic labors for all.

It was two years or more before Mrs. Stowe replied to these words of sympathy.

Orange-blossom time, MANDARIN, *March 18,*
1876.

MY DEAR FRIEND,—I always think of you when the orange trees are in blossom; just now they are fuller than ever, and so many bees are filling the branches that the air is full of a sort of still murmur. And now I am beginning to hear from you every month in Harper's. It is as good as a letter. "Daniel Deronda" has succeeded in awaking in my somewhat worn-out mind an interest. So many stories are tramping over one's mind in every modern magazine nowadays that one is macadamized, so to speak. It takes something unusual to make a sensation. This does excite and interest me, as I wait for each number with eagerness. I wish I could endow you with our long winter weather,—not winter, except such as you find in Sicily. We live here from November to June, and my husband sits outdoors on the veranda and reads all day. We emigrate in solid family: my two dear daughters, husband, self, and servants come together to spend the winter here, and so together to our Northern home in summer. My twin daughters relieve me from all domestic care; they are lively, vivacious, with a real genius for practical life. We have around us a little settlement of neighbors, who like ourselves have a winter home here, and live an easy, undress, picnic kind of life, far from the world and its cares. Mr. Stowe has been busy on eight volumes of Görres on the mysticism of the Middle Ages. This Görres was Professor of Philosophy at Munich, and he reviews the whole ground of the shadow-land between the natural and the supernatural,—ecstacy, trance, prophecy, miracles, spiritualism, the stigmata, etc. He was a devout Roman Catholic, and the so-called facts that he reasons on seem to me quite amazing; and yet the possibilities that lie between inert matter and man's living, all-powerful, immortal soul may make almost anything credible. The soul at times can do anything with matter. I have been busying myself with Sainte-Beuve's seven volumes on the Port Royal development. I like him (Sainte-Beuve). His capacity of seeing, doing justice to all kinds of natures and sentiments, is wonderful. I am sorry he is no longer our side the veil.

There is a redbird (cardinal grosbeak) singing in the orange trees fronting my window, so sweetly and insistently as to almost stop my writing. I hope, dear friend, you are well— better than when you wrote last.

It was very sweet and kind of you to write what you did last. I suppose it is so long ago you may have forgotten, but it was a word of tenderness and sympathy about my brother's trial; it was womanly, tender, and sweet, such as at heart you are. After all, my love of you is greater than my admiration, for I think it more and better to be really a woman worth loving than to have read Greek and German and written books. And in this last book I read, I feel more with you in some little, fine points,—they stare at me as making an amusing exhibition. For, my dear, I feel myself at last as one who has been playing and picnicking on the shores of life, and waked from a dream late in the afternoon to find that everybody almost has gone over to the beyond. And the rest are sorting their things and packing their trunks, and waiting for the boat to come and take them.

It seems now but a little time since my brother Henry and I were two young people together. He was my two years junior, and nearest companion out of seven brothers and three sisters. I taught him drawing and heard his Latin lessons, for you know a girl becomes mature and womanly long before a boy. I saw him through college, and helped him through the difficult love affair that gave him his wife; and then he and my husband had a real German, enthusiastic love for each other, which ended in making me a wife. Ah! in those days we never dreamed that he, or I, or any of us, were to be known in the world. All he seemed then was a boy full of fun, full of love, full of enthusiasm for protecting abused and righting wronged people, which made him in those early days write editorials, and wear arms and swear himself a special policeman to protect the poor negroes in Cincinnati, where we then lived, when there were mobs instigated by the slaveholders of Kentucky.

Then he married, and lived a missionary life in the new West, all with a joyousness, an enthusiasm, a chivalry, which made life bright and vigorous to us both. Then in time he was called to Brooklyn, just as the crisis of the great anti-slavery battle came on, and the Fugitive Slave Law was passed. I was then in Maine, and I well remember one snowy night his riding till midnight to see me, and then our talking, till near morning, what we could do to make headway against the horrid cruelties that were being practiced against the defenseless blacks. My husband was then away lecturing, and my heart was burning itself out in indignation and anguish. Henry told me then that he meant to fight that battle in New York; that he would have a church that would stand by him to resist the tyrannic dictation of Southern slaveholders. I said: "I, too, have begun to do something; I have begun a story, trying to set forth the sufferings and wrongs of the slaves." "That's right, Hattie," he said; "finish it, and I will scatter it thick as the leaves of

Vallambrosa," and so came "Uncle Tom," and Plymouth Church became a stronghold where the slave always found refuge and a strong helper. One morning my brother found sitting on his doorstep poor old Paul Edmonson, weeping; his two daughters, of sixteen and eighteen, had passed into the slave warehouse of Bruin & Hill, and were to be sold. My brother took the man by the hand to a public meeting, told his story for him, and in an hour raised the two thousand dollars to redeem his children. Over and over again, afterwards, slaves were redeemed at Plymouth Church, and Henry and Plymouth Church became words of hatred and fear through half the Union. From that time until we talked together about the Fugitive Slave Law, there was not a pause or stop in the battle till we had been through the war and slavery had been wiped out in blood. Through all he has been pouring himself out, wrestling, burning, laboring everywhere, making stump speeches when elections turned on the slave question, and ever maintaining that the cause of Christ was the cause of the slave. And when all was over, it was he and Lloyd Garrison who were sent by government once more to raise our national flag on Fort Sumter. You must see that a man does not so energize without making many enemies. Half of our Union has been defeated, a property of millions annihilated by emancipation, a proud and powerful slave aristocracy reduced to beggary, and there are those who never saw our faces that, to this hour, hate him and me. Then he has been a progressive in theology. He has been a student of Huxley, and Spencer, and Darwin,— enough to alarm the old school,—and yet remained so ardent a supernaturalist as equally to repel the radical destructionists in religion. He and I are Christ-worshippers, adoring Him as the Image of the Invisible God and all that comes from believing this. Then he has been a reformer, an advocate of universal suffrage and woman's rights, yet not radical enough to please that reform party who stand where the Socialists of France do, and are for tearing up all creation generally. Lastly, he has had the misfortune of a popularity which is perfectly phenomenal. I cannot give you any idea of the love, worship, idolatry, with which he has been overwhelmed. He has something magnetic about him that makes everybody crave his society,—that makes men follow and worship him. I remember being at his house one evening in the time of early flowers, and in that one evening came a box of flowers from Maine, another from New Jersey, another from Connecticut,—all from people with whom he had no personal acquaintance, who had read something of his and wanted to send him some token. I said, "One would think you were a *prima donna*. What does make people go on so about you?"

My brother is hopelessly generous and confiding. His inability to believe evil is something incredible, and so has come all this suffering. You said you hoped I should be at rest when the first investigating committee and Plymouth Church cleared my brother almost by acclamation. Not so. The enemy have so committed themselves that either they or he must die, and there has followed two years of the most dreadful struggle. First, a legal trial of six months, the expenses of which on his side were one hundred and eighteen thousand dollars, and in which he and his brave wife sat side by side in the court-room, and heard all that these plotters, who had been weaving their webs for three years, could bring. The foreman of the jury was offered a bribe of ten thousand dollars to decide against my brother. He sent the letter containing the proposition to the judge. But with all their plotting, three fourths of the jury decided against them, and their case was lost. It was accepted as a triumph by my brother's friends; a large number of the most influential clergy of all denominations so expressed themselves in a public letter, and it was hoped the thing was so far over that it might be lived down and overgrown with better things.

But the enemy, intriguing secretly with all those parties in the community who wish to put down a public and too successful man, have been struggling to bring the thing up again for an ecclesiastical trial. The cry has been raised in various religious papers that Plymouth Church was in complicity with crime,—that they were so captivated with eloquence and genius that they refused to make competent investigation. The six months' legal investigation was insufficient; a new trial was needed. Plymouth Church immediately called a council of ministers and laymen, in number representing thirty-seven thousand Congregational

Christians, to whom Plymouth Church surrendered her records,—her conduct,—all the facts of the case, and this great council unanimously supported the church and ratified her decision; recognizing the fact that, in all the investigations hitherto, nothing had been proved against my brother. They at his request, and that of Plymouth Church, appointed a committee of five to whom within sixty days any one should bring any facts that they could prove, or else forever after hold their peace. It is thought now by my brother's friends that this thing must finally reach a close. But you see why I have not written. This has drawn on my life—my heart's blood. He is myself; I know you are the kind of woman to understand me when I say that I felt a blow at him more than at myself. I, who know his purity, honor, delicacy, know that he has been from childhood of an ideal purity,—who reverenced his conscience as his king, whose glory was redressing human wrong, who spake no slander, no, nor listened to it.

Never have I known a nature of such strength, and such almost childlike innocence. He is of a nature so sweet and perfect that, though I have seen him thunderously indignant at moments, I never saw him fretful or irritable,—a man who continuously, in every little act of life, is thinking of others, a man that all the children on the street run after, and that every sorrowful, weak, or distressed person looks to as a natural helper. In all this long history there has been no circumstance of his relation to any woman that has not been worthy of himself,—pure, delicate, and proper; and I know all sides of it, and certainly should not say this if there were even a misgiving. Thank God, there is none, and I can read my New Testament and feel that by all the beatitudes my brother is blessed.

His calmness, serenity, and cheerfulness through all this time has uplifted us all. Where he was, there was no anxiety, no sorrow. My brother's power to console is something peculiar and wonderful. I have seen him at death-beds and funerals, where it would seem as if hope herself must be dumb, bring down the very peace of Heaven and change despair to trust. He has not had less power in his own adversity. You cannot conceive how he is beloved, by those even who never saw him,—old, paralytic, distressed, neglected people, poor seamstresses, black people, who have felt these arrows shot against their benefactor as against themselves, and most touching have been their letters of sympathy. From the first, he has met this in the spirit of Francis de Sales, who met a similar plot,—by silence, prayer, and work, and when urged to defend himself said "God would do it in his time." God was the best judge how much reputation he needed to serve Him with.

In your portrait of Deronda, you speak of him as one of those rare natures in whom a private wrong bred no bitterness. "The sense of injury breeds, not the will to inflict injuries, but a hatred of all injury;" and I must say, through all this conflict my brother has been always in the spirit of Him who touched and healed the ear of Malchus when he himself was attacked. His friends and lawyers have sometimes been aroused and sometimes indignant with his habitual caring for others, and his habit of vindicating and extending even to his enemies every scrap and shred of justice that might belong to them. From first to last of this trial, he has never for a day intermitted his regular work. Preaching to crowded houses, preaching even in his short vacations at watering places, carrying on his missions which have regenerated two once wretched districts of the city, editing a paper, and in short giving himself up to work. He cautioned his church not to become absorbed in him and his trials, to prove their devotion by more faithful church work and a wider charity; and never have the Plymouth missions among the poor been so energetic and effective. He said recently, "The worst that can befall a man is to stop thinking of God and begin to think of himself; if trials make us self-absorbed, they hurt us." Well, dear, pardon me for this outpour. I loved you—I love you—and therefore wanted you to know just what I felt. Now, dear, this is over, don't think you must reply to it or me. I know how much you have to do,—yes, I know all about an aching head and an overtaxed brain. This last work of yours is to be your best, I think, and I hope it will bring you enough to buy an orange grove in Sicily, or somewhere else, and so have lovely weather such as we have.

Your ancient admirer, who usually goes to bed at eight o'clock, was convicted by me of sitting up after eleven over the last installment of "Daniel Deronda," and he is full of it. We think well of Guendoline, and that she isn't much more than young ladies in general so far.

Next year, if I can possibly do it, I will send you some of our oranges. I perfectly long to have you enjoy them.

Your very loving
H. B. STOWE.

P. S. I am afraid I shall write you again when I am reading your writings, they are so provokingly suggestive of things one wants to say.

H. B. S.

In her reply to this letter Mrs. Lewes says, incidentally: "Please offer my reverential love to the Professor, and tell him I am ruthlessly proud of having kept him out of his bed. I hope that both you and he will continue to be interested in my spiritual children."

After Mr. Lewes's death, Mrs. Lewes writes to Mrs. Stowe:—

THE PRIORY, 21 NORTH BANK, *April 10, 1879.*

MY DEAR FRIEND,—I have been long without sending you any sign (unless you have received a message from me through Mrs. Fields), but my heart has been going out to you and your husband continually as among the chief of the many kind beings who have given me their tender fellow-feeling in my last earthly sorrow. . . . When your first letter came, with the beautiful gift of your book, I was unable to read any letters, and did not for a long time see what you had sent me. But when I did know, and had read your words of thankfulness at the great good you have seen wrought by your help, I felt glad, for your sake first, and then for the sake of the great nation to which you belong. The hopes of the world are taking refuge westward, under the calamitous conditions, moral and physical, in which we of the elder world are getting involved. . . .

Thank you for telling me that you have the comfort of seeing your son in a path that satisfies your best wishes for him. I like to think of your having family joys. One of the prettiest photographs of a child that I possess is one of your sending to me. . . .

Please offer my reverential, affectionate regards to your husband, and believe me, dear friend,

Yours always gratefully,
M. L. LEWES.

As much as has been said with regard to spiritualism in these pages, the subject has by no means the prominence that it really possessed in the studies and conversations of both Professor and Mrs. Stowe.

Professor Stowe's very remarkable psychological development, and the exceptional experiences of his early life, were sources of conversation of unfailing interest and study to both.

Professor Stowe had made an elaborate and valuable collection of the literature of the subject, and was, as Mrs. Stowe writes, "over head and ears in *diablerie*."

It is only just to give Mrs. Stowe's views on this perplexing theme more at length, and as the mature reflection of many years has caused them to take form.

In reference to professional mediums, and spirits that peep, rap, and mutter, she writes:—

"Each friend takes away a portion of ourselves. There was some part of our being related to him as to no other, and we had things to say to him which no other would understand or appreciate. A portion of our thoughts has become useless and burdensome, and again and again, with involuntary yearning, we turn to the stone at the door of the sepulchre. We lean against the cold, silent marble, but there is no answer,—no voice, neither any that regardeth.

"There are those who would have us think that in *our* day this doom is reversed; that there are those who have the power to restore to us the communion of our lost ones. How many a heart, wrung and tortured with the anguish of this fearful silence, has throbbed with strange, vague hopes at the suggestion! When we hear sometimes of persons of the strongest and clearest minds becoming credulous votaries of certain spiritualist circles, let us not wonder: if we inquire, we shall almost always find that the belief has followed some stroke of death; it is only an indication of the desperation of that heart-hunger which in part it appeases.

"Ah, *were* it true! Were it indeed so that the wall between the spiritual and material is growing thin, and a new dispensation germinating in which communion with the departed blest shall be among the privileges and possibilities of this our mortal state! Ah, were it so that when we go forth weeping in the gray dawn, bearing spices and odors which we long to pour forth for the beloved dead, we should indeed find the stone rolled away and an angel sitting on it!

"But for us the stone must be rolled away by an *unquestionable* angel, whose countenance is as the lightning, who executes no doubtful juggle by pale moonlight or starlight, but rolls back the stone in fair, open morning, and sits on it. Then we could bless God for his mighty gift, and with love, and awe, and reverence take up that blessed fellowship with another life, and weave it reverently and trustingly into the web of our daily course.

"But no such angel have we seen,—no such sublime, unquestionable, glorious manifestation. And when we look at what is offered to us, ah! who that had a friend in heaven could wish them to return in such wise as this? The very instinct of a sacred sorrow seems to forbid that our beautiful, our glorified ones should stoop lower than even to the medium of their cast-off bodies, to juggle, and rap, and squeak, and perform mountebank tricks with tables and chairs; to recite over in weary sameness harmless truisms, which we were wise enough to say for ourselves; to trifle, and banter, and jest, or to lead us through endless moonshiny mazes. Sadly and soberly we say that, if this be communion with the dead, we had rather be without it. We want something a little in advance of our present life, and not below it. We have read with some attention weary pages of spiritual communication purporting to come from Bacon, Swedenborg, and others, and long accounts from divers spirits of things seen in the spirit land, and we can conceive of no more appalling prospect than to have them true.

"If the future life is so weary, stale, flat, and unprofitable as we might infer from these readings, one would have reason to deplore an immortality from which no suicide could give an outlet. To be condemned to such eternal prosing would be worse than annihilation.

"Is there, then, no satisfaction for this craving of the soul? There is One who says: "I am he that liveth and was dead, and behold I am alive for evermore, and I have the keys of hell and of death;" and this same being said once before: "He that loveth me shall be loved of my Father, and I will love him and will manifest myself unto him." This is a promise direct and personal; not confined to the first apostles, but stated in the most general way as attainable by any one who loves and does the will of Jesus. It seems given to us as some comfort for the unavoidable heart-breaking separations of death that there should be, in that dread unknown, one all-powerful Friend with whom it is possible to commune, and from whose spirit there may come a response to us. Our Elder Brother, the partaker of our nature, is not only in the spirit land, but is all-powerful there. It is he that shutteth and no man openeth, and openeth and no man shutteth. He whom we have seen in the flesh, weeping over the grave of Lazarus, is he who hath the keys of hell and of death. If we cannot commune with our friends, we can at least commune with Him to whom they are present, who is intimately with them as with us. He is the true bond of union between the spirit world and our souls; and one blest hour of prayer, when we draw near to Him and feel the breadth, and length, and depth, and heighth of that love of his that passeth knowledge, is better than all those incoherent, vain, dreamy glimpses with which longing hearts are cheated.

"They who have disbelieved all spiritual truth, who have been Sadduceeic doubters of either angel or spirit, may find in modern spiritualism a great advance. But can one who has ever really had communion with Christ, who has said with John, "Truly our fellowship is with the Father and the Son,"—can such an one be satisfied with what is found in the modern circle?

"For Christians who have strayed into these inclosures, we cannot but recommend the homely but apt quotation of old John Newton:—

"'What think ye of Christ is the test
To try both your word and your scheme.'

"In all these so-called revelations, have there come any echoes of the *new song* which no man save the redeemed from earth could learn; any unfoldings of that love that passeth knowledge,—anything, in short, such as spirits might utter to whom was unveiled that which eye hath not seen nor ear heard, neither hath entered the heart of man to conceive? We must confess that all those spirits that yet have spoken appear to be living in quite another sphere from John or Paul.

"Let us, then, who long for communion with spirits, seek nearness to Him who has promised to speak and commune, leaving forever this word to his church:—

"'I will not leave you comfortless. I will come to you.'"

CHAPTER XXI

CLOSING SCENES, 1870-1889

LITERARY LABORS.—COMPLETE LIST OF PUBLISHED
BOOKS.—FIRST READING TOUR.—PEEPS BEHIND THE
CURTAIN.—SOME NEW ENGLAND CITIES.—A LETTER
FROM MAINE.—PLEASANT AND UNPLEASANT
READINGS.—SECOND TOUR.—A WESTERN JOURNEY.—
VISIT TO OLD SCENES.—CELEBRATION OF SEVENTIETH
BIRTHDAY.—CONGRATULATORY POEMS FROM MR.
WHITTIER AND DR. HOLMES.—LAST WORDS.

BESIDES the annual journeys to and from Florida, and her
many interests in the South, Mrs. Stowe's time between 1870 and
1880 was largely occupied by literary and kindred labors. In the
autumn of 1871 we find her writing to her daughters as follows
regarding her work:—

"I have at last finished all my part in the third book of mine
that is to come out this year, to wit 'Oldtown Fireside Stories,' and
you can have no idea what a perfect luxury of rest it is to be free
from all literary engagements, of all kinds, sorts, or descriptions. I
feel like a poor woman I once read about,—

"'Who always was tired,
'Cause she lived in a house
Where help wasn't hired,'

and of whom it is related that in her dying moments,

"'She folded her hands
With her latest endeavor,
Saying nothing, dear nothing,
Sweet nothing forever.'

"I am in about her state of mind. I luxuriate in laziness. I do not want to do anything or go anywhere. I only want to sink down into lazy enjoyment of living."

She was certainly well entitled to a rest, for never had there been a more laborious literary life. In addition to the twenty-three books already written, she had prepared for various magazines and journals an incredible number of short stories, letters of travel, essays, and other articles. Yet with all she had accomplished, and tired as she was, she still had seven books to write, besides many more short stories, before her work should be done. As her literary life did not really begin until 1852, the bulk of her work has been accomplished within twenty-six years, as will be seen from the following list of her books, arranged in the chronological order of their publication:—

- 1833. An Elementary Geography.

- 1843. The Mayflower.

- 1852. Uncle Tom's Cabin.

- 1853. Key to Uncle Tom's Cabin.

- 1854. Sunny Memories.

- 1856. Dred.

- 1858. Our Charley.

- 1859. Minister's Wooing.

- 1862. Pearl of Orr's Island.

- 1863. Agnes of Sorrento.

- 1864. House and Home Papers.

- 1865. Little Foxes.

- 1866. Nina Gordon (Formerly "Dred").

- 1867. Religious Poems.

- 1867. Queer Little People.

- 1868. The Chimney Corner.

- 1868. Men of Our Times.

- 1869. Oldtown Folks.

- 1870. Lady Byron Vindicated.

- 1871. The History of the Byron Controversy (London).

- 1870. Little Pussy Willow.

- 1871. Pink and White Tyranny.

- 1871. Old Town Fireside Stories.

- 1872. My Wife and I.

- 1873. Palmetto Leaves.

- 1873. Library of Famous Fiction.

- 1875. We and Our Neighbors.

- 1876. Betty's Bright Idea.

- 1877. Footsteps of the Master.

- 1878. Bible Heroines.

- 1878. Poganuc People.

- 1881. A Dog's Mission.

In 1872 a new and remunerative field of labor was opened to Mrs. Stowe, and though it entailed a vast amount of weariness and hard work, she entered it with her customary energy and enthusiasm. It presented itself in the shape of an offer from the American Literary (Lecture) Bureau of Boston to deliver a course of forty readings from her own works in the principal cities of the New England States. The offer was a liberal one, and Mrs. Stowe accepted it on condition that the reading tour should be ended in time to allow her to go to her Florida home in December. This being acceded to, she set forth and gave her first reading in Bridgeport, Conn., on the evening of September 19, 1872.

The following extracts from letters written to her husband while on this reading tour throw some interesting gleams of light on the scenes behind the curtain of the lecturer's platform. From Boston, October 3d, she writes: "Have had a most successful but fatiguing week. Read in Cambridgeport to-night, and Newburyport to-morrow night." Two weeks later, upon receipt of a letter from her husband, in which he fears he has not long to live, she writes from Westfield, Mass:—

"I have never had a greater trial than being forced to stay away from you now. I would not, but that my engagements have involved others in heavy expense, and should I fail to fulfill them, it would be doing a wrong.

"God has given me strength as I needed it, and I never read more to my own satisfaction than last night.

"Now, my dear husband, please do *want*, and try, to remain with us yet a while longer, and let us have a little quiet evening together before either of us crosses the river. My heart cries out for a home with you; our home together in Florida. Oh, may we see it again! Your ever loving wife."

From Fitchburg, Mass., under date of October 29th, she writes:—

"In the cars, near Palmer, who should I discover but Mr. and Mrs. J. T. Fields, returning from a Western trip, as gay as a troubadour. I took an empty seat next to them, and we had a jolly ride to Boston. I drove to Mr. Williams's house, where I met the Chelsea agent, who informed me that there was no hotel in Chelsea, but that they were expecting to send over for me. So I turned at once toward 148 Charles Street, where I tumbled in on the Fields before they had got their things off. We had a good laugh, and I received a hearty welcome. I was quickly installed in my room, where, after a nice dinner, I curled up for my afternoon nap. At half-past seven the carriage came for me, and I was informed that I should not have a hard reading, as they had engaged singers to take part. So, when I got into the carriage, who should I find, beshawled, and beflowered, and betoggled in blue satin and white lace, but our old friend —— of Andover concert memory, now become Madame Thingumbob, of European celebrity. She had studied in Italy, come out in Milan, sung there in opera for a whole winter, and also in Paris and London.

"Well, she sings very sweetly and looks very nice and pretty. Then we had a little rosebud of a Chelsea girl who sang, and a pianist. I read 'Minister's Housekeeper' and Topsy, and the audience was very jolly and appreciative. Then we all jogged home."

The next letter finds Mrs. Stowe in Maine, and writing in the cars between Bangor and Portland. She says:—

MY DEAR HUSBAND,—Well, Portland and Bangor are over, and the latter, which I had dreaded as lonesome and far off, turned out the pleasantest of any place I have visited yet. I stayed at the Fays; he was one of the Andover students, you remember; and found a warm, cosy, social home. In the evening I met an appreciative audience, and had a delightful reading. I read Captain Kittridge, apparently to the great satisfaction of the people, who laughed heartily at his sea stories, and the "Minister's Housekeeper" with the usual success, also Eva and Topsy.

One woman, totally deaf, came to me afterwards and said: "Bless you. I come jist to see you. I'd rather see you than the Queen." Another introduced her little girl named Harriet Beecher Stowe, and another, older, named Eva. She said they had traveled fifty miles to hear me read. An incident like that appeals to one's heart, does it not?

The people of Bangor were greatly embarrassed by the horse disease; but the mayor and his wife walked over from their house, a long distance off, to bring me flowers, and at the reading he introduced me. I had an excellent audience notwithstanding that it rained tremendously, and everybody had to walk because there were no horses. The professors called on me, also Newman Smith, now a settled minister here.

Everybody is so anxious about you, and Mr. Fay made me promise that you and I should come and spend a week with them next summer. Mr. Howard, in Portland, called upon me to inquire for you, and everybody was so delighted to hear that you were getting better.

It stormed all the time I was in Portland and Bangor, so I saw nothing of them. Now I am in a palace car riding alongside the Kennebec, and recalling the incidents of my trip. I certainly had very satisfactory houses; and these pleasant little visits, and meetings with old acquaintance, would be well worth having, even though I had made nothing in a pecuniary sense. On the whole it is as easy a way of making money as I have ever tried, though no way of making money is perfectly easy,—there must be some disagreeables. The lonesomeness of being at a hotel in dull weather is one, and in Portland it seems there is nobody now to invite us to their homes. Our old friends there are among the past. They have gone on over the river. I send you a bit of poetry that pleases me. The love of the old for each other has its poetry. It is something sacred and full of riches. I long to be with you, and to have some more of our good long talks.

The scenery along this river is very fine. The oaks still keep their leaves, though the other trees are bare; but oaks and pines make a pleasant contrast. We shall stop twenty minutes at Brunswick, so I shall get a glimpse of the old place.

Now we are passing through Hallowell, and the Kennebec changes sides. What a beautiful river! It is now full of logs and rafts. Well, I must bring this to a close. Good-by, dear, with unchanging love. Ever your wife.

From South Framingham, Mass., she writes on November 7th:—

Well, my dear, here I am in E.'s pretty little house. He has a pretty wife, a pretty sister, a pretty baby, two nice little boys, and a lovely white cat. The last is a perfect beauty! a Persian, from a stock brought over by Dr. Parker, as white as snow, with the softest fur, a perfect bunch of loving-kindness, all purr and felicity. I had a good audience last evening, and enjoyed it. My audiences, considering the horse disease and the rains, are amazing. And how they do laugh! We get into regular gales.

E. has the real country minister turn-out: horse and buggy, and such a nice horse too. The baby is a beauty, and giggles, and goos, and shouts inquiries with the rising inflection, in the most inspiring manner.

November 13. Wakefield. I read in Haverhill last night. It was as usual stormy. I had a good audience, but not springy and inspiriting like that at Waltham. Some audiences seem to put spring into one, and some to take it out. This one seemed good but heavy. I had to lift them, while in Framingham and Waltham they lifted me.

The Lord bless and keep you. It grieves me to think you are dull and I not with you. By and by we will be together and stay together. Good-by dear. Your ever loving wife,

H. B. S.

November 24. "I had a very pleasant reading in Peabody. While there visited the library and saw the picture of the Queen that she had painted expressly for George Peabody. It was about six inches square, enameled on gold, and set in a massive frame of solid gold and velvet. The effect is like painting on ivory. At night the picture rolls back into a safe, and great doors, closed with a combination lock, defend it. It reminded me of some of the foreign wonders we have seen.

"Well, my course is almost done, and if I get through without any sickness, cold, or accident, how wonderful it will seem. I have never felt the near, kind presence of our Heavenly Father so much as in this. 'He giveth strength to the faint, and to them of no might He increaseth strength.' I have found this true all my life."

From Newport she writes on November 26th:—

"It was a hard, tiring, disagreeable piece of business to read in New London. Had to wait three mortal hours in Palmer. Then a slow, weary train, that did not reach New London until after dark. There was then no time to rest, and I was so tired that it did seem as though I could not dress. I really trembled with fatigue. The hall was long and dimly lighted, and the people were not seated compactly, but around in patches. The light was dim, except for a great flaring gas jet arranged right under my eyes on the reading desk, and I did not see a creature whom I knew. I was only too glad when it was over and I was back again at my hotel. There I found that I must be up at five o'clock to catch the Newport train.

"I started for this place in the dusk of a dreary, foggy morning. Traveled first on a ferry, then in cars, and then in a little cold steamboat. Found no one to meet me, in spite of all my writing, and so took a carriage and came to the hotel. The landlord was very polite to me, said he knew me by my trunk, had been to our place in Mandarin, etc. All I wanted was a warm room, a good bed, and unlimited time to sleep. Now I have had a three hours' nap, and here I am, sitting by myself in the great, lonely hotel parlor.

"Well, dear old man, I think lots of you, and only want to end all this in a quiet home where we can sing 'John Anderson, my Jo' together. I check off place after place as the captive the days of his imprisonment. Only two more after to-night. Ever your loving wife."

Mrs. Stowe made one more reading tour the following year, and this time it was in the West. On October 28, 1873, she writes from Zanesville, Ohio, to her son at Harvard:—

You have been very good to write as often as you have, and your letters, meeting me at different points, have been most cheering. I have been tired, almost to the last degree. Read two successive evenings in Chicago, and traveled the following day for thirteen hours, a distance of about three hundred miles, to Cincinnati. We were compelled to go in the most uncomfortable cars I ever saw, crowded to overflowing, a fiend of a stove at each end burning up all the air, and without a chance to even lay my head down. This is the grand route between Chicago and Cincinnati, and we were on it from eight in the morning until nearly ten at night.

Arrived at Cincinnati we found that George Beecher had not received our telegram, was not expecting us, had no rooms engaged for us, and that we could not get rooms at his boarding-place. After finding all this out we had to go to the hotel, where, about eleven o'clock, I crept into bed with every nerve aching from fatigue. The next day was dark and rainy, and I lay in bed most of it; but when I got up to go and read I felt only half rested, and was still so tired that it seemed as though I could not get through.

Those who planned my engagements failed to take, into account the fearful distances and wretched trains out here. On none of these great Western routes is there a drawing-room car. Mr. Saunders tried in every way to get them to put one on for us, but in vain. They are all reserved for the night trains; so that there is no choice except to travel by night in sleeping cars, or take such trains as I have described in the daytime.

I had a most sympathetic audience in Cincinnati; they all seemed delighted and begged me to come again. The next day George took us for a drive out to Walnut Hills, where we saw the seminary buildings, the house where your sisters were born, and the house in which we afterwards lived. In the afternoon we had to leave and hurry away to a reading in Dayton. The next evening another in Columbus, where we spent Sunday with an old friend.

By this time I am somewhat rested from the strain of that awful journey; but I shall never again undertake such another. It was one of those things that have to be done once, to learn not to do it again. My only reading between Columbus and Pittsburgh is to be here in Zanesville, a town as black as Acheron, and where one might expect to see the river Styx.

Later. I had a nice audience and a pleasant reading here, and to-day we go on to Pittsburgh, where I read to-morrow night.

I met the other day at Dayton a woman who now has grandchildren; but who, when I first came West, was a gay rattling girl. She was one of the first converts of brother George's seemingly obscure ministry in the little new town of Chillicothe. Now she has one son who is a judge of the supreme court, and another in business. Both she and they are not only Christians, but Christians of the primitive sort, whose religion is their all; who triumph and glory in tribulation, knowing that it worketh patience. She told me, with a bright sweet calm, of her husband killed in battle the first year of the war, of her only daughter and two grandchildren dying in the faith, and of her own happy waiting on God's will, with bright hopes of a joyful reunion. Her sons are leading members of the Presbyterian Church, and most active in stirring up others to make their profession a reality, not an empty name. When I thought that all this came from the conversion of one giddy girl, when George seemed to be doing so little, I said, "Who can measure the work of a faithful minister?" It is such living witnesses that maintain Christianity on earth.

Good-by. We shall soon be home now, and preparing for Florida. Always your own loving mother,

H. B. S.

Mrs. Stowe never undertook another reading tour, nor, after this one, did she ever read again for money, though she frequently contributed her talent in this direction to the cause of charity.

The most noteworthy event of her later years was the celebration of the seventieth anniversary of her birthday. That it might be fittingly observed, her publishers, Messrs. Houghton, Mifflin & Co. of Boston, arranged a reception for her in form of a garden party, to which they invited the *literati* of America. It was held on June 14, 1882, at "The Old Elms," the home of Ex-Governor Claflin of Massachusetts, in Newtonville, one of Boston's most beautiful suburbs. Here the assembly gathered to do honor to Mrs. Stowe, that lovely June afternoon, comprised two hundred of the most distinguished and best known among the literary men and women of the day.

From three until five o'clock was spent socially. As the guests arrived they were presented to Mrs. Stowe by Mr. H. O. Houghton, and then they gathered in groups in the parlors, on the verandas, on the lawn, and in the refreshment room. At five o'clock they assembled in a large tent on the lawn, when Mr. Houghton, as host, addressed to his guest and her friends a few words of congratulation and welcome. He closed his remarks by saying:—

"And now, honored madam, as

"'When to them who sail
Beyond the Cape of Hope, and now are past
Mozambic, off at sea northeast winds blow
Sabean odors from the spicy shore
Of Arabie the blest,'

so the benedictions of the lowly and the blessings of all conditions of men are brought to you to-day on the wings of the wind, from every quarter of the globe; but there will be no fresher laurels to crown this day of your rejoicing than are brought by those now before you, who have been your co-workers in the strife; who have wrestled and suffered, fought and conquered, with you; who rank you with the Miriams, the Deborahs, and the Judiths of old; and who now shout back the refrain, when you utter the inspired song:—

"'Sing ye to the Lord, for he hath triumphed gloriously.'

.   .   .   .

'The Almighty Lord hath disappointed them by the hand of a woman.'"

In reply to this Mrs. Stowe's brother, Henry Ward Beecher, said: "Of course you all sympathize with me to-day, but, standing in this place, I do not see your faces more clearly than I see those of my father and my mother. Her I only knew as a mere babe-child. He was my teacher and my companion. A more guileless soul than he, a more honest one, more free from envy, from jealousy, and from selfishness, I never knew. Though he thought he was great by his theology, everybody else knew he was great by his religion. My mother is to me what the Virgin Mary is to a devout Catholic. She was a woman of great nature, profound as a philosophical thinker, great in argument, with a kind of intellectual imagination, diffident, not talkative,—in which respect I take after her,—the woman who gave birth to Mrs. Stowe, whose graces and excellences she probably more than any of her children—we number but thirteen—has possessed. I suppose that in bodily resemblance, perhaps, she is not like my mother, but in mind I presume she is most like her. I thank you for my father's sake and for my mother's sake for the courtesy, the friendliness, and the kindness which you give to Mrs. Stowe."

The following poem from John Greenleaf Whittier was then read:—

"Thrice welcome from the Land of Flowers
And golden-fruited orange bowers
To this sweet, green-turfed June of ours!
To her who, in our evil time,
Dragged into light the nation's crime
With strength beyond the strength of men,

And, mightier than their sword, her pen;
To her who world-wide entrance gave
To the log cabin of the slave,
Made all his wrongs and sorrows known,
And all earth's languages his own,—
North, South, and East and West, made all
The common air electrical,
Until the o'ercharged bolts of heaven
Blazed down, and every chain was riven!

"Welcome from each and all to her
Whose Wooing of the Minister
Revealed the warm heart of the man
Beneath the creed-bound Puritan,
And taught the kinship of the love
Of man below and God above;
To her whose vigorous pencil-strokes
Sketched into life her Oldtown Folks,
Whose fireside stories, grave or gay,
In quaint Sam Lawson's vagrant way,
With Old New England's flavor rife,
Waifs from her rude idyllic life,
Are racy as the legends old
By Chaucer or Boccaccio told;
To her who keeps, through change of place
And time, her native strength and grace,
Alike where warm Sorrento smiles,
Or where, by birchen-shaded isles
Whose summer winds have shivered o'er
The icy drift of Labrador,
She lifts to light the priceless Pearl
Of Harpswell's angel-beckoned girl.
To her at threescore years and ten
Be tributes of the tongue and pen,
Be honor, praise, and heart thanks given,
The loves of earth, the hopes of heaven!

"Ah, dearer than the praise that stirs
The air to-day, our love is hers!
She needs no guaranty of fame

Whose own is linked with Freedom's name.
Long ages after ours shall keep
Her memory living while we sleep;
The waves that wash our gray coast lines,
The winds that rock the Southern pines
Shall sing of her; the unending years
Shall tell her tale in unborn ears.
And when, with sins and follies past,
Are numbered color-hate and caste,
White, black, and red shall own as one,
The noblest work by woman done."

It was followed by a few words from Dr. Oliver Wendell
Holmes, who also read the subjoined as his contribution to the
chorus of congratulation:—

"If every tongue that speaks her praise
For whom I shape my tinkling phrase
Were summoned to the table,
The vocal chorus that would meet
Of mingling accents harsh or sweet,
From every land and tribe, would beat
The polyglots of Babel.

"Briton and Frenchman, Swede and Dane,
Turk, Spaniard, Tartar of Ukraine,
Hidalgo, Cossack, Cadi,
High Dutchman and Low Dutchman, too,
The Russian serf, the Polish Jew,
Arab, Armenian, and Mantchoo
Would shout, 'We know the lady.'

"Know her! Who knows not Uncle Tom
And her he learned his gospel from,
Has never heard of Moses;
Full well the brave black hand we know
That gave to freedom's grasp the hoe
That killed the weed that used to grow
Among the Southern roses.

"When Archimedes, long ago,

Spoke out so grandly, '*Dos pou sto*,—
Give me a place to stand on,
I'll move your planet for you, now,'—
He little dreamed or fancied how
The *sto* at last should find its *pou*
For woman's faith to land on.

"Her lever was the wand of art,
Her fulcrum was the human heart,
Whence all unfailing aid is;
She moved the earth! Its thunders pealed
Its mountains shook, its temples reeled,
The blood-red fountains were unsealed,
And Moloch sunk to Hades.

"All through the conflict, up and down
Marched Uncle Tom and Old John Brown,
One ghost, one form ideal;
And which was false and which was true,
And which was mightier of the two,
The wisest sibyl never knew,
For both alike were real.

"Sister, the holy maid does well
Who counts her beads in convent cell,
Where pale devotion lingers;
But she who serves the sufferer's needs,
Whose prayers are spelt in loving deeds,
May trust the Lord will count her beads
As well as human fingers.

"When Truth herself was Slavery's slave
Thy hand the prisoned suppliant gave
The rainbow wings of fiction.
And Truth who soared descends to-day
Bearing an angel's wreath away,
Its lilies at thy feet to lay
With heaven's own benediction."

 Poems written for the occasion by Mrs. A. D. T. Whitney, Miss
Elizabeth Stuart Phelps, Mr. J. T. Trowbridge, Mrs. Allen (Mrs.

Stowe's daughter), Mrs. Annie Fields, and Miss Charlotte F. Bates, were also read, and speeches were made by Judge Albion W. Tourgée and others prominent in the literary world.

Letters from many noted people, who were prevented from being present by distance or by other engagements, had been received. Only four of them were read, but they were all placed in Mrs. Stowe's hands. The exercises were closed by a few words from Mrs. Stowe herself. As she came to the front of the platform the whole company rose, and remained standing until she had finished. In her quiet, modest, way, and yet so clearly as to be plainly heard by all, she said:—

"I wish to say that I thank all my friends from my heart,—that is all. And one thing more,—and that is, if any of you have doubt, or sorrow, or pain, if you doubt about this world, just remember what God has done; just remember that this great sorrow of slavery has gone, gone by forever. I see it every day at the South. I walk about there and see the lowly cabins. I see these people growing richer and richer. I see men very happy in their lowly lot; but, to be sure, you must have patience with them. They are not perfect, but have their faults, and they are serious faults in the view of white people. But they are very happy, that is evident, and they do know how to enjoy themselves,—a great deal more than you do. An old negro friend in our neighborhood has got a new, nice two-story house, and an orange grove, and a sugar-mill. He has got a lot of money, besides. Mr. Stowe met him one day, and he said, 'I have got twenty head of cattle, four head of "hoss," forty head of hen, and I have got ten children, all *mine, every one mine*.' Well, now, that is a thing that a black man could not say once, and this man was sixty years old before he could say it. With all the faults of the colored people, take a man and put him down with nothing but his hands, and how many could say as much as that? I think they have done well.

"A little while ago they had at his house an evening festival for their church, and raised fifty dollars. We white folks took our carriages, and when we reached the house we found it fixed nicely. Every one of his daughters knew how to cook. They had a good place for the festival. Their suppers were spread on little white tables with nice clean cloths on them. People paid fifty cents for supper. They got between fifty and sixty dollars, and had one of the best frolics you could imagine. They had also for supper ice-cream, which they made themselves.

"That is the sort of thing I see going on around me. Let us never doubt. Everything that ought to happen is going to happen."

Mrs. Stowe's public life ends with the garden party, and little more remains to be told. She had already, in 1880, begun the task of selection from the great accumulation of letters and papers relating to her life, and writes thus to her son in Saco, Maine, regarding the work:—

September 30, 1880.

MY DEAR CHARLEY,—My mind has been with you a great deal lately. I have been looking over and arranging my papers with a view to sifting out those that are not worth keeping, and so filing and arranging those that are to be kept, that my heirs and assigns may with the less trouble know where and what they are. I cannot describe (to you) the peculiar feelings which this review occasions. Reading old letters—when so many of the writers are gone from earth, seems to me like going into the world of spirits—letters full of the warm, eager, anxious, busy life, that is *forever* past. My own letters, too, full of by-gone scenes in my early life and the childish days of my children. It is affecting to me to recall things that strongly moved me years ago, that filled my thoughts and made me anxious when the occasion and emotion have wholly vanished from my mind. But I thank God there is *one* thing running through all of them from the time I was thirteen years old, and that is the intense unwavering sense of Christ's educating, guiding presence and care. It is *all* that remains now. The romance of my youth is faded, it looks to me now, from my years, so *very* young— those days when my mind only lived in *emotion*, and when my letters never were dated, because they were only histories of the *internal*, but now that I am no more and never can be young in this world, now that the friends of those days are almost all in eternity, what remains?

> Through life and through death, through
> sorrowing, through sinning,

Christ shall suffice me as he hath sufficed.
Christ is the end and Christ the beginning,
The beginning and end of all is Christ.

THE LATER HARTFORD HOME.

I was passionate in my attachments in those far back years, and as I have looked over files of old letters, they are all gone (except one, C. Van Rensselaer), Georgiana May, Delia Bacon, Clarissa Treat, Elisabeth Lyman, Sarah Colt, Elisabeth Phenix, Frances Strong, Elisabeth Foster. I have letters from them all, but they have been long in spirit land and know more about how it is there than I do. It gives me a sort of dizzy feeling of the shortness of life and nearness of eternity when I see how many that I have traveled with are gone within the veil. Then there are all my own letters, written in the first two years of marriage, when Mr. Stowe was in Europe and I was looking forward to motherhood and preparing for it—my letters when my whole life was within the four walls of my nursery, my thoughts absorbed by the developing character of children who have now lived their earthly life and gone to the eternal one,—my two little boys, each in their way good and lovely, whom Christ has taken in youth, and my little one, my first Charley, whom He took away before he knew sin or sorrow,— then my brother George and sister Catherine, the one a companion of my youth, the other the mother who assumed the care of me after I left home in my twelfth year—and they are gone. Then my blessed father, for many years so true an image of the Heavenly Father,—in all my afflictions he was afflicted, in all my perplexities he was a sure and safe counselor, and he too is gone upward to join the angelic mother whom I scarcely knew in this world, who has been to me only a spiritual presence through life.

In 1882 Mrs. Stowe writes to her son certain impressions derived from reading the "Life and Letters of John Quincy Adams," which are given as containing a retrospect of the stormy period of her own life-experience.

"Your father enjoys his proximity to the Boston library. He is now reading the twelve or fourteen volumes of the life and diary of John Q. Adams. It is a history of our country through all the period of slavery usurpation that led to the war. The industry of the man in writing is wonderful. Every day's doings in the house are faithfully daguerreotyped,—all the mean tricks, contrivances of the slave-power, and the pusillanimity of the Northern members from day to day recorded. Calhoun was then secretary of state. Under his connivance even the United States census was falsified, to prove that freedom was bad for negroes. Records of deaf, dumb, and blind, and insane colored people were distributed in Northern States, and in places where John Q. Adams had means of *proving* there were no negroes. When he found that these falsified figures had been used with the English embassador as reasons for admitting Texas as a slave State, the old man called on Calhoun, and showed him the industriously collected *proofs* of the falsity of this census. He says: 'He writhed like a trodden rattlesnake, but said the census was full of mistakes; but one part balanced another,—it was not worth while to correct them.' His whole life was an incessant warfare with the rapidly advancing spirit of slavery, that was coiling like a serpent around everything.

"At a time when the Southerners were like so many excited tigers and rattlesnakes,—when they bullied, and scoffed, and sneered, and threatened, this old man rose every day in his place, and, knowing every parliamentary rule and tactic of debate, found means to make himself heard. Then he presented a petition from *negroes*, which raised a storm of fury. The old man claimed that the right of petition was the right of every human being. They moved to expel him. By the rules of the house a man, before he can be expelled, may have the floor to make his defense. This was just what he wanted. He held the floor for *fourteen days*, and used his wonderful powers of memory and arrangement to give a systematic, scathing history of the usurpations of slavery; he would have spoken fourteen days more, but his enemies, finding the thing getting hotter and hotter, withdrew their motion, and the right of petition was gained.

"What is remarkable in this journal is the minute record of going to church every Sunday, and an analysis of the text and sermon. There is something about these so simple, so humble, so earnest. Often differing from the speaker—but with gravity and humility—he seems always to be so self-distrustful; to have such a sense of sinfulness and weakness, but such trust in God's fatherly mercy, as is most beautiful to see. Just the record of his Sunday sermons, and his remarks upon them, would be most instructive to a preacher. He was a regular communicant, and, beside, attended church on Christmas and Easter,—I cannot but love the old man. He died without seeing even the dawn of liberty which God has brought; but oh! I am sure he sees it from above. He died in the Capitol, in the midst of his labors, and the last words he said were, 'This is the last of earth; I am content.' And now, I trust, he is with God.

"All, all are gone. All that raged; all that threatened; all the cowards that yielded; truckled, sold their country for a mess of pottage; all the *men* that stood and bore infamy and scorn for the truth; all are silent in dust; the fight is over, but eternity will never efface from their souls whether they did well or ill—whether they fought bravely or failed like cowards. In a sense, our lives are irreparable. If we shrink, if we fail, if we choose the fleeting instead of the eternal, God may forgive us; but there must be an eternal regret! This man lived for humanity when hardest bestead; for truth when truth was unpopular; for Christ when Christ stood chained and scourged in the person of the slave."

In the fall of 1887 she writes to her brother Rev. Dr. Edward Beecher of Brooklyn, N. Y.:—

49 FOREST STREET, HARTFORD, CONN., *October 11, 1887.*

DEAR BROTHER,—I was delighted to receive your kind letter. *You* were my earliest religious teacher; your letters to me while a school-girl in Hartford gave me a high Christian aim and standard which I hope I have never lost. Not only did they do me good, but also my intimate friends, Georgiana May and Catherine Cogswell, to whom I read them. The simplicity, warmth, and childlike earnestness of those school days I love to recall. I am the *only one living* of that circle of early friends. *Not one* of my early schoolmates is living,—and now Henry, younger by a year or two than I, has gone—my husband also. I often think, *Why* am I spared? Is there yet anything for me to do? I am thinking with my son Charles's help of writing a review of my life, under the title, "Pebbles from the Shores of a Past Life."

Charlie told me that he has got all written up to my twelfth or thirteenth year, when I came to be under sister Catherine's care in Hartford. I am writing daily my remembrances from that time. You were then, I think, teacher of the Grammar School in Hartford. . . .

So, my dear brother, let us keep good heart; no evil can befall us. Sin alone is evil, and from that Christ will keep us. Our journey is *so* short!

I feel about all things now as I do about the things that happen in a hotel, after my trunk is packed to go home. I may be vexed and annoyed . . . but what of it! I am going home soon.

Your affectionate sister,
HATTIE.

To a friend she writes a little later:—

"I have thought much lately of the possibility of my leaving you all and going home. I am come to that stage of my pilgrimage that is within sight of the River of Death, and I feel that now I must have all in readiness day and night for the messenger of the King. I have sometimes had in my sleep strange perceptions of a vivid spiritual life near to and with Christ, and multitudes of holy ones, and the joy of it is like no other joy,—it cannot be told in the language of the world. What I have then I *know* with absolute certainty, yet it is so unlike and above anything we conceive of in this world that it is difficult to put it into words. The inconceivable loveliness of Christ! It seems that about Him there is a sphere where the enthusiasm of love is the calm habit of the soul, that without words, without the necessity of demonstrations of affection, heart beats to heart, soul answers soul, we respond to the Infinite Love, and we feel his answer in us, and there is no need of words. All seemed to be busy coming and going on ministries of good, and passing each gave a thrill of joy to each as Jesus, the directing soul, the centre of all, "over all, in all, and through all," was working his beautiful and merciful will to redeem and save. I was saying as I awoke:—

""Tis joy enough, my all in all,
At thy dear feet to lie.
Thou wilt not let me lower fall,
And none can higher fly.'

"This was but a glimpse; but it has left a strange sweetness in my mind."

FOOTNOTES

This geography was begun by Mrs. Stowe during the summer of 1832, while visiting her brother William at Newport, R. I. It was completed during the winter of 1833, and published by the firm of Corey, Fairbank & Webster, of Cincinnati.

A ridiculous book from which Mr. Stowe derived endless amusement.

Salmon P. Chase.

The governess, Miss Anna Smith.

An old colored woman.

Wife of Professor Upham of Bowdoin College.

Her brother George's only child.

Bancroft's funeral oration on Lincoln.

Greeley's *American Conflict*, vol. i. p. 65.

Introduction to Illustrated Edition of *Uncle Tom*, p. xiii. (Houghton, Osgood & Co., 1879.)

Afterwards embodied in the *Key to Uncle Tom's Cabin*.

Author of *Spanish Conquest in America.*—ED.

Students in the Seminary.

The Pearl of Orr's Island.

Andrew Johnson.

Die Christliche Mystik, by Johann Joseph Görres, Regensburg, 1836-42.

George Eliot's Life, edited by J. W. Cross, vol. i.

Die Christliche Mystik.

Professor Stowe.

Uncle Tom's Cabin, new edition, with introduction.

Professor Stowe died August, 1886.

CPSIA information can be obtained
at www.ICGtesting.com
Printed in the USA
BVHW041255240922
647922BV00004B/72

9 789353 292188